taste of home
TREASURY OF Christmas RECIPES

Senior Vice President, Editor in Chief:
CATHERINE CASSIDY
Vice President, Executive Editor/books:
HEIDI REUTER LLOYD
Food Director: DIANE WERNER RD
Senior Editor/Books: MARK HAGEN
Editor: JEAN STEINER
Associate Editor: BETH KONG
Art Directors: LORI ARNDT, GRETCHEN TRAUTMAN
Content Production Supervisor: JULIE WAGNER
Recipe Asset System Manager: COLEEN MARTIN
Premedia Supervisor: SCOTT BERGER
Recipe Testing and Editing: TASTE OF HOME TEST KITCHEN
Food Photography: TASTE OF HOME PHOTO STUDIO
Administrative Assistant: BARB CZYSZ

North American Chief Marketing Officer: LISA KARPINSKI
Vice President/Book Marketing: DAN FINK
Creative Director/Creative Marketing: JIM PALMEN

THE READER'S DIGEST ASSOCIATION, INC.
President and Chief Executive Officer:
MARY G. BERNER
President, North American Affinities:
SUZANNE M. GRIMES

5400 S. 60th St., Greendale WI 53129

International Standard Book Number (10): 0-89821-410-6
International Standard Book Number (13): 978-0-89821-410-9
Library of Congress Control Number: 2004093536

Printed in China.
9 10 8

Table of Contents

You'll Treasure this Special Christmas Collection Filled with 734 Festive Recipes...

THINK OF IT as our gift to you during this busy holiday season!

We all have our "must-haves" we make for family and friends year after year, and Christmas wouldn't be the same without these seasonal favorites. But we're always eager to try out newfound recipes on them as well, dishes that will win their hearty approval and earn a place in our annual holiday "lineup".

That's why we're so excited to present *Taste of Home Treasury of Christmas Recipes* to you! Over the years, *Taste of Home* magazine readers have shared the special recipes their families ask them to make every Christmas season...and we've compiled the very best ones into this big colorful cookbook. It's brimming with 734 festive recipes!

Your gang is going to love these great-tasting dishes. How can we be so sure? Because each is already the tried-and-true favorite of a fellow cook's family. Our Test Kitchen staff prepared and tried every dish, too, to guarantee you'll have delicious results when you make them in your own kitchen.

Any of the 93 appetizers and beverages found inside are so flavorful and filling, they could make a merry meal all by themselves...but they will also whet guests' appetites for the main courses to come. This recipe collection serves up 52 mouth-watering entrees, as well as 33 refreshing salads and 53 side dishes and condiments to round out a meal. Everyone will still have room for a little dessert, though, when you set out any of the 78 luscious pies, cakes, puddings and more featured here.

Christmas morning will be extra-special with this book's 89 brunch items to choose from. Your family will have a hard time deciding whether to head for the presents or the eye-opening buffet table first!

Speaking of presents, 72 oven-fresh breads, 92 beautiful morsels of candy and 87 scrumptious cookies and bars make thoughtful gifts you can give to friends, co-workers, church members and more...what Christmas would be complete without these traditional treats?

Even more homemade goodies are tucked inside a separate chapter called "Gifts from the Kitchen"...85 of them in fact. You will have gift-giving wrapped up with the creative mix ideas and from-scratch jams, spiced nuts, seasonings and classic fruitcake!

All the ingredients for a happy holiday season are at your fingertips with *Taste of Home Treasury of Christmas Recipes*—the largest Christmas cookbook we've ever published! It's sure to be one "must-have" you grab when you prepare for each holiday season.

Appetizers & Beverages

Bread Pot Fondue

(Pictured above)

Bring this fun fondue to a buffet or potluck and you'll be the toast of the gathering. Folks always ask for the recipe. —*Terry Christensen, Roy, Utah*

2 cups (8 ounces) shredded cheddar cheese
1-1/2 cups (12 ounces) sour cream
2 packages (3 ounces *each*) cream cheese, softened
1/4 pound chopped fully cooked ham
1/2 cup finely chopped green onions
1 can (4 ounces) chopped green chilies
1 teaspoon Worcestershire sauce
1 round loaf (1 to 1-1/2 pounds) Italian bread
Assorted fresh vegetables

In a mixing bowl, combine the first three ingredients. Stir in ham, onions, chilies and Worcestershire sauce; set aside. Cut top fourth off loaf of bread; carefully hollow out top and bottom, leaving a 1/2-in. shell. Cube removed bread; set aside.

Spoon ham mixture into the bottom shell, mounding slightly. Replace top; wrap tightly with a double layer of heavy-duty foil. Bake at 350° for 1 to 1-1/2 hours. Stir before serving. Serve with reserved bread cubes and vegetables. **Yield:** 4 cups.

Zippy Cheese Log

Due to popular demand, my pretty cheese log has become a tasty tradition at our women's Christmas brunch. As soon as the ladies try a bite, I start getting requests for the recipe. —*Evangeline Rew*
Manassas, Virginia

2 packages (8 ounces *each*) cream cheese, softened
1 cup small-curd cottage cheese
1 envelope Parmesan Italian salad dressing mix
4 tablespoons minced fresh parsley, *divided*
1/2 cup minced fully cooked ham
1/2 cup chopped walnuts
Assorted crackers

In a mixing bowl, beat cream cheese, cottage cheese and salad dressing mix until smooth. Line the bottom and sides of a 13-in. x 9-in. x 2-in. pan with waxed paper. Spread cheese mixture evenly in pan. Cover and refrigerate for 1 hour.

Remove waxed paper with cheese from pan. Sprinkle 2 tablespoons parsley in a 13-in. x 1-in. strip 1/2 in. from one long edge. Sprinkle ham over remaining cheese mixture. Starting with parsley edge, carefully roll up jelly-roll style.

Combine walnuts and remaining parsley; roll log in parsley mixture. Cut log in half; wrap and refrigerate for at least 4 hours. Serve with crackers. **Yield:** 2 cheese logs (about 1-3/4 cups each).

Rosy Holiday Punch

With its tangy juice and lovely blush color, this punch is fun to serve anytime. It's a refreshing beverage to go with a holiday meal or the season's sweet treats.
—*Linda Ault, Newberry, Indiana*

1 bottle (32 ounces) cranberry juice
1 can (12 ounces) frozen orange juice concentrate, thawed
2 tablespoons sugar
1/4 teaspoon ground allspice

1 bottle (1 liter) ginger ale, chilled
Lemon and orange slices, optional

In a large container, combine cranberry juice, orange juice concentrate, sugar and allspice; mix well. Cover and chill at least 2 hours. Just before serving, add ginger ale; mix well. Garnish with lemon and orange slices if desired. **Yield:** 18-20 servings (about 1/2 cup each).

Chili Cups

Nothing tickles appetites quicker than these spicy tidbits. It's like eating chili in a muffin. I like assembling and freezing them ahead of time to beat the Christmas rush in my kitchen. —*Diane Hixon Niceville, Florida*

1 pound ground beef
1 medium green pepper, diced
1 medium onion, diced
3 garlic cloves, minced
1 can (8 ounces) tomato sauce
2 tablespoons water
1/2 teaspoon salt
1/2 to 1 teaspoon ground cumin
1/2 teaspoon dried oregano
1/4 teaspoon celery seed
1/4 teaspoon dill weed
1/8 to 1/4 teaspoon cayenne pepper
2 loaves (1 pound *each*) sliced Italian bread
Grated Parmesan cheese

In a large skillet, cook the beef, green pepper, onion and garlic over medium heat until the meat is no longer pink; drain. Stir in tomato sauce, water and seasonings. Bring to a boil over medium heat. Reduce heat; cover and simmer for 30 minutes, stirring occasionally.

Meanwhile, cut 2-1/2-in. circles from the bread slices using a biscuit cutter. Press the circles into greased miniature muffin cups. Bake at 400° for 5-6 minutes or until lightly toasted. Remove from the tins and cool on wire racks.

Fill each bread cup with about 1 tablespoon of the chili mixture; sprinkle with Parmesan cheese. Broil for 2-3 minutes or until the cheese is golden brown. **Yield:** about 5 dozen.

Editor's Note: Some slices of bread will yield two 2-1/2-in. circles and some slices only one. There may be bread slices left over.

Bacon-Wrapped Scallops with Cream Sauce

(Pictured below)

Although the rich seafood tidbits look complicated, they're actually easy to assemble and cook. The dipping sauce, with its hints of mustard and maple syrup, complements the scallops nicely. It's a unique appetizer. —*Barb Horstmeier, Freeport, Illinois*

10 bacon strips
10 large sea scallops
1 cup heavy whipping cream
2 tablespoons Dijon mustard
2 tablespoons maple syrup
1/8 teaspoon salt

Place bacon in an ungreased 15-in. x 10-in. x 1-in. baking pan. Bake at 350° for 7-10 minutes or until partially cooked and lightly browned. Drain on paper towels. Wrap each strip of bacon around a scallop; secure with toothpicks.

In a saucepan, bring cream to a boil. Reduce heat; simmer, uncovered, until cream is reduced to 3/4 cup, about 8 minutes. Stir in the mustard, syrup and salt. Bring to a boil and boil for 2 minutes. Meanwhile, place the scallops on a greased baking sheet. Bake at 400° for 8-12 minutes or until firm and opaque. Serve with the cream sauce. **Yield:** 10 appetizers.

Dilly Shrimp

A friend shared the recipe for this hors d'oeuvre. The zesty sauce complements the shrimp nicely and guarantees they'll be gobbled up. —*Diana Holmes Hubertus, Wisconsin*

1-1/2 cups mayonnaise
1/2 cup sour cream
1/3 cup lemon juice
1/4 cup sugar
1 large red onion, thinly sliced
2 tablespoons dill weed
1/4 teaspoon salt
32 medium cooked shrimp (about 2 pounds), peeled and deveined

In a bowl, combine the mayonnaise, sour cream, lemon juice and sugar. Stir in the onion, dill, salt and shrimp. Cover and refrigerate for 8 hours or overnight. Serve with toothpicks. **Yield:** 10 servings.

Mushroom Crescents

(Pictured below)

These tasty appetizers are popular at holiday parties. They can be prepared ahead and reheated. —*Mavis Diment Marcus, Iowa*

1 package (8 ounces) cream cheese, softened
1/2 cup butter, softened
1-1/2 cups all-purpose flour

FILLING:
1/2 pound fresh mushrooms, finely chopped
1 medium onion, finely chopped
2 tablespoons butter
1 package (3 ounces) cream cheese, cubed
1/2 teaspoon salt
1/4 teaspoon dried thyme
1/8 teaspoon pepper
1 egg, lightly beaten
1 teaspoon water

In a mixing bowl, beat cream cheese and butter until smooth; stir in flour. Cover and refrigerate dough for at least 1 hour. Meanwhile, in a skillet or saucepan over medium heat, saute mushrooms and onion in butter until tender. Remove from the heat. Add cream cheese, salt, thyme and pepper; stir until cheese is melted. Cool to room temperature.

On a floured surface, roll dough to 1/8-in. thickness. Cut into 3-in. circles. Combine egg and water; lightly brush edges of circles. Place about 1 teaspoon of filling in center of each circle. Fold over; seal edges. Brush with egg mixture. Bake at 400° for 15-20 minutes or until golden brown. **Yield:** about 4 dozen.

Chocolate-Raspberry Fondue

You don't need a fancy fondue pot to make this melt-in-your-mouth concoction. I serve the dip in my small slow cooker. Folks love the chocolate-raspberry combination. —*Heather Maxwell, Fort Riley, Kansas*

1 package (14 ounces) caramels*
2 cups (12 ounces) semisweet chocolate chips
1 can (12 ounces) evaporated milk
1/2 cup butter
1/2 cup seedless raspberry jam
Assorted fruit *or* pound cake cubes

In a large saucepan, combine the first five ingredients. Cook over low heat until the caramels, chocolate chips and butter are melted, about 15 minutes. Stir until smooth. Transfer to a small slow cooker or fondue pot. Serve warm with fruit or pound cake. **Yield:** 5 cups.

***Editor's Note:** This recipe was tested with Hershey caramels.

Curried Chicken Triangles

Plain refrigerated crescent rolls shape up festively into these time-saving treats. Serve the savory triangles warm, then just stand back and watch them as they quickly vanish. —*Anne Marie Cardilino Kettering, Ohio*

2 tubes (8 ounces *each*) refrigerated crescent rolls
1 can (5 ounces) white chicken, undrained
1 can (8 ounces) sliced water chestnuts, drained and chopped
1 cup (4 ounces) shredded Swiss cheese
1/2 cup chopped green onions
1/3 cup mayonnaise
1 teaspoon lemon juice
1/2 teaspoon curry powder
1/2 teaspoon garlic salt
Paprika, optional

Separate crescent dough; cut each piece into four triangles. Place on greased baking sheets. In a bowl, break up chicken. Add the water chestnuts, cheese, onions, mayonnaise, lemon juice, curry powder and garlic salt; mix well.

Drop by rounded teaspoonfuls onto triangles. Sprinkle with paprika if desired. Bake at 350° for 12-15 minutes or until edges are lightly browned. Serve warm. **Yield:** about 5-1/2 dozen.

Six-Layer Dip

(Pictured above right)

Tortilla chips make great scoopers for this dip, which is a family favorite after we open Christmas gifts. Sometimes I serve it in a glass bowl, just to show off the pretty layers. —*Etta Gillespie, San Angelo, Texas*

2 medium ripe avocados, peeled and sliced
2 tablespoons lemon juice
1/2 teaspoon garlic salt
1/8 teaspoon hot pepper sauce
1 cup (8 ounces) sour cream
1 can (2-1/4 ounces) chopped ripe olives, drained
1 jar (16 ounces) thick and chunky salsa, drained
2 medium tomatoes, seeded and chopped
1 cup (4 ounces) shredded cheddar cheese
Tortilla chips

In a bowl, combine the avocados, lemon juice, garlic salt and hot pepper sauce; mash well. Spoon into a deep-dish 10-in. pie plate or serving bowl. Layer with sour cream, olives, salsa, tomatoes and cheese. Cover and refrigerate for at least 1 hour. Serve with chips. **Yield:** 20 servings.

Planning Your Party

For an appetizer buffet that serves as the meal, offer five or six different appetizers (including some substantial selections) and plan on eight to nine pieces per guest. If you'll also be serving a meal, two to three pieces per person is sufficient.

In order to appeal to everyone's tastes and diets, have a balance of hearty and low-calorie appetizers as well as hot and cold choices.

Eggnog Dip

I put together a cookbook of my grandma's Christmas recipes that includes this classic eggnog appetizer. Serve it as a dip with fresh fruit or drizzle it over cake for dessert.
—Sharon MacDonnell, Lantzville, British Columbia

1-1/2 cups eggnog*
2 tablespoons cornstarch
1/2 cup sour cream
1/2 cup heavy whipping cream
1 tablespoon sugar
1/2 teaspoon rum extract, optional
Assorted fruit and pound cake cubes

In a saucepan, combine the eggnog and cornstarch until smooth. Bring to a boil; boil and stir for 2 minutes. Remove from the heat; stir in sour cream. Cool completely.

In a mixing bowl, beat whipping cream and sugar until stiff peaks form. Fold into eggnog mixture with extract if desired. Cover and refrigerate overnight. Serve with fruit and pound cake cubes. **Yield:** about 2-1/2 cups.

***Editor's Note:** This recipe was tested with commercially prepared eggnog.

Tangy Mozzarella Bites

(Pictured above)

I adapted this recipe from one I found years ago, substituting ingredients most people have on hand. I like to serve it with crackers or small bread slices.
—Julie Wasem, Aurora, Nebraska

1/4 cup olive oil
1 to 2 teaspoons balsamic vinegar
1 garlic clove, minced
1 teaspoon dried basil
1 teaspoon coarsely ground pepper
1 pound mozzarella cheese, cut into 1/2-inch cubes

In a bowl, combine the oil, vinegar, garlic, basil and pepper. Add the cheese and toss to coat. Cover and refrigerate for at least 1 hour. Serve with toothpicks. **Yield:** about 3 cups.

Holiday Mushroom Appetizers

A friend served these wedges at an open house. With English muffins as a base, they're quick and convenient to make and sure to be a hit with mushroom lovers.
—Patricia Kile, Greentown, Pennsylvania

4 ounces fresh mushrooms, finely chopped
1/4 cup butter, softened, *divided*
1 jar (5 ounces) sharp American cheese spread
1-1/2 teaspoons mayonnaise
1/2 teaspoon seasoned salt
1/2 teaspoon Italian seasoning
1/4 teaspoon garlic salt
6 English muffins, split

In a small skillet, saute mushrooms in 1 tablespoon butter; drain and cool. In a bowl, combine the cheese spread, mayonnaise, seasoned salt, Italian seasoning, garlic salt, mushroom mixture and remaining butter. Spread onto cut side of each muffin; cut each into

eight wedges. Place on a baking sheet. Broil 4 in. from the heat for 4 minutes or until golden brown. Refrigerate any leftovers. **Yield:** 4 dozen.

Pizza Swirls

My children helped me dream up this snappy bread that tastes like pizza. The from-scratch flavor makes it a family favorite, but it's great for parties, too.
—Linda Gerrald, Nacogdoches, Texas

1 package (1/4 ounce) active dry yeast
1-1/3 cups warm water (110° to 115°)
1/4 cup vegetable oil
1/2 teaspoon sugar
1/2 teaspoon salt
3-3/4 to 4-1/4 cups all-purpose flour

SAUCE:

1/4 cup chopped onion
2 garlic cloves, minced
1 can (8 ounces) tomato sauce
1/4 teaspoon dried basil

TOPPINGS:

4 cups (16 ounces) shredded mozzarella cheese, *divided*
2 packages (3 ounces *each*) sliced pepperoni
1 can (2-1/4 ounces) chopped ripe olives, drained

In a mixing bowl, dissolve yeast in warm water. Add oil, sugar, salt and 2 cups flour; beat until smooth. Stir in enough remaining flour to form a soft dough. Turn onto a floured surface; knead until smooth and elastic, about 6-8 minutes. Place in a greased bowl, turning once to grease top. Cover and let rise in a warm place until doubled, about 1 hour. Punch dough down. Turn onto a floured surface; divide in half. Roll each portion into a 12-in. x 8-in. rectangle; set aside.

For sauce, combine onion and garlic in a microwave-safe dish. Cover; microwave on high for 1 minute. Add tomato sauce and basil; cover and cook at 50% power for 3 minutes or until bubbly. Spoon over crust to within 1/2 in. of edges. Sprinkle with 3 cups mozzarella cheese, pepperoni and olives.

Roll up jelly-roll style, starting with a long side; pinch seam to seal. Cut each roll into 12 slices. Place cut side down on a greased baking sheet. Sprinkle with remaining cheese. Bake at 400° for 15 minutes or until crust is golden and cheese is melted. Serve warm. **Yield:** 2 dozen.

Salmon Canapes

(Pictured below)

This appealing appetizer, with its delicate smoked salmon taste and dash of holiday color, is simply irresistible! *—Dorothy Anderson, Ottawa, Kansas*

1 can (7-1/2 ounces) red salmon, drained, skin and bones removed
2 tablespoons minced celery
2 tablespoons minced green onions with tops
3 tablespoons mayonnaise
1/2 teaspoon lemon juice
1/4 teaspoon salt
1/8 teaspoon pepper
1/8 teaspoon Liquid Smoke, optional
1 small cucumber, thinly sliced
Snack rye bread, toast *or* crackers
Fresh dill *or* parsley sprigs *and/or* sliced pimientos

In a bowl, combine the salmon, celery and onions. Add the mayonnaise, lemon juice, salt, pepper and Liquid Smoke if desired; mix well. Cover and chill at least 1 hour.

Just before serving, place the cucumber slices on bread or crackers and top with the salmon mixture. Garnish with dill, parsley and/or pimientos. **Yield:** 1 cup spread.

Fiesta Pinwheels

(Pictured below)

Whenever I serve these make-ahead appetizers, they disappear fast. When a friend at the office shared them with me, I knew in one bite I'd be bringing her recipe home for the holidays. —*Diane Martin*
Brown Deer, Wisconsin

- **1 package (8 ounces) cream cheese, softened**
- **1/2 cup sour cream**
- **1/4 cup picante sauce**
- **2 tablespoons taco seasoning**
- **Dash garlic powder**
- **1 can (4-1/2 ounces) chopped ripe olives, drained**
- **1 can (4 ounces) chopped green chilies**
- **1 cup (4 ounces) finely shredded cheddar cheese**
- **1/2 cup thinly sliced green onions**
- **8 flour tortillas (10 inches)**
- **Salsa**

In a small mixing bowl, beat cream cheese, sour cream, picante sauce, taco seasoning and garlic powder until smooth. Stir in olives, chilies, cheese and onions. Spread about 1/2 cup on each tortilla. Roll up jelly-roll style; wrap in plastic wrap. Refrigerate for 2 hours or overnight. Slice into 1-in. pieces. Serve with salsa. **Yield:** about 5 dozen.

Editor's Note: Pinwheels may be prepared ahead and frozen. Thaw in the refrigerator.

Festive Fruit 'n' Franks

A zesty mix of apricot preserves, pineapple, mandarin oranges and apple gives a sweet treatment to cocktail franks. Serve this and you'll receive compliments galore.
—*Edie DeSpain, Logan, Utah*

- **1 tablespoon cornstarch**
- **1/3 cup lemon juice**
- **1 jar (10 to 12 ounces) apricot preserves**
- **1/2 teaspoon ground cinnamon**
- **1 package (12 ounces) miniature smoked sausage links**
- **1 can (8 ounces) pineapple chunks, drained**
- **1 can (11 ounces) mandarin oranges, drained**
- **1 large red apple, cut into chunks**

In a saucepan, combine cornstarch and lemon juice until smooth. Add the preserves and cinnamon. Bring to a boil over medium heat; cook and stir for 2 minutes or until thickened.

Add sausage and pineapple; stir to coat. Cook for 5 minutes or until heated through. Just before serving, stir in oranges and apple. Serve warm. Refrigerate any leftovers. **Yield:** 10-12 servings.

Hammettes

With the flavor of roasted ham in bite-size morsels, these hammettes are a nice change from traditional party meatballs. They're a popular snack that appeals to most palates. —*Marguerite Jensen, Rockford, Illinois*

- **2 eggs**
- **1 cup milk**
- **2 cups dry bread crumbs**
- **1-1/2 pounds ground fully cooked ham (6 cups)**
- **1 pound ground pork**
- **1 cup packed brown sugar**
- **1/2 cup vinegar**
- **1/2 cup pineapple juice**
- **1 teaspoon ground mustard**
- **6 whole cloves**

In a bowl, beat eggs and milk. Add the bread crumbs, ham and pork; mix well. Using about 3 tablespoons for each, shape mixture into logs. Place in a lightly greased 15-in. x 10-in. x 1-in. baking pan. Bake, uncovered, at 350° for 30 minutes.

Meanwhile, in a saucepan, bring the brown sugar,

vinegar, pineapple juice, mustard and cloves to a boil. Pour over logs. Cover and bake at 350° for 1-1/4 hours, basting occasionally with sauce. Uncover and bake 15 minutes longer. Discard cloves. Serve warm. **Yield:** about 3-1/2 dozen.

Tangy Pork Meatballs

Yuletide buffet "grazers" stampede for these meatballs! The mouth-watering morsels go so fast, I often make several batches at once. Barbecue sauce adds a nice bite to the mildly seasoned ground pork.
—Katie Koziolek, Hartland, Minnesota

2 eggs, beaten
2/3 cup dried bread crumbs
2 tablespoons dried minced onion
2 teaspoons seasoned salt
2 pounds ground pork
SAUCE:
1-1/2 cups ketchup
1 can (8 ounces) tomato sauce
3 tablespoons Worcestershire sauce
2 to 3 tablespoons cider vinegar
2 teaspoons Liquid Smoke, optional

In a bowl, combine the eggs, bread crumbs, onion and salt. Crumble pork over mixture and mix well. Shape into 3/4-in. balls; place on a greased 15-in. x 10-in. x 1-in. baking pan. Bake at 400° for 15 minutes or until the meat is no longer pink.

Meanwhile, in a large saucepan, combine sauce ingredients. Simmer, uncovered, for 10 minutes, stirring occasionally. Add meatballs. Serve in a slow cooker or chafing dish. **Yield:** about 7-1/2 dozen.

Crisp Cheese Twists

(Pictured above right)

These golden twists are always popular. We like them alongside chili and soup. My husband and daughter usually try to sneak a few from the cooling rack when I make them.
—Kelly-Ann Gibbons
Prince George, British Columbia

1-1/4 cups all-purpose flour
1/2 cup cornmeal
1 teaspoon salt
1/4 cup shortening
1-1/4 cups shredded cheddar cheese
1/3 cup cold water
Grated Parmesan cheese, optional

In a large bowl, combine the flour, cornmeal and salt. Cut in shortening until mixture resembles coarse crumbs. Stir in cheddar cheese. Sprinkle with 1/3 cup water. Toss with a fork (if dough is dry, add water, 1 teaspoon at a time, until dough forms a ball). Wrap tightly in plastic wrap; refrigerate for 1 hour or until firm.

Divide dough in half. On a lightly floured surface, roll each portion into an 11-in. x 10-in. rectangle. Cut into 5-in. x 1/2-in. strips. Carefully twist each strip and place on greased baking sheets, pressing ends down.

Bake at 425° for 7-9 minutes or until golden brown. Immediately sprinkle twists with Parmesan cheese if desired. Cool on wire racks. Store in an airtight container. **Yield:** about 7 dozen.

Fruity Cranberry Punch

(Pictured above)

The women's group from our church has held its Christmas potluck at my home for more than 20 years. I never fail to serve this rich and creamy fruit punch...everyone enjoys it. —*Joann Dudgeon, Mendon, Ohio*

4 cups cranberry juice, chilled
4 cups pineapple juice, chilled
2 cups sugar, *divided*
1 to 2 teaspoons almond extract
1/2 gallon strawberry ice cream, softened
2 cups heavy whipping cream
1 liter ginger ale, chilled

In a large punch bowl, combine juices, 1-1/2 cups sugar, almond extract and ice cream. Refrigerate until serving. Just before serving, beat cream in a mixing bowl. Gradually add the remaining sugar, beating until soft peaks form. Whisk gently into chilled juice mixture. Add ginger ale. Refrigerate any leftovers. **Yield:** about 7 quarts.

Festive Turkey Meatballs

Turkey gives a different twist to these slightly sweet and spicy meatballs. For the holidays, I serve them on a tray lined with parsley and garnished with red pepper or pimientos. —*Audrey Thibodeau, Mesa, Arizona*

1 egg, beaten
1/2 cup dry bread crumbs
1/4 cup finely chopped onion
1/2 teaspoon curry powder
1/4 teaspoon ground ginger
1/4 teaspoon ground cinnamon
1/8 teaspoon salt
1/4 teaspoon pepper
1 pound ground turkey

SAUCE:

1 cup honey
1/4 cup Dijon mustard
1/2 teaspoon curry powder
1/2 teaspoon ground ginger

In a bowl, combine the first eight ingredients. Add turkey; mix well. Form into 1-in. balls. Place in a greased 13-in. x 9-in. x 2-in. baking dish. Bake, uncovered, at 350° for 20-25 minutes or until juices run clear.

Meanwhile, combine sauce ingredients in a small saucepan; cook and stir until heated through. Brush meatballs with 1/4 cup sauce; return to the oven for 10 minutes. Serve remaining sauce with meatballs for dipping. **Yield:** about 2-1/2 dozen.

Cheese Olive Appetizers

Here's a quick way to dress up a hot roll mix. The crust smothered in a cheese topping will make company think you've fussed. —*Marian Platt, Sequim, Washington*

1 package (16 ounces) hot roll mix
3/4 cup warm water (110° to 115°)
1 egg
1/4 cup butter, melted
1 cup (4 ounces) shredded cheddar cheese
1 tablespoon poppy seeds

TOPPING:

2 cups (8 ounces) shredded cheddar cheese

1 cup sliced stuffed olives
1/3 cup butter, melted
1 egg, beaten
1 tablespoon dried minced onion
1 teaspoon Worcestershire sauce

In a large bowl, dissolve yeast from hot roll mix in warm water. Add egg, butter, cheese and poppy seeds. Add flour from mix; blend well. Press into a greased 15-in. x 10-in. x 1-in. baking pan. Cover and let rise in a warm place until doubled, about 45 minutes.

Combine topping ingredients; spread over dough. Bake at 400° for 20-25 minutes or until golden. Cut into squares; serve warm. **Yield:** about 4 dozen.

Hot Buttered Lemonade

Since my husband had fond childhood memories of this winter warmer-upper, I simmered up a batch. It's delicious, simple to prepare for drop-in guests and sets a soothing holiday mood. —Jennifer Jones, Springfield, Missouri

3 cups water
3/4 cup lemon juice
2/3 cup sugar
1-1/2 teaspoons grated lemon peel
1 tablespoon butter
4 cinnamon sticks (4 inches), optional

In a saucepan over medium heat, simmer water, lemon juice, sugar and lemon peel until sugar is dissolved. Pour into mugs; dot each with butter. Serve with a cinnamon stick if desired. **Yield:** 4 servings (about 1 cup each).

Crab-Stuffed Cherry Tomatoes

(Pictured below)

For a little something special, I include these petite pleasers on the menu of our holiday parties. Our six children and 15 grandkids eat them up warm and juicy from the oven. —Marcia Keckhaver, Burlington, Wisconsin

1 pint cherry tomatoes
1 can (6 ounces) crabmeat, drained, flaked and cartilage removed
1/2 cup diced green pepper
2 green onions, diced
2 tablespoons Italian-seasoned bread crumbs
1 teaspoon white wine vinegar
1/2 teaspoon dried parsley flakes
1/4 teaspoon dill weed
1/8 teaspoon salt, optional

Cut a thin slice off tops of tomatoes and carefully scoop out insides; invert on paper towels to drain. In a small bowl, combine remaining ingredients; mix well. Stuff tomatoes; place in an ungreased 13-in. x 9-in. x 2-in. baking dish. Bake, uncovered, at 350° for 8-10 minutes or until heated through. Serve warm. **Yield:** about 1-1/2 dozen.

Snow Punch

(Pictured below)

As pretty as a fresh snowdrift, this frothy, fruity punch has been a Christmas tradition in our family for years—but it's a light, refreshing thirst-quencher in any season.
—Eloise Neeley, Norton, Ohio

1 cup lemon juice
5 medium ripe bananas
1 cup sugar
2 cups half-and-half cream
1 liter lemon-lime soda, chilled
1 pint lemon *or* pineapple sherbet
1/4 cup flaked coconut, optional

In a blender or food processor, cover and process the lemon juice, bananas and sugar. Add cream; blend until smooth. Cover and refrigerate. Just before serving, pour banana mixture into a punch bowl. Stir in soda. Top with lemon sherbet and coconut if desired. **Yield:** 2-1/2 quarts.

Bacon-Wrapped Water Chestnuts

A sweet glaze coats these crunchy appetizers that get gobbled up at parties as soon as I put them on the plate. —Penny Patterson, Kent City, Michigan

1-1/2 pounds sliced bacon
3 cans (8 ounces *each*) whole water chestnuts, drained and halved
1-1/2 cups packed brown sugar
3/4 cup ketchup
3/4 cup mayonnaise*

Cut bacon strips into thirds. Wrap each strip around a water chestnut and secure with a toothpick. Place in an ungreased 13-in. x 9-in. x 2-in. baking dish. Bake, uncovered, at 400° for 30-35 minutes or until bacon is crisp, turning once; drain.

Meanwhile, combine the remaining ingredients; pour over water chestnuts. Bake 6-8 minutes longer or until hot and bubbly. **Yield:** about 8-1/2 dozen.

***Editor's Note:** Reduced-fat or fat-free mayonnaise may not be substituted for regular mayonnaise.

Savory Mushroom Tartlets

My husband likes to say, "I bet you can't eat just one of these appetizers!" And he's right. Folks always come back for more. —Judi Vreeland, Alamo, California

48 thin slices white bread, cut into 3-inch rounds
1/2 cup butter, softened, *divided*
3 tablespoons finely chopped green onions
1/2 pound fresh mushrooms, finely chopped
2 tablespoons all-purpose flour
1 cup heavy whipping cream
2 tablespoons snipped chives
1 tablespoon minced fresh parsley
1/2 teaspoon lemon juice
1/2 teaspoon salt
Dash cayenne pepper
2 tablespoons Parmesan cheese, optional

Spread one side of the bread rounds with 1/4 cup butter; place buttered side up in lightly greased miniature muffin cups. Bake at 400° for 10 minutes

or until lightly browned. Cool for 2 minutes before removing to wire racks.

In a saucepan, saute onions in the remaining butter for 3 minutes. Add mushrooms; saute for 10-12 minutes or until mushroom liquid has evaporated. Remove from the heat; stir in flour and cream until blended. Bring to a boil; boil and stir for 2 minutes or until thickened. Add chives, parsley, lemon juice, salt and cayenne; mix well. Cool slightly.

Place bread cups on a baking sheet; fill with mushroom mixture. Sprinkle with Parmesan cheese if desired. Bake at 350° for 10 minutes. Broil 4 in. from the heat for 2 minutes or until lightly browned. **Yield:** 4 dozen.

Dried Beef Spread

This tasty spread is handy because you can make it ahead. For a festive presentation, chill it for an hour or two, shape it into a ball and roll it in chopped nuts.
—Margaret Sas, Ocean City, Maryland

1 package (2-1/2 ounces) sliced dried beef
2 packages (8 ounces *each*) cream cheese, cubed
2 tablespoons milk
1 tablespoon chopped green onion
1/2 teaspoon dill weed
1/4 teaspoon hot pepper sauce
Crackers *or* party rye bread

Place beef in a food processor or blender; cover and process until chopped. Add the cream cheese, milk, onion, dill and hot pepper sauce; cover and process until well blended. Serve with crackers or bread. **Yield:** 2 cups.

Appetizer Crab Pizza

(Pictured above right)

Guests will know you fussed when they bite into a wedge of this rich, golden pizza with a made-from-scratch crust.
—Heidi Ralston, Tionesta, Pennsylvania

3 to 3-1/2 cups all-purpose flour
1 package (1/4 ounce) active dry yeast
1 teaspoon sugar
1/2 teaspoon salt
1 cup water
2 tablespoons olive oil

TOPPINGS:
2 packages (8 ounces *each*) cream cheese, softened
2 cans (6 ounces *each*) crabmeat, drained, flaked and cartilage removed *or* 2 cups chopped imitation crabmeat
1/4 cup milk
1 cup (4 ounces) crumbled feta cheese
1 teaspoon dried basil
1 teaspoon dried oregano
1/2 teaspoon garlic powder
1 cup (4 ounces) shredded Swiss cheese, *divided*

In a large mixing bowl, combine 1-1/2 cups flour, yeast, sugar and salt. In a saucepan, heat water and oil to 120°-130°. Add to dry ingredients; beat on medium speed for 3 minutes. Stir in enough remaining flour to form a soft dough. Turn onto a floured surface; knead until smooth and elastic, about 8 minutes. Place in a greased bowl, turning once to grease top. Cover and let rise in a warm place until doubled, about 1 hour.

Punch dough down; divide in half. On a floured surface, roll each piece into a 13-in. circle; transfer to two 12-in. pizza pans. Build up edge slightly. Prick dough thoroughly with a fork. Bake crusts at 450° for 10-12 minutes or until lightly browned.

Combine the cream cheese, crab, milk, feta cheese, basil, oregano and garlic powder; spread half of the mixture over each crust. Sprinkle each with 1/2 cup Swiss cheese. Bake 10-12 minutes longer or until crust is golden and cheese is melted. Cut into wedges. **Yield:** 2 pizzas (8-10 servings each).

Sweet 'n' Sour Sausage

(Pictured above)

A sweet sauce and merry Christmas colors make this fruit-and-sausage combo a trusted holiday crowd-pleaser. Hearty enough to serve for brunch, it always disappears in a twinkling! —*Mary Poninski Whittington, Illinois*

2 cans (8 ounces *each*) pineapple chunks
2 tablespoons cornstarch
1/2 teaspoon salt
1/2 cup maple syrup
1/3 cup water
1/3 cup cider vinegar
1 large green pepper, cut into 1-inch pieces
2 packages (8 ounces *each*) brown-and-serve sausage links
1/2 cup red maraschino cherries, halved

Drain the pineapple, reserving juice. Set the pineapple and juice aside. In a large saucepan, combine the cornstarch, salt, maple syrup, water, vinegar and reserved pineapple juice until smooth. Bring to a boil; cook and stir for 2 minutes or until thickened. Add the green pepper; cook 2 minutes longer.

Meanwhile, in a skillet, brown sausage; drain. Cut each link into thirds. Add the sausage, cherries and reserved pineapple to saucepan; heat through. Serve with toothpicks. **Yield:** 4-6 servings.

Crunchy Combo

My husband and our four sons enjoy this mix any time of year. What's more, the snack carries well to gatherings and makes a nice present when packaged in pretty tins. —*Gloria Schmitz, Elkhart, Indiana*

6 cups toasted oat cereal*
1-1/2 cups miniature pretzels
1-1/2 cups Cheetos
1/2 cup butter, melted
1/4 cup grated Parmesan cheese
1/2 teaspoon garlic salt
1/2 teaspoon onion salt
1/2 teaspoon Italian seasoning, optional

In a large bowl, combine the cereal, pretzels and Cheetos. Combine the remaining ingredients; pour over cereal mixture and stir to coat. Spread into an ungreased 15-in. x 10-in. x 1-in. baking pan. Bake at 275° for 30 minutes, stirring every 10 minutes. Cool. Store in an airtight container. **Yield:** about 9 cups.

***Editor's Note:** This recipe was tested with Quaker Toasted Oatmeal Squares.

Cheesy Mushroom Morsels

There's plenty of happy munching all around the table when I dish up these luscious morsels. Ideal for a large crowd, they taste like quiche without the crust or the fuss. —*Marian Platt, Sequim, Washington*

1 pound fresh mushrooms, sliced
1 large onion, chopped
2 garlic cloves, minced
1/2 cup butter
1 large green pepper, chopped
10 eggs
4 cups (16 ounces) shredded Monterey Jack cheese
2 cups (16 ounces) small-curd cottage cheese
1/2 cup all-purpose flour
1 teaspoon baking powder

3/4 teaspoon salt
3/4 teaspoon dried basil
3/4 teaspoon ground nutmeg

In a large skillet, saute the mushrooms, onion and garlic in butter until tender. Add the green pepper; saute 1 minute longer. Remove from the heat; drain. In a large bowl, beat eggs. Stir in the cheeses, flour, baking powder, salt, basil and nutmeg. Add mushroom mixture. Pour into a greased 15-in. x 10-in. x 1-in. baking pan.

Bake, uncovered, at 350° for 30-35 minutes or until edges are golden and a knife inserted near the center comes out clean. Let stand for 15 minutes. Cut into squares; serve warm. **Yield:** about 12 dozen.

Creamy Shrimp Mousse

Folks will think you're spoiling them when you serve this wonderful shrimp mousse! Molded in a ring, it looks fancy even as it feeds a crowd. —Eloise Bingenheimer Salem, Oregon

1 can (10-3/4 ounces) condensed cream of mushroom soup, undiluted
1 package (8 ounces) cream cheese, cubed
1 cup mayonnaise
1 envelope unflavored gelatin
6 tablespoons cold water
1 can (6 ounces) small shrimp, rinsed and drained *or* 1/3 cup frozen small cooked shrimp, thawed
3/4 cup chopped onion
1/2 cup chopped celery
Lettuce leaves
Fresh parsley, optional
Assorted crackers

In a saucepan, combine the soup, cream cheese and mayonnaise. Cook and stir over medium heat until smooth; remove from the heat. In a small saucepan, sprinkle the gelatin over water; let stand for 1 minute. Heat on low until the gelatin is dissolved. Transfer to a mixing bowl; cool slightly.

Add the shrimp, onion, celery and cream cheese mixture. Transfer to a 6-cup mold coated with nonstick cooking spray. Cover; refrigerate for 4 hours or overnight. Unmold onto a lettuce-lined serving plate. Garnish with parsley if desired. Serve with crackers. Refrigerate leftovers. **Yield:** 5 cups.

Ham 'n' Cheese Quiches

(Pictured below)

When I need a festive finger food, this recipe's the one I reach for. With cheese in both the crust and the filling, eating one quiche naturally leads to another. —Virginia Abraham, Vicksburg, Mississippi

1/2 cup cold butter
1 jar (5 ounces) process sharp cheddar cheese spread
1 cup all-purpose flour
2 tablespoons cold water

FILLING:

1 egg
1/2 cup milk
1/4 teaspoon salt
1/2 cup finely chopped fully cooked ham
1/2 cup shredded Monterey Jack cheese
1 tablespoon minced fresh parsley, optional

In a bowl, cut butter and cheese spread into flour until well blended. Add water and toss with a fork until a ball forms. Refrigerate for 1 hour. Press tablespoonfuls onto the bottom and up the sides of greased miniature muffin cups.

In a bowl, beat the egg, milk and salt. Stir in the ham, cheese and parsley if desired. Spoon a rounded teaspoonful into each shell. Bake at 350° for 28-32 minutes or until golden brown. Let stand 5 minutes before serving. **Yield:** 2 dozen.

Bacon Cheese Wreath

(Pictured below)

My grandmother makes this smoky bacon and Parmesan spread for parties and holiday get-togethers. For a pretty Yuletide presentation, accent the cream cheese wreath with parsley and pimientos. —*Lisa Carter*
Warren, Indiana

2 packages (8 ounces *each*) cream cheese, softened
1/2 cup mayonnaise
1/3 cup grated Parmesan cheese
1/4 cup sliced green onions, optional
10 bacon strips, cooked and crumbled
Parsley sprigs and diced pimientos, optional
Assorted crackers

In a small mixing bowl, beat the cream cheese, mayonnaise, Parmesan cheese and onions if desired; mix well. Stir in bacon. Cover and refrigerate for 1-2 hours.

Invert a small bowl in the center of a serving platter. Drop cream cheese mixture by rounded tablespoonfuls around edge of bowl. Remove bowl. Smooth cream cheese mixture, forming a wreath. Garnish with parsley and pimientos if desired. Serve with crackers. **Yield:** about 3 cups.

Sesame Ham Pinwheels

Rounding out a spread at our house is the task of these ham and cheese goodies rolled in sesame seeds. Not only are these appetizers delicious, they're pretty, too!
—*Kathleen Lally, Columbus, Ohio*

1 tube (8 ounces) refrigerated crescent rolls
1 cup (4 ounces) finely shredded cheddar *or* Swiss cheese
4 thin slices fully cooked ham
2 teaspoons prepared mustard
1 egg white
1/4 cup sesame seeds

Unroll crescent rolls and divide into four rectangles; seal perforations. Sprinkle with cheese. Top with ham; spread mustard over ham. Roll up from a short side; pinch seam to seal. Cut each into five slices.

In a shallow bowl, beat egg white. Roll dough edges of each slice in egg white, then in sesame seeds. Place on a greased baking sheet. Bake at 350° for 15 minutes or until bottoms are golden brown. **Yield:** 20 appetizers.

Date Snack Crackers

These delicious tidbits add a sweet element to a holiday lineup. The dates and nuts taste wonderful topped with fluffy frosting. And since the two toppings can be stored separately in the fridge, you don't have to make them all at once. —*Nettie Vandy, Lexington, Kentucky*

1 can (14 ounces) sweetened condensed milk
1-1/2 cups chopped dates
1-1/2 cups chopped walnuts
1 package (10 ounces) butter-flavored crackers
2 packages (3 ounces *each*) cream cheese, softened

2-1/2 cups confectioners' sugar
1/2 teaspoon vanilla *or* coconut extract

In a bowl, combine the milk, dates and walnuts. Cover and refrigerate for 3 hours or until firm. Spread level teaspoonfuls on each cracker. Place crackers on greased baking sheets. Bake at 350° for 8-10 minutes. Remove to wire racks to cool.

For frosting, beat cream cheese in a mixing bowl. Gradually add sugar and vanilla; beat until smooth. Spread over crackers. Store in the refrigerator. **Yield:** about 8 dozen.

Curried Chutney Cheese Spread

It's impossible to stop eating this distinctive spread once you start. I like it because it's an eye-catching dish to serve, and it has an intriguing blend of flavors and textures. People have fun guessing the ingredients.
—Leslie Suffich, Mobile, Alabama

2 packages (8 ounces *each*) cream cheese, cubed
2 cups (8 ounces) shredded cheddar cheese
1/3 cup apple juice
2 tablespoons Worcestershire sauce
2 teaspoons vanilla extract
1 teaspoon curry powder
1/2 teaspoon salt
1 jar (9 ounces) mango chutney
1/2 cup chopped green onions
1/2 cup flaked coconut
1/2 cup finely chopped unsalted peanuts
Assorted crackers

In a blender or food processor, combine the first seven ingredients. Cover and process until smooth. Spread into a 1/2-in.-thick circle on a 10-in. serving plate. Cover and refrigerate. Just before serving, spread chutney over cheese mixture. Sprinkle with onions, coconut and peanuts. Serve with crackers. **Yield:** about 5 cups.

Cranberry Tea

(Pictured above right)

This colorful tea with its sweet spicy flavor is a great winter warmer-upper. The aroma is sure to bring guests to the table! *—Kathy Traetow, Waverly, Iowa*

1 bottle (32 ounces) cranberry juice
2 cups sugar
1 can (6 ounces) frozen orange juice concentrate
1 can (6 ounces) frozen lemonade concentrate
1/3 cup red-hot candies
1 cinnamon stick
2 whole cloves

In a 3-qt. saucepan, combine all ingredients; bring to a boil over medium heat. Boil for 7 minutes, stirring occasionally. Remove cinnamon and cloves.

To serve, mix 1 cup concentrate and 2 cups water; heat through. Store concentrate in a covered container in the refrigerator. **Yield:** 18 cups (1-1/2 quarts concentrate).

Ice Ring Idea

An ice ring can add a festive touch to punch while keeping it cold. Fill a ring mold about half full with water or juice; freeze until slushy. Place fresh cranberries or other fruit and mint sprigs or lemon leaves around the ring. Add water until the mold is full; freeze until solid.

Festive Vegetable Dip

(Pictured above)

I like to serve this well-seasoned dip with veggies. It rounds out a holiday snack buffet in a festive way when it's served in hollowed-out green and red bell peppers. —*Mary Pollard, Crossville, Tennessee*

1 cup mayonnaise
1/2 cup sour cream
2 tablespoons minced fresh parsley
1 tablespoon minced chives
1 teaspoon dried minced onion
1/2 teaspoon lemon juice
1/2 teaspoon Worcestershire sauce
1/4 teaspoon salt
1/4 teaspoon paprika
1/8 teaspoon curry powder
1/8 teaspoon pepper
1 medium green pepper
1 medium sweet red pepper
Assorted raw vegetables

In a large bowl, combine the first 11 ingredients. Cover and refrigerate for at least 1 hour. Lay green pepper on its side; with a sharp knife, make a horizontal slice just above stem. Remove top piece; save for another use. Remove membrane and seeds. Repeat with red pepper. Fill peppers with dip. Serve with vegetables. **Yield:** 1-1/2 cups.

Zippy Cheese Bites

You'll need just four ingredients to assemble this extra-rich blend. Picante sauce adds a little kick to the cheesy squares that are wonderful served warm on crackers. —*Bernita Ebel, Norfolk, Nebraska*

5 eggs
3 cups (12 ounces) shredded Monterey Jack cheese
3 cups (12 ounces) shredded cheddar cheese
3/4 cup picante sauce
Assorted crackers

In a bowl, beat eggs; add cheeses. Pour half into a greased 13-in. x 9-in. x 2-in. baking dish. Spoon picante sauce over top. Top with remaining egg mixture.

Bake, uncovered, at 350° for 25-30 minutes or until a knife inserted near the center comes out clean. Let stand for 15 minutes. Cut into 1-in. squares. Serve warm on crackers. Refrigerate any leftovers. **Yield:** about 9-1/2 dozen.

Party Barbecued Franks

These peachy little franks disappear quickly whenever I serve them. The sweet and tangy sauce appeals to all ages. —Dorothy Anderson, Ottawa, Kansas

2 teaspoons cornstarch
2 tablespoons cold water
1 jar (18 ounces) peach preserves
1 cup barbecue sauce
2 packages (1 pound *each*) miniature hot dogs *or* smoked sausage links

In a large saucepan, combine the cornstarch and water until smooth. Stir in the preserves and barbecue sauce. Bring to a boil; cook and stir for 2 minutes or until thickened. Stir in hot dogs until coated. Cover and cook for 5 minutes or until heated through. **Yield:** 20 servings.

Cheesy Sausage Dip

The garlic really comes through in this crowd-pleasing cheese dip. It's one of our family's all-time favorites. I serve it in a slow cooker with a basket of tortilla chips alongside. —Curtis Cole, Dallas, Texas

1 pound ground beef
1 pound bulk pork sausage
2 tablespoons all-purpose flour
1 can (10-3/4 ounces) condensed cream of mushroom soup, undiluted
1 can (10 ounces) diced tomatoes and green chilies, undrained
1 medium onion, chopped
1 tablespoon garlic powder
2 pounds process cheese, cubed
Tortilla chips

In a large saucepan, cook beef and sausage over medium heat until no longer pink; drain. Sprinkle with flour. Add the soup, tomatoes, onion and garlic powder; mix well.

Bring to a boil; cook and stir for 2 minutes or until thickened. Reduce heat. Stir in the cheese until melted. Serve warm with tortilla chips. Refrigerate any leftovers. **Yield:** 8 cups.

Everything Nice Nuts

(Pictured below)

I wasn't satisfied with any spiced nut recipes I tried, so I created my own crunchy concoction. They're great to take to a party. —Janet Forden, Okotoks, Alberta

1/2 cup packed brown sugar
1/2 teaspoon ground cinnamon
1/4 teaspoon ground allspice
1/8 teaspoon ground cardamom
1/8 teaspoon ground cloves
4-1/2 teaspoons water
2 cups mixed nuts

In a microwave-safe bowl, combine the first six ingredients. Microwave, uncovered, on high for 1 minute. Stir; heat 30-60 seconds longer or until syrupy. Add nuts; stir to coat. Spread into a microwave-safe 9-in. pie plate. Microwave, uncovered, on high for 4 to 4-1/2 minutes or until syrup is bubbly. Immediately spread onto a greased baking sheet. When cool, break apart. **Yield:** 2 cups.

Editor's Note: This recipe was tested in an 850-watt microwave.

Colorful Shrimp Spread

(Pictured below)

A friend gave me the recipe for this scrumptious shrimp spread topped with mozzarella cheese and veggies. When I take it to a party or potluck, I never bring left-overs home. —Irene Smazal, Prineville, Oregon

1 package (8 ounces) cream cheese, softened
1 bottle (12 ounces) seafood sauce
1 can (6 ounces) small shrimp, rinsed and drained *or* 1/3 cup small frozen cooked shrimp, thawed
2 cups (8 ounces) shredded mozzarella cheese
3/4 cup chopped green pepper
1 medium tomato, chopped
4 green onions, sliced
Fresh rosemary and cilantro, optional
Assorted crackers

In a mixing bowl, beat cream cheese until smooth. Spread on a 12-in. round serving platter to within 2 in. of edge. In bowl, combine the seafood sauce and shrimp; spread over the cream cheese.

Sprinkle with mozzarella cheese, green pepper, tomato and onions. Garnish with rosemary and cilantro if desired. Serve with crackers. Refrigerate any leftovers. **Yield:** 8-12 servings.

Southwestern Appetizer Triangles

A nifty cross between egg rolls and tacos, these triangles are fun to serve, especially at the holidays. My mom created the recipe years ago, much to the delight of my family. Since I began making them, my husband insists we have them on Sundays during football season as well as for holiday celebrations. —Sheila Pope Preston, Idaho

1 pound ground beef
1 medium onion, chopped
Salt and pepper to taste
1 can (16 ounces) refried beans
1-1/2 cups (6 ounces) shredded cheddar cheese
1 cup salsa
1 can (4 ounces) diced jalapeno peppers, drained
2 packages (12 ounces *each*) wonton wrappers*
Oil for deep-fat frying
Additional salsa

In a skillet over medium heat, cook beef, onion, salt and pepper until meat is no longer pink; drain. Add the beans, cheese, salsa and jalapenos. Cook and stir over low heat until the cheese is melted. Remove from the heat; cool for 10 minutes.

Place a teaspoonful of beef mixture in the center of each wonton wrapper. Moisten edges with water. Fold wontons in half, forming a triangle. In an electric skillet or deep-fat fryer, heat 1 in. of oil to 375°. Fry wontons, a few at a time, for 2-3 minutes or until golden brown. Drain on paper towels. Serve warm with salsa. **Yield:** about 7-1/2 dozen.

***Editor's Note:** Fill wonton wrappers a few at a time, keeping others covered until ready to use.

Pineapple Cranberry Punch

Combining refreshing pineapple flavor with the zing of cranberry juice is how I created an easy-to-fix sipper to take to holiday parties. —Paula Zsiray, Logan, Utah

1 bottle (64 ounces) cranberry juice, chilled, *divided*
1 can (20 ounces) crushed pineapple, undrained

1 can (46 ounces) pineapple juice, chilled
1 liter ginger ale, chilled

Combine 2 cups cranberry juice and the crushed pineapple. Pour into a 6-cup ring mold; freeze. Just before serving, combine pineapple juice and remaining cranberry juice in a punch bowl; stir in ginger ale. Add the ice ring. **Yield:** about 3-1/2 quarts.

Cheesy Artichoke Garlic Loaf

Even people who don't like artichokes will enjoy slices of this delicious bread. The soft interior is rich with sour cream, three kinds of cheese and other goodies. —Diane Hixon, Niceville, Florida

1 loaf (20 inches) French bread, halved lengthwise
1/2 cup butter
6 garlic cloves, minced
2 tablespoons sesame seeds
1-1/2 cups (12 ounces) sour cream
1/4 cup grated Parmesan cheese
2 tablespoons minced fresh parsley *or* 2 teaspoons dried parsley flakes
2 teaspoons lemon-pepper seasoning
2 cups (8 ounces) cubed Monterey Jack cheese
1 can (14 ounces) water-packed artichoke hearts, rinsed, drained and chopped
1 can (2-1/4 ounces) sliced ripe olives, drained
1 cup (4 ounces) shredded cheddar cheese
1 medium tomato, chopped
Additional parsley

Carefully hollow out top and bottom of bread, leaving 1/4-in. shells; set aside. Cut removed bread into small cubes. In a skillet, melt butter. Add the bread cubes, garlic and sesame seeds; cook and stir until butter is absorbed. Remove from the heat.

In a bowl, combine the sour cream, Parmesan, parsley, lemon-pepper, Monterey Jack cheese, artichokes, olives and bread mixture. Spoon into bread shells; sprinkle with cheddar cheese.

Place on ungreased baking sheets. Bake at 350° for 30 minutes or until heated through. Sprinkle with tomato and additional parsley. Refrigerate any leftovers. **Yield:** 10-12 servings.

Party Chicken Wings

(Pictured above)

These moist wings—marinated overnight in a mixture of soy sauce, mustard and brown sugar—are excellent party appetizers. At our house, they're a must for holiday gatherings. —Marian Slattery Whitewater, Wisconsin

12 whole chicken wings* (about 2 pounds)
3/4 cup soy sauce
1/4 cup water
1/2 cup packed brown sugar
1 tablespoon Dijon mustard
1 teaspoon garlic powder

Cut chicken wings into three sections; discard wing tip section. In a bowl, combine remaining ingredients. Set aside 1/4 cup for basting; cover and refrigerate. Place the wings in a large resealable plastic bag. Pour the remaining marinade over wings; turn to coat. Seal and refrigerate overnight.

Drain and discard marinade. Place the wings in a shallow baking pan. Bake, uncovered, at 375° for 1 hour, brushing several times with reserved soy sauce mixture during the last 30 minutes of baking. Refrigerate any leftovers. **Yield:** 2 dozen.

***Editor's Note:** 2 pounds of uncooked chicken wing sections (wingettes) may be substituted for the whole chicken wings. Omit the first step of the recipe.

Pinecone-Shaped Spread

(Pictured above)

Spreading Christmas cheer is deliciously simple with this holiday novelty. Originally my mother's recipe, it always gets raves. —Lisa Pointer, Leadore, Idaho

1 package (8 ounces) cream cheese, softened
1/2 cup mayonnaise
5 bacon strips, cooked and crumbled
1 tablespoon finely chopped green onion
1/2 teaspoon dill weed
1/8 teaspoon pepper
1-1/4 cups whole unblanched almonds, toasted
Fresh rosemary sprigs, optional
Assorted crackers *or* raw vegetables

In a bowl, combine the cream cheese, mayonnaise, bacon, onion, dill and pepper; chill. Form into two pinecone shapes on a serving platter. Beginning at the narrow end of each shape, arrange almonds in overlapping rows. Garnish with rosemary if desired. Serve with crackers or vegetables. **Yield:** 1-1/2 cups.

Hot Apple Punch

(Pictured above)

With its soothing cinnamon seasoning, this fresh and flavorful apple punch is a must for Christmastime. —Dawn Supina, Edmonton, Alberta

2 cinnamon sticks (about 3 inches *each*), broken
10 whole cloves
6 whole allspice *or* 2 whole nutmeg
2 quarts apple juice
Additional cinnamon sticks, optional

Place the cinnamon sticks, cloves and allspice on a double thickness of cheesecloth; bring up the corners and tie with string to form a bag. Place in a large saucepan with apple juice (or place loose spices in pan and strain before serving). Bring to a boil.

Reduce heat; cover and simmer for 30 minutes. Remove spice bag. Serve punch hot in mugs. Garnish with cinnamon sticks if desired. **Yield:** 2 quarts.

Artichoke Dip

Crackers make great dippers for this creamy appetizer (chips and breadsticks work well, too). It's become the traditional introduction to our family's Christmas Eve dinner. —*Mrs. William Garner, Austin, Texas*

1 can (14 ounces) water-packed artichoke hearts, rinsed, drained and chopped
1 cup mayonnaise
1/3 to 1/2 cup grated Parmesan cheese
1 garlic clove, minced
Dash hot pepper sauce
Paprika, optional
Assorted crackers

In a bowl, combine the artichokes, mayonnaise, Parmesan cheese, garlic and hot pepper sauce. Transfer to a greased 1-qt. baking dish. Sprinkle with paprika if desired. Bake, uncovered, at 325° for 30 minutes. Serve warm with crackers. **Yield:** 2 cups.

Spinach Cheese Puffs

Friends and family request that I make these golden brown puffs every year on Christmas Eve. The tasty little treats are so good, you can't help but pop them in your mouth. —*Patricia Gould Canaan, New Hampshire*

1 cup milk
1/2 cup butter
1 teaspoon salt
1 cup all-purpose flour
4 eggs
1 package (10 ounces) frozen chopped spinach, thawed and well drained
1 cup (4 ounces) shredded Swiss cheese
1/2 cup grated Parmesan cheese

In a saucepan, bring the milk, butter and salt to a boil over medium heat. Add flour all at once and stir until a smooth ball forms. Remove from the heat; let stand for 5 minutes. Add eggs, one at a time, beating well after each addition. Continue beating until the mixture is smooth and shiny. Stir in spinach and cheeses.

Line baking sheets with foil and grease the foil. Drop batter by tablespoonfuls 1-1/2 in. apart onto prepared baking sheets. Bake at 375° for 23-28 minutes or until puffed and golden brown. Remove to wire racks. Serve warm. Refrigerate any leftovers. **Yield:** about 3-1/2 dozen.

Orange-Ginger Fruit Dip

(Pictured below)

A platter piled high with colorful cut-up fruit surrounding a bowl of this fluffy no-fuss dip will sweeten any holiday buffet table. It's a great way to get kids to eat fruit, too! —*Trisha Faulk, Athens, Michigan*

1 package (8 ounces) cream cheese, softened
1 jar (7 ounces) marshmallow creme
1 tablespoon grated orange peel
1/8 teaspoon ground ginger
Assorted fresh fruit

In a mixing bowl, beat cream cheese until smooth. Beat in the marshmallow creme, orange peel and ginger. Cover and refrigerate until serving. Serve with fruit. **Yield:** 2-1/2 cups.

Chicken Wings with Spicy Apricot Sauce

(Pictured below)

Everyone gobbles these up at Christmas potlucks! My mother gave me the recipe for this anytime appetizer with its flavorful sweet-and-sour sauce. —*Shirley Eckert Crestline, Ohio*

40 whole chicken wings (about 8 pounds)
1-1/2 cups cornstarch
1 tablespoon baking powder
1-1/2 teaspoons salt
1/2 teaspoon pepper
1/2 teaspoon sugar
3 eggs, beaten
Oil for deep-fat frying
SAUCE:
1 cup (3 ounces) dried apricots
1-1/4 cups water
2 tablespoons sugar
2 tablespoons cider vinegar
2 tablespoons honey
1/8 to 1/4 teaspoon cayenne pepper

Cut chicken wings into three sections; discard wing tip section. In a large resealable plastic bag, combine cornstarch, baking powder, salt, pepper and sugar. Dip chicken pieces in eggs, then coat generously with cornstarch mixture. In an electric skillet or deep-fat fryer, heat oil to 350°. Fry chicken wings, a few at a time, for about 9 minutes or until juices run clear. Drain on paper towels. Keep warm.

Meanwhile, combine apricots and water in a saucepan; bring to a boil. Reduce heat; cover and simmer until apricots are tender. Transfer to a blender or food processor. Add sugar, vinegar, honey and cayenne; puree until smooth. Cool slightly. Serve with chicken wings. **Yield:** 6 dozen.

Editor's Note: 8 pounds of uncooked chicken wing sections (wingettes) may be substituted for the whole chicken wings. Omit the first step of the recipe. The sauce can be made ahead, covered and refrigerated. Reheat and thin with a little water if necessary.

Cheesy Party Puffs

The first time I made these puffs for friends, all eight couples asked for the recipe! They're so tasty and quick to make in the busy holiday season, and everyone loves them. —*JoAnn Rohde, Vestal, New York*

1 tube (7-1/2 ounces) refrigerated buttermilk biscuits
5 pieces (5 ounces) string cheese, cut into fourths
3 to 4 tablespoons prepared Italian salad dressing
1/4 cup grated Parmesan cheese
Pizza sauce *or* ranch salad dressing, optional

Cut each biscuit in half; flatten each piece into a 2-1/2-in. circle. Place a piece of cheese in the center of each. Bring dough around cheese; pinch edges to seal. Roll in salad dressing. Dip the top of each ball in Parmesan cheese; place seam side down on a greased baking sheet.

Bake at 375° for 8-10 minutes or until golden brown. Serve with pizza sauce or ranch dressing if desired. **Yield:** 5 servings.

Dill Vegetable Dip

A friend gave me this zesty dip recipe many years ago, and now I serve it every year at our holiday open house.
—Karen Gardiner, Eutaw, Alabama

1 cup (8 ounces) sour cream
1/2 cup mayonnaise
1 tablespoon finely chopped onion
2 teaspoons dried parsley flakes
1 teaspoon dill weed
1 teaspoon seasoned salt
Assorted fresh vegetables

In a bowl, combine the first six ingredients; mix well. Cover and refrigerate. Serve with vegetables. **Yield:** 1-1/2 cups.

Crab Roll-Ups

These festive pinwheels are the perfect finger food for the buffet table. Chutney is a wonderful surprise in the flavorful filling. Chock-full of goodies, they won't last long.
—Emily Scott Kort, Washington, Michigan

1 package (10 ounces) frozen chopped spinach, thawed and squeezed dry
1 package (1.7 ounces) vegetable soup mix
1/2 cup mayonnaise
1/2 cup sour cream
1 package (8 ounces) imitation crabmeat, chopped
1 package (8 ounces) cream cheese, softened
1/4 cup mango chutney *or* chutney of your choice
1/8 teaspoon garlic powder
1/8 teaspoon onion powder
12 flour tortillas (8 inches)

In a bowl, combine the spinach, soup mix, mayonnaise and sour cream; cover and refrigerate for 1 hour. In another bowl, combine the crab, cream cheese, chutney, garlic powder and onion powder; cover and refrigerate for 1 hour.

Spread the spinach mixture on six tortillas. Spread the crab mixture on remaining tortillas. Place one crab tortilla over each spinach tortilla. Roll up tightly, jelly-roll style, and wrap in plastic wrap. Refrigerate for at least 30 minutes. Cut each roll into seven slices. Refrigerate any leftovers. **Yield:** about 7 dozen.

Bacon Cheese Spread

(Pictured above)

Each year, I share Christmas cheer by setting up a buffet at my family's hardware store. This spread is always a hit!
—Sharon Bickett, Chester, South Carolina

1 package (12 ounces) bacon strips, chopped
1/2 cup chopped pecans *or* almonds, toasted
4 cups (1 pound) shredded sharp cheddar cheese
2 cups mayonnaise
1 small onion, chopped
2 tablespoons finely chopped sweet red pepper
1/8 teaspoon cayenne pepper
Assorted crackers

Cook bacon until crisp; drain. Mix with the next six ingredients. Serve with crackers. **Yield:** 4 cups.

16 slices bread
1 cup mayonnaise
1 package (3 ounces) cream cheese, softened
1/3 cup grated Parmesan cheese
2 teaspoons grated onion
1/8 teaspoon cayenne pepper
Additional Parmesan cheese

Using a 2-in. round or diamond cookie cutter, cut shapes from bread slices. Place on ungreased baking sheets. Bake at 300° for 8-10 minutes or until toasted.

Meanwhile, in a small mixing bowl, combine the mayonnaise, cream cheese, Parmesan cheese, onion and cayenne. Spread on bread. Sprinkle with additional Parmesan. Broil 4 in. from the heat for 2-3 minutes or until golden brown and bubbly. Serve warm. **Yield:** about 3 dozen.

Creamy Guacamole Spread

(Pictured above)

All my brothers and sisters like to bring appetizers to our Christmas gatherings. This delectable dip came from my brother. It can be attractively displayed on lettuce with tomato wedges. —Lynn Thomas Lakewood, New York

2 large ripe avocados, peeled and cubed
1/2 cup mayonnaise
1/4 cup chopped onion
2 teaspoons lemon juice
2 teaspoons Worcestershire sauce
1 teaspoon salt
1 teaspoon hot pepper sauce
Assorted raw vegetables *or* tortilla chips

In a blender or food processor, combine the first seven ingredients. Cover and process until smooth. Serve with vegetables or chips. **Yield:** 2 cups.

Parmesan Puffs

These scrumptious puffs come from the oven golden brown and bubbly. I make them often to serve at parties. For a change of pace, I'll use Swiss cheese instead of Parmesan. —Patricia Brewer, Clanton, Alabama

Hot Bean Dip

My hearty dip is extra smooth, thanks to the cream cheese and sour cream I add. It's easy to assemble ahead and then bake before serving. People keep dipping until the dish is empty. —Donna Trout, Las Vegas, Nevada

1 can (16 ounces) refried beans
1 package (8 ounces) cream cheese, softened
1 cup (8 ounces) sour cream
1 can (4 ounces) chopped green chilies
3/4 cup salsa
3 tablespoons taco seasoning
6 green onions, chopped
Tortilla chips

In a mixing bowl, combine the first six ingredients; mix well. Transfer to a greased shallow 2-qt. baking dish. Sprinkle with onions. Bake, uncovered, at 350° for 25-30 minutes or until heated through. Serve with tortilla chips. **Yield:** 5 cups.

Warm Bacon Cheese Spread

This creamy spread, made with Monterey Jack and Parmesan cheeses, is sure to warm up your next holiday party. Guests never wander too far from the table when I put out this fragrant dip. —Bonnie Hawkins Burlington, Wisconsin

1 unsliced round loaf (1 pound) Italian bread
2 cups (8 ounces) shredded Monterey Jack cheese
1 cup (4 ounces) shredded Parmesan cheese
1 cup mayonnaise*
1/4 cup chopped onion
5 bacon strips, cooked and crumbled
1 garlic clove, minced

Cut top fourth off loaf of bread; carefully hollow out bottom, leaving a 1-in. shell. Cube removed bread and set aside.

Combine the remaining ingredients; spoon into bread bowl. Replace top. Place on an ungreased baking sheet. Bake at 350° for 1 hour or until heated through. Serve with reserved bread cubes. **Yield:** 2 cups.

***Editor's Note:** Reduced-fat or fat-free mayonnaise may not be substituted for regular mayonnaise.

Pizza Poppers

(Pictured below)

Both my husband and I are big pizza fans, so we created these pizza rolls that we like to take to parties. I think they'd be fun to set out for Santa to enjoy, along with his milk and cookies! —*Denise Sargent*
Pittsfield, New Hampshire

4 to 4-1/2 cups all-purpose flour
1/3 cup sugar
1 package (1/4 ounce) active dry yeast
1 teaspoon dried oregano
1/2 teaspoon salt
1 cup water
1 tablespoon shortening
1 egg
3 cups (12 ounces) shredded mozzarella cheese
1-1/3 cups minced pepperoni (about 5 ounces)
2 cups pizza sauce, warmed

In a mixing bowl, combine 2 cups of flour, sugar, yeast, oregano and salt. Heat water and shortening to 120°-130°; add to flour mixture along with the egg. Beat on medium speed for 1 minute. Stir in cheese and pepperoni; mix well. Add enough remaining flour to form a soft dough.

Turn onto a floured surface; knead until smooth and elastic, about 6-8 minutes. Place in a greased bowl, turning once to grease top. Cover and let rise in a warm place until doubled, about 1 hour.

Punch dough down; divide into four portions. Cut each portion into eight pieces; roll each piece into a 12-in. rope. Tie into a loose knot, leaving two long ends. Fold top end under roll; bring bottom end up. Press into center of roll. Place on greased baking sheets. Cover; let rise until doubled, 30 minutes. Bake at 375° for 10-12 minutes or until golden brown. Serve warm with pizza sauce. **Yield:** 32 appetizers.

Nutty Stuffed Mushrooms

(Pictured below)

Basil, Parmesan cheese and mushrooms blend together well, while buttery pecans give these treats a surprising crunch. Our children, grandchildren and great-grandchildren always ask for them! —Mildred Eldred Union City, Michigan

18 to 20 large fresh mushrooms
1 small onion, chopped
3 tablespoons butter
1/4 cup dry bread crumbs
1/4 cup finely chopped pecans
3 tablespoons grated Parmesan cheese
1/4 teaspoon salt
1/4 teaspoon dried basil
Dash cayenne pepper

Remove stems from mushrooms; set caps aside. Finely chop stems; place in a paper towel and squeeze to remove any liquid. In a skillet, saute chopped mushrooms and onion in butter for 5 minutes or until tender. Remove from the heat; set aside.

In a small bowl, combine the bread crumbs, pecans, Parmesan cheese, salt, basil and pepper; add the mushroom mixture. Stuff firmly into the mushroom caps. Place in a greased 15-in. x 10-in. x 1-in. baking pan. Bake, uncovered, at 400° for 15-18 minutes or until tender. Serve hot. **Yield:** 18-20 servings.

Cranberry Orange Punch

This tangy punch is festive, refreshing and easy to prepare. I float orange wedges studded with cloves in the pitcher or bowl as a garnish. And instead of plain ice cubes, I add frozen orange juice cubes. —Sandy McKenzie, Braham, Minnesota

2 bottles (32 ounces *each*) cranberry juice, chilled
1 cup lemon juice
2/3 cup sugar
2 cans (12 ounces *each*) orange soda, chilled
Ice cubes
Whole cloves and orange wedges, optional

In a large punch bowl or several pitchers, combine the cranberry juice, lemon juice and sugar; stir until sugar is dissolved. Just before serving, add orange soda and ice. If desired, insert cloves into orange wedges for garnish. **Yield:** about 3-1/2 quarts.

Creamy Shrimp Dip

I first tasted this seafood dip at a family reunion and requested the recipe right away. It's since become a fixture at our Christmas Day celebration, partly because it's so easy, but mostly because it's so yummy! —Pam Clayton, Brownsboro, Texas

1 package (8 ounces) cream cheese, softened
1/2 cup mayonnaise
4 green onions, chopped
1/2 teaspoon celery seed
1/2 teaspoon garlic powder

2 cans (6 ounces *each*) tiny shrimp, rinsed and drained
Potato chips *or* crackers

In a bowl, combine the first five ingredients; mix well. Stir in shrimp. Refrigerate until serving. Serve with chips or crackers. **Yield:** 2 cups.

Crab-Stuffed Deviled Eggs

For a little something special, I like to include this appealing appetizer in holiday buffets. Guests really go for the creamy crab filling with almonds and celery that add a fun crunch. —Inez Orsburn, De Motte, Indiana

12 hard-cooked eggs
1 can (6 ounces) crabmeat, drained, flaked and cartilage removed *or* 1 cup finely chopped imitation crabmeat
2/3 cup mayonnaise
1/2 cup finely chopped celery
1/2 cup chopped slivered almonds
2 tablespoons finely chopped green pepper
1/2 teaspoon salt

Slice eggs in half lengthwise. Remove yolks and set whites aside. In a bowl, mash yolks. Stir in the crab, mayonnaise, celery, almonds, green pepper and salt. Stuff or pipe into egg whites. Refrigerate until serving. **Yield:** 2 dozen.

Pineapple Smokies

(Pictured above)

These sausages in a tangy-sweet sauce make an excellent holiday snack. The recipe is quick and easy but makes lots. —Dorothy Anderson, Ottawa, Kansas

1 cup packed brown sugar
3 tablespoons all-purpose flour
2 teaspoons ground mustard
1 cup pineapple juice
1/2 cup vinegar
1-1/2 teaspoons soy sauce
2 pounds mini smoked sausage links

In a large saucepan, combine sugar, flour and mustard. Gradually stir in pineapple juice, vinegar and soy sauce. Bring to a boil over medium heat, stirring occasionally. Boil for 2 minutes, stirring constantly.

Add sausages; stir to coat. Cook for 5 minutes or until heated through. Serve warm. **Yield:** about 8 dozen.

Snow Pea Holiday Wreath

(Pictured above)

Santa himself might stop to sample this pretty-as-a-picture finger food! Crunchy green pea pods and juicy red tomatoes add a naturally fresh, festive holiday note to my buffet table. —Carol Schneck, Stockton, California

1 package (3 ounces) cream cheese, softened
1/4 teaspoon garlic powder
1/4 teaspoon seasoned salt
1/2 pound fresh snow peas, strings removed
2 cups grape *or* cherry tomatoes

In a small mixing bowl, combine the cream cheese, garlic powder and seasoned salt. Place mixture in a pastry bag or heavy-duty plastic bag with a small star tip. Pipe about 1/4 teaspoon of mixture onto the wide end of each pea pod. Arrange pods on a serving platter with cheese mixture toward the outside of the platter; fill center with tomatoes. **Yield:** 20 servings.

Homemade Smoked Almonds

Mom passed this recipe on to me—much to my husband's delight! We like to take the flavorful nuts to all sorts of gatherings, from fancy holiday affairs to casual luncheons. —Sheila Flodin, Farmington, Minnesota

1 egg white
2 teaspoons garlic powder
2 teaspoons celery salt
1/4 teaspoon salt
1/2 teaspoon Liquid Smoke
3 cups whole unblanched almonds, toasted and cooled

In a bowl, whisk egg white until foamy. Add the garlic powder, celery salt, salt and Liquid Smoke; stir until blended. Add almonds and stir until well coated.

Evenly spread the almonds in a 15-in. x 10-in. x 1-in. baking pan coated with nonstick cooking spray. Bake at 300° for 30 minutes, stirring every 10 minutes. Cool completely. Store in an airtight container. **Yield:** 3 cups.

Coconut Chicken Bites

These tender nuggets are great for nibbling, thanks to the coconut, cumin, celery salt and garlic powder that season them. I've served the bites several times for parties, and everyone enjoyed them. —Linda Schwarz Bertrand, Nebraska

2 cups flaked coconut
1 egg
2 tablespoons milk
3/4 pound boneless skinless chicken breasts, cut into 3/4-inch pieces
1/2 cup all-purpose flour
Oil for deep-fat frying
1 teaspoon celery salt
1/2 teaspoon garlic powder
1/2 teaspoon ground cumin

In a blender or food processor, process coconut until finely chopped. Transfer to a bowl and set aside. In another bowl, combine egg and milk. Toss chicken with flour; dip in egg mixture, then in coconut. Place in a single layer on a baking sheet. Refrigerate for 30 minutes.

In an electric skillet or deep-fat fryer, heat 2 in. of oil to 375°. Fry chicken, a few pieces at a time, for 1-1/2 minutes on each side or until golden brown. Drain on paper towels; place in a bowl. Sprinkle with celery salt, garlic powder and cumin; toss to coat. Serve warm. **Yield:** about 3 dozen.

Tasty Tortilla Roll-Ups

Celebrate the season in Southwestern style with these tasty pinwheel roll-ups. They're simple to make, easy for guests to handle and look so colorful on a serving tray or buffet table. —J. O'Neall, Westminster, Colorado

2 packages (one 8 ounces, one 3 ounces) cream cheese, softened
1/4 cup minced green onions
3 tablespoons chopped green chilies *or* jalapeno peppers*
3 tablespoons chopped ripe olives
3 tablespoons diced pimientos, drained
3 tablespoons finely chopped pecans *or* walnuts
1/8 teaspoon garlic powder
5 flour tortillas (8 inches)

In a small mixing bowl, beat cream cheese. Stir in green onions, green chilies, olives, pimientos, pecans and garlic powder. Spread over tortillas. Roll up tightly. Wrap in plastic wrap. Refrigerate for at least 2 hours. Cut into 1/2-in. pieces. **Yield:** 2-1/2 dozen.

***Editor's Note:** When cutting or seeding hot peppers, use rubber or plastic gloves to protect your hands. Avoid touching your face.

Ranch Jalapeno Dip

(Pictured below)

My family often asks me to make this zippy ranch-style dip. The recipe, from a local Mexican restaurant, stirs up a creamy blend that tastes great with crunchy tortilla chips or raw vegetables. —Charolette Westfall Houston, Texas

1 envelope original ranch salad dressing mix
2 pickled jalapeno peppers, seeded
1 jalapeno pepper, seeded
2 tablespoons minced fresh cilantro
Tortilla chips

In a blender or food processor, prepare the ranch salad dressing according to package directions. Add peppers and cilantro; cover and process for 2-3 minutes or until combined. Cover and refrigerate for at least 1 hour. Serve with tortilla chips. **Yield:** 2-1/2 cups.

Editor's Note: When cutting or seeding hot peppers, use rubber or plastic gloves to protect your hands. Avoid touching your face.

Bacon Rounds

(Pictured below)

On my family's list of favorite nibbles, this appetizer is tops. I've served the satisfying canapes at showers and brunches. They're convenient to make for parties because they can be made ahead and kept on hand in the freezer. —*Edie Despain, Logan, Utah*

1 cup mayonnaise
1 tablespoon grated Parmesan cheese
2 teaspoons Worcestershire sauce
1/4 teaspoon paprika
1/8 teaspoon celery seed
1/8 teaspoon garlic powder
1/8 teaspoon pepper
2 cups (8 ounces) shredded cheddar cheese
8 bacon strips, cooked and crumbled
1/3 cup chopped salted peanuts
4 green onions, thinly sliced
24 small French bread slices *or* 12 slices white bread
Additional sliced green onions, optional

In a bowl, combine the first seven ingredients; mix well. Stir in cheese, bacon, peanuts and onions; mix well. Spread over bread. Sprinkle with additional onions if desired. Place on ungreased baking sheets. Bake at 400° for 8-10 minutes or until lightly browned. If using white bread, cut into quarters. **Yield:** 4 dozen.

Editor's Note: Rounds may be frozen before baking. Bake at 400° for 10-12 minutes or until lightly browned (they do not need to be thawed first).

Hot Mustard Popcorn

When friends pop in at Yuletide, I like to dish up yummy munchies like this one. Mixed with zippy seasoning, it's best enjoyed with a thirst-quenching beverage. —*Diane Hixon, Niceville, Florida*

1 teaspoon ground mustard
1/2 teaspoon dried thyme
1/2 teaspoon salt
1/4 teaspoon pepper
Dash cayenne pepper
3 quarts freshly popped popcorn

Combine the first five ingredients. Place popcorn in a large bowl; add seasonings and toss. **Yield:** 3 quarts.

Sausage Bacon Tidbits

These taste-tempting tidbits come gift-wrapped. The savory sausage stuffing rolled up in bacon makes an irresistible combination that everyone loves. —*Doris Heath, Bryson City, North Carolina*

1-1/2 cups herb-seasoned stuffing mix
1/4 cup butter
1/4 cup water
1/4 pound bulk pork sausage
1 egg, beaten
1 pound sliced bacon

Place stuffing mix in a large bowl. In a saucepan, heat butter and water until butter is melted. Pour over stuffing. Add sausage and egg; mix well. Refrigerate for at least 1 hour.

Shape into 1-in. balls. Cut bacon strips in half; wrap a strip around each stuffing ball and secure with a toothpick. Place in an ungreased 15-in. x 10-in. x 1-in. baking pan. Bake, uncovered, at 375° for 20 minutes. Turn; bake 15 minutes longer or until bacon is crisp. Drain on paper towels; serve warm. **Yield:** about 2-1/2 dozen.

Christmas Cheese Balls

(Pictured above)

Christmas at our house just wouldn't be complete without these rich cheese balls. Friends and family ask for them every year, and I can make three gifts from just one recipe. —Margie Cadwell, Eastman, Georgia

4 packages (8 ounces *each*) cream cheese, softened
4 cups (1 pound) shredded cheddar cheese
1 cup chopped pecans
1/4 cup evaporated milk
1 can (2-1/4 ounces) chopped ripe olives, drained
2 garlic cloves, minced
1/2 teaspoon salt
Minced fresh parsley, chopped pecans and paprika
Assorted crackers

In a small mixing bowl, beat the cream cheese and cheddar cheese. Stir in the pecans, milk, olives, garlic and salt. Divide into thirds; roll each into a ball. Roll one ball in parsley and one in nuts. Sprinkle one with paprika. Cover and refrigerate. Remove from the refrigerator 15 minutes before serving. Serve with crackers. **Yield:** 3 cheese balls.

Cheese Ball Basics

To keep your hands and the countertop clean, spoon cheese mixture onto a piece of plastic wrap. Working from the underside of the wrap, pat the mixture into a ball. Complete the recipe as directed.

Allow cheese balls, dips and spreads that contain cream cheese to stand at room temperature 15 minutes before serving for easier spreading and more flavor.

Elegant Cheese Torte

(Pictured above)

Rich and creamy, this eye-catching torte makes quite an impression. Every time I take it to a party, it receives rave reviews! —*Donna Cline, Pensacola, Florida*

4 packages (8 ounces *each*) cream cheese, softened
1 cup butter, softened
2 teaspoons coarsely ground pepper
1 jar (5-3/4 ounces) stuffed olives, drained and chopped
8 cups (32 ounces) shredded sharp cheddar cheese, room temperature
3/4 cup apple cider, room temperature
2-1/4 teaspoons paprika
1 cup chopped pecans, toasted
Grapes and assorted crackers

In a mixing bowl, beat cream cheese and butter until smooth. Remove 3-1/2 cups to a small bowl; stir in pepper and set aside. Fold olives into remaining cream cheese mixture. Spread evenly over bottom of a 9-in. springform pan; set aside.

In a mixing bowl, beat cheddar cheese, cider and paprika on low speed for 1 minute. Beat on high until almost smooth. Spread half over olive layer. Top with peppered cheese mixture. Top with remaining cheddar mixture. Cover with plastic wrap; refrigerate for 6 hours or until firm. Place on serving plate and remove sides of pan. Press pecans into top; garnish with grapes. Serve with crackers. **Yield:** 24-30 servings.

Sausage-Filled Stars

My family loves these snacks with a savory sausage-cheese filling. The star shape makes them perfect for Christmas. —*Minnie Bell Millsaps, McCaysville, Georgia*

1 pound bulk sausage
1-1/2 cups (6 ounces) shredded cheddar cheese
1-1/2 cups (6 ounces) shredded Monterey Jack cheese
1 medium sweet red pepper, diced
1 medium green pepper, diced
1 can (4 ounces) chopped green chilies, drained
1 can (4-1/2 ounces) chopped ripe olives, drained
1 envelope ranch salad dressing mix
48 wonton wrappers
Vegetable oil

In a skillet, cook sausage until no longer pink; drain. Add cheeses, peppers, chilies, olives and dressing mix; mix well. Set aside. Brush both sides of wrappers with oil; press onto the bottom and up the sides of greased muffin cups.

Bake at 350° for 5 minutes or until golden brown. Transfer to a baking sheet. Fill each with about 2 tablespoons of the sausage mixture. Bake for 5 minutes or until heated through. Serve warm. **Yield:** 4 dozen.

Strawberry Dip

Fresh and fruity, this versatile dip lends a hint of summertime to Yuletide. It's light in taste and pretty in holiday pink. —*Doris Soliwoda, La Mesa, California*

1 package (8 ounces) cream cheese, softened
1/2 cup sour cream
1 carton (6 ounces) lemon yogurt
1/4 cup mashed strawberries
3 tablespoons honey
1 tablespoon maple syrup
Fresh fruit

In a mixing bowl, beat cream cheese and sour cream until smooth. Add yogurt, strawberries, honey and syrup; mix well. Refrigerate for 4 hours. Stir before serving. Serve with fruit. **Yield:** about 2 cups.

Creamy Herb Slices

These dressed-up slices of French bread go well with soup or salad...or can be served as an appetizer. I have to move fast after putting them out or there are none left for me! —*Kelly Schulz, Oak Forest, Illinois*

1 package (8 ounces) cream cheese, softened
1 tablespoon minced fresh parsley
1 tablespoon minced chives
2 teaspoons chopped green onion
2 garlic cloves, minced
1 teaspoon dill weed
1/2 teaspoon pepper
1 loaf (1/2 pound) French bread

In a small bowl, combine the first seven ingredients. Cut bread into 1/2-in. slices; spread each slice with 1 tablespoon cream cheese mixture. Place on ungreased baking sheets. Bake at 400° for 7 minutes or broil for 2 minutes or until golden brown. **Yield:** about 22 appetizers.

Zesty Marinated Shrimp

(Pictured below)

These easy shrimp look impressive on a buffet table and taste even better! The zesty sauce has a wonderful spicy citrus flavor. I especially like this recipe because I can prepare it ahead of time. —*Mary Jane Guest Alamosa, Colorado*

1/2 cup vegetable oil
1/2 cup lime juice
1/2 cup thinly sliced red onion
6 lemon slices
1 tablespoon minced fresh parsley
1/2 teaspoon salt
1/2 teaspoon dill weed
1/8 teaspoon hot pepper sauce
2 pounds medium shrimp, cooked, peeled and deveined

In a large bowl, combine the first eight ingredients. Stir in shrimp. Cover and refrigerate for 4 hours, stirring occasionally. Drain before serving. **Yield:** 12 servings.

Mocha Eggnog

(Pictured below)

This chocolaty twist on traditional eggnog will spread good cheer at your Christmas or New Year's celebration. My family makes a batch each year to sip while opening presents. —Beth Ann Hill, Dayton, Ohio

5 cups chocolate milk
4 cups eggnog*
1 cup heavy whipping cream, ***divided***
2 tablespoons instant coffee granules
2-1/2 teaspoons vanilla extract
1 teaspoon rum extract

In a large saucepan, combine the milk, eggnog, 1/2 cup cream and coffee granules; heat through. Remove from the heat; stir in vanilla and rum extracts. In a small mixing bowl, beat the remaining cream until stiff peaks form. Garnish eggnog with the whipped cream. **Yield:** 2-1/2 quarts.

***Editor's Note:** This recipe was tested with commercially prepared eggnog.

Pizza Bread

My moist, cheesy bread is a fun appetizer that I also use to complement Italian dishes, like lasagna and spaghetti and meatballs, and main-dish salads. This pull-apart bread is wonderful to eat warm from the oven. —Carla Hodenfield, Mandan, North Dakota

2 teaspoons yellow cornmeal
1 tube (12 ounces) refrigerated biscuits
1/2 cup pizza sauce
3/4 cup shredded mozzarella cheese

Sprinkle cornmeal on the bottom of a greased 8-in. square baking pan. Cut each biscuit into quarters; toss with pizza sauce. Place in pan; sprinkle with cheese. Bake at 400° for 14 minutes or until golden brown. **Yield:** 8-10 servings.

Spicy Pineapple Spread

Want a sweet-and-spicy treat? Set out my spread! It features a delicious mixture of warm fruit preserves, zesty horseradish and mustard, which you pour over cream cheese and serve with crackers. —Mavis Diment, Marcus, Iowa

1/4 cup apple jelly
1/4 cup pineapple preserves
4 to 5 teaspoons prepared horseradish
4 to 5 teaspoons ground mustard
1 package (8 ounces) cream cheese, softened
Assorted crackers

In a saucepan, combine jelly, preserves, horseradish and mustard. Cook and stir over medium-low heat until blended. Cover and refrigerate for 1 hour. Spoon over cream cheese. Serve with crackers. **Yield:** about 2/3 cup.

Ricotta Tart

(Pictured above)

Guests will think you fussed when they bite into a wedge of this cheesy tart. It's so simple to make with prepared pie pastry. —Teri Rasey-Bolf, Cadillac, Michigan

2 eggs
1 cup ricotta cheese
1 cup (4 ounces) shredded sharp cheddar cheese
2 tablespoons salsa
1/2 teaspoon salt
1/2 teaspoon pepper
Pastry for a single-crust pie (9 inches)

In a bowl, beat eggs. Add the cheeses, salsa, salt and pepper; mix well. Roll out pastry into a 12-in. circle on a foil-lined baking sheet. Spread with cheese mixture to within 1 in. of edge. Fold edge of pastry over outer edge of filling.

Bake at 400° for 22-26 minutes or until golden brown. Let stand for 5 minutes before cutting into wedges. Refrigerate any leftovers. **Yield:** 8-12 servings.

Hot Cranberry Cider

Adding colorful appeal to a wintertime or holiday meal is easy—just turn to this tasty cider that I developed myself. The addition of cranberry juice gives it lots of flavor and fun holiday color. —Anna Mary Beiler Strasburg, Pennsylvania

3 quarts unsweetened apple juice *or* cider
1 quart cranberry juice
2 to 3 whole cloves
1 cinnamon stick (3-1/2 inches)

Combine the apple juice, cranberry juice, cloves and cinnamon stick in a large kettle; bring to a boil. Boil for 5 minutes. Reduce heat; cover and simmer for 30 minutes. Remove the cloves and cinnamon stick before serving. Serve warm. **Yield:** 25-30 servings (1 gallon).

Olive Cheese Nuggets

More than 20 years ago, I tried these olive-stuffed treats for a holiday party. Friends are still asking me to bring them to get-togethers. —*Lavonne Hartel, Williston, North Dakota*

2 cups (8 ounces) shredded cheddar cheese
1-1/4 cups all-purpose flour
1/2 cup butter, melted
1/2 teaspoon paprika
36 stuffed olives

In a small mixing bowl, beat cheese, flour, butter and paprika until blended. Pat olives dry; shape 1 teaspoon of cheese mixture around each. Place 2 in. apart on ungreased baking sheets. Bake at 400° for 12-15 minutes or until golden brown. **Yield:** 3 dozen.

Piquant Meatballs

These meatballs, baked in a well-seasoned sauce, are always on the menu for our family's informal Christmas Eve get-togethers. Leftovers, if there are any, are a cinch to reheat in a slow cooker. —*Jennifer Wunderl, San Angelo, Texas*

1 can (16 ounces) jellied cranberry sauce
1 bottle (12 ounces) chili sauce
1 tablespoon lemon juice
2 eggs, lightly beaten
1 cup crushed cornflakes
1/3 cup ketchup
1/3 cup dried parsley flakes
3 tablespoons soy sauce
2 tablespoons dried minced onion
3/4 teaspoon salt
1/2 teaspoon pepper
1/4 teaspoon garlic powder
2 pounds lean ground beef

In a saucepan, combine cranberry sauce, chili sauce and lemon juice. Bring to a boil over medium heat; cook and stir until smooth. Set aside.

In a bowl, combine the next nine ingredients; add beef and mix well. Shape into 1-in. balls. Place in a greased 13-in. x 9-in. x 2-in. baking dish. Pour sauce over meatballs. Bake, uncovered, at 350° for 40-50 minutes or until the meatballs are no longer pink and sauce is bubbly. **Yield:** 4 dozen.

Fireside Clam Logs

These snacks taste great after a frolic in the snow. What's more, I found a way to make them even easier. After shaping them, I cover and refrigerate them until ready to bake. —*Mrs. Chester Forwood, Merced, California*

3 cans (6-1/2 ounces *each*) chopped clams, rinsed and drained
1/2 cup mayonnaise
1/3 cup sliced green onions
1/3 cup grated Parmesan cheese
1 teaspoon Worcestershire sauce
3/4 teaspoon garlic powder
1/2 teaspoon hot pepper sauce
24 thin slices sandwich bread, crusts removed
1/3 cup butter, melted

In a medium bowl, combine the first seven ingredients; mix well. Chill until ready to use. Flatten each slice of bread with a rolling pin; spread with 1 tablespoon of clam mixture. Roll up jelly roll style and cut in half. Place 1 in. apart on a greased baking sheet; brush with butter. Bake at 425° for 10-12 minutes or until lightly browned. Serve immediately. **Yield:** 4 dozen.

Taco Party Wings

Even though winter doesn't cool down all that much in this part of the country, I still like to serve snacks with added warmth, like these zesty party wings. —*Betty Riley, Phoenix, Arizona*

12 whole chicken wings* (about 2-1/2 pounds)
1/4 cup cornmeal
1 envelope taco seasoning
2 teaspoons dried parsley flakes
3/4 teaspoon salt

Cut chicken wings into three sections; discard wing tip section. Combine remaining ingredients in a bowl or plastic bag; add chicken wings and stir or shake to coat. Place in a single layer on two greased 15-in. x 10-in. x 1-in. baking pans.

Bake at 350° for 25 minutes; turn and bake 10 minutes or until chicken juices run clear. **Yield:** 6-8 servings.

***Editor's Note:** 2-1/2 pounds of uncooked chicken wing sections (wingettes) may be substituted for the whole chicken wings. Omit the first step of the recipe.

Salads

Spectacular Citrus Salad

A delightfully different salad is what I was looking for when I came across the original version of this recipe. I altered it a bit to fit my taste. —*Debbie Crutcher*
Tulsa, Oklahoma

1/2 cup vegetable oil
1/4 cup orange juice
2 tablespoons honey
2 tablespoons lime juice
2 teaspoons poppy seeds
1 teaspoon grated orange peel
1/2 teaspoon grated lime peel
12 cups torn red and green leaf lettuce
3 medium oranges, peeled and sectioned
3/4 cup thinly sliced red onion
2/3 cup pecan halves, toasted

In a jar with tight-fitting lid, combine the first seven ingredients; shake well. In a large salad bowl, combine lettuce, oranges, onion and pecans. Add dressing and toss to coat; serve immediately. **Yield:** 10-12 servings.

Bacon-Swiss Tossed Salad

(Pictured above)

This recipe came from a cookbook compiled by the women of our church in my hometown of Chico, California. It's pretty and tasty. Best of all, it can be put together a couple of hours before serving. When it's time, a simple toss and it's ready. —*Cathee Bethel*
Philomath, Oregon

1/2 cup mayonnaise
1 tablespoon sugar
1/4 teaspoon salt
1/4 teaspoon pepper
6 cups mixed salad greens
1 medium red onion, sliced
1 package (10 ounces) frozen peas, thawed
8 ounces sliced Swiss cheese, julienned
1 pound bacon, cooked and crumbled

In a small bowl, combine mayonnaise, sugar, salt and pepper. In a large salad bowl, layer a third of the greens and a third of the mayonnaise mixture, onion, peas and cheese. Repeat the layers twice. Cover and refrigerate for at least 2 hours. Just before serving, add the bacon and toss. **Yield:** 6-8 servings.

Orange-Cranberry Tossed Salad

Candied cranberries and mandarin oranges sparkle like jewels in this merry Christmas salad. —*Bernice Weir*
Hot Springs Village, Arkansas

2 cups fresh *or* frozen cranberries, thawed
1 cup sugar
3 tablespoons orange juice
2 tablespoons cider vinegar
2 tablespoons honey
1 teaspoon poppy seeds
1 teaspoon ground mustard
Dash salt and pepper
3/4 cup vegetable oil
2 heads Boston *or* Bibb lettuce, torn
1 can (11 ounces) mandarin oranges, drained

For candied cranberries, place cranberries in a baking pan; sprinkle with sugar. Cover tightly with foil and bake at 350° for 30 minutes, stirring every 15 minutes. Place in a single layer on greased aluminum foil; cool for at least 30 minutes.

For salad dressing, combine orange juice, vinegar,

honey, poppy seeds, mustard, salt and pepper in a small bowl. Slowly whisk in oil. Just before serving, toss lettuce, oranges and dressing in a large bowl. Sprinkle with candied cranberries. **Yield:** 12 servings.

Festive Fruit Salad

Here's a salad that won't remain on the dinnertime sidelines. Each time I serve it, it earns lots of compliments. —*Peggy Feist, Eatonton, Georgia*

- **3/4 cup sugar**
- **1/3 cup all-purpose flour**
- **1 cup milk**
- **1 can (20 ounces) crushed pineapple, drained**
- **2 tablespoons butter**
- **4 medium unpeeled red apples, cut into chunks**
- **1 cup green grapes**
- **1 cup chopped pecans, toasted**
- **1/4 cup red maraschino cherries, quartered**
- **1/4 cup green maraschino cherries, quartered**

In a saucepan, combine sugar and flour. Stir in milk and pineapple until blended. Bring to a boil over medium heat, stirring constantly. Cook and stir for 2 minutes or until thickened. Remove from the heat; add butter. Cool.

In a bowl, combine the apples, grapes, pecans and cherries. Add dressing; stir to coat. Cover and refrigerate until serving. **Yield:** 10-12 servings.

Curly Endive Salad

(Pictured below)

My wife grows herbs in our tiny city garden. I use her fresh oregano and mint to season this unique salad I created years ago. —*Roger Burch, Staten Island, New York*

- **4 cups torn curly endive, Belgian endive *and/or* escarole**
- **1/4 cup chopped red onion**
- **24 whole stuffed olives**
- **2 tablespoons olive oil**
- **1 tablespoon red wine vinegar**
- **3 tablespoons minced fresh oregano *or* 3 teaspoons dried oregano**
- **1 tablespoon minced fresh mint *or* 1 teaspoon dried mint flakes**
- **1/4 teaspoon salt**
- **1/8 teaspoon pepper**
- **2 ounces crumbled feta cheese**

In a salad bowl, toss endive, onion and olives. In a jar with a tight-fitting lid, combine oil, vinegar, oregano, mint, salt and pepper; shake well. Drizzle over salad and toss to coat. Top with cheese. **Yield:** 4 servings.

Lime Strawberry Surprise

(Pictured below)

Eye-catching in Christmas colors, this dish looks deliciously decorative on the table. Its combination of fruitiness and nutty crunch is surprisingly simple to create.
—Arline Wertz, Millington, Tennessee

1 package (3 ounces) lime gelatin
1 can (8 ounces) crushed pineapple, drained
1 package (8 ounces) cream cheese, softened
1/2 cup mayonnaise
1/2 cup chopped pecans
1 package (3 ounces) strawberry *or* cherry gelatin

Prepare lime gelatin according to package directions. Refrigerate until partially set, about 1 hour. Stir in pineapple. Pour into an 8-cup bowl or mold. Cover and refrigerate until firm, about 3 hours.

Beat cream cheese and mayonnaise until smooth; stir in pecans. Spread over lime gelatin. Refrigerate until firm, about 2 hours.

Prepare strawberry gelatin according to package directions; cool slightly. Carefully pour over cream cheese layer. Refrigerate until firm, about 3 hours or overnight. **Yield:** 8-10 servings.

Editor's Note: This recipe was doubled for a 4-qt. trifle bowl.

Greens with Creamy Celery Dressing

I love to top green salads with this slightly sweet, simple-to-fix dressing. My grandchildren request it all the time! *—Bertille Cooper, St. Inigoes, Maryland*

1/2 cup mayonnaise
1/2 cup sour cream
2 tablespoons sugar
1 tablespoon lemon juice
1 tablespoon orange juice
1 teaspoon celery seed
6 cups torn salad greens
3 green onions, sliced

In a bowl, whisk together the first six ingredients. In a salad bowl, combine the greens and onions. Drizzle with 1/3 cup dressing and toss to coat. Store leftover dressing in the refrigerator. **Yield:** 6 servings (1 cup dressing).

Christmas Salad

I enjoy entertaining during the holidays and always include this colorful salad on the menu. The red pepper and water chestnuts add a sweet crunch while the homemade vinaigrette gives this salad a savory zest.
—Jan Renaud, Lisle, Illinois

CRANBERRY VINAIGRETTE:
1/4 cup white wine vinegar
1/2 cup fresh *or* frozen cranberries, thawed
2 green onions, cut into 1-inch pieces
1 tablespoon sugar
1-1/2 teaspoons Dijon mustard
1/2 teaspoon salt
1/4 teaspoon pepper
1/4 teaspoon rubbed sage, crushed
3/4 cup olive oil

SALAD:
12 cups mixed salad greens
1 small sweet red pepper, chopped
1 can (8 ounces) sliced water chestnuts, drained, optional
Grated *or* shredded Parmesan cheese, optional

In a blender, combine the first eight ingredients. With the blender on high speed, gradually add the oil through the cap opening; process until smooth. Chill until serving.

In a large salad bowl, combine greens, red pepper and water chestnuts if desired. Sprinkle with Parmesan if desired. Serve with cranberry vinaigrette. **Yield:** 12 servings (1 cup vinaigrette).

Ambrosia Waldorf Salad

(Pictured at right)

A light, lovely pink salad, this recipe puts a different spin on traditional Waldorf salad. It is super served with roast turkey or baked ham. My family didn't think they liked cranberries until they tried this sweet, crunchy salad.
—Janet Smith, Smithton, Missouri

2 cups fresh *or* frozen cranberry halves
1/2 cup sugar
3 cups miniature marshmallows
2 cups diced unpeeled apples
1 cup seedless green grape halves
3/4 cup chopped pecans
1 can (20 ounces) pineapple tidbits, drained
1 cup heavy whipping cream, whipped
Shredded *or* flaked coconut

Combine cranberries and sugar. In a large bowl, combine the marshmallows, apples, grapes, pecans and pineapple. Add cranberries and mix well. Fold in whipped cream. Cover and chill. Sprinkle with coconut before serving. **Yield:** 12-14 servings.

Cranberry Mousse Salad

My sister and I discovered this recipe while looking for something different to serve at holiday time. The fruity flavor of the festive-looking salad goes especially well with poultry or pork.
—Sue Warner
Garner, North Carolina

1 package (6 ounces) strawberry gelatin
3/4 cup boiling water
1 can (16 ounces) whole-berry cranberry sauce
2 tablespoons lemon juice
1 teaspoon grated lemon peel
1/4 teaspoon ground nutmeg
1 can (20 ounces) crushed pineapple
2 cups (16 ounces) sour cream
1/2 cup chopped pecans

In a bowl, dissolve the gelatin in boiling water. Add the cranberry sauce, lemon juice, lemon peel and nutmeg; mix well. Drain pineapple; add juice to gelatin mixture and set pineapple aside. Chill until syrupy.

Whisk in sour cream. Add the pineapple and pecans. Pour into an 8-cup mold coated with nonstick cooking spray. Refrigerate until firm. **Yield:** 10-12 servings.

shake well. Toss pear slices with lemon juice; drain. In a salad bowl, combine the salad greens, pears, pecans and raspberries. Sprinkle with cheese. Drizzle with dressing. **Yield:** 8 servings.

Red and Green Apple Salad

Even though this colorful salad is perfect at Christmastime, it's so good I fix it throughout the year for buffets. —Fayellen McFarlane Kitimat, British Columbia

3 medium unpeeled green apples, coarsely chopped
3 medium unpeeled red apples, coarsely chopped
2 tablespoons lemon juice
1 cup (8 ounces) sour cream
1/4 cup mayonnaise
1 cup chopped dates
1 cup chopped walnuts
20 red maraschino cherries, halved
20 green maraschino cherries, halved

In a large bowl, toss apples with lemon juice. Cover and refrigerate. Just before serving, combine sour cream and mayonnaise. Pour over apples and toss to coat. Stir in dates, nuts and cherries. **Yield:** 10 servings.

Pecan-Pear Tossed Salad

(Pictured above)

To save time, I prepare the ingredients and dressing the day before, then combine them just before serving. This salad has become a star at family gatherings. Once, when I forgot to bring it, dinner was postponed so I could go get it! —Marjean Claassen, Sedgwick, Kansas

2 tablespoons fresh raspberries
3/4 cup olive oil
3 tablespoons cider vinegar
2 tablespoons plus 1 teaspoon sugar
1/4 to 1/2 teaspoon pepper
SALAD:
4 medium ripe pears, thinly sliced
2 teaspoons lemon juice
8 cups torn salad greens
2/3 cup pecan halves, toasted
1/2 cup fresh raspberries
1/3 cup (2 ounces) crumbled feta cheese

Press raspberries through a sieve, reserving juice. Discard seeds. In a jar with a tight-fitting lid, combine oil, vinegar, sugar, pepper and reserved raspberry juice;

Eggnog Molded Salad

This gelatin salad looks so lovely on a platter and tastes good with the fruit and a hint of eggnog flavor. It goes well with any meal because it's refreshing. —Alice Ceresa, Rochester, New York

1 teaspoon unflavored gelatin
1/4 cup water
1 can (15-1/4 ounces) sliced pears
1 package (6 ounces) lemon gelatin
1 cup (8 ounces) sour cream
3/4 cup eggnog*
1 can (11 ounces) mandarin oranges, drained
Orange slices, maraschino cherries and mint leaves, optional

In a small bowl, combine gelatin and water; set aside. Drain pears, reserving juice; set pears aside. Add enough water to juice to measure 2 cups. Pour into a saucepan; bring to a boil. Remove from the heat; stir in gelatin mixture and lemon gelatin until completely dissolved. Cool for about 15 minutes.

Stir in sour cream and eggnog until well blended. Chill until partially set. Cut the oranges and pears into chunks; add to eggnog mixture. Pour into a 6-cup mold coated with nonstick cooking spray. Chill until firm. Garnish with oranges, cherries and mint if desired. **Yield:** 10-12 servings.

***Editor's Note:** This recipe was tested with commercially prepared eggnog.

Cranberry-Orange Relish

I always include this delicious fruity relish as part of our special Christmas Eve dinner. —Vonna Wendt Ephrata, Washington

- **1 unpeeled navel orange**
- **2 cups fresh *or* frozen cranberries**
- **1 unpeeled medium red apple**
- **1 package (3 ounces) raspberry gelatin**
- **1-1/3 cups boiling water**
- **1 can (20 ounces) crushed pineapple, undrained**
- **1/2 cup chopped walnuts**

Slice the orange into eighths; finely chop in a food processor. Add cranberries and process until chopped. Slice apple into eighths; add to orange mixture and process until chopped.

In a large bowl, dissolve gelatin in boiling water; stir in pineapple and orange mixture. Chill for at least 4 hours. Just before serving, stir in nuts. **Yield:** 12 servings.

Tart Cherry Salad

(Pictured at right)

This recipe has been in my family for years; we especially use it during the holiday season. It's pleasantly tart and a perfect complement to any meal. —Bea Wittman, Ridgway, Pennsylvania

- **2 cans (14-1/2 ounces *each*) pitted tart cherries**
- **2 cans (8 ounces *each*) crushed pineapple**
- **1 cup sugar**
- **2 packages (6 ounces *each*) cherry gelatin**
- **3 cups ginger ale**
- **3/4 cup flaked coconut**
- **1 cup chopped nuts, optional**

Drain cherries and pineapple, reserving juices. Set fruit aside. Add enough water to combined juices to make 3-1/4 cups; pour into a saucepan. Add sugar; bring to a boil. Remove from the heat; stir in gelatin until dissolved. Add the cherries, pineapple and ginger ale. Chill until partially set.

Stir in coconut and nuts if desired. Pour into a 3-qt. mold or 13-in. x 9-in. x 2-in. pan coated with nonstick cooking spray. Chill until firm, about 3 hours. **Yield:** 16-18 servings.

Unmolding Gelatin Salads

Dip the mold in a sink or large pan of warm water for just a few seconds or until the edges of the gelatin salad begin to release from the side of the mold. Place a serving platter over the mold and invert. Carefully lift the mold from the salad.

Marinated Italian Pasta Salad

(Pictured below)

When I have guests coming over or a busy day ahead, I like to make this pasta salad because I prepare it the day before. —*Gail Buss, Westminster, Maryland*

1 package (16 ounces) medium shell pasta
1/4 pound hard salami, cubed
1/4 pound sliced pepperoni, halved
1 block (4 ounces) provolone cheese, cubed
4 medium tomatoes, seeded and chopped
4 celery ribs, chopped
1 medium green pepper, chopped
1/2 cup sliced stuffed olives
1/2 cup sliced ripe olives
1 bottle (8 ounces) Italian salad dressing
2 teaspoons dried oregano
1/2 teaspoon pepper

Cook pasta according to package directions; rinse in cold water and drain. Place in a large bowl; add salami, pepperoni, cheese, vegetables and olives. Add salad dressing, oregano and pepper; toss to coat. Cover and refrigerate overnight. **Yield:** 12-16 servings.

Colorful Coleslaw

We enjoy the interesting blend of flavors and textures in this crisp cabbage slaw. It adds nice color and refreshing crunch to our Christmas feast.
—*Audrey Thibodeau, Mesa, Arizona*

3 cups shredded green cabbage
3 cups shredded red cabbage
3 tablespoons minced fresh parsley
1 carton (8 ounces) lemon yogurt
1 tablespoon sugar
1 tablespoon lemon juice
1 teaspoon ground mustard
1/4 teaspoon salt
1/4 teaspoon pepper
1 cup halved seedless red grapes
1/4 cup slivered almonds, toasted
1 teaspoon sesame seeds

In a bowl, combine cabbage and parsley. Combine the yogurt, sugar, lemon juice, mustard, salt and pepper; pour over cabbage mixture and toss to coat. Cover and refrigerate for 6-8 hours. Just before serving, add grapes, almonds and sesame seeds; mix well. **Yield:** 8-10 servings.

Snow-White Salad

I love to collect recipes for all kinds of occasions. This sweet gelatin salad is one I often make for Christmas, decorating it with halved red candied cherries for "holly berries" and green candied cherries cut into "leaves".
—*Sharon McClatchey, Muskogee, Oklahoma*

2 envelopes unflavored gelatin
1/2 cup cold water
1 can (20 ounces) crushed pineapple, undrained
1/4 cup sugar
2 packages (8 ounces *each*) cream cheese, softened
1 jar (7 ounces) marshmallow creme
2 envelopes whipped topping mix
Red and green candied cherries, optional

In a small bowl, combine gelatin and water; set aside. In a saucepan, bring pineapple and sugar to a boil. Remove from the heat; stir in gelatin mixture until completely dissolved. In a mixing bowl, beat cream cheese. Add marshmallow creme and pineapple mixture. Refrigerate for 30 minutes. Prepare whipped topping according to package directions; fold into pineapple mixture.

Pour into an ungreased 13-in. x 9-in. x 2-in. dish. Cover and refrigerate overnight. Decorate with cherries if desired. **Yield:** 16 servings.

Cinnamon Apple Salad

(Pictured at right)

The color of this salad complements the holiday season. It's very pretty. I also like that I can fix it a day ahead of time, especially when preparing a big holiday meal. —*Lisa Andis Morristown, Indiana*

1/2 cup red-hot candies
1 cup boiling water
1 package (3 ounces) lemon gelatin
1 cup applesauce
1 package (8 ounces) cream cheese, softened
1/2 cup mayonnaise
1/2 cup chopped pecans
1/4 cup chopped celery

In a bowl, dissolve candies in water (reheat if necessary). Add gelatin; stir to dissolve. Stir in applesauce. Pour half into an 8-in. square pan that has been lightly coated with nonstick cooking spray. Refrigerate until firm. Cover and set remaining gelatin mixture aside at room temperature.

Meanwhile, combine the cream cheese, mayonnaise, pecans and celery; spread over chilled gelatin mixture. Carefully pour remaining gelatin mixture over cream cheese layer. Chill overnight. **Yield:** 9 servings.

Festive Pea Salad

Colorful and dressed up enough for Christmas, here's an easy-to-make salad that is wonderful year-round. The green peas and red onion make it especially festive. —*J. O'Neall, Westminster, Colorado*

1 package (16 ounces) frozen petite peas, thawed

1-1/2 cups fresh snow peas, trimmed and halved
1 cup halved thinly sliced red onion
1 jar (2 ounces) diced pimientos, drained
1/3 cup mayonnaise
1/3 cup sour cream
1 teaspoon minced fresh mint
1/4 teaspoon salt
1/8 teaspoon white pepper
Dash to 1/8 teaspoon ground nutmeg
5 bacon strips, cooked and crumbled

In a large bowl, combine the peas, onion and pimientos. In a small bowl, combine the mayonnaise, sour cream, mint, salt, pepper and nutmeg. Pour over pea mixture; toss to coat. Cover and refrigerate for at least 1 hour. Just before serving, stir in the bacon. **Yield:** 8-10 servings.

Sweet Potato Apple Salad

(Pictured above)

Pairing a seasonal fruit and vegetable makes for a very pretty and unusual salad to accompany a turkey dinner. The poppy seed dressing has a citrus tang and really brings out the flavor. —*Dorothy Smith*
El Dorado, Arkansas

- **6 medium sweet potatoes (about 2-1/2 pounds)**
- **1/2 cup olive oil**
- **1/4 cup orange juice**
- **1 tablespoon sugar**
- **1 tablespoon white wine vinegar**
- **1 tablespoon Dijon mustard**
- **1 tablespoon finely chopped onion**
- **1-1/2 teaspoons poppy seeds**
- **1 teaspoon grated orange peel**
- **1/2 teaspoon grated lemon peel**
- **2 medium tart apples (about 3/4 pound), chopped**
- **2 green onions, thinly sliced**

In a large saucepan, cook sweet potatoes in boiling salted water until just tender, about 20 minutes. Cool completely. Meanwhile, in a jar with a tight-fitting lid, combine the next nine ingredients; shake well. Peel potatoes; cut each in half lengthwise, then into 1/2-in. slices.

In a 4-qt. bowl, layer a fourth of the sweet potatoes, apples and onions; drizzle with a fourth of the salad dressing. Repeat layers three times. Refrigerate for 1-2 hours. Toss before serving. **Yield**: 8-10 servings.

Cranberry Delight

This holiday salad stars cranberries in a tart ruby topping that sits on a snow-white cream cheese layer.
—*Billie Wilson, Murray, Kentucky*

- **1 cup graham cracker crumbs (about 16 crackers)**
- **1/4 cup butter, melted**
- **2 cups fresh *or* frozen cranberries**
- **1 cup sugar**
- **1/2 cup water**
- **1/3 cup chopped pecans**
- **3 tablespoons orange marmalade**
- **1 package (8 ounces) cream cheese, softened**
- **1/3 cup confectioners' sugar**
- **1 tablespoon milk**

1 teaspoon vanilla extract
1 cup heavy whipping cream, whipped

Combine crumbs and butter; press into an ungreased 8-in. square baking dish. Chill. In a saucepan, combine cranberries, sugar and water; bring to a boil. Reduce heat and simmer for 20 minutes. Remove from the heat. Stir in pecans and marmalade; refrigerate until completely cool.

Meanwhile, combine cream cheese, confectioners' sugar, milk and vanilla in a mixing bowl; beat until smooth. Fold in whipped cream. Spread over crust. Top with cranberry mixture. Refrigerate for at least 2 hours. **Yield:** 8 servings.

Holiday Broccoli Salad

What could be more Christmasy than a red and green dish? Plus, once people taste this crisp lightly dressed salad, I never have to worry about leftovers.
—Luann Kessi, Eddyville, Oregon

4-1/2 cups broccoli florets
3 cups chopped sweet red pepper
10 bacon strips, cooked and crumbled
1/3 cup sliced green onions
1/4 cup chopped pecans
3/4 cup mayonnaise
1 tablespoon red wine vinegar
Dash pepper

In a large bowl, combine the first five ingredients. In a small bowl, combine the mayonnaise, vinegar and pepper until smooth. Pour over broccoli mixture; toss to coat. Cover and refrigerate until serving. **Yield:** 16 servings.

Cherry Cola Salad

This tempting gelatin salad has a big cherry flavor and a fun zing from the cola. My two small children are always happy to see this salad on the table. We think it tastes great with or without the whipped topping.
—Betty Aman, Center, North Dakota

1 package (6 ounces) cherry gelatin
1-1/2 cups boiling water
1-1/2 cups cola
1 can (21 ounces) cherry pie filling
Whipped topping, optional

Dissolve gelatin in water. Add cola and pie filling; mix well. Pour into an 8-in. square baking dish. Refrigerate until firm. Garnish with whipped topping if desired. **Yield:** 8-10 servings.

Turkey Mandarin Salad

(Pictured below)

A refreshing, interesting combination of turkey, pasta and fruit with a lightly sweet dressing makes this a family favorite. I found the recipe in an old church cookbook.
—Bernice Smith, Sturgeon Lake, Minnesota

2 cups cubed cooked turkey
1 tablespoon finely chopped onion
1/2 teaspoon salt
1 cup seedless red grape halves
1 cup diced celery
1 can (15 ounces) mandarin oranges, drained
1 cup cooked macaroni
3/4 cup mayonnaise
3/4 cup heavy whipping cream, whipped
1/3 cup slivered almonds
Toasted almonds, optional

In a large bowl, combine turkey, onion and salt; mix well. Add grapes, celery, oranges and macaroni; toss lightly to mix. Cover and refrigerate. Just before serving, combine mayonnaise and whipped cream; fold into salad along with almonds. Top with toasted almonds if desired. **Yield:** 6-8 servings.

Winter Cabbage Salad

(Pictured below)

My mother made this recipe for as long as I can remember. She'd serve it as a vegetable, salad or garnish at family meals, ladies' church luncheons and potluck parties. —*Eleanor Shuknecht, Elba, New York*

2 cups cider vinegar
1 cup sugar
2 tablespoons salt
1 tablespoon mustard seed
3/4 teaspoon celery seed
1/2 teaspoon ground turmeric
10 cups thinly sliced cabbage (about 2-1/4 pounds)
3 medium onions, thinly sliced
2 medium sweet red peppers, thinly sliced
1 medium green pepper, thinly sliced

In a saucepan, bring the first six ingredients to a boil. Reduce heat; simmer, uncovered, for 5 minutes. Remove from the heat and allow to cool. In a large bowl, combine cabbage, onions and peppers. Pour vinegar mixture over vegetables and stir to coat. Cover and refrigerate overnight. **Yield:** 16-20 servings.

Italian Salad

This salad's easy on the hostess since the dressing is made ahead. What's more, it's popular with everyone I know who tastes it. —*Sandy Moran Manteno, Illinois*

1 cup olive oil
6 tablespoons red wine vinegar
1 jar (4 ounces) diced pimientos, drained
1 garlic clove, minced
1/3 cup grated Parmesan cheese
1/2 teaspoon salt
1/4 teaspoon pepper
1 can (14 ounces) water-packed artichoke hearts, rinsed, drained and quartered
1 medium red onion, halved and sliced
16 to 18 cups torn salad greens
Additional Parmesan cheese, optional

In a jar with a tight-fitting lid, combine the first seven ingredients and shake well. In a bowl, combine the artichoke hearts and onion. Add the salad dressing and toss gently. Cover and refrigerate for at least 8 hours or overnight.

Just before serving, pour the artichoke mixture over the salad greens and toss to coat. Sprinkle with additional Parmesan cheese if desired. **Yield:** 14-16 servings.

Christmas Broccoli Salad

Horseradish gives this well-seasoned salad a special zing. The radishes and broccoli add a festive Yule flair.
—Terri Puffenbarger, Blue Grass, Virginia

3/4 cup cold water
3 egg yolks
3 tablespoons vinegar
2 tablespoons sugar
1 tablespoon cornstarch
3/4 teaspoon salt
2 tablespoons prepared horseradish
4 cups broccoli florets (about 1 medium bunch)
Grated radishes

In a blender, combine the first six ingredients; cover and process until smooth. Transfer to a saucepan; cook and stir over low heat until a thermometer reads 160° and mixture is thickened. Stir in horseradish. Cover and refrigerate until chilled.

Meanwhile, place the broccoli in a saucepan; add 1 in. of water. Bring to a boil; reduce heat. Cover and simmer for 5-8 minutes or until crisp-tender. Rinse with cold water; drain well. Transfer to a serving bowl; cover and refrigerate. Just before serving, spoon sauce over broccoli. Garnish with radishes. **Yield:** 4 servings.

Holiday Tossed Salad

I served this fresh and colorful blend at a New Year's dinner party, and it was an instant success.
—Carol Dilcher, Emmaus, Pennsylvania

1 package (10 ounces) Italian-blend salad greens
1 package (5 ounces) spring mix salad greens
2 cans (11 ounces *each*) mandarin oranges, drained
1-1/2 cups dried cranberries
1 medium red apple, chopped
1 cup chopped walnuts
1/3 cup shredded cheddar cheese
1 bottle (8 ounces) raspberry vinaigrette

In a large bowl, toss the greens, oranges, cranberries, apple, walnuts and cheese. Drizzle with vinaigrette just before serving; toss to coat. **Yield:** 12 servings.

Fruited Wild Rice Salad

(Pictured above)

I created this salad recipe to feature wild rice, a delicious state crop. The apples and pecans in this salad give it some crunch. *—Larren Wood, Nevis, Minnesota*

DRESSING:
1/3 cup orange juice
1/4 cup olive oil
2 tablespoons honey
SALAD:
1 cup uncooked wild rice
2 medium apples, chopped
Juice of 1 lemon
1 cup golden raisins
1 cup seedless red grapes, halved
2 tablespoons *each* minced fresh mint, parsley and chives
Salt and pepper to taste
1 cup pecan halves

Combine dressing ingredients; set aside. Cook rice according to package directions; drain and set aside to cool. In a large bowl, toss apples with lemon juice. Add raisins, grapes, mint, parsley, chives and rice. Add dressing and toss. Season with salt and pepper.

Cover and refrigerate several hours or overnight. Just before serving, add pecans and toss lightly. **Yield:** 8-10 servings.

Salad with Honey-Mustard Dressing

This salad is one of my most-requested recipes. The from-scratch dressing, hard-cooked eggs and sugar-coated almonds can all be prepared ahead of time, so it can be made at the last minute. —Chris Rufener Rittman, Ohio

1 cup vegetable oil
1/2 cup plus 3 tablespoons sugar, *divided*
1/4 cup vinegar
1/4 cup honey
2 tablespoons lemon juice
1 teaspoon onion powder
1 teaspoon salt
1 teaspoon celery seed
1 teaspoon ground mustard
1 teaspoon paprika
1/2 cup slivered almonds
9 cups torn romaine
1 cup (4 ounces) shredded cheddar cheese
2 hard-cooked eggs, diced

In a saucepan, combine the oil, 1/2 cup sugar, vinegar, honey, lemon juice and seasonings; cook and stir until sugar is dissolved. Remove from the heat; set aside to cool.

In a skillet over low heat, cook almonds and remaining sugar until nuts are glazed; cool. In a salad bowl, toss the romaine, cheese and almonds. Top with eggs. Drizzle with dressing. Serve immediately. Refrigerate any leftover dressing. **Yield:** 10-12 servings.

Festive Potato Salad

Every member of my family and all my friends like creamy-type potato salads. So I make mine often for parties, potlucks and many other special occasions, especially Christmas. It's usually partially eaten before I can even announce, "It's ready"! —Gloria Warczak Cedarburg, Wisconsin

8 medium red potatoes, cooked and cubed
2 celery ribs with leaves, thinly sliced
2 green onions with tops, chopped
4 hard-cooked eggs, chopped
1/2 cup chopped peeled cucumber
1/4 cup chopped sweet red pepper
1/4 cup chopped green pepper
1-1/4 cups mayonnaise
1/4 cup sour cream
1/4 cup plain yogurt
1 tablespoon *each* minced fresh basil, marjoram and dill *or* 1 teaspoon *each* dried basil, marjoram and dill weed
1 teaspoon sugar
1/2 teaspoon salt
1/2 teaspoon pepper
4 plum tomatoes, coarsely chopped
1 cup frozen peas, thawed
1 cup (4 ounces) shredded cheddar cheese

In a large bowl, combine the potatoes, celery, onions, eggs, cucumber, and red and green pepper. In another bowl, combine the mayonnaise, sour cream, yogurt and seasonings. Pour over the potato mixture and toss to coat. Gently stir in the tomatoes, peas and cheese. Cover and refrigerate until serving. **Yield:** 14 servings.

Turkey Almond Salad

Whenever we have leftover turkey in the refrigerator, especially around the holidays, this is the first recipe I reach for. Chow mein noodles, almonds and sesame seeds add a nice crunch. —Donna Rear, Olds, Alberta

3 cups cubed cooked turkey
2 cups shredded cabbage
3/4 cup diced celery
1/4 cup sliced green onions
1-1/2 cups chow mein noodles
1/2 cup slivered almonds, toasted
2 tablespoons sesame seeds, toasted
DRESSING:
2/3 cup mayonnaise
1 tablespoon milk
2 teaspoons prepared mustard
1-1/2 teaspoons sugar
1/2 teaspoon salt
1/4 teaspoon pepper

In a large bowl, toss together the turkey, cabbage, celery and green onions. In another bowl, combine the mayonnaise, milk, mustard, sugar, salt and pepper. Pour over the turkey mixture. Chill for several hours.

Just before serving, add the chow mein noodles, almonds and sesame seeds and toss to mix. **Yield:** 6 servings.

Side Dishes & Condiments

Curried Squash Soup

(Pictured above)

Cayenne pepper gives a little kick to bowls of this pretty golden soup, a first course that everyone seems to love. It can be made several days ahead to fit a busy schedule, then heated up whenever needed.
—Evelyn Southwell, Etters, Pennsylvania

1 butternut squash (about 1-3/4 pounds)
1 large onion, chopped
2 garlic cloves, minced
2 tablespoons vegetable oil
1 tablespoon all-purpose flour
1 teaspoon salt
1 teaspoon curry powder
1/8 teaspoon cayenne pepper
5 cups chicken broth
1 bay leaf
CILANTRO CREAM TOPPING:
1/2 cup sour cream
1/4 cup heavy whipping cream
1/4 cup minced fresh cilantro

Cut squash in half lengthwise; discard seeds. Place squash cut side down in a greased or foil-lined baking pan. Bake, uncovered, at 400° for 40-50 minutes or until tender. When cool enough to handle, scoop out pulp; set aside.

In a large saucepan, saute onion and garlic in oil until tender. Add the flour, salt, curry powder and cayenne until blended. Stir in broth. Add bay leaf. Bring to a boil; cook and stir for 2 minutes or until thickened. Reduce heat; simmer, uncovered, for 20 minutes. Discard bay leaf. Cool to room temperature.

In a blender or food processor, place half of the broth mixture and squash; cover and process until smooth. Repeat with remaining broth mixture and squash. Return to the saucepan; heat through. Combine the topping ingredients; place a dollop on each serving. **Yield:** 6 servings.

Mushroom Barley Bake

I first tasted this barley bake when my daughter, a busy nurse, mother and farm wife, made it one night. Its tempting flavor prompted the whole family to ask for seconds.
—Jean Simons, Winnipeg, Manitoba

3/4 pound fresh mushrooms, sliced
2 medium onions, chopped
1/4 cup butter
1-1/2 cups medium pearl barley
1 jar (2 ounces) diced pimientos, drained
6 teaspoons chicken bouillon granules, ***divided***
4 cups boiling water, ***divided***

In a skillet, saute mushrooms and onions in butter until tender. Stir in barley and pimientos. Transfer to a greased 13-in. x 9-in. x 2-in. baking dish. Dissolve 3 teaspoons bouillon in 2 cups water; stir into barley mixture. Cover and bake at 325° for 1 hour.

Dissolve remaining bouillon in remaining water; stir into barley mixture. Bake, uncovered, 30 minutes longer or until liquid is absorbed and barley is tender. **Yield:** 8-10 servings.

Cauliflower Au Gratin

The first time I made this rich side dish for a big family meal, it was an instant hit. When everyone had eaten their fill, there was a lively discussion on who would be the lucky one to take home the leftovers!
—Kathryn Herman, Villisca, Iowa

1 medium head cauliflower (about 1-1/2 pounds), broken into florets
2 garlic cloves, minced
6 tablespoons butter
2 tablespoons all-purpose flour
1-1/2 cups milk
4 bacon strips, cooked and crumbled
1/4 teaspoon salt
1/8 teaspoon pepper
Dash cayenne pepper
1 cup (4 ounces) shredded Swiss cheese

In a large saucepan, bring cauliflower and 1 in. of water to a boil. Reduce heat; cover and cook for 6-7 minutes or until crisp-tender. Drain well; set aside. In another saucepan, saute garlic in butter for 1 minute. Stir in flour until blended; gradually add milk. Bring to a boil; cook and stir for 2 minutes or until thickened.

Remove from the heat; stir in cauliflower, bacon, salt, pepper and cayenne. Pour into a greased 1-1/2-qt. baking dish. Sprinkle with cheese. Bake, uncovered, at 400° for 15-20 minutes or until cheese is melted. **Yield:** 5-7 servings.

Holiday Hominy

I was looking for an attractive holiday dish that didn't repeat the red of beets, the orange of yams or the green of broccoli. So I developed this one, featuring the glow of golden hominy. —*Sara Crowley, Tyler, Texas*

1/2 cup butter
1/2 cup all-purpose flour
3 cups milk
1 to 1-1/2 teaspoons seasoned salt
1 to 1-1/2 teaspoons coarsely ground pepper
2 cups cubed process cheese (Velveeta)
5 cans (15-1/2 ounces *each*) yellow hominy, drained
Paprika

In a large saucepan, melt butter; stir in flour until smooth. Gradually add milk, seasoned salt and pepper. Bring to a boil; cook and stir for 2 minutes or until thickened. Stir in cheese until melted.

Place hominy in a greased 13-in. x 9-in. x 2-in. baking dish. Pour cheese sauce over hominy. Bake, uncovered, at 350° for 25 minutes. Sprinkle with paprika. Bake 10 minutes longer or until heated through. **Yield:** 12-14 servings.

Carrot Souffle

(Pictured below)

This recipe is rooted in my backyard garden. It's an excellent way to dress up veggies. My six grandchildren are happy to eat their carrots when they're dished up like this. —*Martha Sorrell, Louisville, Kentucky*

1-1/2 cups soft bread crumbs
1 cup milk
3 eggs, *separated*
2 cups finely grated carrots
1/2 cup finely chopped celery
3 tablespoons minced fresh parsley
1 tablespoon grated onion
1 teaspoon salt
1/4 teaspoon pepper
1/4 teaspoon cream of tartar

In a bowl, soak bread crumbs in milk. Lightly beat egg yolks; add to crumbs with carrots, celery, parsley, onion, salt and pepper. Mix well. In a mixing bowl, beat egg whites and cream of tartar until stiff peaks form. Gently fold into carrot mixture.

Transfer to a greased 2-qt. baking dish. Bake, uncovered, at 325° for 40-45 minutes or until a knife inserted near the center comes out clean. **Yield:** 6-8 servings.

Festive Cauliflower Casserole

(Pictured below)

My family asks for this dish every Christmas. It complements turkey or ham and can be put together the day before the meal—a real convenience for a cook when the holiday rush is in full swing.
—Nancy McDonald, Burns, Wyoming

1 large head cauliflower (2 pounds), cut into florets
1/4 cup diced green pepper
1 jar (4-1/2 ounces) sliced mushrooms, drained
1/4 cup butter
1/3 cup all-purpose flour
3/4 teaspoon salt
2 cups milk
1 jar (2 ounces) diced pimientos, drained
1 cup (4 ounces) shredded Swiss cheese, *divided*

Cook cauliflower in boiling salted water until crisp-tender; drain. Place in a greased 1-1/2-qt. baking dish. In a saucepan over medium heat, saute green pepper and mushrooms in butter until tender. Add flour and salt; stir until blended. Gradually add milk; bring to a boil, stirring constantly. Cook and stir 2 minutes more or until thickened. Remove from the heat; add pimientos. Stir in 3/4 cup cheese until melted; pour over cauliflower.

Cover and bake at 350° for 20 minutes. Sprinkle with remaining cheese; bake, uncovered, for 10-15 minutes or until cheese is melted. **Yield:** 6-8 servings.

Sweet Potato Apple Dressing

This dressing is simply the greatest. It's easy to make, creates a heavenly aroma when baking and combines two traditional favorites—sweet potatoes and dressing—into one special dish. Folks always give it rave reviews. *—Gail Prather, Bethel, Minnesota*

1-1/2 cups chopped green onions
2 celery ribs, chopped
1/2 cup butter
3 cups diced cooked sweet potatoes
3 medium tart apples, peeled and diced
4 cups soft bread cubes
1/2 cup chopped walnuts
3 eggs, lightly beaten
1/4 cup minced fresh parsley
2 teaspoons dried thyme
1 teaspoon rubbed sage
1/2 teaspoon salt
1/2 teaspoon pepper
1/4 teaspoon ground nutmeg

In a skillet, saute onions and celery in butter until tender. Transfer to a large bowl; add the sweet potatoes, apples, bread cubes and walnuts. Add eggs; toss to coat. Stir in the remaining ingredients.

Spoon into a greased 2-1/2-qt. baking dish. Cover and bake at 350° for 40 minutes. Uncover; bake 10 minutes longer or until lightly browned. **Yield:** 10-12 servings.

Elegant Mushroom Soup

This easy recipe turns commonplace ingredients into a wonderfully tasty soup. My family is delighted whenever they see it simmering on the stove.
—Marjorie Jaeger, Enderlin, North Dakota

1 large onion, chopped
1/2 pound fresh mushrooms, sliced

2 tablespoons butter
2 tablespoons all-purpose flour
1/4 teaspoon pepper
1/8 teaspoon salt
1 cup milk
1 cup chicken broth
1 tablespoon minced fresh parsley
Ground nutmeg, optional
Sour cream

In a large saucepan, saute onion and mushrooms in butter for 3 minutes or until onion is tender. Stir in flour, pepper and salt; gradually add milk and broth.

Bring to a boil; cook and stir for 2 minutes or until thickened. Add parsley and nutmeg if desired. Top individual servings with a dollop of sour cream. **Yield:** 2-3 servings.

Fancy Brussels Sprouts

Here's a great way to dress up brussels sprouts. Almonds give this rich creamy dish a nutty texture and flavor.
—Lucy Meyring, Walden, Colorado

1-1/4 pounds fresh brussels sprouts *or* 1 package (18 ounces) frozen brussels sprouts
1 can (10-3/4 ounces) condensed cream of mushroom soup, undiluted
1/4 cup milk
1 cup (4 ounces) shredded sharp cheddar cheese
1/8 teaspoon salt
1/8 teaspoon pepper
1 can (8 ounces) sliced water chestnuts, drained
1/2 cup slivered almonds, toasted

Cut an X in the core of each brussels sprout; cook brussels sprouts in boiling water. Meanwhile, in a saucepan over medium heat, combine the soup, milk, cheese, salt and pepper; cook and stir until cheese is melted. Drain brussels sprouts; transfer to a serving dish. Add water chestnuts and cheese sauce. Sprinkle with almonds. Serve immediately. **Yield:** 6-8 servings.

Cranberry Chutney

(Pictured above)

Its beautiful ruby hue makes this chutney ideal for the holiday season on a variety of meats.
—June Formanek, Belle Plaine, Iowa

1 pound fresh *or* frozen cranberries
2-1/2 cups sugar
1 cup water
1/2 teaspoon salt
1/2 teaspoon *each* ground cinnamon and cloves
1 medium onion, chopped
1 medium tart apple, peeled and cubed
1 medium pear, peeled and cubed
1 cup raisins
1/4 cup lemon juice
1 tablespoon grated lemon peel
1/2 cup chopped walnuts
Cooked pork chops *or* roast turkey *or* chicken

In a saucepan, combine the cranberries, sugar, water, salt, cinnamon and cloves. Bring to a boil; reduce heat. Simmer, uncovered, for 10 minutes. Add the onion, apple and pear; cook for 5 minutes. Remove from the heat; stir in raisins, lemon juice and peel. Cover and refrigerate for 8 hours or overnight. Just before serving, stir in the walnuts. Serve with meat. **Yield:** about 7 cups.

Spinach Spirals with Mushroom Sauce

(Pictured above)

I never thought I liked spinach until I tried these pretty spirals topped with a creamy mushroom sauce! It is a delicious dish to serve at a festive gathering.
—Mrs. Archie Potts, San Antonio, Texas

- **3/4 pound fresh mushrooms, sliced**
- **1/4 cup butter**
- **3 tablespoons all-purpose flour**
- **1 cup chicken broth**
- **1 cup half-and-half cream**
- **2 tablespoons sherry *or* additional chicken broth**
- **1 teaspoon Dijon mustard**
- **1/2 teaspoon lemon juice**

SPINACH ROLL:

- **1/2 cup dry bread crumbs**
- **3 packages (10 ounces *each*) frozen chopped spinach, thawed and squeezed dry**
- **6 tablespoons butter, melted**
- **1/4 teaspoon salt**
- **1/8 teaspoon pepper**
- **1/8 teaspoon ground nutmeg**
- **4 eggs, *separated***
- **1/4 cup grated Parmesan cheese**

In a large skillet, saute mushrooms in butter for 2-3 minutes. Stir in flour until blended; cook 2-3 minutes longer or until liquid is absorbed. Gradually stir in broth and cream. Bring to a boil. Remove from the heat; stir in the sherry or additional broth, mustard and lemon juice. Cool for 15 minutes.

Grease and line a 15-in. x 10-in. x 1-in. baking pan with parchment paper; grease the paper. Sprinkle with bread crumbs; set aside. In a large bowl, combine spinach, butter, salt, pepper, nutmeg and egg yolks. In a small mixing bowl, beat egg whites on high speed until stiff peaks form. Gradually fold into spinach mixture. Gently spoon over bread crumbs; press down lightly. Sprinkle with Parmesan cheese.

Bake at 350° for 12-15 minutes or until center springs back when lightly touched. Cover with a piece of greased foil; immediately invert pan onto foil. Gently peel away parchment paper. Spread 1 cup mushroom sauce over spinach mixture to within 1 in. of edges. Roll up jelly-roll style, starting with a short side and peeling foil away while rolling. Cut into slices. Reheat remaining mushroom sauce; serve with spinach spirals. **Yield**: 12 servings.

Golden Squash Bake

I save this memorable casserole for the holidays. We all look forward to it! The squash has a slight tang from sour cream, and allspice lends delightful aroma and flavor. *—Mary McKay, Sault Saint Marie, Ontario*

1/2 cup chopped onion
2 tablespoons butter
3 cups cooked mashed winter squash
1 cup (8 ounces) sour cream
1 teaspoon salt
1/4 to 1/2 teaspoon ground allspice
1/4 teaspoon pepper
1 tablespoon grated Parmesan cheese

In a skillet, saute onion in butter until tender. Remove from the heat. Stir in squash, sour cream, salt, allspice and pepper. Transfer to a greased 1-qt. baking dish; sprinkle with Parmesan cheese. Bake, uncovered, at 375° for 25-30 minutes. **Yield:** 6-8 servings.

Glazed Dijon Carrots

I not only serve these sweet glazed carrots during the holidays, but many times throughout the year as well. It's delightfully different and it tastes so good.
—Teri Lindquist, Gurnee, Illinois

1 package (16 ounces) baby carrots
1/2 cup water
3 tablespoons butter
2 tablespoons brown sugar
1 tablespoon Dijon mustard
1/2 teaspoon ground ginger
1/4 teaspoon salt

In a saucepan, bring carrots and water to a boil. Reduce heat; cover and cook for 10-12 minutes or until tender. Drain. Place carrots in a serving dish and keep warm.

In the same pan, melt butter. Add brown sugar, mustard, ginger and salt; cook and stir over medium heat until sugar is dissolved. Pour over carrots and toss to coat. **Yield:** 4-6 servings.

Broccoli Elegant

(Pictured at right)

My family loves this creamy vegetable side dish. As pretty as it is tasty, it's an extra-special way to serve broccoli, and it really dresses up a table.
—Carolyn Griffin, Macon, Georgia

3 cups water
1/2 cup plus 2 tablespoons butter, *divided*
2 packages (6 ounces *each*) corn bread stuffing mix
2 packages (10 ounces *each*) frozen broccoli spears, cooked and drained
2 tablespoons all-purpose flour
1/2 teaspoon chicken bouillon granules
1/4 teaspoon salt
1-1/3 cups milk
1 package (3 ounces) cream cheese, softened and cubed
2 green onions, sliced
1/2 cup shredded cheddar cheese
1/8 teaspoon paprika

In a saucepan over medium heat, combine water, 1/4 cup butter and seasoning packet from stuffing mixes; bring to a boil. Remove from the heat; add stuffing crumbs and toss. Let stand 5 minutes. Spoon stuffing around edges of a greased 13-in. x 9-in. x 2-in. baking dish. Place broccoli spears in center of dish.

In a saucepan over medium heat, melt remaining butter. Add flour, bouillon and salt; stir to form a smooth paste. Gradually add milk, stirring constantly; bring to a boil. Cook and stir for 2 minutes or until thickened. Add cream cheese; stir until melted. Add onions; mix well.

Pour over center of broccoli. Cover and bake at 350° for 20-25 minutes or until heated through. Sprinkle with cheese and paprika. **Yield:** 8-10 servings.

Glazed Whole Beets

(Pictured below)

This recipe came from my mother and was always a favorite holiday side dish when I was growing up. The glaze is such a wonderfully quick and easy way to dress up canned beets. —*Sylvia Lepczyk, Pittsburgh, Pennsylvania*

3 cans (15 ounces *each*) whole beets
5 teaspoons sugar
1 tablespoon all-purpose flour
1/4 teaspoon salt
1 tablespoon cider vinegar

Drain beets, reserving 2/3 cup juice. In a large skillet, combine the sugar, flour and salt. Stir in vinegar and reserved beet juice until smooth. Bring to a boil; cook and stir for 2 minutes or until thickened. Add beets; reduce heat. Cook, uncovered, for 4-5 minutes or until heated through. **Yield:** 6 servings.

Creamy Cheese Soup

We have a large family, so I always plan a big holiday menu. This time-saving first course is enjoyed by everyone, including the cook! —*Jan Campbell, Purvis, Mississippi*

1/3 cup *each* chopped carrots, celery and green onions
1/2 cup water
1 cup chopped onion
1/2 cup butter
3/4 cup all-purpose flour
4 cups milk
3 cups chicken broth
1 jar (16 ounces) process cheese sauce
1/8 teaspoon cayenne pepper

In a saucepan, bring carrots, celery, green onions and water to a boil; reduce heat. Simmer until crisp-tender; drain. Place in a blender or food processor; puree until smooth.

In a 3-qt. saucepan over medium heat, saute onion in butter. Add flour; stir to form a smooth paste. Gradually add milk and broth, stirring constantly; bring to a boil. Cook and stir 2 minutes or until thickened; reduce heat. Add cheese sauce, cayenne and pureed vegetables. Stir until cheese is melted. **Yield:** 8-10 servings (2-1/2 quarts).

Herbed Vegetable Squares

Flavorful veggies form the foundation for this side dish, which I like to serve with beef and chicken. —*Dorothy Pritchett, Wills Point, Texas*

1 package (10 ounces) frozen chopped spinach, thawed and drained
2 tablespoons vegetable oil
1-1/2 cups chopped zucchini
1 package (10 ounces) frozen cut green beans, thawed
1 large onion, chopped
1/4 cup water
1 garlic clove, minced
1-1/2 teaspoons dried basil
1-1/2 teaspoons salt
1/8 teaspoon pepper
1/8 teaspoon ground nutmeg
4 eggs
1/4 cup grated Parmesan cheese
Paprika

Squeeze spinach dry. In a skillet, saute spinach in oil for 2 minutes. Stir in zucchini, beans, onion, water, garlic, basil, salt, pepper and nutmeg. Cover and simmer for 10 minutes, stirring occasionally. Remove from the heat. In a bowl, beat eggs; gradually stir in 1-1/2 cups vegetable mixture. Return all to pan and mix well.

Transfer to a greased 11-in. x 7-in. x 2-in. baking dish. Place in a 13-in. x 9-in. x 2-in. baking dish; fill the larger dish with hot water to a depth of 1 in. Bake at 350° for 25-30 minutes or until a knife inserted near the center comes out clean. Sprinkle with the Parmesan cheese and paprika. Let stand 10 minutes before cutting. **Yield:** 6-8 servings.

Swiss Bean Casserole

This delicious creamy and cheesy side dish is too rich to serve often, so I save it for Christmas.
—Eleanor McCutcheon, Monticello, Florida

2 tablespoons chopped onion
1/3 cup butter
1/3 cup all-purpose flour
1 teaspoon salt
1/2 teaspoon white pepper
1/2 teaspoon ground mustard
2 cups milk
1-1/2 cups (6 ounces) shredded Swiss cheese
1 package (16 ounces) frozen French-style green beans, thawed and drained
1/4 cup slivered almonds, toasted

In a large saucepan, saute onion in butter until tender. Stir in the flour, salt, pepper and mustard until blended. Gradually add milk. Bring to a boil; cook and stir for 2 minutes or until thickened and bubbly. Reduce heat to low; stir in cheese just until melted.

Stir in beans until coated. Transfer to a greased 2-qt. baking dish. Sprinkle with almonds. Bake, uncovered, at 350° for 25-30 minutes or until bubbly. **Yield:** 6-8 servings.

Neapolitan Potatoes

(Pictured above right)

One taste of these yummy potatoes and I pestered my friend for months to give me the recipe! The tantalizing blend of flavors complements any festive entree.
—Kristi Beneschan, Lincoln, Nebraska

1/2 cup grated Parmesan cheese
3 garlic cloves, minced
1/2 cup minced fresh basil
1/4 cup minced fresh parsley
2 teaspoons minced fresh oregano
1-1/2 teaspoons salt
1 teaspoon pepper
7 tablespoons olive oil, ***divided***
6 cups thinly sliced red potatoes (about 2 pounds)
1 can (14-1/2 ounces) diced tomatoes, drained

In a bowl, combine the first seven ingredients; set aside. Grease a shallow 2-1/2-qt. baking dish with 1 tablespoon oil.

Place a third of the potatoes and tomatoes in prepared dish. Drizzle with 2 tablespoons oil; sprinkle with a third of the cheese mixture. Repeat the layers twice. Cover and bake at 350° for 55-65 minutes or until the potatoes are tender. **Yield:** 6-8 servings.

Pecan-Corn Bread Dressing

(Pictured above)

Plenty of pecans and bacon give this stuffing a unique flavor, while using a packaged mix cuts down on the preparation time. Our Taste of Home Test Kitchen came up with the savory recipe, which will come in handy during the holidays.

3 cups water
1/2 cup butter
1 package (16 ounces) corn bread stuffing
10 bacon strips, diced
1 cup chopped celery
1-1/2 cups chopped green onions
1/2 cup coarsely chopped pecans
1/2 teaspoon salt
1/4 teaspoon pepper

In a large saucepan, bring water and butter to a boil. Remove from the heat and stir in stuffing mix; cover and set aside. In a large skillet, cook bacon until crisp; remove with a slotted spoon to drain on paper towels. Discard all but 3 tablespoons of drippings; cook celery in drippings over medium heat for 5 minutes. Add onions and cook 5 minutes or until celery is tender, stirring constantly.

Add to the corn bread mixture along with pecans, salt, pepper and bacon; mix well. Pour into a greased 2-qt. casserole. Cover and bake at 325° for 45 minutes. **Yield:** 8 cups.

Spinach Potatoes

This potato dish is considered a special treat even by my grandchildren and great-grandchildren. It came to me from a dear friend who was raised on a farm in Kansas, and it's one of my personal favorites. The creamy spuds, spinach and melted cheese provide down-home flavor that can't be beat. —Adele Brooks, La Palma, California

6 to 8 potatoes, peeled, cooked and mashed
3/4 cup sour cream
1/2 cup butter, melted
2 tablespoons sugar
2 teaspoons salt
1/4 teaspoon pepper
1 package (10 ounces) frozen chopped spinach, cooked and drained
2 tablespoons minced chives
1-1/4 teaspoons dill weed
1 cup (4 ounces) shredded cheddar cheese

In a bowl, combine the potatoes, sour cream, butter, sugar, salt and pepper. Add the spinach, chives and dill. Spoon into a greased 2-1/2-qt. baking dish. Sprinkle with cheese. Bake, uncovered, at 400° for 12-17 minutes or until heated through. **Yield:** 8-10 servings.

Festive Peas and Onions

The first time I tried this recipe, my friend finished half of it while my back was turned! That was over 30 years ago, but the dish is just as popular today as it was then. —Carmella Robichaud
Richibucto, New Brunswick

1 package (16 ounces) frozen pearl onions
2 cups water
1 package (10 ounces) frozen peas, thawed
1 can (10-3/4 ounces) condensed cream of celery soup, undiluted
1 jar (2 ounces) diced pimientos, *divided*
1/3 cup shredded sharp cheddar cheese

In a covered saucepan, cook the onions in water for 25 minutes or until tender. Drain, reserving 1/4 cup liquid. Combine the onions, peas, soup, 2 tablespoons pimientos and reserved cooking liquid; stir to coat.

Transfer to a greased 1-1/2-qt. baking dish. Bake, uncovered, at 350° for 35 minutes. Sprinkle with cheese and remaining pimientos. Bake 5 minutes longer or until cheese is melted. **Yield:** 4-6 servings.

Cheesy Rosemary Potatoes

Turning plain potatoes into spectacular spuds is what happens whenever I follow this recipe. The cheese and seasonings make them rich and flavorful. —Jacqueline Thompson Graves Lawrenceville, Georgia

1 medium onion, thinly sliced
3 to 4 garlic cloves, minced
1 tablespoon olive oil
4 large potatoes, peeled and diced
1 teaspoon seasoned salt
1/8 teaspoon pepper
1/2 teaspoon grated lemon peel
2 cups (8 ounces) shredded cheddar cheese, *divided*
1/4 cup dry bread crumbs
1 tablespoon butter, melted
1/2 teaspoon dried rosemary, crushed

In a large skillet or saucepan, saute onion and garlic in oil until tender. Add potatoes, seasoned salt, pepper and lemon peel. Remove from the heat. Spoon half into a greased 1-1/2-qt. baking dish. Sprinkle with 1 cup cheese. Repeat the layers.

Combine bread crumbs, butter and rosemary; sprinkle over cheese. Cover and bake at 400° for 40 minutes. Uncover and bake 20 minutes longer or until potatoes are tender. **Yield:** 8-10 servings.

Cranberry Rice Pilaf

(Pictured below)

This deliciously different pilaf gets its festive color from tart cranberries, while brown rice provides wholesome flavor. It's excellent alongside poultry.
—S. Sonnon, Peru, Illinois

1 cup chicken broth
1/2 cup orange juice
2 tablespoons sugar
1-1/2 cups uncooked instant brown rice
1/2 cup fresh *or* frozen cranberries, thawed
1 tablespoon butter
2 tablespoons sliced almonds, toasted

In a saucepan, bring the broth, orange juice and sugar to a boil. Stir in the rice, cranberries and butter. Reduce heat; cover and cook for 5-8 minutes or until water is absorbed. Remove from the heat and let stand for 5 minutes. Sprinkle with almonds. **Yield:** 4 servings.

Onion-Stuffed Acorn Squash

(Pictured below)

Acorn squash are such a treat any time of year, especially when dressed up for the holidays with a special stuffing. I found this recipe in an old cookbook that was handed down to me. —*Barb Zamowski Rockford, Illinois*

3 small acorn squash, halved and seeded
1 egg, beaten
1/4 teaspoon salt
1/8 teaspoon pepper
1 teaspoon chicken bouillon granules
2 tablespoons boiling water
1/4 cup chopped onion
2 tablespoons butter
1 cup crushed sage stuffing mix

Invert squash in a greased 15-in. x 10-in. x 1-in. baking pan. Fill pan with hot water to a depth of 1/4 in. Bake, uncovered, at 400° for 30 minutes or until tender. When cool enough to handle, scoop out pulp, leaving a 1/4-in. shell (pulp will measure about 3 cups). Place shells cut side up in a greased 15-in. x 10-in. x 1-in. baking pan; set aside.

In a bowl, combine pulp, egg, salt and pepper. Dissolve bouillon in water; add to squash mixture. In a small saucepan, saute onion in butter until tender; stir in stuffing mix. Set aside 1/4 cup for topping; add remaining stuffing mixture to squash mixture. Spoon into shells. Sprinkle with reserved stuffing mixture. Bake, uncovered, at 400° for 20 minutes or until heated through. **Yield:** 6 servings.

Editor's Note: The squash mixture may be baked in a greased 1-qt. baking dish instead of in the shells.

Nutty Sweet Potato Bake

Even people who say they don't like traditional sweet potato dishes come back for more of this yummy casserole. —*Dorothy Pritchett, Wills Point, Texas*

4 eggs
1 cup sugar
1 cup milk
1/4 cup butter, melted
6 cups cubed cooked sweet potatoes *or* 2 cans (40 ounces *each*) cut yams, drained

TOPPING:

1 cup all-purpose flour
1 cup packed brown sugar
1/2 cup butter, melted
1 cup chopped pecans

In a large bowl, beat eggs. Add sugar, milk and butter; mix well. Add sweet potatoes and mix gently. Pour into a greased 13-in. x 9-in. x 2-in. baking dish.

For topping, combine flour and sugar in a small bowl. Stir in butter and pecans; mix well. Sprinkle over sweet potatoes. Bake, uncovered, at 350° for 55-65 minutes or until a knife inserted near the center comes out clean. **Yield:** 16 servings.

Broccoli Artichoke Casserole

A creamy mellow sauce draped over bold-tasting broccoli and artichokes makes this a great addition to any meal. —*Sue Braunschweig, Delafield, Wisconsin*

3 packages (10 ounces *each*) frozen broccoli spears, thawed and drained
2 cans (14 ounces *each*) water-packed artichoke hearts, rinsed and drained
1-1/2 cups mayonnaise*
1/2 cup butter
1/2 cup grated Parmesan cheese
4 teaspoons lemon juice
1/2 teaspoon celery salt
1/2 cup slivered almonds, optional
2 tablespoons diced pimientos, optional

Arrange broccoli and artichokes in a greased shallow 2-1/2-qt. baking dish; set aside. In a saucepan, combine mayonnaise, butter, cheese, lemon juice and celery salt. Cook and stir over low heat until butter is melted and sauce is heated through (do not boil). Pour over broccoli and artichokes. Sprinkle with almonds and pimientos if desired. Bake, uncovered, at 350° for 30-40 minutes or until broccoli is crisp-tender. **Yield:** 8-10 servings.

*__Editor's Note:__ Reduced-fat or fat-free mayonnaise is not recommended for this recipe.

Perfect Scalloped Oysters

My husband, children and grandchildren all look forward to this easy seafood side dish. It's one I've made for well over 30 years. —*Alice King, Nevada, Ohio*

2 cups crushed butter-flavored crackers (about 54)
1/2 cup butter, melted
1/2 teaspoon salt
Dash pepper
1 pint shucked oysters *or* 2 cans (8 ounces *each*) whole oysters
1 cup heavy whipping cream
1/4 teaspoon Worcestershire sauce

Combine cracker crumbs, butter, salt and pepper; sprinkle a third into a greased 1-1/2-qt. baking dish. Arrange half of the oysters over crumbs. Top with another third of the crumb mixture and the remaining oysters.

Combine cream and Worcestershire sauce; pour over oysters. Top with remaining crumb mixture. Bake, uncovered, at 350° for 30-40 minutes or until top is golden brown. **Yield:** 8 servings.

Lemon-Dilled Brussels Sprouts

(Pictured above)

Brussels sprouts get dressed up for the holidays when I make this flavorful dish. Lemon and dill season the buttery sauce, and chopped walnuts add just the right crunch. —*Marlyn Duff, New Berlin, Wisconsin*

1-1/2 pounds fresh brussels sprouts
1/3 cup butter
2 tablespoons lemon juice
1 teaspoon dill weed
1/2 teaspoon salt
1/8 teaspoon pepper
2 tablespoons finely chopped walnuts

Cut an X in the core of each brussels sprout. In a saucepan, bring brussels sprouts and 1 in. of water to a boil. Reduce heat; cover and simmer for 8-10 minutes or until tender.

Meanwhile, in another saucepan, melt the butter. Stir in the lemon juice, dill, salt and pepper; cook and stir for 1 minute. Drain the sprouts; add to the butter mixture and toss to coat. Sprinkle with walnuts. **Yield:** 4-6 servings.

Rich 'n' Creamy Potato Casserole

My husband, a pastor, and our three children enjoy these potatoes so much that I don't wait until the holidays to make them. —Mary White, Pawnee City, Nebraska

6 medium potatoes
2 cups (16 ounces) sour cream
2 cups (8 ounces) shredded cheddar cheese
4 tablespoons butter, melted, *divided*
3 green onions, thinly sliced
1 teaspoon salt
1/4 teaspoon pepper

Place potatoes in a saucepan; cover with salted water. Bring to a boil. Reduce heat; cover and simmer until tender. Drain and cool. Peel and grate potatoes; place in a bowl. Add the sour cream, cheddar cheese, 3 tablespoons butter, green onions, salt and pepper.

Transfer to a greased 2-1/2-qt. baking dish. Drizzle with remaining butter. Bake, uncovered, at 350° for 30-35 minutes or until heated through. Refrigerate any leftovers. **Yield:** 8-10 servings.

Festive Corn

(Pictured above)

For a deluxe side dish that's easy yet has big impact, I whip up this recipe. It features corn and peppers in a comforting cream cheese sauce. —Joy Beck Cincinnati, Ohio

1/4 cup chopped green pepper
1/4 cup chopped sweet red pepper
2 green onions, thinly sliced
2 tablespoons butter
1 package (8 ounces) cream cheese, cubed
2/3 cup milk
3/4 teaspoon salt
1/8 teaspoon pepper
1/2 teaspoon dill weed
1 package (16 ounces) frozen corn, thawed

In a saucepan over medium heat, saute peppers and onions in butter until tender. Add cream cheese, milk, salt, pepper and dill. Cook and stir over low heat until cheese is melted. Add corn; heat through. **Yield:** 6-8 servings.

Potato Stuffing

It wouldn't be Christmas in our family without this satisfying stuffing made from potatoes. —Lorraine Taylor, East Hartland, Connecticut

8 cups riced cooked potatoes
4 cups fine soft bread crumbs
2 large onions, chopped
1 cup butter
1 cup egg substitute
1 to 2 tablespoons poultry seasoning
2 teaspoons salt
1/2 teaspoon pepper
1 turkey (10 to 12 pounds)

In a bowl, combine the potatoes and crumbs; set aside. In a skillet, saute onions in butter until tender; add to potato mixture. Stir in egg substitute, poultry seasoning, salt and pepper. Stuff turkey.

Skewer and fasten openings. Tie drumsticks together. Place with breast side up on a rack in a roasting pan. Cover and bake at 325° for 3 to 3-3/4 hours or until a meat thermometer reads 180° for the turkey and 165° for the stuffing. **Yield:** 8-10 servings.

Editor's Note: Stuffing may also be baked in a greased 2-1/2-qt. baking dish. Cover and bake at 325° for 30 minutes. Uncover; bake 10-15 minutes longer.

Vegetable-Stuffed Baked Onions

(Pictured below)

Stuffed with carrots, red pepper, diced bacon and bread crumbs, these elegant baked onions will dress up any special-occasion meal. My mother often pulled out this recipe when company was coming. —Ruth Andrewson Peck, Idaho

8 to 10 medium onions, peeled
4 bacon strips, diced
3/4 cup finely chopped carrots
1/2 cup finely chopped sweet red pepper
1-1/2 cups soft bread crumbs
1/3 cup minced fresh parsley
3 tablespoons butter, melted
1-1/2 teaspoons salt
1/2 teaspoon pepper
3/4 cup beef broth

Cut 1/2 in. off the top of each onion; trim bottom so onion sits flat. Scoop out center, leaving a 1/2-in. shell. Chop removed onion; set 1/2 cup aside (discard remaining onion or save for another use). Place onion shells in a Dutch oven or large saucepan and cover with water. Bring to a boil; reduce heat and cook for 8-10 minutes.

Meanwhile, in a large skillet, cook bacon over medium heat until crisp. Remove to paper towels; drain, reserving 1 teaspoon drippings. In the drippings, saute chopped onion, carrots and red pepper for 8 minutes or until tender. Remove from the heat; stir in the bread crumbs, parsley, butter, salt, pepper and bacon.

Drain onion shells; fill each with about 1/3 cup vegetable mixture. Place in an ungreased shallow 3-qt. baking dish. Pour broth over onions. Cover and bake at 350° for 45-50 minutes or until heated through. **Yield:** 8-10 servings.

Pimiento Green Beans

(Pictured below)

Here's an easy way to turn everyday green beans into a special side dish. Pimientos, Parmesan cheese and chicken broth add savory flavor and a dash of color.
—Lyn McAllister, Mt. Ulla, North Carolina

2 pounds fresh green beans, cut into 2-inch pieces
1 can (14-1/2 ounces) chicken broth
1/2 cup chopped onion
1 jar (2 ounces) chopped pimientos, drained
1/2 teaspoon salt
1/8 to 1/4 teaspoon pepper
1/4 cup shredded Parmesan cheese

In a large saucepan, bring beans, broth and onion to a boil. Reduce heat; cover and cook for 10-15 minutes or until crisp-tender. Drain. Stir in the pimientos, salt and pepper. Sprinkle with Parmesan cheese. **Yield:** 10 servings.

Swiss Scalloped Potatoes

(Pictured below)

If you're a fan of French onion soup, you'll love this layered potato casserole. My family really enjoys it with ham, turkey or pork roast. —*Shirley Awood Glaab*
Hattiesburg, Mississippi

5 medium potatoes (about 3 pounds), peeled and thinly sliced
1 small onion, thinly sliced
1 jar (4 ounces) diced pimientos, drained
3 garlic cloves, minced
2 cups (8 ounces) shredded Swiss cheese, *divided*
3/4 teaspoon salt
1/4 teaspoon pepper
1 can (14-1/2 ounces) chicken broth
2 tablespoons butter

In a greased shallow 3-qt. baking dish, layer a third of the potatoes, onion, pimientos, garlic and Swiss cheese; sprinkle with 1/4 teaspoon salt and a dash of pepper. Repeat layers once. Top with remaining potatoes, onion, pimientos, garlic, salt and pepper. Pour broth over the top; dot with butter. Bake, uncovered, at 375° for 1 hour.

Sprinkle with remaining cheese. Bake 30 minutes longer or until liquid is absorbed and cheese is melted. Let stand for 10 minutes before serving. **Yield:** 8 servings.

Potato Cheese Casserole

This rich flavorful side dish is a Christmas tradition at our house. Plain potatoes are the start, but they get dressed up with a creamy cheese sauce and colorful ingredients like peppers and chives. —*Jane Luxem*
Green Bay, Wisconsin

4 pounds potatoes, peeled
1 package (8 ounces) cream cheese, softened
1/2 cup butter, softened
1/4 cup milk
1 to 1-1/4 teaspoons salt
1/4 teaspoon pepper
1 cup chopped green pepper
1/2 cup shredded cheddar cheese
1/2 cup grated Parmesan cheese
1/2 cup snipped chives
1 jar (2 ounces) diced pimientos, drained

Cook potatoes in boiling water until tender; drain and mash. Add cream cheese, butter, milk, salt and pepper; mix well. Stir in the green pepper, cheeses, chives and pimientos. Spread in a greased 13-in. x 9-in. x 2-in. baking dish. Bake, uncovered, at 350° for 50-60 minutes or until browned and heated through. **Yield:** 12-15 servings.

Crimson Chutney

The apples give my cranberry chutney a pleasant crunch. I especially like this recipe because I can make it weeks ahead. —*Linda Shaffer*
Crossville, Tennessee

3-1/2 cups (12 ounces) fresh *or* frozen cranberries
1 cup sugar
1 cup water
1/2 cup packed brown sugar
1/2 cup raisins
2 teaspoons ground cinnamon
1-1/2 teaspoons ground ginger
1/2 teaspoon ground cloves
1/4 teaspoon ground allspice
1 cup chopped peeled apples

In a large saucepan over medium heat, combine the first nine ingredients. Cook, uncovered, for 15 minutes, stirring occasionally. Add apples.

Reduce heat; cover and simmer 10 minutes. Pour into jars or plastic containers; cover and refrigerate up to 3 weeks. Do not freeze. **Yield:** 3-1/2 cups.

***Editor's Note:** A 10-ounce package of frozen spinach, thawed and squeezed dry, may be substituted for the fresh spinach.

Savory Onions And Spinach

This delicious mixture of onions and spinach, draped in a rich Parmesan cream sauce, looks as festive as it tastes. —*Sue Smith, Norwalk, Connecticut*

2 pounds frozen pearl onions
1 garlic clove, minced
3 tablespoons butter, ***divided***
1 package (10 ounces) fresh spinach*
3/4 cup grated Parmesan cheese, ***divided***
1/4 cup heavy whipping cream
Salt and pepper to taste
3 tablespoons dry bread crumbs

Cook onions according to package directions; drain well and set aside. In a saucepan, saute garlic in 2 tablespoons butter for 1-2 minutes. Add spinach; cook and stir until spinach is wilted and liquid evaporates, about 3 minutes. Stir in 1/2 cup of Parmesan cheese and the cream. Stir in onions, salt and pepper.

Place in a greased shallow 2-qt. baking dish. Combine bread crumbs and remaining cheese; sprinkle over onion mixture. Dot with remaining butter. Bake, uncovered, at 400° for 20 minutes or until golden brown. Serve with a slotted spoon. **Yield:** 8 servings.

Spiced Squash Rings

(Pictured above)

If you're tired of traditional sweet potatoes, this side dish is a tasty alternative. The cornmeal gives it a pleasant texture, and there's a nice balance between sweetness and spice. —*Kathy Biesheuvel, Broadus, Montana*

2 medium acorn squash
2 eggs
1/4 cup milk
1/2 cup cornmeal
1/4 cup packed brown sugar
3/4 teaspoon ground cinnamon
1/4 teaspoon salt
1/4 teaspoon ground nutmeg
1/3 cup butter, melted

Wash squash. Cut into 1/2-in. rings; remove and discard seeds and membranes. In a shallow dish, beat eggs and milk. In another shallow dish, combine the cornmeal, brown sugar, cinnamon, salt and nutmeg; mix well. Dip squash rings into egg mixture, then into cornmeal mixture; turn to coat.

Place in a greased 15-in. x 10-in. x 1-in. baking pan; drizzle with butter. Cover and bake at 400° for 25 minutes. Uncover; bake 10 minutes longer or until the squash is tender. **Yield:** 6-8 servings.

Cranberry Sweet Potato Bake

(Pictured above)

Sweet potatoes and tart cranberries are a feast for the eyes as well as the palate in this appealing side dish. It's scrumptious served with any holiday meal.
—Patricia Kile, Greentown, Pennsylvania

1-1/2 pounds sweet potatoes
1-1/2 cups fresh *or* frozen cranberries
2/3 cup sugar
1/3 cup orange juice
1 teaspoon salt
1 tablespoon butter
1-1/2 cups granola cereal

In a large saucepan, cover sweet potatoes with water; bring to a boil. Reduce heat; cover and simmer for 30 minutes or until tender. Drain and cool. Peel potatoes; cut into 1-in. pieces.

Combine cranberries, sugar, orange juice and salt; place half in a greased 11-in. x 7-in. x 2-in. baking dish. Top with half of the sweet potatoes. Repeat layers. Dot with butter.

Cover and bake at 350° for 25 minutes or until cranberries are tender. Uncover and sprinkle with granola; return to the oven for 10 minutes. **Yield:** 6-8 servings.

Jeweled Ham Glaze

When it comes to creating a gorgeous holiday entree, this glaze is tops. If your kitchen time's limited, try preparing it ahead so it's on hand in the refrigerator.
—Marian Platt, Sequim, Washington

1 jar (12 ounces) currant jelly
1/2 cup light corn syrup
1/4 cup lemon juice
1/2 teaspoon grated lemon peel
1/4 teaspoon ground cloves
1/4 teaspoon ground cinnamon
1/4 teaspoon ground allspice
1-1/3 cups chopped mixed candied fruit

In a saucepan, combine the first seven ingredients. Bring to a boil; reduce heat. Simmer, uncovered, for 5-7 minutes. Remove from the heat. Add candied fruit and mix well. Spoon glaze over ham during the last 30 minutes of baking time. **Yield:** 2-1/2 cups.

CORN SPOON BREAD

Here's a comforting side dish that has saved quite a few ordinary meals at our house. To spice it up a bit for Christmas, I stir in a can of holly-green chopped chilies. It's as good for breakfast as it is at lunch or dinner.
—Ruth Campbell, Staunton, Virginia

3 eggs, *separated*
1-1/2 cups milk
3/4 cup cornmeal
3/4 teaspoon salt
1 can (14-3/4 ounces) cream-style corn
2 tablespoons butter, softened
3/4 teaspoon baking powder

In a mixing bowl, beat egg whites until stiff peaks form; set aside. In another bowl, beat egg yolks; set aside. In a saucepan, bring milk to a boil. Add cornmeal and salt. Reduce heat; cook and stir for 1 minute or until thickened. Remove from the heat. Stir in the corn, butter and baking powder. Stir in egg yolks. Fold in egg whites.

Transfer to a greased 11-in. x 7-in. x 2-in. baking dish. Bake, uncovered, at 350° for 30-35 minutes or just until set. Serve immediately with a spoon. **Yield:** 6-8 servings.

SAVORY WILD RICE CASSEROLE

Seasoned with sage and tasty pork sausage, this filling rice casserole is a hearty accompaniment to roast turkey, chicken or duck. I especially like the crunch that the sliced water chestnuts add.
—Carol King
Onalaska, Wisconsin

3 cups water
1 cup uncooked wild rice
1/4 teaspoon salt
1 pound bulk pork sausage
1 medium onion, chopped
1 can (14-1/2 ounces) chicken broth
1 can (10-3/4 ounces) condensed cream of chicken soup, undiluted
1 can (8 ounces) mushroom stems and pieces, drained
1 can (8 ounces) sliced water chestnuts, drained
1 teaspoon rubbed sage

In a saucepan, combine water, rice and salt; bring to a boil. Reduce heat; cover and simmer for 55-60 minutes or until rice is tender. Meanwhile, in a skillet, cook sausage and onion until meat is no longer pink; drain. Add broth, soup, mushrooms, water chestnuts, sage and rice. Transfer to a greased 3-qt. baking dish. Bake, uncovered, at 350° for 45-50 minutes or until heated through. **Yield:** 8-10 servings.

HOLIDAY PEAS AND RICE

(Pictured below)

With all the fuss that goes into holiday meals, it's nice to find a side dish like this that's both satisfying and simple. The pimientos and peas nestle among rice delightfully seasoned with sage and chicken broth.
—Patricia Rutherford, Winchester, Illinois

1/2 cup uncooked long grain rice
1/8 teaspoon rubbed sage
2 tablespoons butter
1 can (14-1/2 ounces) chicken broth
1 cup fresh *or* frozen peas
2 tablespoons diced pimientos

In a saucepan, saute rice and sage in butter until rice is lightly browned. Add broth; bring to a boil. Reduce heat; cover and simmer for 20 minutes. Add peas; simmer, uncovered, 10 minutes longer or until heated through, stirring occasionally. Stir in pimientos. **Yield:** 4-6 servings.

Raisin-Studded Apple Stuffing

This is the only stuffing my family will permit on our holiday table. With Italian sausage and a blend of so many great flavors, it's almost a meal in itself. No wonder it won first prize in a local recipe contest!
—Teri Lindquist, Gurnee, Illinois

1 cup raisins
1-1/2 cups orange juice, *divided*
2 cups chopped celery
1 large onion, chopped
1 cup butter, *divided*
1 pound bulk Italian sausage
1 package (14 ounces) crushed herb-seasoned stuffing
4 medium tart apples, peeled and chopped
1 cup chopped pecans
2 cups chicken broth
2 teaspoons dried thyme
1/2 teaspoon pepper

In a saucepan, bring raisins and 1 cup orange juice to a boil. Remove from the heat; set aside (do not drain). In a skillet, saute celery and onion in 1/2 cup butter until tender. Transfer to a large bowl.

In same skillet, cook sausage over medium heat until no longer pink; drain. Add sausage, stuffing, apples, pecans, remaining orange juice and reserved raisins to celery mixture. In a saucepan, melt remaining butter; add broth, thyme and pepper. Pour over stuffing mixture; mix well.

Place in two greased 13-in. x 9-in. x 2-in. baking dishes. Cover and bake at 325° for 1 hour. Uncover; bake 10 minutes longer or until lightly browned. Refrigerate any leftovers. **Yield:** 18 cups.

Carrot Ring

(Pictured below)

Carrots become everyone's favorite when they're baked in this slightly sweet, lighter-than-air ring. Our holiday meal wouldn't be complete without it.
—Elaine Strassburger, Madison, Wisconsin

2 pounds carrots, peeled, cooked and mashed
3/4 cup half-and-half cream
3 eggs, beaten
1-1/2 teaspoons minced fresh parsley
1 teaspoon finely chopped onion
1/2 teaspoon salt
1/4 teaspoon pepper
1 package (10 ounces) frozen peas, cooked

Combine the first seven ingredients. Pour into a 6-cup ring mold coated with nonstick cooking spray. Bake, uncovered, at 350° for 35-40 minutes or until a knife inserted near the center comes out clean. Let stand for 10 minutes; unmold onto a serving plate. Fill the center with peas. **Yield:** 8-10 servings.

Citrus Carrots And Sprouts

I love serving brussels sprouts this way. The carrots and orange peel sweeten them up just right, while the hot pepper sauce adds a bit of zip.
—Sherri Gentry, Dallas, Oregon

1 pound fresh brussels sprouts, halved
1 pound fresh baby carrots
1/4 cup butter, melted
1 tablespoon grated orange peel
1 tablespoon minced fresh parsley
1/2 teaspoon salt
5 to 6 drops hot pepper sauce

Place the brussels sprouts and the carrots in a large saucepan with a small amount of water; cover and cook until tender, about 20 minutes.

Meanwhile, combine the remaining ingredients. Drain vegetables; add the butter mixture and toss to coat. **Yield:** 6-8 servings.

Cranberry Applesauce

Instead of the usual canned jellied cranberry sauce, I serve this refreshing from-scratch alternative. It's not too sweet and not too sour, plus it's a snap to make. The cranberries add fun Christmas color. *—Trisha Czyz Baldwinsville, New York*

1/2 cup plus 2 tablespoons water
1/2 cup plus 2 tablespoons sugar
5 medium Golden Delicious apples (about 2-1/2 pounds), peeled and chopped
1-1/4 cups fresh *or* frozen cranberries
1/2 teaspoon grated lemon peel
1 teaspoon minced fresh gingerroot
1/4 teaspoon ground cinnamon

In a large saucepan over medium heat, cook and stir water and sugar until sugar is dissolved. Add apples; cover and cook for 5 minutes, stirring often. Add cranberries; cover and cook until apples are tender and berries pop, about 15 minutes.

Mash until sauce reaches desired consistency. Stir in lemon peel, ginger and cinnamon. Cook, uncovered, 5 minutes longer. Serve warm or refrigerate until serving. **Yield:** 3-1/2 cups.

Twice-Baked Potatoes Supreme

(Pictured above)

On Christmas Day, we invite all our nearby relatives to dinner. One way I make the meal memorable is with this side dish that combines mashed and baked potatoes.
—Ruth Andrewson, Leavenworth, Washington

8 large baking potatoes
1/4 cup butter, softened
1/2 teaspoon garlic powder
1/2 teaspoon salt
1/2 teaspoon dried oregano
1/4 teaspoon cayenne pepper
1/8 teaspoon celery salt
1/3 to 1/2 cup milk
Grated Parmesan cheese
Paprika, optional

Pierce the potatoes with a fork. Bake at 400° for 60-70 minutes or until tender. Cut potatoes in half lengthwise; scoop out pulp, leaving a thin shell. Set shells aside. In a large bowl, mash pulp; add butter, garlic powder, salt, oregano, cayenne, celery salt and enough milk to make a smooth filling.

Stuff or pipe into shells; place in two greased 13-in. x 9-in. x 2-in. baking pans. Sprinkle with Parmesan cheese and paprika if desired. Bake, uncovered, at 350° for 20-25 minutes or until heated through. **Yield:** 16 servings.

Holiday Fruit Soup

I remember eating this soup every Christmas while I was a girl. I considered it a real treat. My mother, who was born in Sweden, made this soup during the holidays, and now I carry on the family tradition. —Eunice Jacobson
Wildrose, North Dakota

- **1 pound mixed dried fruit**
- **3/4 cup pearl tapioca**
- **6 cups water, *divided***
- **5 medium tart apples, peeled and cubed**
- **1 cup sugar**
- **Ground cinnamon**

Place fruit, tapioca and 4 cups water in a large saucepan. Cover and let stand overnight. Add apples, sugar and remaining water; bring to a boil. Reduce heat; cover and simmer for 1 hour or until tapioca is transparent. Add additional water if necessary. Serve warm or cold with a dash of cinnamon. **Yield:** 8-10 servings.

Whipped Squash

This is an excellent way to serve butternut squash. Its rich flavor and golden harvest color really come through in this smooth vegetable side dish.
—Dorothy Pritchett, Wills Point, Texas

- **1 butternut squash (about 2-1/2 pounds), peeled, seeded and cubed**
- **3 cups water**
- **3/4 teaspoon salt, optional, *divided***
- **2 tablespoons butter**
- **1 tablespoon brown sugar**
- **1/8 to 1/4 teaspoon ground nutmeg**

In a saucepan over medium heat, bring squash, water and 1/2 teaspoon of salt if desired to a boil. Reduce heat; cover and simmer for 20 minutes or until the squash is tender. Drain; transfer to a mixing bowl. Add butter, brown sugar, nutmeg and remaining salt if desired; beat until smooth. **Yield:** 6 servings.

Maple Baked Onions

I created this side dish to make use of the great maple syrup we have here in Vermont. My family loves this recipe, and I like the fact that it's so easy to prepare.
—Donna Kurant, West Rutland, Vermont

- **6 large sweet onions, sliced 1/2 inch thick**
- **1/3 cup maple syrup**
- **1/4 cup butter, melted**

Layer onions in a greased 13-in. x 9-in. x 2-in. baking dish. Combine syrup and butter; pour over onions. Bake, uncovered, at 425° for 40-45 minutes or until tender. **Yield:** 8-10 servings.

Creamy Vegetable Casserole

Even kids will eat their veggies when you serve them this way, covered in a creamy cheese sauce and topped with crushed crackers. They just might ask for seconds!
—Maxine Simes, Sidney, Ohio

- **1 package (24 ounces) frozen California-blend vegetables**
- **1 can (10-3/4 ounces) condensed cream of celery soup, undiluted**
- **1 jar (8 ounces) process cheese sauce**
- **1/2 cup finely crushed butter-flavored crackers (about 13 crackers)**
- **2 tablespoons butter, melted**

Prepare vegetables according to package directions; drain. In a bowl, combine soup and cheese sauce. Add vegetables and stir to coat. Transfer to a greased shallow 2-qt. baking dish. Toss cracker crumbs and butter; sprinkle over the top. Bake, uncovered, at 350° for 30 minutes or until heated through. **Yield:** 6 servings.

Sprucing Up Vegetables

Try these tasty toppings for basic hot cooked vegetables.

Combine 1/4 cup plain dry bread crumbs, 1-1/2 teaspoons melted butter, 1/2 teaspoon dried parsley flakes and a dash of salt. Sprinkle over cooked vegetables.

Melt 1/4 cup butter over low heat; stir in 1/2 teaspoon garlic powder, 2 tablespoons lemon juice, 1 tablespoon slivered toasted almonds, 1 tablespoon minced chives or 1 tablespoon grated Parmesan cheese. Drizzle over cooked vegetables.

Prepare a packaged white, hollandaise or bernaise sauce mix as directed and serve over your vegetable of choice.

Main Dishes

Roast Chicken with Creole Stuffing

(Pictured above)

I've used this recipe ever since I roasted my first chicken. The combination of shrimp, sausage, ham, vegetables and seasonings makes the stuffing unique and delicious. —*Ruth Bates, Temecula, California*

1-1/2 cups uncooked brown rice
2 fresh Italian sausage links
2 tablespoons vegetable oil
1 cup chopped onion
5 garlic cloves, minced
1/2 cup diced green pepper
1/2 cup diced sweet red pepper
1 can (14-1/2 ounces) diced tomatoes, undrained
1 tablespoon lemon juice
1 teaspoon dried basil
1/2 teaspoon sugar
1/2 teaspoon hot pepper sauce
1/2 teaspoon chicken bouillon granules
1/4 teaspoon chili powder
1/4 teaspoon pepper
1/8 teaspoon dried thyme
1-1/4 teaspoons salt, *divided*
1 cup diced fully cooked ham
1 cup frozen cooked small shrimp, thawed, optional
3 tablespoons minced fresh parsley
1 roasting chicken (5 to 6 pounds)
1/2 teaspoon paprika
Dash pepper

In a large saucepan, cook rice according to package directions. Meanwhile, in a skillet, cook sausages in oil. Remove sausages, reserving drippings. When cool enough to handle, cut sausages in half lengthwise, then into 1/4-in. pieces; set aside. Saute onion, garlic and peppers in drippings until tender, about 4 minutes. Add the next nine ingredients and 1 teaspoon salt; cook and stir for 5 minutes. Add to the cooked rice. Stir in ham, shrimp if desired, parsley and sausage; mix lightly.

Just before baking, stuff the chicken with about 3-1/2 cups stuffing. Place remaining stuffing in a greased 1-1/2-qt. baking dish; cover and refrigerate. Place chicken on a rack in a roasting pan; tie drumsticks together. Combine paprika, pepper and remaining salt; rub over chicken.

Bake, uncovered, at 350° for 1-1/2 hours, basting every 30 minutes. Cover and bake 1-1/2 hours longer or until juices run clear. Bake additional stuffing for the last 40 minutes of baking time, uncovering during the last 10 minutes. **Yield:** 8-10 servings (8 cups stuffing).

Swedish Meatballs

I can still remember Mother making this delicious recipe. It's such wonderful family fare, we still enjoy warming up with it on cold winter nights! —*Ruth Andrewson*
Leavenworth, Washington

1 egg
1/2 cup milk
3/4 cup dry bread crumbs
3/4 cup finely chopped onion
1 teaspoon Worcestershire sauce
1 teaspoon salt
1/2 to 3/4 teaspoon ground allspice
1/4 teaspoon pepper
1-1/2 pounds ground beef
3/4 pound ground pork
1 tablespoon vegetable oil
1 can (10-3/4 ounces) condensed cream of mushroom soup, undiluted
1/2 cup water
Hot cooked noodles

In a bowl, combine the first eight ingredients. Crumble meat over mixture; mix well. Shape into 1-1/2-in. balls. In a large skillet, brown meatballs in oil in small batches over medium heat; drain.

Place meatballs in a greased 2-qt. baking dish. Combine the soup and water; pour over the meatballs. Bake, uncovered, at 350° for about 40-45 minutes or until the meat is no longer pink. Serve over noodles. **Yield:** 10 servings.

Mustard-Glazed Ham

Holiday ham gets a sweet and tangy taste from this honey of a glaze. I make sure to have extra on hand because my family likes to use it as a dipping sauce.
—*Dawn Wood, Machiasport, Maine*

1 boneless fully cooked ham (about 5 pounds)
3/4 cup honey mustard*
1/4 cup packed brown sugar
2 tablespoons orange juice
1/8 teaspoon ground cloves
Pinch allspice

Place ham on a rack in a shallow roasting pan. Bake at 325° for 1 hour. In a small bowl, combine the remaining ingredients. Spoon about 1/3 cup over ham. Bake 15 minutes longer or until a meat thermometer reads 140° and ham is heated through. Heat remaining glaze to serve with sliced ham. **Yield:** about 16 servings (1 cup sauce).

***Editor's Note:** As a substitute for honey mustard, combine 1/3 cup each honey and Dijon mustard.

Shrimp in Cream Sauce

(Pictured below)

Looking for an extra-special Christmas Eve entree to delight your crowd? My family loves this rich shrimp dish. We enjoy it over golden egg noodles. —*Jane Birch*
Edison, New Jersey

2 tablespoons butter
1/3 cup all-purpose flour
1-1/2 cups chicken broth
4 garlic cloves, minced
1 cup heavy whipping cream
1/2 cup minced fresh parsley
2 teaspoons paprika
Salt and pepper to taste
2 pounds large uncooked shrimp, peeled and deveined
Hot cooked noodles *or* rice

In a saucepan, melt butter; stir in flour until smooth. Gradually add broth and garlic. Bring to a boil; cook and stir 2 minutes or until thickened. Remove from heat. Stir in cream, parsley, paprika, salt and pepper.

Cut shrimp lengthwise but not all the way through; spread to butterfly. Place cut side down in a greased 13-in. x 9-in. x 2-in. baking dish. Pour cream sauce over shrimp. Bake, uncovered, at 400° for 15-18 minutes or until shrimp turn pink. Serve over noodles or rice. **Yield:** 8 servings.

Orange-Glazed Cornish Hens

(Pictured below)

One year, I served this recipe and got nothing but raves. My family prefers these moist glazed hens instead of turkey. —Mary Jo Hopkins, Hobart, Indiana

1 cup finely chopped onion
1 cup finely chopped celery
1/2 cup sliced almonds
1/2 cup butter
3 cups cooked rice
4 teaspoons sugar
1 teaspoon salt
1/2 teaspoon dried thyme
1/4 cup grated orange peel
4 Cornish game hens (about 20 ounces *each*)
GLAZE:
1 cup orange juice
1/4 cup honey
1/4 cup vegetable oil
1 tablespoon grated orange peel

In a skillet, saute the onion, celery and almonds in butter. Add rice, sugar, salt, thyme and orange peel; mix well. Loosely stuff hens. Place, breast side up, on a rack in a shallow baking pan. In a small bowl, combine glaze ingredients; spoon some over hens.

Bake, uncovered, at 350° for 40 minutes. Cover; bake 40 minutes longer until juices run clear, brushing often with remaining glaze. **Yield:** 4 servings.

Hot Turkey Salad Sandwiches

Our family looks forward to these day-after-Christmas sandwiches featuring leftover turkey. When presented alongside coleslaw and cranberry sauce, they make another meal worth celebrating. —Jeanne Lester Newport News, Virginia

2 to 3 cups diced cooked turkey
2 celery ribs, diced
1 small onion, diced
2 hard-cooked eggs, chopped
3/4 cup mayonnaise
1/2 teaspoon salt
1/4 teaspoon pepper
6 hamburger buns, split

In a bowl, combine the turkey, celery, onion, eggs, mayonnaise, salt and pepper. Spoon into buns. Wrap each in foil. Bake at 400° for 20-25 minutes or until heated through. **Yield:** 6 servings.

Sirloin with Sour Cream Sauce

My in-laws raise beef for all their children, so I'm always looking for new ways to cook steak. This is an absolute favorite. It's so easy to fix, and the result is a tender steak smothered in a creamy onion and mushroom sauce. The aroma alone makes my husband's mouth water! —Kim Schmitt, Bellingham, Washington

3 tablespoons all-purpose flour, *divided*
1/2 teaspoon salt
1/2 teaspoon pepper
1/2 teaspoon paprika
1-1/2 pounds boneless beef sirloin steak, cut into serving-size pieces
2 tablespoons vegetable oil
1/2 cup chopped onion
2 cups sliced fresh mushrooms
1 garlic clove, minced
2/3 cup water, *divided*
2 tablespoons brown sugar
2 tablespoons soy sauce
1 teaspoon Dijon mustard
1/2 cup sour cream
Hot cooked noodles *or* rice

In a large resealable plastic bag, combine 2 tablespoons flour, salt, pepper and paprika; add beef and toss to coat. In a skillet, brown beef on all sides in oil. Add the onion, mushrooms, garlic, 1/2 cup water, brown sugar, soy sauce and mustard; cover and simmer for 10-15 minutes or until meat is tender. Remove meat to a serving platter and keep warm.

Combine remaining flour and water until smooth; stir into skillet. Bring to a boil; cook and stir for 2 minutes or until thickened. Reduce heat; stir in sour cream. Heat gently (do not boil). Serve beef and sauce over noodles. **Yield:** 4-6 servings.

Baked Chicken Amandine

On busy winter evenings, this saucy casserole is a minute-saving mainstay. Often, I serve it with twice-baked potatoes, salad and dessert. It's fine for family, company and potlucks. —Pauline Strickland, Friendship, Wisconsin

3 to 4 cups cubed cooked chicken
1 package (10 ounces) frozen chopped broccoli, thawed
2 cans (10-3/4 ounces *each*) condensed cream of chicken soup, undiluted
1 cup mayonnaise*
2 cups (8 ounces) shredded cheddar cheese
1 cup crushed butter-flavored crackers (about 25)
1/4 cup butter, melted
1/2 cup sliced almonds

In a greased 13-in. x 9-in. x 2-in. baking dish, layer chicken and broccoli. In a bowl, combine soup and mayonnaise; spoon over the broccoli. Sprinkle with cheese. Combine the crackers and butter; sprinkle over the cheese. Top with almonds. Bake, uncovered, at 350° for 45-50 minutes or until golden brown. **Yield:** 6-8 servings.

***Editor's Note:** Reduced-fat or fat-free mayonnaise may not be substituted for regular mayonnaise.

After-Christmas Turkey Potpie

(Pictured above right)

Need ways to use up leftover turkey? This is what I like to do. The cubed poultry, tender vegetables and herbs encased in a flaky crust is a favorite at our house. —Leona Luecking, West Burlington, Iowa

1 cup sliced carrots
1 cup finely chopped onion
1/2 cup chopped celery
1/2 teaspoon dried thyme
1/8 teaspoon pepper
3 tablespoons butter
2 cups cubed cooked turkey
1 tablespoon all-purpose flour
1 can (10-3/4 ounces) condensed golden mushroom soup, undiluted
1 cup frozen cut green beans, cooked and drained
Pastry for double-crust pie (9 inches)
1 tablespoon milk

In a skillet, saute carrots, onion, celery, thyme and pepper in butter until vegetables are crisp-tender. In a large resealable plastic bag, combine turkey and flour; shake to coat. Add turkey, soup and green beans to the vegetable mixture; mix well.

Line a 9-in. pie plate with bottom crust. Add turkey mixture. Roll out remaining pastry to fit top of pie; seal and flute edges. Cut slits in pastry. Brush with milk. Cover edges loosely with foil. Bake at 350° for 55-65 minutes or until golden brown. Serve warm. **Yield:** 6 servings.

Beef Rouladen

(Pictured above)

Our family was poor when I was growing up in Germany, so we ate garden vegetables for many weekday meals. When Mother made meat for a Sunday dinner, it was a terrific treat. My favorite is this tender beef dish, which gets great flavor from Dijon mustard.
—Karin Cousineau, Burlington, North Carolina

1/4 cup Dijon mustard
8 slices top round steak, 1/4 inch thick (about 2 pounds)
Salt and pepper to taste
8 bacon strips
1 large onion, cut into thin wedges
3 tablespoons vegetable oil
3 cups beef broth
1/3 cup all-purpose flour
1/2 cup water
Chopped fresh parsley, optional

Lightly spread mustard on each slice of steak; sprinkle with salt and pepper. Place 1 bacon strip and a few onion wedges on each slice; roll up and secure with toothpicks. Brown in a skillet in oil; drain. Add broth; bring to a boil. Reduce heat; cover and simmer for 1-1/2 hours or until meat is tender. Remove meat and keep warm.

Combine flour and water until smooth; stir into broth. Bring to a boil, stirring constantly until thickened and bubbly. Remove toothpicks from meat and return to gravy; heat through. Sprinkle with parsley if desired. **Yield:** 8 servings.

Pork Loin Supper

A hint of cinnamon gives additional flavor to this tender roast, while the vegetables and dried fruits add extra goodness. This recipe was given to me by my aunt over 30 years ago. It's a complete meal in one pan.
—Lois McAtee, Oceanside, California

1 teaspoon salt
1 teaspoon pepper
1 teaspoon garlic powder
1 teaspoon paprika
1 bone-in pork loin roast (about 4-1/2 pounds)
6 medium potatoes, peeled and cut into 1-inch pieces
6 medium carrots, cut into 1/2-inch pieces
12 pitted prunes
12 dried apricots
1 thin lemon slice
2 cans (10-1/2 ounces *each*) condensed beef broth, undiluted
1/4 cup butter, melted
1/2 teaspoon ground cinnamon

Combine salt, pepper, garlic powder and paprika; rub over roast. Place in a shallow roasting pan. Arrange vegetables and fruit around roast. Combine broth, butter and cinnamon; pour over vegetable mixture.

Cover and bake at 350° for 45 minutes. Uncover; bake 1-1/2 hours longer or until a meat thermometer reads 160°, basting often. Cover and let stand for 10 minutes before carving. **Yield:** 8-10 servings.

Christmas Seafood Soup

For as long as I can remember, we always had this wonderful main-dish seafood soup on Christmas Day. In our part of the country, where winters are long and cold, this sure warms us up.
—Sue Bridley, Dennison, Minnesota

2 cans (6-1/2 ounces *each*) chopped clams
2 cups diced peeled potatoes
2 cups chopped celery
2 cups diced carrots
1/2 cup water
2 cups milk
1 package (5 ounces) frozen cooked salad shrimp, thawed

4 bacon strips, cooked and crumbled
2 teaspoons minced fresh parsley
Salt and pepper to taste

Drain the clams, reserving juice; set clams aside. In a large saucepan or Dutch oven, combine clam juice, potatoes, celery, carrots and water. Bring to a boil. Reduce heat; cover and cook for 15 minutes or until vegetables are tender. Add the milk, shrimp, bacon, parsley, salt, pepper and reserved clams; heat through. **Yield:** 7 servings.

Wild Goose with Giblet Stuffing

(Pictured below)

This recipe is one of our favorite ways to prepare goose for the holidays. My husband does a lot of hunting, so I'm always looking for new ways to fix game.
—Louise Laginess, East Jordan, Michigan

1 dressed wild goose (6 to 8 pounds)
Lemon wedges
Salt

STUFFING:
Goose giblets
2 cups water
10 cups crumbled corn bread
2 large tart apples, chopped
1 large onion, chopped
1/3 cup minced fresh parsley
1 to 2 tablespoons rubbed sage
1 teaspoon salt
1/4 teaspoon pepper
1/4 teaspoon garlic powder
Butter, softened

Rub inside goose cavity with lemon and salt; set aside. In a saucepan, cook giblets in water until tender, about 20-30 minutes. Remove giblets with a slotted spoon and reserve liquid. Chop giblets and place in a large bowl; add corn bread, apples, onion, parsley, sage, salt, pepper and garlic powder. Add enough of the reserved cooking liquid to make a moist stuffing; toss gently.

Stuff the body and neck cavity; truss openings. Place goose, breast side up, on a rack in a shallow roasting pan. Spread with butter. Bake, uncovered, at 325° for 2-1/2 to 3 hours or until fully cooked and tender. If goose is an older bird, add 1 cup of water to pan and cover for last hour. **Yield:** 6-8 servings.

Quail in Mushroom Gravy

(Pictured below)

We live in an area with many Southern plantations, and quail are abundant. I cook this tasty dish with rich mushroom gravy often when my two boys are home. They think it makes a great meal. —Jean Williams Hurtsboro, Alabama

3/4 cup all-purpose flour, *divided*
1 teaspoon salt
1/2 teaspoon pepper
6 dressed quail (1/3 to 1/2 pound *each*)
1/2 cup butter
1/2 pound fresh mushrooms, sliced
2 cups chicken broth
2 teaspoons minced fresh thyme *or* 3/4 teaspoon dried thyme
Hot cooked noodles, optional

Combine 1/2 cup flour, salt and pepper; coat each quail. Melt butter in a skillet; brown the quail. Transfer to an ungreased 2-1/2-qt. baking dish. In the pan drippings, saute the mushrooms until tender. Add remaining flour and stir to make a smooth paste. Add broth and thyme, stirring constantly. Bring to a boil; boil for 1 minute or until thickened. Pour over the quail. Cover and bake at 350° for 40-50 minutes or until tender and juices run clear. Serve over noodles if desired. **Yield:** 6 servings.

Apricot-Glazed Pork Loin Roast

A nice alternative for a special dinner during the Yuletide season or any other time of year, this pork roast gets its fruity flavor and lovely golden color from apricot nectar. I serve it often to guests. —Ramona Stude Mineral Point, Wisconsin

1 bone-in pork loin roast (4 to 5 pounds)
1/2 teaspoon salt
1/2 teaspoon pepper
2/3 cup packed brown sugar
2 tablespoons cornstarch
1-1/4 teaspoons ground mustard
2 cups apricot nectar
4 teaspoons cider vinegar

Sprinkle roast with salt and pepper. Place on a rack in a shallow roasting pan. Bake, uncovered, at 350° for 1-1/2 hours. In a saucepan, combine the brown sugar, cornstarch and mustard. Stir in apricot nectar and vinegar until smooth. Bring to a boil over medium heat; cook and stir for 2 minutes or until thickened.

Spoon 1/2 cup glaze over roast. Bake 20 minutes longer or until a meat thermometer reads 160°. Let stand for 10-15 minutes before slicing. Serve with remaining glaze. **Yield:** 8 servings.

Honey-Glazed Turkey

Even during the holidays, my husband wouldn't eat turkey until I tried this recipe. Now, he loves it! The sweet and spicy glaze gives the turkey a wonderful flavor. —Mary Smolka, Spring Grove, Illinois

2 cups chopped onion
1-1/2 cups chopped celery
1/2 cup butter
12 cups unseasoned stuffing croutons *or* dry bread cubes
1 tablespoon poultry seasoning
2 teaspoons chicken bouillon granules

1 teaspoon pepper
1 teaspoon dried rosemary, crushed
1 teaspoon lemon-pepper seasoning
1/2 teaspoon salt
2 to 2-1/2 cups boiling water
1 turkey (14 to 16 pounds)

GLAZE:

1/2 cup honey
1/2 cup Dijon mustard
1-1/2 teaspoons dried rosemary, crushed
1 teaspoon onion powder
1/2 teaspoon salt
1/4 teaspoon garlic powder
1/4 teaspoon pepper

In a large skillet, saute onion and celery in butter until tender. Pour into a large bowl. Add the next seven ingredients; mix well. Stir in enough water until stuffing has reached desired moistness. Just before baking, stuff the turkey. Skewer openings; tie drumsticks together. Place on a rack in a roasting pan. Cover lightly with a tent of aluminum foil. Bake at 325° for 4 hours.

Combine glaze ingredients. Pour over turkey. Bake an additional 1 to 1-1/2 hours, basting if needed, or until a meat thermometer reads 185°. Remove all stuffing. If desired, thicken drippings for gravy. **Yield:** 12-14 servings (about 12 cups stuffing).

Editor's Note: Stuffing may be baked in a greased 3-qt. covered baking dish at 325° for 70 minutes (uncover the last 10 minutes). Turkey may also be prepared in an oven roasting bag. Pour glaze over stuffed turkey and bake according to package directions.

Stuffed Crown Roast of Pork

(Pictured above right)

I first made this recipe on Christmas...the oohs and aahs from my family were a delight! In addition to the holidays, I sometimes make a crown roast for Sunday dinner. It reminds me of my childhood, when Sunday suppers were always special. —*Marianne Severson West Allis, Wisconsin*

1 crown roast of pork (about 8 pounds)
1 pound ground pork
1/2 pound bulk pork sausage
3/4 cup finely chopped onion
3 tablespoons butter
1/2 cup diced peeled apple
1/4 cup finely chopped celery
1-1/2 cups soft bread crumbs
1/2 cup minced fresh parsley
1-1/2 teaspoons salt
1/2 teaspoon pepper
1/2 teaspoon rubbed sage
Spiced crab apples, optional

Tie roast and place on a rack in a large roasting pan. Cover the bone ends with foil. Bake at 350° for 2 hours. Meanwhile, in a large skillet, cook the pork and sausage until no longer pink; drain and set aside. In the same skillet, saute onion in butter until tender. Add apple and celery; cook for 5 minutes. Remove from heat. Add the cooked pork and sausage, crumbs, parsley, salt, pepper and sage; mix well.

Remove roast from the oven. Carefully press a double layer of heavy-duty foil into the center of roast to form a base for stuffing. Spoon the stuffing lightly into crown. Return to oven and bake for 1 hour more or until a meat thermometer reads 160°-170°. Transfer to serving platter. Garnish with spiced crab apples if desired. Cut between the ribs to serve. **Yield:** 16-20 servings.

Turkey Pasta Supreme

(Pictured above)

Since this dish combines turkey and pasta, even our children love it. It's fun to make turkey a different way, and you can't beat the creamy, cheesy sauce. This recipe also helps stretch my meal budget. —*Cassie Dion*
South Burlington, Vermont

3/4 pound uncooked turkey breast
2 garlic cloves, minced
2 tablespoons butter
1-1/4 cups heavy whipping cream
2 tablespoons minced fresh basil *or* 2 teaspoons dried basil
1/4 cup grated Parmesan cheese
Dash pepper
3 to 4 cups hot cooked pasta

Cut turkey into 2-in. x 1/4-in. pieces. In a skillet, saute turkey and garlic in butter until turkey is browned and no longer pink, about 6 minutes. Add cream, basil, Parmesan and pepper; bring to a boil. Reduce heat; simmer for 3 minutes, stirring frequently. Stir in pasta and toss to coat. Serve immediately. **Yield:** 4 servings.

Christmas Day Chicken

I've been fixing this delicious chicken for Christmas dinner for over 10 years. It's convenient since you refrigerate it overnight, then simply coat with crumbs and bake. It comes out crispy on the outside and tender and juicy on the inside. —*Marcia Larson, Batavia, Illinois*

16 boneless skinless chicken breast halves
2 cups (16 ounces) sour cream
1/4 cup lemon juice
4 teaspoons Worcestershire sauce
2 teaspoons celery salt
2 teaspoons pepper
2 teaspoons paprika
1 teaspoon seasoned salt
1 teaspoon garlic salt
1-1/2 to 2 cups finely crushed Waverly crackers
1/2 cup vegetable oil
1/2 cup butter, melted

Place the chicken in two large resealable plastic bags. In a bowl, combine the sour cream, lemon juice, Worcestershire sauce and seasonings. Pour over chicken; seal bags and refrigerate overnight.

Drain and discard marinade. Coat chicken with cracker crumbs; place in two greased 13-in. x 9-in. x 2-in. baking dishes. Combine oil and butter; drizzle over chicken. Bake, uncovered, at 350° for 50-60 minutes or until juices run clear. **Yield:** 16 servings.

Oven-Barbecued Ribs

My mom made these tender ribs for special Sunday suppers when we were growing up. My family's eyes light up when I bring a plate of these ribs to the table, and company never suspects how easy they are to prepare.
—Yvonne White, Williamson, New York

3 to 4 pounds country-style pork ribs
1-1/2 cups water
1 cup ketchup
1/3 cup Worcestershire sauce
1 teaspoon salt
1 teaspoon chili powder
1/2 teaspoon onion powder
1/8 teaspoon hot pepper sauce

Place ribs in a greased roasting pan. Bake, uncovered, at 350° for 45 minutes. Meanwhile, in a saucepan, combine the remaining ingredients. Bring to a boil; cook for 1 minute. Drain ribs. Spoon sauce over ribs. Cover and bake for 1-1/2 hours. Uncover; bake 30 minutes longer, basting once. **Yield:** 4-6 servings.

Currant-Glazed Cornish Hens

(Pictured at right)

I served this to my husband the very first Christmas we were married. It's been a family favorite ever since! *—Lori Bluml, Carroll, Iowa*

1 package (6 ounces) long grain and wild rice mix
1 medium onion, chopped
1/2 pound fresh mushrooms, sliced
1/4 cup chopped celery
2 tablespoons vegetable oil
1/2 cup chopped pecans, toasted
2 tablespoons minced fresh parsley
1/4 teaspoon dried thyme
1/4 teaspoon dried marjoram
4 Cornish game hens
2 tablespoons butter, softened

CURRANT SAUCE:

1/2 cup currant jelly
2 tablespoons lemon juice
1 tablespoon butter
1 tablespoon cornstarch
1/4 cup cider vinegar
1 teaspoon salt
3 whole cloves

Prepare rice according to package directions. In a large skillet, saute onion, mushrooms and celery in oil until tender. Remove from the heat; add rice, pecans, parsley, thyme and marjoram. Stuff hens; rub skin with butter. Place on a rack in a shallow baking pan. Bake, uncovered, at 350° for 30 minutes.

Meanwhile, for sauce, heat jelly, lemon juice and butter in a small saucepan until melted. Combine cornstarch, vinegar, salt and cloves until smooth; add to pan. Bring to a boil; boil for 2 minutes.

After hens have baked for 30 minutes, baste with sauce and bake 30 minutes longer or until juices run clear. Bake extra stuffing in a greased 1-qt. covered baking dish at 350° for 30 minutes. **Yield:** 4 servings.

Cider-Roasted Chicken

(Pictured below)

I make this savory roast chicken only for special occasions such as Christmas. I found the recipe in the first real good cookbook I owned, and my six children savor every bite. —*Mary Dunphy Stephenville, Newfoundland*

1 whole roasting chicken (5 to 7 pounds)
1/4 cup butter
2-1/2 cups apple cider
6 to 8 small unpeeled red potatoes, quartered
6 to 8 small onions, peeled and quartered
1 to 2 medium green peppers, cut into strips
6 to 8 bacon strips
2 to 4 small tomatoes, quartered

Place chicken in a roasting pan; dot with butter. Bake, uncovered, at 375° for 15 minutes. Reduce heat to 325°; bake for 2 hours. Pour cider over chicken. Add potatoes, onions and peppers to the pan; place bacon over chicken breast.

Bake 1 hour longer, basting often. Add tomatoes to the pan. Bake 30 minutes longer or until a meat thermometer reads 180°. Cover and let stand 10 minutes before carving. Thicken the pan juices for gravy if desired. **Yield:** 6 servings.

Stuffed Bone-In Ham

Scored with a simple but delicious stuffing, this glazed ham makes such an elegant statement when you set it on your holiday table! It's become a Yuletide tradition at our house. —*Rebecca Watts, Laneville, Texas*

1 medium onion, finely chopped
1/2 cup finely chopped celery
2 tablespoons minced fresh parsley
1/2 cup butter
1/4 cup egg substitute
3/4 cup milk
1 teaspoon rubbed sage
1/2 teaspoon dried thyme
1/4 teaspoon salt
6 cups soft bread cubes (1/4-inch cubes)
1 shank half bone-in fully cooked ham (about 12 pounds)

GLAZE:
1/2 cup packed brown sugar
1/4 cup orange juice
1/4 cup dark corn syrup

In a large skillet, saute the onion, celery and parsley in butter until vegetables are tender. In a bowl, combine the egg substitute, milk, sage, thyme and salt. Add bread cubes and vegetable mixture; toss to combine.

From the cut end of the ham, cut five parallel wedges, about 1-1/2 in. apart, 1/2 in. wide and 1-1/2 in. deep. Repeat in the opposite direction, making diamond shapes. Spoon stuffing into slits. Place ham on a rack in a shallow roasting pan. Cover loosely with a foil tent. Bake at 325° for 2-1/4 hours.

In a saucepan, combine the glaze ingredients. Cook and stir over medium heat until sugar is dissolved. Remove foil from ham; drizzle glaze over top. Bake 30-45 minutes longer or until a meat thermometer reads 140°. Let stand for 10 minutes before slicing. **Yield:** 15-18 servings.

Special Roast Turkey

Before putting my turkey in the oven, I pour on a savory sauce that adds a pleasant citrus-soy sauce flavor and helps hold the other seasonings I sprinkle on. —*Gloria Warczak, Cedarburg, Wisconsin*

1 turkey (12 to 14 pounds)
2 cups water
2-1/2 cups chicken broth, *divided*

1-1/2 cups orange juice, *divided*
4 tablespoons soy sauce, *divided*
1 tablespoon chicken bouillon granules
1 teaspoon dried minced onion
1/2 teaspoon garlic powder

ORANGE GIBLET GRAVY:
3/4 cup chicken broth
1/4 cup orange juice
2 teaspoons Worcestershire sauce
1/2 teaspoon dried thyme
1/2 teaspoon sugar
1/4 teaspoon pepper
3 tablespoons cornstarch
1/2 cup water

Place turkey on a greased rack in a roasting pan. Add water, giblets and neck to pan. Combine 1-1/4 cups broth, 3/4 cup orange juice and 2 tablespoons soy sauce; pour over turkey. Combine bouillon, onion and garlic powder; sprinkle over turkey. Bake, uncovered, at 325° for 3-1/2 hours, basting every 30 minutes. When turkey begins to brown, cover lightly with foil.

Remove giblets and neck when tender; set aside for gravy. Combine remaining broth, orange juice and soy sauce. Remove foil from turkey; pour broth mixture over turkey. Bake 30 minutes longer or until a meat thermometer reads 180°. For gravy, remove meat from neck and discard the bones.

Chop giblets and neck meat; set aside. In a saucepan, combine 2 cups pan juices, broth, orange juice and Worcestershire sauce; mix well. Stir in thyme, sugar and pepper. Combine cornstarch and water until smooth. Whisk into broth mixture; bring to a boil. Cook and stir for 2 minutes. Stir in reserved giblets and neck meat. Carve turkey; serve with gravy. **Yield:** 8 servings.

Meaty Stuffed Onions

(Pictured above right)

I won a prize for this mouth-watering main dish in a contest sponsored by our local newspaper. I got the recipe from my mother-in-law, who's originally from Italy. —*Lorraine Grass, Allentown, Pennsylvania*

4 large sweet onions
1 pound ground beef
1/2 pound bulk pork sausage
1 package (10 ounces) frozen chopped spinach, thawed and drained
5 slices day-old bread, crumbled
1/2 to 2/3 cup beef broth
1/2 cup grated Parmesan cheese
1 egg, beaten
1 tablespoon minced fresh parsley
1/2 teaspoon salt
1/4 teaspoon pepper
1/8 teaspoon ground nutmeg

Peel onions and cut 1/2 in. off tops and bottoms. Place onions in a large saucepan. Cover with boiling water. Cook until tender, about 20 minutes; drain. Cool slightly. Carefully remove inside layers of onion, separating into eight individual shells (refrigerate remaining onion for another use). Drain on paper towels.

In a skillet, cook beef and sausage over medium heat until no longer pink; drain. Add spinach; cook and stir for 2 minutes. Remove from the heat; stir in the remaining ingredients. Spoon into the onion shells. Place in a greased 13-in. x 9-in. x 2-in. baking pan. Bake, uncovered, at 350° for 15-20 minutes or until heated through and lightly browned. **Yield:** 8 servings.

Cranberry Chicken

(Pictured above)

My husband loves chicken when it's nice and moist, like it is in this recipe. I serve it over hot fluffy rice with a salad and warm rolls on the side. The ruby-red sauce has a tart, cinnamony flavor. —*Dorothy Bateman*
Carver, Massachusetts

1/2 cup all-purpose flour
1/2 teaspoon salt
1/4 teaspoon pepper
6 boneless skinless chicken breast halves
1/4 cup butter
1 cup fresh *or* frozen cranberries
1 cup water
1/2 cup packed brown sugar
Dash ground nutmeg
1 tablespoon red wine vinegar, optional
Hot cooked rice

In a shallow dish, combine flour, salt and pepper; dredge chicken. In a skillet, melt butter over medium heat. Brown chicken on both sides. Remove and keep warm. In the same skillet, add the cranberries, water, brown sugar, nutmeg and vinegar if desired. Cook and stir until the cranberries pop, about 5 minutes.

Return chicken to skillet. Cover and simmer for 20-30 minutes or until chicken is tender, basting occasionally with the sauce. Serve over rice. **Yield:** 4-6 servings.

Porcupine Meatballs

These well-seasoned meatballs in a rich tomato sauce are one of my mom's best main dishes. I used to love this meal when I was growing up. I made it at home for our children, and now my daughters make it for their families. —*Darlis Wilfer*
Phelps, Wisconsin

1/2 cup uncooked long grain rice
1/2 cup water
1/3 cup chopped onion
1 teaspoon salt
1/2 teaspoon celery salt
1/8 teaspoon pepper
1/8 teaspoon garlic powder
1 pound ground beef
2 tablespoons vegetable oil
1 can (15 ounces) tomato sauce
1 cup water
2 tablespoons brown sugar
2 teaspoons Worcestershire sauce

In a bowl, combine the first seven ingredients. Add beef and mix well. Shape into 1-1/2-in. balls. In a large skillet, brown meatballs in oil; drain. Combine remaining ingredients; pour over meatballs. Reduce heat; cover and simmer for 1 hour or until meat is no longer pink. **Yield:** 4-6 servings.

Christmas Chicken Cordon Bleu

Christmas Eve wouldn't be complete without my dad's chicken cordon bleu! My husband tries all year to talk Dad into also making this scrumptious main dish for other occasions. It's a definite family favorite.
—*Vickie Lemos, Modesto, California*

6 boneless skinless chicken breast halves
3 thin slices fully cooked ham, halved
3 slices Swiss cheese, halved
1/2 cup all-purpose flour
1/2 teaspoon salt
1/4 teaspoon paprika
1 egg
2 tablespoons milk
3/4 cup dry bread crumbs
3 tablespoons butter
1 cup chicken broth
2 tablespoons dried parsley flakes
Hot cooked rice
1 can (10-3/4 ounces) condensed cream of chicken soup, undiluted
1/2 cup sour cream

Flatten chicken breasts to 1/4-in. thickness; top each with one piece of ham and one piece of cheese. Fold chicken around ham and cheese; secure with toothpicks. In a shallow bowl, combine flour, salt and paprika. In another bowl, beat egg and milk. Dredge chicken in flour mixture, dip in egg mixture, then roll in bread crumbs.

In a large skillet over medium heat, brown chicken in butter. Add broth and parsley. Cover and simmer over medium-low heat for 50-60 minutes or until chicken juices run clear. Remove toothpicks. Place rice on a serving platter; top with chicken and keep warm. In the same skillet, combine soup and sour cream; heat through but do not boil. Pour over chicken and rice. **Yield:** 6 servings.

Flavorful Lamb Chops

(Pictured below)

These aren't your ordinary lamb chops. I flavor them with juice squeezed from oranges and limes we grow ourselves plus a generous dash of caraway. The chops always turn out nice and tender. —Margaret Pache, Mesa, Arizona

2 tablespoons orange juice
2 tablespoons lime juice
1-1/2 teaspoons caraway seeds
1/2 teaspoon grated orange peel
6 loin lamb chops (about 1-3/4 pounds)
1 tablespoon vegetable oil
1/2 teaspoon salt
1/2 teaspoon pepper
1/2 cup chicken broth
Fresh orange slices and parsley sprigs, optional

In a large resealable plastic bag, combine the first four ingredients and then add lamb chops. Seal and refrigerate overnight, turning once. Drain, reserving marinade.

In a nonstick skillet over medium-high heat, brown chops in oil. Season with salt and pepper. Remove chops and keep warm. Add broth and reserved marinade to the skillet; bring to a rolling boil. Return chops to pan; reduce heat. Cover and simmer for 20 minutes. Uncover and simmer 10 minutes longer. Serve chops with pan juices. Garnish with oranges and parsley if desired. **Yield:** 6 servings.

Chicken Kiev

(Pictured below)

A favorite aunt shared this special recipe with me. It makes attractive individual servings fancy enough to be served for company. They have great flavor and are always a hit. —*Lynne Peterson, Salt Lake City, Utah*

1/4 cup butter, softened
1 tablespoon grated onion
1 tablespoon chopped fresh parsley
1/2 teaspoon garlic powder
1/2 teaspoon dried tarragon
1/4 teaspoon pepper
6 boneless skinless chicken breast halves
1 egg
1 tablespoon milk
1 envelope (2-3/4 ounces) seasoned chicken coating mix

Combine the butter, onion, parsley, garlic powder, tarragon and pepper. Shape mixture into six pencil-thin strips about 2 in. long; place on waxed paper. Freeze until firm, about 30 minutes. Flatten each chicken breast to 1/4 in. Place one butter strip in the center of each chicken breast. Fold long sides over butter; fold ends up and secure with a toothpick.

In a bowl, beat egg and milk; place coating mix in another bowl. Dip chicken in egg mixture, then roll in coating mix. Place chicken, seam side down, in a greased 13-in. x 9-in. x 2-in. baking pan. Bake, uncovered, at 425° for 35-40 minutes or until chicken juices run clear. Remove the toothpicks before serving. **Yield:** 6 servings.

Microwave Directions (timing based on a 700-watt oven): Place chicken in a greased glass pie plate. Microwave on high for 4 minutes. Turn plate; microwave for 3-4 minutes or until juices run clear. Let stand 5 minutes.

Sausage-Stuffed Squash

This delicious, satisfying meal-in-one is easy to prepare. The green of the squash remains true to color through the cooking process, so it's pretty on the plate. It's a favorite when I'm cooking for just the two of us.
—*Linda Gaido, New Brighton, Pennsylvania*

1 acorn squash (2 to 2-1/2 pounds)
Salt and pepper to taste
12 ounces bulk pork sausage
1 egg
2 tablespoons brown sugar
2 garlic cloves, minced
1/3 cup dry bread crumbs

Cut squash in half lengthwise; remove seeds. Sprinkle with salt and pepper. In a small bowl, combine the sausage, egg, brown sugar, garlic and bread crumbs; mix well. Spoon into squash halves; place in a small shallow baking dish. Bake, uncovered, at 350° for 1-1/2 hours or until squash is tender. **Yield:** 2 servings.

Cranberry-Glazed Pork Roast

My family loves pork prepared in this festive way. You'll find that this succulent roast, with its tangy ruby glaze, is an entree that you, too, will be proud to serve at the holidays year after year. —*Theresa Pearson Ogilvie, Minnesota*

1 boneless pork loin roast (3-1/2 to 4 pounds)
12 small whole onions
1 can (16 ounces) whole-berry cranberry sauce
1/4 cup orange juice
2 teaspoons cornstarch
1/2 to 1 teaspoon grated orange peel
1/4 teaspoon ground cinnamon
1/8 teaspoon salt

Place roast, fat side up, in a greased roasting pan. Bake, uncovered, at 325° for 45 minutes. Place onions around roast; cover and bake for 30 minutes.

Meanwhile, in a saucepan, combine cranberry sauce, orange juice, cornstarch, orange peel, cinnamon and salt; mix well. Bring to a boil over medium heat; boil and stir for 2 minutes or until thickened. Spoon 3/4 cup over roast and onions; set remaining sauce aside.

Bake, basting occasionally, 30-45 minutes longer or until a meat thermometer reads 160°-170° and onions are tender. Let stand 15 minutes before slicing. Heat reserved sauce; serve with roast and onions. **Yield:** 12-14 servings.

Herb-Crusted Roast Beef

(Pictured above right)

It's over 15 years now I've been married to a man who loves beef. For a long time, though, I was reluctant to cook a roast for fear of ruining a nice cut of meat. Finally, I started experimenting and this recipe was the rewarding result. —*Teri Lindquist, Gurnee, Illinois*

1 boneless rump roast (4-1/2 to 5 pounds)
2 garlic cloves, minced
2 tablespoons Dijon mustard
2 tablespoons lemon juice
2 tablespoons olive oil
2 tablespoons Worcestershire sauce
1 tablespoon dried parsley flakes
1 teaspoon dried basil
1 teaspoon salt
1 teaspoon pepper
1/2 teaspoon dried tarragon
1/2 teaspoon dried thyme
2-1/3 cups water, *divided*
2 teaspoons beef bouillon granules
1/4 to 1/3 cup all-purpose flour

Place roast with fat side up in an ungreased roasting pan. Combine the next five ingredients; pour over roast. Combine parsley, basil, salt, pepper, tarragon and thyme; rub over roast. Bake, uncovered, at 325° for 1-3/4 to 2-1/4 hours or until meat reaches desired doneness (for rare, a meat thermometer should read 140°; medium, 160°; well-done, 170°). Remove to a warm serving platter. Let stand for 10-15 minutes.

Meanwhile, add 2 cups water and bouillon to pan drippings; bring to a boil. Combine flour and remaining water until smooth; gradually add to pan. Cook and stir until bubbly and thickened. Slice roast; serve with gravy. **Yield:** 10-12 servings.

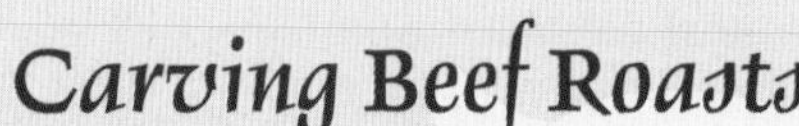

Carving Beef Roasts

To carve boneless roasts, cut the meat into 1/4-inch slices, making vertical cuts across the grain. If the roast is tied, remove the string as you carve to help hold the roast together.

Turkey Croquettes With Cranberry Salsa

(Pictured above)

This is a great way to use up leftover turkey during the holidays. But my kids love the croquettes so much, I make them year-round. —*Jacque Capurro Anchorage, Alaska*

1/3 cup chopped onion
2 tablespoons butter
1/4 cup all-purpose flour
1/4 cup milk
1/4 cup chicken broth
2 cups finely chopped cooked turkey
1/2 cup mashed sweet potato
1/2 teaspoon salt
1/4 teaspoon pepper
1/8 teaspoon cayenne pepper

SALSA:
3/4 cup chopped tart green apple
1 tablespoon lemon juice
1/2 cup chopped cranberries
2 green onions, chopped
2 jalapeno peppers, seeded and chopped*
3 tablespoons golden raisins, chopped
1 tablespoon honey

CROQUETTES:
2 eggs
1 tablespoon water
1/2 cup all-purpose flour
1/2 cup dry bread crumbs
Oil for deep-fat frying

In a saucepan, saute onion in butter until tender. Stir in flour until blended. Gradually add milk and broth. Bring to a boil; cook and stir for 2 minutes or until thickened. Remove from the heat; stir in turkey, sweet potato, salt, pepper and cayenne. Cover and refrigerate for 2 hours or until firm. Meanwhile, toss apple with lemon juice in a bowl. Stir in remaining salsa ingredients. Cover and chill for 1 hour.

For croquettes, beat eggs and water in a shallow bowl. Place flour and bread crumbs in separate shallow bowls. Shape turkey mixture into 1-1/2-in. balls. Roll in flour; shake off excess. Roll in egg mixture, then in crumbs.

In an electric skillet or deep-fat fryer, heat 1-1/2 in. of oil to 375°. Fry croquettes for 2 minutes or until golden brown. Drain on paper towels. Serve with salsa. **Yield:** 16 croquettes (2 cups salsa).

***Editor's Note:** When cutting or seeding hot peppers, use rubber or plastic gloves to protect your hands. Avoid touching your face.

Ham Slice with Pineapple-Orange Sauce

A juicy ham slice is just as tasty as a whole ham, and it's easier and faster to prepare. Plus, topped with golden pineapple sauce, this dish is so elegant on the table.
—*Ruth Andrewson, Leavenworth, Washington*

1 fully cooked ham slice (about 1 inch thick and 2 pounds)
1 tablespoon butter
1 can (8 ounces) unsweetened sliced pineapple
1/3 cup orange juice

3 tablespoons brown sugar
2 teaspoons cornstarch
1 teaspoon white wine vinegar
Dash ground ginger

In a skillet, brown ham in butter. Place in a greased 13-in. x 9-in. x 2-in. baking dish. Drain pineapple, reserving juice; set juice aside. Place pineapple over ham; set aside.

In a saucepan, combine orange juice, brown sugar, cornstarch, vinegar, ginger and reserved pineapple juice; mix well. Bring to a boil over medium heat; boil and stir for 2 minutes or until thickened. Pour over ham and pineapple. Bake, uncovered, at 350° for 25-30 minutes or until ham is heated through. **Yield:** 6-8 servings.

Herbed Rib Roast

The mixture of herbs and garlic turns this tender roast into a real treat. Our children and grandchildren look forward to feasting on it at Christmastime and other special family occasions.
—Carol Jackson, South Berwick, Maine

1 boneless rib roast (4 to 5 pounds)
2 to 3 garlic cloves, thinly sliced
1 teaspoon salt
1/2 teaspoon pepper
1/2 teaspoon dried basil
1/2 teaspoon dried parsley flakes
1/2 teaspoon dried marjoram

Cut 15-20 slits in the roast; insert garlic. Combine salt, pepper, basil, parsley and marjoram; rub over roast. Place fat side up on a rack in a roasting pan. Bake, uncovered, at 325° for 2 to 2-1/2 hours or until meat reaches the desired doneness (for rare, a meat thermometer should read 140; medium, 160°; well-done, 170°). **Yield:** 8-10 servings.

Deviled Crab Casserole

(Pictured at right)

After creating this recipe, I later pared it down to serve two. I serve this entree often, since it's so easy to assemble. Along with a green salad, dessert and coffee, this casserole makes a delicious lunch or dinner.
—Helen Bachman, Champaign, Illinois

1 can (6 ounces) crabmeat, drained, flaked and cartilage removed
1 cup dry bread crumbs, *divided*
3/4 cup milk
1/4 cup chopped green onions
2 hard-cooked eggs, chopped
1/2 teaspoon salt
1/4 teaspoon Worcestershire sauce
1/8 teaspoon ground mustard
1/8 teaspoon pepper
6 tablespoons butter, melted, *divided*
Paprika

In a bowl, combine crab, 3/4 cup of bread crumbs, milk, onions, eggs, salt, Worcestershire sauce, mustard and pepper. Add 4 tablespoons of butter; mix well. Spoon into a greased 1-qt. baking dish.

Combine the remaining bread crumbs and butter; sprinkle over casserole. Sprinkle with paprika. Bake, uncovered, at 425° for 16-18 minutes or until golden brown and the edges are bubbly. **Yield:** 2 servings.

Turkey Drumstick Dinner

(Pictured below)

I discovered this recipe a long time ago and love it since it uses tasty, economical turkey drumsticks. Our family and friends enjoy this savory meat and potatoes meal. —*Alice Balliet, Kane, Pennsylvania*

4 uncooked turkey drumsticks (about 3 pounds)
2 tablespoons vegetable oil
1 tablespoon butter
1 medium onion, sliced
1 can (14-1/2 ounces) stewed tomatoes
3 chicken bouillon cubes
1 teaspoon garlic salt
1/2 teaspoon dried oregano
1/2 teaspoon dried basil
4 large potatoes, peeled, cooked and quartered
2 medium zucchini, cut into 3/4-inch slices
2 tablespoons cornstarch
2 tablespoons water
Snipped fresh parsley

In a large skillet, brown the turkey drumsticks in oil and butter. Place in a 3-qt. Dutch oven. Top with onion slices. In the same skillet, heat the tomatoes, bouillon and seasonings until the bouillon is dissolved. Pour over the drumsticks. Cover and bake at 325° for 2 hours, basting once or twice. Add the potatoes and zucchini. Cover and bake for 20 minutes. Remove the drumsticks and vegetables to a serving dish and keep warm.

Combine the cornstarch and water until smooth; stir into tomato mixture. Return to the oven, uncovered, for 10-15 minutes or until slightly thickened. Pour over drumsticks and vegetables. Sprinkle with parsley. **Yield:** 4 servings.

Herbed Beef Rib Roast

This is one of my favorite ways to prepare a roast because it turns out so tender and flavorful. My husband and our six children just love it! —*Donna Conlin Gilmour, Ontario*

1 tablespoon garlic powder
1 tablespoon ground mustard
1 to 2 teaspoons salt
1 to 2 teaspoons pepper
1 beef rib roast (6 to 8 pounds)
1/4 cup water
1/4 cup beef broth
1 tablespoon red wine vinegar

Combine the garlic powder, mustard, salt and pepper; rub over entire roast. Place roast fat side up in a shallow roasting pan. Pour water, broth and vinegar into pan.

Bake, uncovered, at 350° for 2-3/4 to 3 hours, basting frequently with pan juices, or until meat reaches desired doneness (for rare, a meat thermometer should read 140°; medium, 160°; well-done, 170°). Let stand for 10-15 minutes before slicing. **Yield:** 10-12 servings.

Stuffed Beef Tenderloin

As spectacular as it is to the eye, with ham, cheese and spinach peeking out of every slice, there's very little fuss to making this stuffed tenderloin. The meat turns out extremely tender, too. —*Marianne Blackman Fairfield, Connecticut*

1 beef tenderloin (3 pounds)
Celery salt, garlic powder and pepper to taste
1/4 pound sliced provolone cheese

6 cups fresh spinach
1/2 pound thinly sliced fully cooked ham

Cut a lengthwise slit down the center of the tenderloin to within 3/4 in. of bottom; open tenderloin so it lies flat. Flatten to 1/2-in. thickness. Sprinkle with celery salt, garlic powder and pepper. Layer with cheese, spinach and ham; press down gently. Roll up, starting with a long side; secure with string. Sprinkle with additional celery salt, garlic powder and pepper.

Place in a shallow baking pan. Bake, uncovered, at 400° for 35-45 minutes or until meat reaches desired doneness (for rare, a meat thermometer should read 140°; medium, 160°; well-done, 170°). Let stand 10 minutes before slicing. **Yield:** 10-12 servings.

Mom's Best Meat Loaf

(Pictured above)

This is no ordinary-tasting meat loaf—in fact, the recipe is so good it's been passed down in our family for three generations. The zesty seasoning gives the flavor a spark. —*Linda Nilsen, Anoka, Minnesota*

1 cup milk
1 egg, lightly beaten
3/4 cup soft bread crumbs
1 medium onion, chopped
1 tablespoon finely chopped green pepper
1 tablespoon ketchup
1-1/2 teaspoons salt
1 teaspoon prepared horseradish
1 teaspoon sugar
1 teaspoon ground allspice
1 teaspoon dill weed
1-1/2 pounds lean ground beef
Additional ketchup

In a large bowl, combine the first 11 ingredients; add beef and mix well. Press into an ungreased 8-in. x 4-in. x 2-in. loaf pan.

Bake at 350° for 1 hour. Drizzle top of loaf with ketchup; bake 15 minutes more or until meat is no longer pink and a meat thermometer reads 160°. **Yield:** 6-8 servings.

Special Scallops And Chicken

(Pictured above)

I make this main course when I want to wow company. It tastes heavenly, and guests always love it. The subtle flavor of tarragon in the creamy sauce complements the mushrooms, chicken and scallops nicely.
—Sheila Vail, Long Beach, California

1/2 cup all-purpose flour
1/2 teaspoon salt
1/2 teaspoon pepper
6 boneless skinless chicken breast halves
1/2 pound bay scallops
1/4 cup olive oil
1-1/2 cups sliced fresh mushrooms
1 medium onion, chopped
1/4 cup white wine *or* chicken broth
2 teaspoons cornstarch
1/2 cup heavy whipping cream
1 teaspoon dried tarragon
1/2 cup shredded Swiss cheese

In a large resealable plastic bag, combine the flour, salt and pepper. Add chicken and scallops in batches; shake to coat. In a large skillet, saute the chicken and scallops in oil until lightly browned. Transfer to a greased 13-in. x 9-in. x 2-in. baking dish.

In the pan drippings, saute mushrooms and onion. Add wine or broth. Bring to a boil; cook until liquid is reduced to 2 tablespoons. Combine the cornstarch, cream and tarragon until blended; add to skillet. Bring to a boil; cook and stir for 1 minute or until thickened.

Spoon over the chicken and scallops. Sprinkle with cheese. Bake, uncovered, at 375° for 18-20 minutes or until chicken juices run clear. **Yield:** 6 servings.

Duck with Orange Hazelnut Stuffing

For over 50 years, this elegant entree has graced my family's holiday table. The zesty stuffing with its nice nutty crunch complements the slices of moist duck. —Donna Smith, Victor, New York

2 domestic ducklings (4 to 5 pounds *each*)
1 teaspoon salt
STUFFING:
4 cups coarse soft bread crumbs
2 cups chopped peeled tart apple
2 cups chopped toasted hazelnuts
1 cup chopped celery
1/2 cup chopped onion
1/2 cup orange juice
1/2 cup egg substitute
1/4 cup butter, melted
2 to 3 tablespoons lemon juice
2 teaspoons grated orange peel
1-1/2 teaspoons grated lemon peel
1 teaspoon seasoned salt
1/2 teaspoon pepper
1/2 teaspoon dried thyme
1/4 teaspoon ground nutmeg
Additional butter, melted
GRAVY:
3 tablespoons all-purpose flour
1/4 teaspoon salt

1/8 teaspoon pepper
2 cups chicken broth
1/3 cup orange marmalade

Sprinkle the inside of ducks with salt; prick skin several times and set aside. Combine the first 15 stuffing ingredients; spoon into ducks. Place with breast side up on a rack in a large shallow roasting pan. Brush with butter. Bake, uncovered, at 350° for 2 to 2-1/2 hours or until a meat thermometer reads 180° for duck and 165° for stuffing. Remove all stuffing and keep warm.

For gravy, combine 3 tablespoons pan drippings, flour, salt and pepper in a saucepan; stir until smooth. Heat until bubbly, stirring constantly. Gradually add broth. Bring to a boil; cook for 1-2 minutes, stirring constantly. Add marmalade; stir until smooth. Serve with ducks and stuffing. **Yield:** 8 servings.

Asian Spiced Turkey

I have my mother and our Chinese heritage to thank for this moist and savory turkey. The vanilla, aniseed and apple juice make the basting sauce unique.
—K. Fung, Stoneham, Massachusetts

2 to 3 celery ribs
1 to 2 green onions
1 turkey (16 to 20 pounds)
3 cups water, *divided*
1 cup soy sauce
1/4 cup sugar
1/4 cup apple juice
1 teaspoon vanilla extract
1/2 teaspoon garlic powder
1/2 teaspoon ground ginger
1/8 teaspoon aniseed, crushed
1/8 teaspoon *each* ground cinnamon, nutmeg and cloves

Place celery and onions inside the turkey cavity. In a small bowl, combine 1 cup water, soy sauce, sugar, apple juice, vanilla and seasonings; mix well. Place turkey, breast side up, on a rack in a roasting pan; pour remaining water into the pan. Pour 1/4 cup soy sauce mixture into the cavity and another 1/4 cup over turkey; set remaining sauce aside.

Bake, uncovered, at 325° for 3-1/2 to 4 hours or until a meat thermometer reads 180°, basting occasionally with the remaining sauce. When the turkey begins to brown, cover lightly with foil. Cover and let stand for 20 minutes before carving. **Yield:** 18-20 servings.

Wild Rice Shrimp Saute

(Pictured below)

The seafood is so good here in Florida, and shrimp is at the top of our list of favorites. Shrimp and wild rice make a delicious combination. *—Judy Robinette Ommert*
Sebring, Florida

2-1/3 cups water
4 tablespoons butter, *divided*
1 teaspoon lemon juice
1/2 teaspoon Worcestershire sauce
1/2 teaspoon ground mustard
1/4 teaspoon pepper
1 package (6 ounces) long grain and wild rice mix
1 pound uncooked shrimp, peeled and deveined
2 tablespoons chopped green pepper
2 tablespoons chopped green onions

In a saucepan over medium heat, combine water, 1 tablespoon butter, lemon juice, Worcestershire sauce, mustard and pepper; bring to a boil. Add rice with seasoning packet; return to a boil. Reduce heat; cover and simmer for 25-30 minutes or until rice is tender and liquid is absorbed.

Meanwhile, in a skillet over medium heat, melt remaining butter. Add shrimp, green pepper and onions. Cook and stir for 7-9 minutes or until shrimp turn pink and are cooked through. Add rice; heat through. **Yield:** 4 servings.

Cashew Chicken Stir-Fry

(Pictured below)

For me, the hardest part of making this quick dish is keeping the cashews in the cupboard! My husband just loves them, and so do our three girls.
—Vicki Hirschfeld, Hartland, Wisconsin

2 cups chicken broth, *divided*
1 pound boneless skinless chicken breasts, cut into 1/2-inch strips
2 garlic cloves, minced
1/2 cup thinly sliced carrots
1/2 cup sliced celery (1/2-inch pieces)
3 cups broccoli florets
1 cup fresh *or* frozen snow peas
1/4 cup cornstarch
3 tablespoons soy sauce
1/2 teaspoon ground ginger
1-1/2 cups cashews
Hot cooked rice, optional

In a skillet, heat 3 tablespoons of broth. Add chicken; stir-fry over medium heat until no longer pink, about 3-5 minutes. Remove with a slotted spoon and keep warm. Add garlic, carrots and celery to skillet; stir-fry for 3 minutes. Add broccoli and peas; stir-fry for 4-5 minutes or until crisp-tender. Meanwhile, combine the cornstarch, soy sauce, ginger and remaining broth until smooth; add to the skillet with the chicken. Cook and stir for 2 minutes. Stir in cashews. Serve over rice if desired. **Yield:** 4 servings.

Spiced Holiday Ham

This glazed ham is one of my family's favorites, so I serve it often at holiday time. Currant jelly, mustard and brown sugar add a special flavor. *—Eunice Hurt Murfreesboro, Tennessee*

1 bone-in half ham (5 to 7 pounds)
15 whole cloves
1 jar (12 ounces) currant jelly
1 tablespoon brown sugar
1 tablespoon vinegar
1 teaspoon ground mustard
1/4 teaspoon ground cinnamon

Score ham; insert cloves in cuts. Place in a greased 13-in. x 9-in. x 2-in. baking dish. Bake, uncovered, at 325° for 20 minutes per pound.

Combine jelly, sugar, vinegar, mustard and cinnamon; brush half over ham. Bake 15 minutes. Brush remaining jelly mixture over ham. Bake for 15 minutes, basting occasionally, or until a meat thermometer reads 140°. **Yield:** 8-10 servings.

Pork Tenderloin With Mushrooms

Over the years, I've found the trick to serving this tender pork with its onion- and mushroom-flavored gravy is to fix enough for second helpings. —*Dorothe Aigner*
Roswell, New Mexico

2 pork tenderloins (about 1 pound *each*)
3 tablespoons butter
1 teaspoon salt
1/4 teaspoon pepper
1 medium onion, thinly sliced
1-1/2 cups sliced fresh mushrooms
1/2 cup thinly sliced celery
2 tablespoons all-purpose flour
1/2 cup chicken broth
Hot wild rice *or* noodles, optional

In a skillet, brown pork in butter. Transfer meat to an ungreased shallow 1-1/2-qt. baking dish. Sprinkle with salt and pepper; set aside. In the pan drippings, saute the onion, mushrooms and celery until tender.

Combine flour and broth until smooth; add to skillet. Bring to a boil; cook and stir for 2 minutes. Pour over meat. Cover and bake at 325° for 1 hour or until a meat thermometer reads 160°-170°. Let stand 5 minutes before slicing. Serve with rice or noodles if desired. **Yield:** 8 servings.

Braised Lamb Shanks

(Pictured above right)

A friend shared this recipe with me many years ago. These lamb shanks make a hearty meal alongside baked potatoes, a hot vegetable and fresh fruit salad. Of course, I include mint jelly on the side. —*Jeanne McNamara*
Camillus, New York

2 lamb shanks (about 3 pounds)
1 cup beef broth
1/4 cup soy sauce
2 tablespoons brown sugar
1 garlic clove, minced
2 teaspoons prepared mustard

Place lamb in a greased 2-1/2-qt. baking dish. Combine broth, soy sauce, brown sugar, garlic and mustard; pour over meat. Cover and bake at 325° for 1-1/2 to 2 hours or until the meat is tender. **Yield:** 2 servings.

Setting a Festive Mood

Lighting and music can wrap up any holiday gathering in a festive and relaxing atmosphere. Try groupings of bright votive candles or different-sized pillars on a mirrored surface to show off your spread (and your guests) in the best light. For music, what could be nicer than the sounds of the season? Mix instrumental with vocal carols.

Apple-Ham Confetti Loaf

One day I had some ground ham and pork in the refrigerator and was thinking about how to use them together in a recipe. I looked outside at my loaded apple tree and decided to combine the three ingredients into one dish. This is what I came up with. Guests really enjoy the unique combination of ingredients.
—Gloria Snyder, Gastonia, North Carolina

3 eggs
1/4 cup packed brown sugar
2 tablespoons prepared mustard
1 tablespoon soy sauce
1/8 teaspoon pepper
3 cups crushed cornflakes
2/3 cup chopped green pepper
2/3 cup chopped sweet red pepper
2/3 cup chopped yellow pepper
2 cups diced peeled apples
1/2 cup chopped onion
1-1/2 pounds ground ham
1-1/2 pounds ground pork
Orange marmalade *or* apricot preserves

In a bowl, combine the eggs, brown sugar, mustard, soy sauce and pepper; stir in the cornflakes, green, red and yellow peppers, apples and onion. Add ham and pork and mix well. Divide between two ungreased 8-in. x 4-in. x 2-in. loaf pans.

Bake, uncovered, at 350° for 45 minutes. Spoon marmalade or preserves over loaves. Bake 20-30 minutes longer or until a meat thermometer reads 170°. **Yield:** 10-12 servings.

Chicken in Potato Baskets

These petite meat pies with their hash brown crusts are so pretty that I like to serve them for special luncheons and holiday dinners. Chock-full of meat and vegetables in a creamy sauce, they're a meal-in-one...and a great way to use up leftovers. *—Helen Lamison*
Carnegie, Pennsylvania

4-1/2 cups frozen shredded hash brown potatoes, thawed
6 tablespoons butter, melted
1-1/2 teaspoons salt
1/4 teaspoon pepper
FILLING:
1/2 cup chopped onion
1/4 cup butter
1/4 cup all-purpose flour
2 teaspoons chicken bouillon granules
1 teaspoon Worcestershire sauce
1/2 teaspoon dried basil
2 cups milk
3 cups cubed cooked chicken
1 cup frozen peas, thawed

In a bowl, combine the potatoes, butter, salt and pepper. Press into six greased 10-oz. custard cups; set aside.

In a saucepan, saute the onion in butter. Add the flour, bouillon, Worcestershire sauce and basil. Stir in the milk. Bring to a boil; cook and stir for 2 minutes or until thickened. Add chicken and peas. Spoon into prepared crusts. Bake, uncovered, at 375° for 30-35 minutes or until crust is golden brown. **Yield:** 6 servings.

Nutty Turkey Slices

Try this flavorful way to dress up plain turkey breast slices. I guarantee your family is sure to enjoy it as much as mine does. You can really taste the walnuts in the crunchy golden coating. And the gravy is delicious served over the slices. *—Nancy Schmidt*
Center, Colorado

3/4 cup ground walnuts
1/4 cup grated Parmesan cheese
1/2 teaspoon Italian seasoning
1/2 teaspoon paprika
6 turkey breast slices (about 1 pound)
3 tablespoons butter
1 teaspoon cornstarch
1/2 cup chicken broth
2 teaspoons lemon juice

In a shallow bowl, combine the walnuts, Parmesan cheese, Italian seasoning and paprika. Coat both sides of turkey slices with crumb mixture. In a large skillet over medium heat, brown half of the turkey at a time in butter for 6-8 minutes or until juices run clear; remove and keep warm.

In a small bowl, combine the cornstarch, broth and lemon juice until smooth; add to the skillet. Stir to loosen browned bits and bring to a boil; cook and stir for 1 minute. Serve with the turkey slices. **Yield:** 3-6 servings.

Brunch

Gingerbread Pancakes

(Pictured below)

Christmas breakfast is extra festive when these fragrant spiced pancakes are on the menu. We've even made them in the shape of gingerbread men. —Debbie Baxter Gresham, Oregon

- 1 cup all-purpose flour
- 1 tablespoon sugar
- 1 teaspoon baking powder
- 1 teaspoon ground ginger
- 1/2 teaspoon baking soda
- 1/2 teaspoon salt
- 1/2 teaspoon ground cinnamon
- Pinch ground cloves
- 1 cup buttermilk
- 1 egg
- 2 tablespoons molasses
- 1 tablespoon vegetable oil
- Maple syrup and whipped cream, optional

In a bowl, combine the first eight ingredients. Combine buttermilk, egg, molasses and oil; add to dry ingredients and mix well. Pour batter by 1/4 cupfuls onto a lightly greased hot griddle; turn when bubbles form on top of pancakes. Cook until second side is golden brown. Serve with syrup and whipped cream if desired. **Yield:** 8-10 pancakes.

Brunch Pizza

Whenever I entertain guests, this zippy pizza is a definite crowd-pleaser. It also makes a great late-night snack any time of the year! —Janelle Lee Sulphur, Louisiana

- 1 pound bulk pork sausage
- 1 tube (8 ounces) refrigerated crescent rolls
- 1 cup frozen shredded hash browns
- 1 cup (4 ounces) shredded cheddar cheese
- 5 eggs
- 1/4 cup milk
- 1/2 teaspoon salt
- 1/4 teaspoon pepper
- 2 tablespoons grated Parmesan cheese

Cook sausage until no longer pink; drain and set aside. Separate crescent roll dough into eight triangles and place on an ungreased 12-in. round pizza pan with points toward center. Press over the bottom and up the sides to form a crust; seal perforations.

Spoon sausage over crust; sprinkle with hash browns and cheddar cheese. In a bowl, beat eggs, milk, salt and pepper; pour over cheese. Sprinkle with Parmesan. Bake at 375° for 25-30 minutes or until crust is golden. **Yield:** 6-8 servings.

Cheery Cherry Compote

I always get loads of compliments on this sweet, colorful compote with its variety of fruits when I serve it for holiday brunch. It's a quick and easy recipe that only looks like it takes hours. —Jeanee Volkmann, Waukesha, Wisconsin

2-1/2 cups water
2 cups pitted prunes
1-1/2 cups dried apricots
1 can (21 ounces) cherry pie filling
1 can (20 ounces) pineapple chunks, undrained
1/4 cup white grape juice
Lemon slices

In a large saucepan, bring water, prunes and apricots to a boil; reduce heat. Simmer, uncovered, for 10 minutes. Remove from the heat and let stand for 5 minutes; drain.

Add pie filling, pineapple and grape juice; bring to a boil. Reduce heat; cover and simmer for 10 minutes or until fruit is tender. Let stand for 5 minutes. Serve warm; garnish with lemon slices. **Yield:** 10-12 servings.

Blueberry Blintz Souffle

(Pictured at right)

This luscious recipe is one I serve for Christmas and on New Year's, too. The rich blueberry syrup is delicious.
—Toni Anselmo, Rancho Palos Verdes, California

1/4 cup butter, softened
1/3 cup sugar
6 eggs
1-1/2 cups (12 ounces) sour cream
1/2 cup orange juice
1 cup all-purpose flour
2 teaspoons baking powder

FILLING:
2 cups (16 ounces) small-curd cottage cheese
1 package (8 ounces) cream cheese, softened
2 egg yolks
1 tablespoon sugar
1 teaspoon vanilla extract

BLUEBERRY SYRUP:
1 can (15 ounces) blueberries
1/2 cup corn syrup
1 tablespoon cornstarch
1/2 teaspoon lemon juice
Dash salt
Dash ground cinnamon

In a mixing bowl, cream butter and sugar. Add eggs, one at a time, beating well after each addition. Beat in sour cream and orange juice. Combine flour and baking powder; stir into egg mixture. Set aside. Combine filling ingredients in a small mixing bowl; beat until blended. Pour half of the batter into a greased 13-in. x 9-in. x 2-in. baking dish. Top with filling and remaining batter. Bake, uncovered, at 350° for 40-50 minutes or until a knife inserted near the center comes out clean.

Meanwhile, for syrup, drain blueberries, reserving juice; set berries aside. In a saucepan, combine corn syrup, cornstarch, lemon juice, salt, cinnamon and reserved blueberry juice until smooth. Bring to a boil over medium heat; boil and stir for 2 minutes or until thickened. Add blueberries; heat through. Serve warm with the souffle. **Yield:** 12 servings.

Brunch Helper

When selecting recipes to serve for brunch, look for some make-ahead choices as well as some last-minute dishes. Get a head start on as many dishes as possible by chopping, slicing and dicing the night before.

Strawberry Cheesecake French Toast

(Pictured above)

For a tempting breakfast dish that's more like dessert, try this! The rich filling between the French toast slices tastes like cheesecake. And who can resist sweet strawberries? —Darlene Markel, Sublimity, Oregon

1 carton (8 ounces) ricotta cheese
3 tablespoons confectioners' sugar
1 teaspoon vanilla extract
16 slices French bread (1/2 inch thick)
2 eggs
1 cup milk
2 cups sliced fresh *or* frozen strawberries
Additional confectioners' sugar *or* maple syrup
Hot cooked sausage links, optional

In a small bowl, combine ricotta, sugar and vanilla; mix well. Spread 2 tablespoons each on eight slices of bread; cover with remaining bread. In a bowl, beat eggs and milk; soak sandwiches 1-2 minutes per side.

Cook on a hot greased griddle for 5 minutes on each side or until golden brown and heated through. Serve with strawberries. Top with confectioners' sugar or maple syrup. Serve with sausage links if desired. **Yield:** 4-6 servings.

Cranberry Muffins

I always make these delicately flavored muffins for the holidays. With tart ruby cranberries peeking out and a sugar-and-spice topping, they don't last long. —Leona Luecking, West Burlington, Iowa

1/2 cup butter, softened
1 cup sugar
2 eggs
1 teaspoon vanilla extract
1 cup (8 ounces) sour cream
2 cups all-purpose flour
1 teaspoon baking powder
1/2 teaspoon baking soda
1/2 teaspoon ground nutmeg
1/4 teaspoon salt
1 cup chopped fresh *or* frozen cranberries
TOPPING:
2 tablespoons sugar
1/8 teaspoon ground nutmeg

In a mixing bowl, cream butter and sugar. Add eggs and vanilla; mix well. Fold in sour cream. Combine flour, baking powder, baking soda, nutmeg and salt; stir into the creamed mixture just until moistened. Fold in cranberries.

Fill greased or paper-lined muffin cups two-thirds full. Combine topping ingredients; sprinkle over muffins. Bake at 400° for 20-25 minutes or until a toothpick comes out clean. Cool in pan 10 minutes; remove to a wire rack. **Yield:** 1 dozen.

Herbed Sausage Gravy Over Cheese Biscuits

The gang at my house loves anything with biscuits, and this oregano-flavored sausage gravy is the best we've ever tasted! It's a real favorite with my husband and children. —Lynn Crosby, Homerville, Ohio

2 cups all-purpose flour
3 teaspoons baking powder
1/2 teaspoon salt
1/2 cup milk
1/4 cup vegetable oil
2 teaspoons dried oregano
1/2 pound bulk mozzarella cheese, cut into 8 cubes
GRAVY:
1/2 pound bulk pork sausage

3/4 cup milk
1 teaspoon dried oregano
1/4 cup all-purpose flour
1 cup cold water

In a large bowl, combine the flour, baking powder and salt. Stir in milk and oil just until moistened. Turn onto a lightly floured surface. Roll to 1/2-in. thickness; cut with a floured 2-1/2-in. biscuit cutter. Place a pinch of oregano in the center of each biscuit; top with a cheese cube. Moisten edge of dough with water and pull up over cheese, forming a pouch; pinch tightly to seal. Place on a lightly greased baking sheet. Bake at 450° for 12-15 minutes or until golden brown.

Meanwhile, in a skillet, cook the sausage over medium heat until no longer pink; drain. Stir in the milk and oregano. Combine the flour and water until smooth; add to sausage mixture. Bring to a boil; cook and stir for 2 minutes or until thickened. For each serving, spoon about 1/3 cup gravy over two biscuits. **Yield:** 4 servings.

Cinnamon Cream Syrup

The sugar and spice flavor of this syrup enhances waffles, griddle cakes, even cooked oatmeal. I often fix it for brunches. —Vera Reid, Laramie, Wyoming

1 cup sugar
1/2 cup light corn syrup
1/4 cup water
3/4 teaspoon ground cinnamon
1 can (5 ounces) evaporated milk

In a saucepan, combine first four ingredients. Bring to a boil over medium heat; boil and stir for 2 minutes. Cool for 5 minutes. Stir in milk. **Yield:** about 1-2/3 cups.

Jolly Jelly Doughnuts

(Pictured at right)

Just looking at these fat, festive, jelly-filled doughnuts will make your mouth water. Serve them warm and you'll find folks licking sugar from their fingers and asking for more. —Lee Bremson, Kansas City, Missouri

2 packages (1/4 ounce *each*) active dry yeast
2 cups warm milk (110° to 115°)
7 cups all-purpose flour, *divided*
4 egg yolks
1 egg
1/2 cup sugar
1 teaspoon salt
2 teaspoons grated lemon peel
1/2 teaspoon vanilla extract
1/2 cup butter, melted
Oil for deep-fat frying
Red jelly of your choice
Additional sugar

In a large mixing bowl, dissolve yeast in warm milk. Add 2 cups flour; mix well. Let stand in a warm place for 30 minutes. Add the egg yolks, egg, sugar, salt, lemon peel and vanilla; mix well. Beat in butter and remaining flour. Do not knead. Cover and let rise in a warm place until doubled, about 45 minutes.

Punch dough down. On a lightly floured surface, roll out to 1/2-in. thickness. Cut with a 2-1/2-in. biscuit cutter. Place on lightly greased baking sheets. Cover and let rise until nearly doubled, about 35 minutes.

In a deep-fat fryer or electric skillet, heat oil to 375°. Fry doughnuts, a few at a time, for 1-1/2 to 2 minutes on each side or until browned. Drain on paper towels. Cool for 2-3 minutes; cut a small slit with a sharp knife on one side of each doughnut. Using a pastry bag with a small round tip or a small spoon, fill each doughnut with about 1 teaspoon jelly. Carefully roll doughnuts in sugar. Serve warm. **Yield:** about 2-1/2 dozen.

Chocolate Marble Bread

(Pictured below)

My mother made this bread many Sundays for breakfast—and, if I was lucky, there'd be some left to savor Monday and Tuesday mornings as well! Just a whiff of this beautiful bread baking brings back treasured memories. —Rosina Sacks, Copley, Pennsylvania

7 to 7-1/2 cups all-purpose flour
1 package (1/4 ounce) active dry yeast
2 cups milk
1/2 cup sugar
1/4 cup butter
1 teaspoon salt
2 eggs
1/4 cup baking cocoa

GLAZE:

1 cup confectioners' sugar
1 tablespoon milk
1/4 cup chopped walnuts

In a mixing bowl, combine 3 cups flour and yeast. In a saucepan, heat milk, sugar, butter and salt to 120°-130°, stirring constantly. Add to flour mixture; mix well. Beat in eggs on low for 30 seconds; beat on high for 3 minutes. Add enough remaining flour to form a soft dough. Turn onto a floured surface; knead until smooth and elastic, about 6-8 minutes.

Divide dough into thirds. Knead cocoa into one-third of the dough (this may take 5-6 minutes). Shape into a ball. Shape remaining two-thirds dough into one ball. Place each ball in a lightly greased bowl, turning once to grease top. Cover and let rise in a warm place until doubled, about 1-1/4 hours. Punch dough down. Cover and let rest 10 minutes.

On a lightly floured surface, roll white dough into a 20-in. x 10-in. rectangle; repeat with chocolate dough. Place chocolate layer on top of white layer. Starting with long side, roll up jelly-roll style; press edges to seal seam. Cut into 20 slices; place in a greased 10-in. tube pan in three layers. Cover and let rise until nearly doubled, about 30-40 minutes.

Bake at 350° for 40-45 minutes or until lightly browned. Remove from pan immediately; cool on a wire rack. Combine sugar and milk; drizzle over bread. Sprinkle with nuts. **Yield:** 1 loaf.

Spiced Fruit Bowl

Juicy grapes and handy canned peaches and pears are spiced just right in this delicious dish. Allspice, cinnamon and cloves give the fruit a punch of holiday flavor. It's an easy and wonderful way to add fruit to your morning meal. —Linda Cary, Albany, New York

2 cans (29 ounces *each*) sliced peaches
1 can (29 ounces) pear halves
1/4 cup cider vinegar
1/4 teaspoon salt
4 cinnamon sticks (3 inches), broken
3/4 teaspoon whole allspice
1/2 teaspoon whole cloves
1 pound seedless red grapes, halved

Drain juice from peaches and pears into a saucepan; set fruit aside. Add vinegar and salt to juices. Place cinnamon, allspice and cloves on a double thickness of cheesecloth; bring up corners of cloth and tie with string to form a bag. Place in the saucepan. Bring to a boil. Reduce heat; cover and simmer for 10 minutes. Remove from the heat; cool for 15 minutes.

In a large bowl, combine the peaches, pears and grapes. Add the juices and spice bag. Cover and refrigerate for 12 hours or up to 3 days, stirring occasionally. Discard the spice bag before serving. **Yield:** 10-12 servings.

Cranberry Banana Coffee Cake

I make this moist cake for Christmas morning every year. It tastes like banana bread but has a sweet golden topping with a nutty crunch. —*Gloria Friesen*
Casper, Wyoming

1/2 cup butter, softened
1/2 cup sugar
2 eggs
1 teaspoon vanilla extract
2 cups all-purpose flour
2 teaspoons baking powder
1 teaspoon ground cinnamon
1/4 teaspoon salt
1/4 teaspoon ground allspice
2 medium ripe bananas, mashed (about 3/4 cup)
1 cup whole-berry cranberry sauce

TOPPING:
1/2 cup packed brown sugar
1/2 cup chopped pecans
2 tablespoons all-purpose flour
2 tablespoons butter, melted

In a large mixing bowl, cream the butter and sugar. Beat in eggs and vanilla. Combine the dry ingredients; add to the creamed mixture alternately with bananas. Spread into a greased 13-in. x 9-in. x 2-in. baking pan. Top with cranberry sauce.

In a small bowl, combine brown sugar, pecans and flour; stir in butter. Sprinkle over cranberries. Bake at 350° for 45-50 minutes or until a toothpick inserted near the center comes out clean. Cool in pan on a wire rack. **Yield:** 12-15 servings.

Coffee Punch

(Pictured above)

Guests will sing your praises when you ladle out this frothy, frosty, ice cream-coffee punch. Try brewing it with different flavored coffees for a perky pick-me-up.
—*Diane Propst, Denver, North Carolina*

1 quart brewed vanilla-flavored coffee, cooled
1 can (12 ounces) evaporated milk
1/2 cup sugar
1/2 gallon vanilla ice cream, softened
Ground cinnamon

In a large container, combine the coffee, milk and sugar; stir until sugar is dissolved. Spoon ice cream into a punch bowl; pour coffee mixture over the top. Sprinkle with cinnamon. Serve immediately. **Yield:** 2-1/2 quarts.

Breakfast in Bread

I enjoy making this delicious bread since it's very easy and a nice change of pace from sweeter breads. It's a "never-fail" treat, and friends always ask for the recipe. —*Joyce Brown, Warner Robins, Georgia*

6 eggs
1-1/2 cups all-purpose flour
2-1/2 teaspoons baking powder
1/2 teaspoon salt
3/4 cup milk
6 bacon strips, cooked and crumbled
1 cup diced fully cooked ham
1 cup *each* shredded Monterey Jack, Swiss and sharp cheddar cheese

In a large bowl, beat eggs until foamy. Combine flour, baking powder and salt. Gradually add to eggs with milk; mix well. Stir in bacon, ham and cheeses.

Pour into a greased 9-in. x 5-in. x 3-in. loaf pan. Bake at 350° for 50-60 minutes or until a toothpick inserted near the center comes out clean and top is golden brown. Serve warm. **Yield:** 1 loaf.

Holiday Burritos

(Pictured above)

In the Southwest, a breakfast burrito wraps up potatoes, eggs and cheese with a unique "Feliz Navidad" flair! There are many variations, but this is our favorite. —*Antoinette Metzgar, Rio Rancho, New Mexico*

1/4 cup chopped onion
1/2 cup butter
2 pounds red potatoes, cut into 1/2-inch cubes
12 eggs, lightly beaten
1 teaspoon garlic salt
1 teaspoon salt
1/2 teaspoon pepper
2 to 3 cans (4 ounces *each*) chopped green chilies, drained
12 flour tortillas (8 inches), warmed
2 cups (8 ounces) shredded cheddar cheese

In a large skillet, saute the onion in butter until tender. Add the potatoes; cover and cook for 15-20 minutes or until tender. In a bowl, combine the eggs, garlic salt, salt and pepper; pour over potatoes.

Cook and stir over medium heat until the eggs are completely set. Stir in the chilies. Fill each tortilla with about 3/4 cup of the egg mixture and 2 heaping tablespoons of the cheese; roll up tightly. Serve immediately. **Yield:** 12 burritos.

Traditional English Muffins

Our neighbors love these yeast treats I make. They tell me my muffins taste so much better than store-bought ones! —*Loretta Kurtz, Allensville, Pennsylvania*

2 packages (1/4 ounce *each*) active dry yeast
1 tablespoon sugar
3 cups warm water (110° to 115°), *divided*
2 eggs, beaten
2/3 cup honey
1 teaspoon salt
9 to 10 cups all-purpose flour

In a mixing bowl, dissolve yeast and sugar in 2 cups water. Beat in eggs, honey, salt, 2 cups flour and remaining water. Add enough remaining flour to form a soft dough. Turn onto a floured surface; knead until smooth and elastic, about 6-8 minutes. Place in a greased bowl, turning once to grease top. Cover and let rise in a warm place until doubled, about 1 hour.

Punch dough down. On a floured surface, roll to 1/2-in. thickness. Cover and let stand 5 minutes. Cut into 4-in. circles. Place 2 in. apart on greased baking sheets. Bake at 375° for 8 minutes or until bottom

is browned. Turn and bake 7 minutes longer or until second side is browned. Cool on wire racks. To serve, split with a fork and toast. **Yield:** about 3 dozen.

Fruit-Topped Buttermilk Pancakes

Years of trying different pancake recipes hasn't changed my opinion that this classic one is best. A generous dollop of warm fruit on top makes the meal truly special.
—Arlene Butler, Ogden, Utah

1 package (10 ounces) frozen sweetened raspberries, thawed
2 medium ripe bananas, sliced
1 can (8 ounces) pineapple chunks, drained
1/2 cup packed brown sugar
PANCAKES:
1-3/4 cups all-purpose flour
2 tablespoons sugar
2 teaspoons baking powder
1 teaspoon baking soda
1/2 teaspoon salt
2 eggs
2 cups buttermilk
1/4 cup vegetable oil
1/2 teaspoon vanilla extract

In a blender, combine raspberries, bananas, pineapple and brown sugar; cover and process until blended. Transfer to a small saucepan; cook and stir over low heat until heated through. Set aside; keep warm.

For pancakes, combine the dry ingredients in a bowl. In another bowl, beat the eggs, buttermilk, oil and vanilla. Stir into dry ingredients just until moistened. Pour batter by 1/4 cupfuls onto a greased hot griddle. Turn when bubbles form on top; cook until the second side is golden brown. Serve with warm fruit topping. **Yield:** about 1-1/2 dozen pancakes (2-1/2 cups topping).

Petite Sausage Quiches

(Pictured at right)

You won't be able to eat just one of these cute mini quiches. Filled with savory sausage, Swiss cheese and a dash of cayenne, the mouth-watering morsels will disappear fast from the breakfast or buffet table.
—Dawn Stitt, Hesperia, Michigan

1 cup butter, softened
2 packages (3 ounces *each*) cream cheese, softened
2 cups all-purpose flour
FILLING:
6 ounces bulk Italian sausage
1 cup (4 ounces) shredded Swiss cheese
1 tablespoon minced chives
2 eggs
1 cup half-and-half cream
1/4 teaspoon salt
Dash cayenne pepper

In a mixing bowl, beat butter, cream cheese and flour until smooth. Shape tablespoonfuls of dough into balls; press onto the bottom and up the sides of greased miniature muffin cups.

In a skillet, cook sausage over medium heat until no longer pink; drain. Sprinkle sausage, Swiss cheese and chives into muffin cups. In a bowl, beat eggs, cream, salt and pepper. Pour into shells. Bake at 375° for 28-30 minutes or until browned. Serve warm. Refrigerate leftovers. **Yield:** 3 dozen.

Crunchy Orange Muffins

(Pictured below)

The topping on these muffins reminds me of a crumb cake. I like to bake a big batch and store some in the freezer to serve to guests. —*Audrey Thibodeau Fountain Hills, Arizona*

1 cup all-purpose flour
1/2 cup whole wheat flour
1/2 cup packed brown sugar
2 teaspoons baking powder
1 teaspoon ground cinnamon
1/4 teaspoon salt
1/4 teaspoon ground nutmeg
1 egg
1/2 cup vegetable oil
1/2 cup orange juice
1 tablespoon grated orange peel
STREUSEL TOPPING:
1/2 cup packed brown sugar
1/2 cup chopped pecans
1/4 cup all-purpose flour
2 tablespoons butter, melted
1 teaspoon ground cinnamon

In a large bowl, combine the first seven ingredients. In a small bowl, combine the egg, oil, orange juice and peel; stir into dry ingredients just until moistened. Fill greased muffin cups two-thirds full.

Combine topping ingredients; sprinkle heaping tablespoonfuls on each muffin. Bake at 375° for 18-20 minutes or until a toothpick comes out clean. Cool for 5 minutes before removing from pan to a wire rack. **Yield:** about 1 dozen.

Ham and Eggs Tart

This hearty tart ensures a good hot breakfast with a minimum of fuss. It's so versatile that you can add different toppings, such as chopped olives and Monterey Jack cheese. —Marge Scardino, Milwaukee, Wisconsin

1/4 cup chopped onion
1 tablespoon butter
1 cup cubed fully cooked ham
1 tube (8 ounces) refrigerated crescent rolls
4 eggs
1/2 cup milk
1/2 teaspoon salt
1/4 teaspoon pepper
1 cup (4 ounces) shredded Swiss cheese
1 tablespoon minced chives

In a skillet, saute onion in butter until tender. Remove from the heat; stir in ham and set aside. Unroll crescent roll dough into one long rectangle. Press onto the bottom and 1 in. up the sides of a greased 13-in. x 9-in. x 2-in. baking dish; seal seams and perforations. Spread with reserved ham mixture.

In a bowl, beat eggs, milk, salt and pepper; stir in cheese. Pour over ham. Sprinkle with chives. Bake at 375° for 23-28 minutes or until a knife inserted in center comes out clean. Refrigerate leftovers. **Yield:** 8-10 servings.

Swiss Omelet Roll-Up

My family always enjoys this unique omelet on Christmas morning after we've opened gifts. Its special taste and appearance make the preparation time worthwhile. —*Gertrude Dumas, Athol, Massachusetts*

1-1/2 cups mayonnaise,* *divided*
2 tablespoons all-purpose flour

12 eggs, *separated*
1 cup milk
1/2 teaspoon salt
1/8 teaspoon pepper
6 tablespoons chopped green onions, *divided*
1 tablespoon Dijon mustard
1-1/2 cups chopped fully cooked ham
1 cup (4 ounces) shredded Swiss cheese
Fresh oregano *or* parsley, optional

In a saucepan, combine 1/2 cup mayonnaise and flour. In a bowl, whisk egg yolks until thickened; add milk. Pour into mayonnaise mixture; cook over low heat, stirring constantly, until thick. Add salt and pepper. Remove from the heat; cool for 15 minutes. In a mixing bowl, beat egg whites until stiff. Fold into the mayonnaise mixture. Line a 15-in. x 10-in. x 1-in. baking pan with waxed paper; coat paper with nonstick cooking spray. Pour egg mixture into pan. Bake at 425° for 20 minutes or until set.

Meanwhile, in a saucepan over low heat, combine 2 tablespoons onions, mustard and remaining mayonnaise. Remove 3/4 cup for topping; set aside and keep warm. To the remaining sauce, add ham, cheese and remaining onions; cook over low heat until cheese begins to melt.

Remove omelet from oven; turn onto a linen towel. Peel off waxed paper. Spread cheese sauce over warm omelet. Roll up from a short side. Top with reserved mustard sauce. Garnish with oregano or parsley if desired. Serve immediately. **Yield:** 10-12 servings.

***Editor's Note:** Reduced-fat or fat-free mayonnaise may not be substituted for regular mayonnaise.

Maple Butter

It's easy to add maple flavor to the breakfast table with this rich spread. Slather the butter on piping-hot pancakes, waffles and toast. Your family will love it!
—Kathy Scott, Hemingford, Nebraska

1/2 cup butter, softened
1/2 cup sugar
1/2 teaspoon vanilla extract
1/2 teaspoon maple flavoring

In a mixing bowl, cream butter, sugar, vanilla and maple flavoring until smooth. Cover and refrigerate until serving. **Yield:** about 1 cup.

Sunny Pancakes

(Pictured above)

These light, delicate pancakes have a nice citrus flavor that the tangy orange sauce complements.
—Alecia Barlow, Fairborn, Ohio

1-1/4 cups all-purpose flour
3 tablespoons sugar
2-1/2 teaspoons baking powder
3/4 teaspoon salt
1 egg
1 cup orange juice
1/4 cup milk
3 tablespoons vegetable oil
2 to 3 teaspoons finely grated orange peel
ORANGE SAUCE:
1/2 cup sugar
1 tablespoon cornstarch
1/4 teaspoon salt
3/4 cup water
1/2 cup orange juice
2 tablespoons butter
1 tablespoon lemon juice
2 to 3 teaspoons finely grated orange peel

In a large bowl, combine the first four ingredients. In another bowl, combine the egg, orange juice, milk, oil and orange peel; add to dry ingredients just until moistened. Pour batter by 1/4 cupfuls onto a lightly greased hot griddle. Turn when bubbles form on top; cook until second side is golden brown.

Combine sugar, cornstarch and salt in a saucepan. Stir in remaining ingredients. Bring to a boil; cook and stir 2 minutes until thickened. Serve warm with pancakes. **Yield:** 12 pancakes (about 1 cup sauce).

Christmas Fruit Kabobs

(Pictured above)

My chunky fruit skewers are always a hit for brunch, whether served with pastries, quiche or eggs and bacon. They're also excellent appetizers and potluck additions.
—*Lois Rutherford, St. Augustine, Florida*

1/2 fresh pineapple, trimmed and cut into 1-inch chunks
4 kiwifruit, peeled and cut into 1-inch pieces
3 navel oranges, peeled and sectioned
3 medium apples, cut into 1-inch pieces
3 medium firm bananas, cut into 1-inch pieces
1 jar (10 ounces) maraschino cherries, drained

SAUCE:
1 egg yolk
1/4 cup maple syrup *or* honey
2 tablespoons lemon juice
3/4 cup heavy whipping cream, whipped

Alternately thread the fruit onto wooden skewers. Cover and refrigerate until serving. In a saucepan over low heat, cook and stir the egg yolk and maple syrup until a thermometer reads 160°. Remove from the heat; stir in the lemon juice. Cool completely. Fold in the whipped cream. Serve with fruit for dipping. Refrigerate any leftovers. **Yield:** 20 kabobs (about 1 cup sauce).

Spiced Raisin Mini Muffins

These flavorful moist muffins don't crumble when you bite into them. You may want to take them into the living room for munching while opening gifts.
—*Faye Hintz, Springfield, Missouri*

1 cup sugar
1 cup chopped raisins
1 cup water
1/2 cup butter
1 teaspoon ground cinnamon
1/2 teaspoon ground cloves
2 cups all-purpose flour
1 teaspoon baking soda
1/2 teaspoon salt
1 cup chopped walnuts

GLAZE:
1 cup confectioners' sugar
1/2 teaspoon vanilla extract
1 to 2 tablespoons milk

In a saucepan, combine the sugar, raisins, water, butter, cinnamon and cloves. Bring to a boil over medium heat, stirring occasionally. Remove from the heat; cool to room temperature. In a bowl, combine the flour, baking soda and salt. Add raisin mixture; mix well. Stir in walnuts.

Fill greased or paper-lined miniature muffin cups two-thirds full. Bake at 350° for 12-16 minutes or until a toothpick comes out clean. Cool for 5 minutes before removing from pans to wire racks. For glaze, combine the confectioners' sugar, vanilla and enough milk to achieve desired consistency. Drizzle over cooled muffins. **Yield:** about 4-1/2 dozen.

Editor's Note: This recipe does not use eggs.

Christmas Breakfast Casserole

Spicy sausage, herbs and vegetables fill this egg casserole with hearty flavor. I like to make it for my family's Christmas breakfast, but it's delicious any time of day!
—*Debbie Carter, O'Fallon, Illinois*

1 pound bulk Italian sausage
1 cup chopped onion
1 jar (7 ounces) roasted red peppers, drained and chopped, *divided*

1 package (10 ounces) frozen chopped spinach, thawed and well drained
1 cup all-purpose flour
1/4 cup grated Parmesan cheese
1 teaspoon dried basil
1/2 teaspoon salt
8 eggs
2 cups milk
1 cup (4 ounces) shredded provolone cheese

In a skillet, cook sausage and onion until sausage is no longer pink; drain. Transfer to a greased 3-qt. baking dish. Sprinkle with half of the red peppers and all of the spinach. In a mixing bowl, combine flour, Parmesan cheese, basil and salt. Combine eggs and milk; add to dry ingredients and mix well. Pour over spinach.

Bake at 425° for 20-25 minutes or until a knife inserted near center comes out clean. Sprinkle with provolone cheese and remaining red peppers. Bake 2 minutes longer or until cheese is melted. Let stand 5 minutes before cutting. **Yield:** 10-12 servings.

Mix 'n' Match Quiche

(Pictured below)

Combine colorful crabmeat and asparagus to bake this hearty main dish from our Test Kitchen that's both festive and flavorful—or choose your family's favorite ingredients and create your own one-of-a-kind specialty! You'll be surprised at the compliments you'll receive.

1 unbaked pastry shell (9 inches)
1 can (6 ounces) crabmeat, drained, flaked and cartilage removed
1 cup frozen asparagus cuts, thawed
2 tablespoons chopped onion
2 tablespoons chopped sweet red pepper
1 cup (4 ounces) shredded Swiss *or* cheddar cheese
3 eggs
1-1/2 cups half-and-half cream
1/2 teaspoon salt
1/8 teaspoon pepper
1/8 teaspoon ground nutmeg

Do not prick pastry shell; line with a double thickness of heavy-duty foil. Bake at 450° for 5 minutes. Remove foil; bake 5 minutes more. Reduce heat to 325°. Layer crab, asparagus, onion, red pepper and cheese in crust. In a small bowl, beat eggs, cream, salt, pepper and nutmeg; pour over cheese. Bake for 35-45 minutes or until a knife inserted near the center comes out clean. Let stand 10 minutes before cutting. **Yield:** 6-8 servings.

Editor's Note: You can mix and match ingredients to come up with your own personal quiche. For the crab, substitute 8 ounces of browned pork sausage or 1 cup of diced cooked chicken or ham. For the asparagus, substitute 1 cup of frozen broccoli or a broccoli-cauliflower-carrot blend.

Black Forest Waffles

(Pictured below)

With their dark chocolate flavor and cherry and cream topping, these waffles add a fancy touch to brunch with very little effort. —*Edith Johnson Fruita, Colorado*

1-3/4 cups cake flour
6 tablespoons sugar
1 tablespoon baking powder
1/2 teaspoon salt
2 eggs, *separated*
1 cup milk
2 squares (1 ounce *each*) unsweetened baking chocolate
3 tablespoons shortening
1 cup heavy whipping cream, whipped
3 tablespoons confectioners' sugar
1 can (21 ounces) cherry pie filling
Fresh mint, optional

In a mixing bowl, combine flour, sugar, baking powder and salt. Combine egg yolks and milk; stir into dry ingredients. In a double boiler or microwave, melt the chocolate and shortening. Add to batter; mix well. In another mixing bowl, beat egg whites until stiff peaks form; fold into the batter.

Bake in a preheated waffle iron according to manufacturer's directions until browned. Combine whipped cream and confectioners' sugar. Serve waffles topped with whipped cream and pie filling. Garnish with mint if desired. **Yield:** 5 waffles (about 6-3/4 inches).

Sausage Rolls

Handy packaged crescent rolls and prepared sausages make this finger food quick and easy for breakfast or brunch. —*Rita Sherman, Coleville, California*

1 tube (8 ounces) refrigerated crescent rolls
8 brown-and-serve sausage links, cooked
1/8 teaspoon garlic powder
1/8 teaspoon rubbed sage
1 egg
1 tablespoon water
Dried parsley flakes
Paprika

Unroll crescent roll dough and separate into four rectangles; seal perforations. Place two sausage links end to end along the long side of each rectangle. Sprinkle with garlic powder and sage. Roll up jelly-roll style and seal the seam with water. Place seam side down on an ungreased baking sheet.

In a bowl, beat the egg and water; brush over the sausage rolls. Sprinkle with parsley and paprika. Cut into 2-in. pieces. Bake at 375° for 11-13 min-

utes or until golden brown and heated through. **Yield:** about 1 dozen.

Vegetable Frittata

(Pictured at right)

This fresh-tasting dish is an easy all-in-one meal. The bacon, eggs and hash browns make it hearty. The green broccoli and red paprika give it a look that fits the season. —*Alice Parker*
Moultrie, Georgia

4 bacon strips, cut into 1/2-inch pieces
2 cups frozen shredded hash browns, thawed
1 cup chopped broccoli
1/2 cup chopped green pepper
1/2 cup chopped red onion
1/2 to 1 teaspoon dried rosemary, crushed
6 eggs
3 tablespoons water
1/2 teaspoon salt
1/4 teaspoon pepper
1/4 teaspoon paprika

In an 8-in. ovenproof skillet, cook the bacon until crisp. Drain, reserving 2 tablespoons drippings in the skillet. Remove bacon to paper towel. To the skillet, add hash browns, broccoli, green pepper, onion and rosemary; cover and cook over low heat until hash browns are golden brown and vegetables are tender, about 10 minutes. Remove from the heat and set aside.

Beat eggs, water, salt and pepper; pour over hash browns. Top with bacon and paprika. Bake, uncovered, at 350° for 12-15 minutes or until eggs are completely set. **Yield:** 4-6 servings.

Almond Apricot Logs

This is a treat my family insists I make each year for the holidays. We often refer to these sweet bread bites simply as "good things". They're super served warm.
—*L. Kniffin, Hockessin, Delaware*

2 packages (1/4 ounce *each*) active dry yeast
1/3 cup warm water (110° to 115°)
1-1/2 cups warm milk (110° to 115°)
1/3 cup vegetable oil
1/2 cup sugar
2 eggs
2 teaspoons salt
2 teaspoons ground nutmeg
5 to 5-1/2 cups all-purpose flour
1-1/2 cups coarsely chopped dried apricots
1 cup chopped almonds

GLAZE:
1-1/2 cups confectioners' sugar
1/2 teaspoon vanilla extract
2 to 3 tablespoons milk

In a large mixing bowl, dissolve yeast in water. Add milk, oil, sugar, eggs, salt, nutmeg and 2 cups flour. Beat until smooth. Add apricots and almonds. Stir in enough remaining flour to form a soft dough. Turn onto a floured surface; knead until smooth and elastic, about 6-8 minutes. Place in a greased bowl, turning once to grease top. Cover and let rise in a warm place until doubled, 1-1/2 hours.

Punch dough down; let rest for 10 minutes. Turn onto a lightly floured surface. Roll into a 15-in. x 12-in. rectangle. Cut into 3-in. x 1-in. strips. Place 1 in. apart on greased baking sheets. Cover and let rise until doubled, about 30 minutes. Bake at 375° for 15 minutes or until light golden brown. Remove to wire racks.

For glaze, combine the confectioners' sugar, vanilla and enough milk to achieve desired consistency. Brush over warm logs. **Yield:** 5 dozen.

Sparkling Oranges

(Pictured above)

We were living in Texas when I found the recipe for this simple yet elegant salad. I was thrilled—we had a surplus of fresh oranges! Since it's prepared ahead, there's no last-minute fuss. —*Janie Bush*
Weskan, Kansas

8 large oranges, peeled and sectioned
1/2 cup sugar
1/2 cup orange marmalade
1 cup white grape juice
1/2 cup lemon-lime soda
3 tablespoons slivered almonds, toasted
3 tablespoons flaked coconut, toasted

Place orange sections in a large bowl. In a saucepan, combine sugar and marmalade; cook and stir over medium heat until sugar is dissolved. Remove from the heat. Stir in grape juice and soda. Pour over oranges and toss to coat.

Cover and refrigerate overnight. Using a slotted spoon, remove oranges to a serving dish. Sprinkle with almonds and coconut. **Yield:** 8 servings.

Christmas Morning Frittata

Christmas breakfast is especially merry when this colorful frittata is on the menu. It's easy to assemble, so it's perfect for busy mornings. —*Marlene Whyte*
Tisdale, Saskatchewan

1 medium onion, chopped
1 medium green pepper, chopped
1 garlic clove, minced
2 tablespoons butter
1/2 cup chopped tomatoes
1/4 cup minced fresh parsley
5 eggs, lightly beaten
2 cups (8 ounces) shredded mozzarella cheese
1/2 cup soft bread crumbs
1 teaspoon Worcestershire sauce
1/2 to 1 teaspoon salt
1/4 teaspoon pepper

In a skillet, saute the onion, green pepper and garlic in butter for 5 minutes or until tender. Remove from the heat. Stir in tomatoes and parsley; set aside. In a large bowl, combine the remaining ingredients. Stir in reserved vegetables.

Pour into an ungreased 9-in. pie plate. Bake, uncovered, at 350° for 25-30 minutes or until a knife inserted near the center comes out clean. Let stand for 5 minutes before cutting. **Yield:** 6-8 servings.

Buffet Scrambled Eggs

These are my favorite scrambled eggs. The white sauce, flavored with chicken bouillon, keeps the eggs creamy and moist. It's a tasty twist on a morning mainstay.
—*Elsie Beachy, Plain City, Ohio*

4 tablespoons butter, *divided*
2 tablespoons all-purpose flour
1 cup milk
2 teaspoons chicken bouillon granules
8 eggs, beaten
Minced fresh parsley, optional

In a saucepan, melt 2 tablespoons butter. Stir in flour until smooth. Add milk and bouillon. Bring to a boil; cook and stir for 2 minutes or until thickened. Set aside.

In a large skillet, melt remaining butter. Add

eggs; cook over medium heat until eggs begin to set, stirring occasionally. Add white sauce; mix well. Cook until the eggs are completely set. Garnish with parsley if desired. **Yield:** 4 servings.

Farmhouse Omelets

(Pictured below)

We really enjoy eating brunch after church on Sundays, so I make an effort to serve something special. This pretty omelet provides a pleasant blend of tastes and textures. —Roberta Williams, Poplar Bluff, Missouri

4 bacon strips, diced
1/4 cup chopped onion
6 eggs
1 tablespoon water
1/4 teaspoon salt, optional
1/8 teaspoon pepper
Dash hot pepper sauce
3 teaspoons butter, *divided*
1/2 cup cubed fully cooked ham, *divided*
1/4 cup thinly sliced fresh mushrooms, *divided*
1/4 cup chopped green pepper, *divided*
1 cup (4 ounces) shredded cheddar cheese, *divided*

In a skillet, cook bacon over medium heat until crisp. Remove with a slotted spoon to paper towels. Drain, reserving 2 teaspoons drippings. In the drippings, saute onion until tender; set aside.

In a bowl, beat eggs, water, salt if desired, pepper and hot pepper sauce. Melt 1-1/2 teaspoons butter in a 10-in. nonstick skillet over medium heat; add half of the egg mixture. As the eggs set, lift edges, letting uncooked portion flow underneath.

When eggs are set, sprinkle half of the bacon, onion, ham, mushrooms, green pepper and cheese over one side; fold over. Cover and let stand 1-2 minutes or until cheese is melted. Repeat with remaining ingredients for second omelet. **Yield:** 2 omelets.

Stuffed French Toast

Kids like to help stuff the sausage and cheese into the bread, so this is a good holiday treat. I serve it year-round for breakfast when we have guests or on special family occasions. —Heidi Wilcox, Lapeer, Michigan

1 package (8 ounces) brown-and-serve sausage patties
6 slices Italian bread (1-1/2 inches thick)
3 slices Muenster *or* brick cheese, halved
4 eggs
1 cup milk
1 tablespoon sugar
Maple syrup

In a skillet, cook sausage until browned; drain. Cut a pocket in the crust of each slice of bread. Stuff a sausage patty and slice of cheese into each pocket.

In a shallow bowl, beat eggs, milk and sugar. Soak bread for 2 minutes. Fry on a greased griddle over medium heat until golden brown on both sides. Serve with maple syrup. **Yield:** 6 servings.

Ham and Broccoli Strata

(Pictured below)

Entertaining is simplified with this homespun strata that features broccoli, ham and cheese. You assemble it the night before you need it, so there's no last-minute fuss.
—Robin Friedly, Louisville, Kentucky

2 packages (10 ounces *each*) frozen chopped broccoli, thawed and drained
3/4 pound thinly sliced deli ham, cut into 1/2-inch strips
2 cups (8 ounces) shredded Swiss cheese
1 loaf (8 ounces) French bread, cut into 1-inch slices
6 eggs, lightly beaten
2 cups milk
3 tablespoons dried minced onion
3 tablespoons Dijon mustard
1/2 teaspoon hot pepper sauce
1/2 teaspoon paprika

Combine broccoli, ham and cheese; spread half into a greased 13-in. x 9-in. x 2-in. baking dish. Arrange bread slices on top. Cover with remaining broccoli mixture. In a bowl, combine the eggs, milk, onion, mustard and hot pepper sauce. Pour over broccoli mixture. Sprinkle with paprika. Cover and refrigerate overnight.

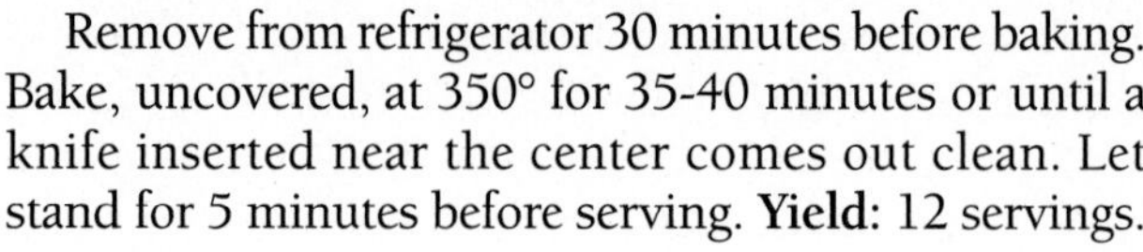

Remove from refrigerator 30 minutes before baking. Bake, uncovered, at 350° for 35-40 minutes or until a knife inserted near the center comes out clean. Let stand for 5 minutes before serving. **Yield:** 12 servings.

Jack Cheese Oven Omelet

Although it's easy, this omelet looks like you fussed. Sometimes I toss in mushrooms and cheddar cheese for a different flavor.
—Laurel Roberts
Vancouver, Washington

8 bacon strips, diced
4 green onions, sliced
8 eggs
1 cup milk
1/2 teaspoon seasoned salt
2-1/2 cups (10 ounces) shredded Monterey Jack cheese, *divided*

In a skillet, cook bacon until crisp. Drain, reserving 1 tablespoon drippings. Set bacon aside. Saute onions in drippings until tender; set aside. In a bowl, beat eggs. Add milk, seasoned salt, 2 cups cheese and sauteed onions. Transfer to a greased shallow 2-qt. baking dish. Bake, uncovered, at 350° for 35-40 minutes. Sprinkle with remaining cheese. **Yield:** 6 servings.

Cheesy Sausage Stromboli

One taste of this yummy sausage loaf at a Christmas party years ago, and I knew I'd be taking the recipe home for the holidays. A hit back then, it's become a family tradition. I like to serve it with hash brown potatoes and a fruit salad.
—Barbara Lindsey, Manvel, Texas

2 pounds bulk pork sausage
1 medium onion, chopped
1/2 cup shredded Colby-Monterey Jack cheese
1/2 cup grated Parmesan cheese
2 eggs, beaten
2 tablespoons minced fresh parsley
1/2 teaspoon salt
1/2 teaspoon hot pepper sauce
1 package (16 ounces) hot roll mix
1 tablespoon butter, melted
Picante sauce

In a skillet, cook sausage and onion over medium heat until meat is no longer pink; drain. Transfer to a bowl. Stir in the cheeses, eggs, parsley, salt and hot pepper sauce; cool.

Prepare hot roll mix according to package directions. Roll dough into a 17-in. x 14-in. rectangle. Spoon filling over dough to within 1 in. of edges. Roll up jelly-roll style, starting with a long side. Seal seams and tuck ends under. Place seam side down on a greased baking sheet. Bake at 400° for 20-25 minutes or until golden brown. Brush with butter. Let stand for 10 minutes before slicing. Serve with picante sauce. **Yield:** 8-10 servings.

Raisin Pinwheel Loaf

These slices are always welcome Christmas morning, especially when they're paired with steaming cups of coffee or tea. —*Jackie van Trigt*
New Hamburg, Ontario

1 cup raisins
1/2 cup ground almonds
1/4 cup sugar
2 egg whites
1/8 teaspoon almond extract
DOUGH:
2 cups all-purpose flour
2 teaspoons baking powder
1/2 teaspoon salt
1/2 cup cold butter
1/2 cup milk
1/4 cup sugar
2 egg yolks
2 teaspoons grated lemon peel
Half-and-half cream
Additional sugar
GLAZE:
1 cup confectioners' sugar
2 tablespoons milk

For filling, combine the first five ingredients in a bowl; set aside. In a large bowl, combine the flour, baking powder and salt. Cut in butter until the mixture resembles coarse crumbs. Add milk, sugar, egg yolks and lemon peel; mix well.

Turn onto a floured surface; knead 12 times. Roll into a 12-in. x 8-in. rectangle. Spread filling to within 1 in. of edges. Roll up, jelly-roll style, starting with a long side; pinch seams to seal and tuck ends under. Place, seam side down, on a greased baking sheet. Brush dough with cream and sprinkle with additional sugar. Bake at 375° for 40-45 minutes or until golden brown (top will crack). Remove to a wire rack. Combine glaze ingredients; drizzle over warm bread. To serve, cut into 1-in. slices. **Yield:** 12 servings.

Creamy Strawberry Breeze

(Pictured above)

Get Christmas Day off to a refreshing start with this frothy fruit drink. For a festive touch, garnish with a strawberry and a dollop of whipped topping. The pretty pink smoothie makes an attractive addition to a Yuletide brunch. —*Amy Cruson, Dodge City, Kansas*

2 cups whole strawberries
2 cups apple juice
3 cups whipped topping

Place half of the strawberries and apple juice in a blender; cover and process until smooth. Add half of the whipped topping; cover and process until blended. Pour into glasses. Repeat. **Yield:** 4 servings.

Citrus Punch

(Pictured above)

This zesty punch is a refreshing addition to my holiday table. I love its fruity flavor and the bright sunshiny color. You can easily double the recipe if you're expecting a larger group. —Dianne Conway, London, Ontario

2 cups orange juice
1 cup grapefruit juice
2 cups pineapple juice
1 cup lemonade
2 cups ginger ale

Chill all ingredients; mix gently in a pitcher or punch bowl. **Yield:** 12-16 servings (2 quarts).

Homemade Sage Sausage Patties

Oregano, garlic and sage add zippy flavor to these quick-to-fix ground pork patties. I've had this Pennsylvania Dutch recipe for years, and it always brings compliments. —Diane Hixon, Niceville, Florida

3/4 cup shredded cheddar cheese
1/4 cup buttermilk
1 tablespoon finely chopped onion
2 teaspoons rubbed sage
3/4 teaspoon salt
3/4 teaspoon pepper
1/8 teaspoon garlic powder
1/8 teaspoon dried oregano
1 pound ground pork

In a bowl, combine the first eight ingredients. Crumble pork over mixture and mix well. Shape into eight 1/2-in. patties. Refrigerate for 1 hour. In a nonstick skillet over medium heat, fry patties for 6-8 minutes on each side or until meat is no longer pink. **Yield:** 8 servings.

Bacon Popovers

Even picky youngsters find the eggs and hint of bacon in these popovers irresistible. For delicious variety, try pairing them with maple syrup or cheese sauce. —Marisa May, Fairport, New York

2 eggs
1 cup milk
1 tablespoon vegetable oil
1 cup all-purpose flour
1/4 teaspoon salt
3 bacon strips, cooked and crumbled

In a mixing bowl, beat the eggs, milk and oil. Beat in flour and salt just until smooth (do not overbeat). Using two 12-cup muffin tins, grease and flour six alternating cups in each pan.

Fill ungreased muffins cups two-thirds full with water. Fill greased muffin cups two-thirds full with batter. Sprinkle bacon over batter. Bake at 400° for 25-30 minutes or until puffed and golden. Serve warm. Refrigerate any leftovers. **Yield:** 1 dozen.

Christmas Coffee Cake

Christmas morning wouldn't be complete at our house without this yummy moist coffee cake. A streusel filling and topping sweetens the delightful cake, and red and green cherries add a festive touch. It's a perfect addition to any holiday breakfast buffet.

—Sue Meckstroth, New Carlisle, Ohio

1 cup pecans, chopped
1/3 cup packed brown sugar
1/4 cup sugar
1/4 cup butter, melted
1 teaspoon ground cinnamon

CAKE:

7 green maraschino cherries, finely chopped
7 red maraschino cherries, finely chopped
1/2 cup shortening
1 cup sugar
2 eggs
1 teaspoon vanilla extract
2-1/4 cups all-purpose flour
1 teaspoon baking powder
1 teaspoon baking soda
1/2 teaspoon salt
1 cup (8 ounces) sour cream

In a small bowl, combine the first five ingredients; mix well. Set aside. Drain cherries on paper towels. In a mixing bowl, cream shortening and sugar. Add eggs, one at a time, beating well after each addition. Add vanilla; mix well. Combine the flour, baking powder, baking soda and salt; add to creamed mixture alternately with sour cream. Fold in cherries.

Pour half of the batter into a greased 9-in. springform pan; sprinkle with half of the pecan mixture. Top with remaining batter and pecan mixture. Bake at 350° for 45-50 minutes or until a toothpick inserted near the center comes out clean. Cool on a wire rack for 10 minutes. Carefully run a knife around edge of pan to loosen. Remove sides of pan just before serving. **Yield:** 12 servings.

Any-Season Fruit Bowl

(Pictured below)

A refreshing fruit salad like this one is a welcome addition to a winter meal. A hint of anise gives it real holiday flavor, and it looks gorgeous on a buffet table.

—Frances Stevenson, McRae, Georgia

2 cups water
1-1/2 cups sugar
1/3 cup lime *or* lemon juice
1 teaspoon anise extract
1/2 teaspoon salt
3 oranges, peeled and sectioned
3 kiwifruit, peeled and sliced
2 grapefruit, peeled and sectioned
2 large apples, cubed
1 pint strawberries, sliced
1 pound green grapes
1 can (20 ounces) pineapple chunks, drained

In a medium saucepan, combine water, sugar, lime juice, anise and salt. Bring to a boil over medium heat; cook for 20 minutes, stirring occasionally. Remove from the heat; cover and refrigerate for 6 hours or overnight. Combine fruit in a large bowl; add dressing and toss to coat. Cover and chill for at least 1 hour. **Yield:** 16-18 servings.

Festive Scrambled Eggs

(Pictured below)

Every bit as quick as scrambled eggs are meant to be, this hearty dish, with red pimientos and green parsley or chives, is nice for hectic Christmas mornings.
—Fern Raleigh, Windom, Kansas

12 eggs
1-1/3 cups milk, ***divided***
1/2 to 1 teaspoon salt
1/4 teaspoon pepper
2 tablespoons diced pimientos
2 tablespoons minced fresh parsley ***or*** **chives**
2 tablespoons all-purpose flour
1/4 cup butter

In a large bowl, beat eggs and 1 cup milk. Add the salt, pepper, pimientos and parsley. In a small bowl, combine flour and remaining milk until smooth; stir into egg mixture. In a large skillet, melt butter over medium heat. Add egg mixture. Cook and stir over medium heat until the eggs are completely set. **Yield:** 6 servings.

Pumpkin Coffee Cake

I created this recipe when I had canned pumpkin on hand and was looking for something different to serve for the holidays. —Hazel Fritchie, Palestine, Illinois

TOPPING:
1/4 cup packed brown sugar
1/4 cup sugar
1/2 teaspoon ground cinnamon
2 tablespoons cold butter
1/2 cup chopped pecans
CAKE:
1/2 cup butter, softened
1 cup sugar
2 eggs
1 cup (8 ounces) sour cream
1/2 cup canned pumpkin
1 teaspoon vanilla extract
2 cups all-purpose flour
1 teaspoon baking soda
1 teaspoon baking powder
1/2 teaspoon pumpkin pie spice
1/4 teaspoon salt

In a small bowl, combine sugars and cinnamon. Cut in the butter until mixture resembles coarse crumbs. Stir in pecans; set aside.

In a mixing bowl, cream butter and sugar. Add eggs, one at a time, beating well after each addition. Combine the sour cream, pumpkin and vanilla; mix well. Combine dry ingredients; add to creamed mixture alternately with sour cream mixture. Beat on low just until blended.

Spread into two greased and floured 8-in. round baking pans. Sprinkle with topping. Bake at 325° for 40-50 minutes or until a toothpick inserted near center comes out clean. **Yield:** 16-20 servings.

Creamy Strawberry Crepes

As special as Christmas morning itself, these delicate crepes add a merry touch of elegance and holiday color to brunch! —Kathy Kochiss, Huntington, Connecticut

4 eggs
1 cup milk
1 cup cold water
2 tablespoons butter, melted
1/4 teaspoon salt
2 cups all-purpose flour
Additional butter

FILLING:
1 package (8 ounces) cream cheese, softened
1-1/4 cups confectioners' sugar
1 tablespoon lemon juice
1 teaspoon grated lemon peel
1/2 teaspoon vanilla extract
4 cups fresh strawberries, sliced, *divided*
1 cup heavy whipping cream, whipped

In a mixing bowl, beat eggs, milk, water, butter and salt. Add flour; beat until smooth. Cover and refrigerate for 1 hour. In an 8-in. nonstick skillet, melt 1 teaspoon butter; pour 2 tablespoons of batter into the center of skillet. Lift and tilt pan to evenly coat bottom. Cook until top appears dry; turn and cook 15-20 seconds longer. Remove to a wire rack. Repeat with remaining batter, adding butter to skillet as needed. When cool, stack crepes with waxed paper or paper towels in between.

For filling, in a small mixing bowl, beat the cream cheese, confectioners' sugar, lemon juice, peel and vanilla until smooth. Fold in 2 cups of berries and the whipped cream. Spoon about 1/3 cup filling down the center of 15 crepes; roll up. Garnish with remaining berries. Freeze remaining crepes for another use. **Yield:** 15 filled crepes.

French Toast with Spiced Butter

My family arrives early on Christmas morning, all of them looking for this delicious French toast with its cinnamon and nutmeg butter. It's easy to make and serve and always a hit! —Mabel Brown, Elmira, Ontario

4 eggs
1 cup milk
2 tablespoons sugar
1/2 teaspoon vanilla extract
6 slices French bread (3/4 inch thick)
2 tablespoons butter
SPICED BUTTER:
1/2 cup butter, softened
1/4 cup confectioners' sugar
1/2 teaspoon ground cinnamon
1/4 teaspoon ground nutmeg
Maple syrup

In a bowl, beat eggs. Whisk in the milk, sugar and vanilla. Arrange bread in a greased 11-in. x 7-in. x 2-in. baking dish; pour egg mixture over top. Turn to coat. Cover and refrigerate overnight.

In a skillet, melt butter over medium heat. Add bread; cook for 3-4 minutes on each side or until golden brown. Meanwhile, in a small mixing bowl, cream the butter, confectioners' sugar, cinnamon and nutmeg. Serve French toast with spiced butter and maple syrup. **Yield:** 3 servings.

Winter Fruit Bowl

(Pictured above)

This fruit salad goes well with any meat dish. The blend of grapefruit and cranberries gives it a tangy flavor and a pretty holiday look. —Margaret Schaeffer, Orlando, Florida

4 medium grapefruit
1/4 cup water
1 cup sugar
1/2 cup orange marmalade
2 cups fresh *or* frozen cranberries
3 medium firm bananas, sliced

Peel and section grapefruit, removing membrane and reserving 1/4 cup juice. In a saucepan, combine water, sugar, marmalade and reserved grapefruit juice; bring to a boil over medium heat. Cook and stir until sugar dissolves. Add cranberries.

Reduce heat to medium; simmer 8-10 minutes or until cranberries pop. Remove from the heat. Gently stir in grapefruit. Chill for at least 1 hour. Stir in bananas just before serving. **Yield:** 8-10 servings.

Orange Blush

(Pictured above)

Your taste buds will enjoy waking up to this drink. It's delicious and simple, yet it adds a special touch to any meal. —*Arsolia Hayden, Owenton, Kentucky*

1 can (12 ounces) frozen orange juice concentrate, thawed
2 cups cranberry juice
1/2 cup sugar
1 liter club soda, chilled
Crushed ice

In a large pitcher or bowl, combine the orange juice concentrate, cranberry juice and sugar. Refrigerate for at least 1 hour. Just before serving, stir in soda. Serve over ice. **Yield:** 6 cups.

Raised Yeast Waffles

These waffles bake up crispy on the outside and light and tender on the inside. Since they aren't too filling, they leave room for sampling the rest of a brunch buffet or for munching on more waffles!
—*Helen Knapp, Fairbanks, Alaska*

1 package (1/4 ounce) active dry yeast
1 teaspoon sugar
1/2 cup warm water (110° to 115°)
2 cups warm milk (110° to 115°)
2 eggs
1/2 cup butter, melted
2 cups all-purpose flour
1 teaspoon salt
1/8 teaspoon baking soda

In a mixing bowl, dissolve yeast and sugar in warm water; let stand for 5 minutes. Beat in milk, eggs and butter. Combine flour, salt and baking soda; stir into yeast mixture just until combined. Cover and let rise in a warm place until doubled, about 45 minutes.

Bake in a preheated waffle iron according to manufacturer's directions until golden brown. **Yield:** 10 waffles.

Corny Potato Frittata

Here's a zesty skillet frittata that's fast, flavorful and easy to fix. It's sure to give your breakfast crowd a hearty, stick-to-the-ribs jump start on busy holiday mornings. —*David Heppner, Brandon, Florida*

6 green onions, sliced
2 garlic cloves, minced
2 tablespoons vegetable oil
1 large potato, peeled and cut into 1/4-inch cubes
2 cups frozen corn, thawed
6 eggs
1 cup (4 ounces) shredded mozzarella cheese
1/2 teaspoon salt
1/4 teaspoon pepper

In a 10-in. ovenproof skillet, cook onions and garlic in oil for 2 minutes. Add potato; cook and stir over low heat for 10 minutes. Add corn; cook and stir for 2 minutes.

In a bowl, beat eggs. Stir in the cheese, salt and pepper. Pour over potato mixture. Cover and cook for 6 minutes or until eggs are nearly set. Meanwhile, preheat broiler. Uncover skillet and place 6 in. from the heat for 2-3 minutes or until eggs are completely set. Cut into wedges. **Yield:** 4-6 servings.

Fruited Ambrosia

This is a great take-along dish for any Yuletide gathering. Crunchy nuts, chewy coconut and fruit galore provide a heavenly blend of textures and flavors.
—Edie DeSpain, Logan, Utah

1 can (14 ounces) sweetened condensed milk
1 cup (8 ounces) plain yogurt
1/2 cup lime juice
2 cans (11 ounces *each*) mandarin oranges, drained
1 can (20 ounces) pineapple chunks, drained
1-1/2 cups halved green grapes
1-1/3 cups flaked coconut
1 cup miniature marshmallows
1 cup chopped pecans
1/2 cup halved maraschino cherries, drained

In a large bowl, combine the milk, yogurt and lime juice. Stir in the remaining ingredients. Cover and refrigerate for up to 3 hours. **Yield:** 10-14 servings.

Apple Cheddar Muffins

If you like tart apples and cheese, you'll love these moist, merry muffins. My family insists I make them for the holidays, but they're so easy to fix that I often whip up a batch or two on camping and canoe trips as well.
—Brenda Hildebrandt, Moosomin, Saskatchewan

2 cups all-purpose flour
1/3 cup sugar
1 teaspoon baking powder
1/2 teaspoon baking soda
1/4 teaspoon salt
1/4 teaspoon ground cinnamon
1-1/2 cups (6 ounces) shredded cheddar cheese, *divided*
1/3 cup grated Parmesan cheese
1 egg
1 cup buttermilk
1/4 cup vegetable oil
2 medium tart apples, peeled and chopped

In a large bowl, combine the first six ingredients; stir in 1 cup cheddar cheese and Parmesan cheese. In a small bowl, beat the egg, buttermilk and oil; stir into dry ingredients just until moistened. Fold in the apples.

Fill greased or paper-lined muffin cups three-fourths full. Sprinkle with the remaining cheddar cheese. Bake at 400° for 20-22 minutes or until a toothpick comes out clean. Cool for 10 minutes; remove from pan to a wire rack. **Yield:** 1 dozen.

Egg Brunch Bake

(Pictured below)

Here's a great way to serve ham and eggs to a crowd, and it's so easy to prepare. Best of all, everyone's eggs will be hot and ready at the same time with this savory, satisfying dish.
—Iva Combs, Medford, Oregon

2 tablespoons butter, melted
2 cups (8 ounces) shredded cheddar cheese
2 cups cubed fully cooked ham
12 eggs
1 can (5 ounces) evaporated milk
2 teaspoons prepared mustard
Salt and pepper to taste

Drizzle butter into a greased shallow 3-qt. baking dish. Sprinkle with cheese and ham. In a mixing bowl, combine the eggs, milk, mustard, salt and pepper; beat well. Pour over ham and cheese.

Bake, uncovered, at 350° for 40-45 minutes or until a knife inserted near the center comes out clean. Let stand for 5-10 minutes before serving. **Yield:** 6-8 servings.

Swedish Cardamom Rolls

(Pictured below)

Raisins, walnuts, orange peel and cardamom give these golden, tender sweet rolls real holiday appeal. Guests are often surprised to learn they're homemade!
—Betty Slavin, Omaha, Nebraska

2 packages (1/4 ounce *each*) active dry yeast
3/4 cup warm water (110° to 115°)
1 cup warm milk (110° to 115°)
3/4 cup sugar
1/2 cup shortening
2 eggs
2 tablespoons grated orange peel
1 to 1-1/2 teaspoons ground cardamom
1 teaspoon salt
6 to 6-1/2 cups all-purpose flour
1/2 cup raisins
1/2 cup chopped walnuts
Additional raisins
1/4 cup butter, melted

In a mixing bowl, dissolve yeast in water. Add milk, sugar, shortening, eggs, orange peel, cardamom, salt and 3-1/2 cups flour; beat until smooth. Stir in raisins, walnuts and enough remaining flour to form a soft dough. Turn onto a floured surface; knead until smooth and elastic, about 6-8 minutes. Place in a greased bowl; turn once to grease top. Cover and let rise in a warm place until doubled, about 1 hour.

Punch dough down; divide into thirds. Roll each into a 12-in. x 10-in. rectangle. Divide in half to form two 12-in. x 5-in. rectangles. Cut each into twelve 5-in. x 1-in. strips; roll strips into 6-in. ropes.

To shape rolls, place two ropes on a greased baking sheet to form an X. Coil each end toward the center. Press a raisin into the center of each coil. Cover and let rise until almost doubled, about 30 minutes. Bake at 400° for 8-10 minutes or until golden brown. Brush with butter. **Yield:** 3 dozen.

Ham and Mushroom Toast

Here's a fast, fun way to use up leftover Christmas ham. The creamy mushroom sauce takes only minutes to put together, and assembling the meat and toast points is easy. *—Winnie Hanzlicek, Great Bend, Kansas*

3 cups sliced fresh mushrooms
1/3 cup butter
2 tablespoons all-purpose flour
1/4 teaspoon salt
1/8 teaspoon pepper
3/4 cup chicken broth
2 cups (16 ounces) sour cream
2 teaspoons snipped chives
1/4 to 1/2 teaspoon dill weed
12 toast points
6 slices fully cooked ham, halved

In a saucepan, saute mushrooms in butter until tender. Stir in flour, salt and pepper until blended. Gradually add broth. Bring to a boil; boil and stir for 2 minutes. Reduce heat to low.

Stir in sour cream, chives and dill; heat through. Place two slices of ham on each toast point; top with mushroom sauce. **Yield:** 6 servings.

Breakfast Sausage Ring

My daughter found this hearty sausage and egg recipe years ago, and our family loves it. It's baked in a ring mold and adds a festive flair to any holiday table. *—Elsie Hofe, Littlestown, Pennsylvania*

2 eggs
1-1/2 cups soft bread crumbs, toasted
1/4 cup chopped onion
1/4 cup minced fresh parsley
2 pounds bulk sage pork sausage
Scrambled eggs
Pimiento strips and additional parsley, optional

In a bowl, combine the eggs, bread crumbs, onion and parsley. Add sausage; mix well. Pat into a greased 6-cup ring mold. Bake at 350° for 20 minutes; drain.

Bake 20-25 minutes longer or until juices run clear. Drain; unmold onto a serving platter. Fill with scrambled eggs. Garnish with pimientos and parsley if desired. **Yield:** 8 servings.

Glazed Doughnuts

(Pictured above)

The coffee-flavored glaze on these moist and tasty doughnuts makes them a perfect way to start off the morning.
—Pat Siebenaler, Westminster, Colorado

2 packages (1/4 ounce *each*) active dry yeast
1/4 cup warm water (110° to 115°)
2 cups warm milk (110° to 115°)
1/2 cup butter
1 cup hot mashed *or* riced potatoes (without added butter *or* seasoning)
3 eggs
1/2 teaspoon lemon extract, optional
1 cup sugar
1-1/2 teaspoons salt
1/2 teaspoon ground cinnamon
9-1/4 to 9-3/4 cups all-purpose flour
COFFEE GLAZE:
6 to 8 tablespoons cold milk
1 tablespoon instant coffee granules
2 teaspoons vanilla extract
3/4 cup butter, softened
6 cups confectioners' sugar
1/2 teaspoon ground cinnamon
Pinch salt
Oil for deep-fat frying

In a large mixing bowl, dissolve yeast in water. Add milk, butter, potatoes, eggs and extract if desired. Add sugar, salt, cinnamon and 3 cups flour; mix well. Add enough remaining flour to form a soft dough. Cover and let rise in a warm place until doubled, about 1 hour. Stir down; roll out on a well-floured surface to 1/2-in. thickness. Cut with a 2-1/2-in. doughnut cutter. Place on greased baking sheets; cover and let rise for 45 minutes.

Meanwhile, for glaze, combine 6 tablespoons milk, coffee and vanilla; stir to dissolve coffee. In a bowl, combine butter, sugar, cinnamon and salt; mix well. Gradually add milk mixture; beat until smooth, adding additional milk to make a dipping consistency.

In an electric skillet or deep-fat fryer, heat oil to 350°. Fry doughnuts, a few at a time, about 1-1/2 minutes per side or until golden. Drain on paper towels. Dip tops in glaze while warm. **Yield:** about 4 dozen.

Bacon Potato Omelet

(Pictured above)

For a fun way to present basic breakfast ingredients—potatoes, eggs and bacon—try my recipe, a family favorite I inherited from my mother-in-law.
—Nancy Meeks, Verona, Virginia

3 bacon strips, diced
2 cups diced peeled potatoes
1 medium onion, chopped
3 eggs, lightly beaten
Salt and pepper to taste
1/2 cup shredded cheddar cheese

In a 9-in. nonstick skillet, cook bacon until crisp. Drain, reserving drippings. Set bacon aside. Cook potatoes and onion in drippings until tender, stirring occasionally. Add eggs, salt and pepper; mix gently.

Cover and cook over medium heat until eggs are completely set. Sprinkle with cheese. Remove from the heat; cover and let stand until cheese is melted. Sprinkle with bacon. Carefully run a knife around edge of skillet to loosen; transfer to a serving plate. Cut into wedges. **Yield:** 3 servings.

Pecan Butter

I came up with this rich, nutty spread as a way to jazz up toast. But my big family also looks for it on my holiday brunch buffet. It's a festive topper for muffins, biscuits, rolls and even slices of pound cake.
—Gladys Chancellor, Laurel, Mississippi

2 cups finely chopped pecans
1 cup butter, softened
1/2 cup confectioners' sugar

In a bowl, combine all ingredients; stir until creamy. Store in the refrigerator. **Yield:** 2 cups.

Merry Christmas Muffins

These moist, fruity muffins are packed with hearty ingredients and spread with a creamy orange-flavored frosting. Served with coffee, they're a favorite.
—Ada Kirkland, Saskatoon, Saskatchewan

2 cups all-purpose flour
1-1/4 cups sugar
2 teaspoons baking soda
1-1/2 teaspoons ground cinnamon
1/2 teaspoon salt
3 eggs
1 cup vegetable oil
2 teaspoons vanilla extract
2 cups grated carrots
1 medium tart apple, peeled and chopped
1/2 cup flaked coconut
1/2 cup chopped dried mixed fruit
1/2 cup raisins
FROSTING:
3 tablespoons butter, softened
1 package (3 ounces) cream cheese, softened
2-1/2 cups confectioners' sugar
1/2 teaspoon orange juice
1/2 teaspoon vanilla extract
Chopped candied cherries

In a large bowl, combine the first five ingredients. In a small bowl, beat eggs, oil and vanilla; stir into dry ingredients just until moistened. Fold in carrots, apple, coconut, fruit and raisins.

Fill paper-lined muffin cups three-fourths full. Bake at 350° for 30 minutes or until a toothpick comes out clean. Cool for 10 minutes; remove from pan to a wire rack to cool completely. Combine butter, cream cheese, sugar, juice and vanilla in a mixing

bowl; beat until smooth and creamy. Spread over muffins. Sprinkle with cherries. **Yield:** 16 muffins.

Old-Fashioned Doughnut Holes

Light and yummy, these doughnut holes go fast! Their old-time goodness comes from mashed potatoes and buttermilk. —*Mrs. Ron Swift, Mapleton, Minnesota*

1-1/2 cups hot mashed potatoes (mashed with milk and butter)
2 cups sugar
1 cup buttermilk
3 eggs
1/3 cup butter, melted
1 teaspoon vanilla extract
5-1/2 cups all-purpose flour
4 teaspoons baking powder
1-1/2 teaspoons baking soda
1 teaspoon salt
1 teaspoon ground cinnamon *or* nutmeg
Oil for deep-fat frying
Additional sugar

In a large bowl, combine the potatoes, sugar, buttermilk, eggs, butter and vanilla. Combine flour, baking powder, baking soda, salt and cinnamon; stir into potato mixture. Refrigerate for 1 hour.

In an electric skillet or deep-fat fryer, heat 1 in. of oil to 375°. Drop batter by rounded teaspoonfuls into oil; fry until browned. Turn with a slotted spoon. Drain on paper towels. Roll in sugar while warm. **Yield:** 13 dozen.

Homemade Pancake Syrup

This simple maple syrup cooks up in minutes but leaves a lasting impression. It's best served hot over waffles or pancakes. —*Jill Hanns, Klamath Falls, Oregon*

3/4 cup packed brown sugar
1/4 cup sugar
3/4 cup water
1/2 cup light corn syrup
1/2 teaspoon maple flavoring
1/2 teaspoon vanilla extract

In a saucepan, combine the sugars, water and corn syrup; bring to a boil over medium heat. Boil for 7 minutes or until slightly thickened. Remove from the heat; stir in maple flavoring and vanilla. Cool for 15 minutes. **Yield:** about 1-1/2 cups.

Citrus Sunshine Punch

(Pictured below)

It's easy to be merry when sipping on this tangy punch from our Taste of Home Test Kitchen. A cool, frothy glass of punch is a terrific way to wake up your taste buds on Christmas or any special day.

1 can (12 ounces) frozen lemonade concentrate, thawed
1 can (12 ounces) frozen limeade concentrate, thawed
1 can (12 ounces) frozen orange juice concentrate, thawed
2 quarts cold water
1 bottle (2 liters) ginger ale, chilled
Ice cubes
1 quart orange sherbet

In a large container, combine concentrates with water; mix well. Chill. Just before serving, add ginger ale and ice cubes. Top with scoops of sherbet. **Yield:** 40 servings (about 1/2 cup each).

Home-for-Christmas Fruit Bake

(Pictured below)

Pop this special dish in the oven and mouths will water in anticipation—the cinnamony aroma is tantalizing! The fruit comes out tender and slightly tart.
—Bonnie Baumgardner, Sylva, North Carolina

1 medium apple, peeled and thinly sliced
1 teaspoon lemon juice
1 can (20 ounces) pineapple chunks
1 can (29 ounces) peach halves, drained
1 can (29 ounces) pear halves, drained
1 jar (6 ounces) maraschino cherries, drained
1/2 cup pecan halves
1/3 cup packed brown sugar
1 tablespoon butter
1 teaspoon ground cinnamon

Toss apple slices with lemon juice. Arrange in a greased 2-1/2-qt. baking dish. Drain pineapple, reserving 1/4 cup juice. Combine pineapple, peaches and pears; spoon over apples. Top with cherries and pecans; set aside.

In a small saucepan, combine brown sugar, butter, cinnamon and reserved pineapple juice. Cook and stir over low heat until sugar is dissolved and butter is melted. Pour over fruit. Bake, uncovered, at 325° for 45 minutes or until apples are tender. Serve warm. **Yield:** 12-14 servings.

Homemade Coffee Mix

Starting with a basic recipe, I created several varieties of creamy coffee drinks. They're great to offer at a get-together or to give as gifts.
—Toye Spence
Baker City, Oregon

BASIC COFFEE MIX:
1/3 cup sugar
1/4 cup non-dairy creamer
1/4 cup instant coffee granules
ADDITIONAL INGREDIENT FOR MOCHA COFFEE:
2 teaspoons baking cocoa

FOR ORANGE CAPPUCCINO COFFEE:
- 6 orange Lifesavers, finely crushed

FOR VIENNESE COFFEE:
- 1/2 teaspoon ground cinnamon

Combine coffee mix ingredients; store in an airtight container. To prepare, combine mix with 8 cups boiling water (or use 2 tablespoons mix per cup); stir until dissolved.

To prepare any of the flavored coffees, add additional ingredient to basic mix before adding water. **Yield:** 8 servings per batch.

Special Long Johns

My husband and I have been making these doughnuts regularly for years. He does the frying and I whip up the frosting. —*Beverly Curp, Festus, Missouri*

- 3 packages (1/4 ounce *each*) active dry yeast
- 1/2 cup warm water (110° to 115°)
- 1/2 cup shortening
- 1 cup boiling water
- 1 cup evaporated milk
- 1/4 teaspoon lemon extract
- 2 eggs
- 1/2 cup sugar
- 2 teaspoons salt
- 1/2 teaspoon ground nutmeg
- 8-1/2 to 9 cups all-purpose flour
- Oil for deep-fat frying

FROSTING:
- 3/4 cup packed brown sugar
- 6 tablespoons butter
- 1/3 cup half-and-half cream
- 3 cups confectioners' sugar
- 1 teaspoon vanilla extract

In a mixing bowl, dissolve yeast in warm water. In a small bowl, combine shortening and boiling water. Stir in milk and extract; cool to 110°-115°. Add to yeast mixture. Beat in eggs, sugar, salt and nutmeg. Add enough flour to form a soft dough. Turn onto a floured surface; knead until smooth and elastic, about 5 minutes. Cover and let rest for 10 minutes.

On a floured surface, roll out dough to an 18-in. x 12-in. rectangle. Cut into 6-in. x 1-in. strips. Cover and let rise in a warm place until doubled, about 1 hour. Heat oil in an electric skillet or deep-fat fryer to 375°. Fry dough strips in oil for 2 minutes or until golden brown, turning once. Drain on paper towels.

For frosting, combine brown sugar, butter and cream in a saucepan. Bring to a boil; boil and stir for 2 minutes. Remove from heat. Stir in confectioners' sugar and vanilla; beat with a portable mixer until creamy. Frost long johns. **Yield:** 3 dozen.

Cinnamon Cream Roll-Ups

(Pictured above)

These fancy breakfast roll-ups are a cinch to make with everyday sandwich bread. Each slice wraps around a rich cream cheese filling, and the cinnamon-sugar coating not only looks pretty, it tastes terrific! —*Helen Clem, Creston, Iowa*

- 1 package (8 ounces) cream cheese, softened
- 1 egg yolk
- 1-1/4 cups sugar, *divided*
- 1 loaf (1 pound) sandwich bread, crusts removed
- 1 tablespoon ground cinnamon
- 1/4 cup butter, melted

In a small mixing bowl, combine the cream cheese, egg yolk and 1/4 cup sugar; mix well. Flatten bread slices with a rolling pin. Spread cream cheese mixture over each slice to within 1/2 in. of edges. Roll up diagonally from point to point.

In a shallow bowl, combine the cinnamon and remaining sugar. Dip roll-ups in melted butter, then in cinnamon-sugar mixture. Place in an ungreased 15-in. x 10-in. x 1-in. baking pan. Bake at 350° for 16-19 minutes or until lightly browned. Remove to wire racks to cool. **Yield:** 8-10 servings.

Fluffy Pink Fruit Salad

Pastel marshmallows give this salad a perky look. It makes enough for a crowd and nicely rounds out a brunch. —*LaDona Merwin Hamilton, Montana*

1 jar (10 ounces) maraschino cherries
1 package (8 ounces) cream cheese, softened
2 cups heavy whipping cream, whipped
1 can (20 ounces) pineapple tidbits, drained
1 can (15-1/4 ounces) fruit cocktail, drained
1 can (15 ounces) sliced peaches, drained and diced
6 medium firm bananas, sliced
3 cups pastel miniature marshmallows

Drain cherries, reserving 1/3 cup juice (save remaining juice for another use). Cut cherries in half; set aside. In a mixing bowl, beat cream cheese and reserved cherry juice until smooth. Fold in whipped cream. Fold in cherries and remaining ingredients. Transfer to a serving bowl. Refrigerate for at least 1 hour. **Yield:** 18-22 servings.

Ambrosia Compote

(Pictured above)

This sparkling fruit salad is versatile and pretty enough for dessert. I like to vary the fruits and will sometimes top them off with a dollop of ginger-laced whipped cream or Yuletide star fruit garnish.
—*Marilou Robinson, Portland, Oregon*

1 can (20 ounces) pineapple chunks
3 medium firm bananas
1 cup seedless red grapes
3 medium navel oranges, peeled and sectioned
1 cup flaked coconut, *divided*
1/2 cup ginger ale, chilled
Sliced star fruit, optional

Drain pineapple, reserving juice in a large bowl. Slice bananas into the bowl; toss to coat. Add the pineapple, grapes, oranges and half of the coconut; toss to coat. Cover and refrigerate for up to 4 hours.

Just before serving, pour ginger ale over salad and sprinkle with remaining coconut. Serve with a slotted spoon. Garnish with star fruit if desired. **Yield:** 6-8 servings.

Cheesy Bacon Muffins

Savory cheese and bacon and a pinch of cayenne pepper give these slightly sweet goodies a flavorful punch. They're versatile—you can serve them for breakfast or brunch or with soup for lunch or supper. They're even good for a late-night snack.
—*Marilyn Gail Sharpless, Bloomington, California*

1-3/4 cups all-purpose flour
1/2 cup shredded sharp cheddar cheese
1/4 cup sugar
2 teaspoons baking powder
1/4 teaspoon salt
1/8 to 1/4 teaspoon cayenne pepper
1 egg
3/4 cup milk
1/3 cup vegetable oil
6 bacon strips, cooked and crumbled

In a large bowl, combine the first six ingredients. In another bowl, combine the egg, milk and oil; stir into dry ingredients just until moistened. Fold in bacon. Fill greased muffin cups two-thirds full. Bake at 375° for 20-25 minutes or until a toothpick comes out clean. **Yield:** 8 muffins.

Two-Cheese Spinach Quiche

This beautiful pie really stars on my holiday brunch buffet. The cheese, ham and spinach flavors blend perfectly. It's easy to prepare besides. —*Patricia Nazaruk Michigan Center, Michigan*

1 unbaked pie pastry (9 inches)
1/2 cup finely shredded Swiss cheese
1/2 cup chopped fresh spinach
1/2 cup sliced fresh mushrooms
1 can (5 ounces) fully cooked ham, flaked*
3 eggs
1 cup half-and-half cream
2 teaspoons all-purpose flour
1/2 teaspoon salt
1/4 cup shredded cheddar cheese

Line the unpricked pastry shell with a double thickness of heavy-duty foil. Bake at 450° for 5 minutes. Remove foil. Bake 5 minutes longer. Remove from the oven; reduce heat to 350°. Combine Swiss cheese, spinach, mushrooms and ham; sprinkle over crust.

In a bowl, beat eggs, cream, flour and salt until smooth; pour over spinach mixture. Sprinkle with cheddar cheese. Bake for 40-45 minutes or until a knife inserted near the center comes out clean. **Yield:** 6-8 servings.

***Editor's Note:** This recipe was tested with Hormel chunk lean ham.

Apple-Cheddar French Toast

(Pictured at right)

Plentiful layers of bread, ham, apple pie filling and more in this sweet-savory dish remind me of lasagna, only for breakfast. I lost count long ago of the number of recipe requests I've received.
—*Lila Hadaway, Polo, Illinois*

2 packages (12-1/2 ounces *each*) frozen French toast
8 ounces thinly sliced fully cooked ham
2-1/2 cups (10 ounces) shredded cheddar cheese, *divided*
1 can (21 ounces) apple pie filling
1 cup granola cereal with raisins
1 cup (8 ounces) sour cream
1/3 cup packed brown sugar

Prepare French toast according to package directions. Place six slices in an ungreased 13-in. x 9-in. x 2-in. baking dish. Top with ham, 2 cups cheese and remaining French toast. Spread pie filling over top; sprinkle with granola.

Bake, uncovered, at 350° for 25 minutes. Sprinkle with remaining cheese; bake 5 minutes longer or until cheese is melted. In a bowl, combine sour cream and brown sugar; serve with French toast. Refrigerate leftovers. **Yield:** 6-8 servings.

Crumb-Topped Baked Pineapple

(Pictured below)

Sweet fruit and a crunchy topping give this comforting side dish plenty of old-fashioned goodness. It's the perfect tummy warmer for any cold-weather occasion.
—Alice Tatro, Geneva, Nebraska

- 1/2 cup sugar
- 2 tablespoons all-purpose flour
- 1 can (20 ounces) pineapple chunks, undrained
- 1 cup (4 ounces) shredded cheddar cheese
- 1/2 cup maraschino cherries, drained
- 3/4 cup dry bread crumbs
- 2 tablespoons butter, melted

In a large bowl, combine the sugar, flour and pineapple; mix well. Stir in cheese and cherries. Transfer to a greased 8-in. square baking dish. Toss bread crumbs and butter; sprinkle over top. Bake, uncovered, at 350° for 30-35 minutes or until golden brown and bubbly. Serve warm. **Yield:** 6-8 servings.

Almond-Topped Spiced Peaches

A dab of cinnamon-flavored sour cream is the perfect complement to these nutty curried peaches. In the oven, the fruit juice forms a wonderful sauce for spooning over each serving. *—Beverly Rogers Orange, California*

- 2 cans (29 ounces *each*) peach halves, drained
- 1/2 cup packed brown sugar
- 1/4 cup butter
- 1/2 to 1 teaspoon curry powder
- 1/4 cup sliced almonds
- 1 cup (8 ounces) sour cream
- 1 teaspoon ground cinnamon

Place peach halves in an ungreased shallow 2-qt. baking dish; set aside. In a saucepan, combine the brown sugar, butter and curry powder. Cook and stir over low heat until sugar is dissolved. Pour over peaches. Sprinkle with almonds.

Bake, uncovered, at 375° for 20 minutes or until heated through. Combine sour cream and cinnamon; serve with peaches. **Yield:** 6-8 servings.

Praline French Toast

There's quite a crowd when our family gathers for Christmas, and I'm always asked to fix this French toast. The praline syrup is a nice change of pace from traditional maple. *—Jean Kruse, Bowling Green, Missouri*

- 9 eggs
- 3 cups half-and-half cream
- 1/3 cup sugar
- 1-1/2 teaspoons vanilla extract
- 1/2 teaspoon ground cinnamon *or* nutmeg
- 24 to 30 slices French bread (3/4 inch thick)

PRALINE SYRUP:

- 1-1/2 cups packed brown sugar
- 1/2 cup corn syrup
- 1/2 cup water
- 1/2 cup chopped pecans, toasted
- 2 tablespoons butter

In a large bowl, lightly beat eggs. Stir in the cream, sugar, vanilla and cinnamon. Arrange bread in a single layer in two greased 15-in. x 10-in. x 1-in. baking pans. Pour egg mixture over bread. Cover and refrigerate overnight.

Remove from the refrigerator 30 minutes before baking. Bake, uncovered, at 400° for 20-25 minutes or until golden brown. Meanwhile, for syrup, combine brown sugar, corn syrup and water in a saucepan. Bring to a boil over medium heat. Reduce heat; simmer, uncovered, for 3 minutes. Stir in pecans and butter; simmer 2 minutes longer. Serve with the French toast. **Yield:** 10-12 servings.

Pumpkin Doughnut Drops

(Pictured at right)

I always have a few special treats handy when the grandchildren visit. These cake doughnuts are a favorite snack. —Beva Staum, Muscoda, Wisconsin

2 eggs
1-1/4 cups sugar
2 tablespoons shortening
1 cup canned pumpkin
2 teaspoons cider vinegar
1 teaspoon vanilla extract
3 cups all-purpose flour
1/2 cup nonfat dry milk powder
3 teaspoons baking powder
1/2 teaspoon salt
1/2 teaspoon ground cinnamon
1/2 teaspoon ground nutmeg
1/2 cup lemon-lime soda
Oil for deep-fat frying
Additional sugar

In a mixing bowl, beat the eggs, sugar and shortening. Add the pumpkin, vinegar and vanilla. Combine the dry ingredients; add to the pumpkin mixture alternately with soda.

In an electric skillet or deep-fat fryer, heat oil to 375°. Drop teaspoonfuls of batter, a few at a time, into hot oil. Fry for 1 minute on each side or until golden brown. Drain on paper towels; roll in sugar while warm. **Yield:** about 7 dozen.

Swiss Bake

This creamy, comforting potato dish has been a family favorite since my daughter got the recipe from a friend years ago. —Maxine Kenning, Hutchinson, Minnesota

1 package (26 ounces) frozen shredded hash browns, thawed
2 cups (8 ounces) shredded Swiss cheese
1 package (10 ounces) frozen chopped broccoli, thawed and well drained
2 cups heavy whipping cream
1/2 cup chopped onion
1/2 cup butter, melted
1 teaspoon salt
1/4 teaspoon pepper

Combine all ingredients; pour into a greased 13-in. x 9-in. x 2-in. baking dish. Bake, uncovered, at 350° for 1 hour or until golden brown. **Yield:** 10-12 servings.

Deep-Fat Frying

It is important to follow the temperature recommended in recipes for heating oil. If oil is too hot, the foods will brown too fast and not be done in the center. If the oil is below temperature, the foods will absorb oil and taste greasy.

Hearty Ham Casserole

(Pictured above)

I first made this filling casserole for a camping trip with friends, adding potatoes and soup to stretch the recipe. It was a big hit. It's a great all-in-one meal that's sure to please your hungry eaters all year-round.
—Sharon Cobb, Fairfax, Vermont

4 medium potatoes
1 package (10 ounces) frozen chopped broccoli
1/4 cup finely chopped onion
3 tablespoons butter, *divided*
1 tablespoon all-purpose flour
1/8 teaspoon pepper
1 cup milk
1/2 cup shredded cheddar cheese
2 cups cubed fully cooked ham
1 can (10-3/4 ounces) condensed cream of mushroom soup, undiluted
1/4 cup dry bread crumbs

Cook potatoes in boiling salted water until tender; drain. Peel and cube; set aside. Cook broccoli according to package directions, omitting salt; drain and set aside. In a large skillet, saute onion in 2 tablespoons butter until tender. Add flour and pepper; stir until blended. Gradually add milk; cook and stir until mixture boils and thickens. Remove from heat; stir in cheese until melted. Stir in ham, soup, potatoes and broccoli.

Transfer to a greased 2-1/2-qt. baking dish. Melt remaining butter; toss with the bread crumbs. Sprinkle over top of casserole. Bake, uncovered, at 350° for 20-30 minutes or until heated through. **Yield:** 6-8 servings.

Overnight Sticky Rolls

Smiles will greet you when you serve these yummy rolls. Seasoned with cinnamon and baked in a rich, gooey syrup, the goodies please everyone I know!
—K. Baldwin, Wildomar, California

5-1/2 to 6 cups all-purpose flour
2 tablespoons sugar
2 packages (1/4 ounce *each*) active dry yeast
2 teaspoons salt
1-3/4 cups milk
1/2 cup water
3 tablespoons shortening
3/4 cup butter, *divided*
1 cup packed brown sugar
2 tablespoons corn syrup
1 cup pecan halves *or* walnut pieces
FILLING:
1/2 cup sugar
1 teaspoon ground cinnamon

In a mixing bowl, combine 2-1/2 cups flour, sugar, yeast and salt. In a saucepan, heat milk, water and shortening to 120°-130°. Add to the flour mixture. Beat on low speed for 2 minutes; beat on medium for 3 minutes. Add enough remaining flour to form a soft dough. Turn onto a floured surface; knead until smooth and elastic, about 6-8 minutes. Place in a greased bowl, turning once to grease top. Cover and let rise in a warm place until doubled, about 1 hour.

Meanwhile, in a saucepan, combine 1/2 cup butter, brown sugar and corn syrup. Cook and stir over medium-low heat until sugar is dissolved and butter is melted. Pour into two greased 13-in. x 9-in. x 2-in. baking pans. Sprinkle with pecans.

Punch dough down. Turn onto a floured surface; divide dough in half. Roll each portion into a 12-in. x 8-in. rectangle. Spread with remaining butter to within 1/2 in. of edges. Combine sugar and cinnamon; sprinkle over butter. Roll up, jelly-roll style, starting with a long side; pinch seams to seal.

Cut into 1-in. slices. Place rolls, cut side down, in prepared pans. Cover and refrigerate overnight. Remove from refrigerator 20 minutes before baking. Bake at 400° for 20-25 minutes or until golden brown. Invert onto a serving platter. **Yield:** 2 dozen.

Plum Sausage Bites

Packed with perky flavor and a thick sauce that clings to the sausage, these links are a must for my brunches and potlucks. Plus, the recipe couldn't be much simpler to make. —Heidi Fisher, Victoria, British Columbia

2 to 2-1/2 pounds uncooked pork sausage links, cut into 1-inch pieces
1 cup plum, apple *or* grape jelly
2 tablespoons soy sauce
1 tablespoon Dijon mustard

In a large skillet, cook sausage over medium heat until no longer pink; drain and set sausage aside. In the same skillet, combine the jelly, soy sauce and mustard; mix well. Simmer, uncovered, for 5 minutes, stirring occasionally. Return sausage to the pan and heat through. Refrigerate any leftovers. **Yield:** 18-22 servings.

Bacon 'n' Egg Pizza

(Pictured below)

Pizza for breakfast? Kids especially will enjoy the bacon, cheese, hash browns and eggs layered on a pizza-like crust. —Georgiann Franklin, Canfield, Ohio

1 tube (8 ounces) refrigerated crescent rolls
12 bacon strips, cooked and crumbled
1 cup frozen shredded hash brown potatoes
3/4 cup shredded cheddar cheese
4 eggs
2 tablespoons milk
1/2 cup grated Parmesan *or* Romano cheese

Unroll crescent roll dough into one long rectangle. Press onto bottom and 1/2 in. up sides of a greased 13-in. x 9-in. x 2-in. baking pan. Seal seams and perforations. Sprinkle with bacon, potatoes and cheddar. In a bowl, beat eggs and milk. Pour over cheddar cheese. Sprinkle with Parmesan. Bake, uncovered, at 375° for 25-30 minutes or until eggs are set. **Yield:** 8 servings.

Christmas Brunch Casserole

No one leaves the table hungry when I serve this savory casserole. In fact, folks rave about it! What I like as much as the taste is that I can prepare it ahead of time. —*Mary Eckler, Louisville, Kentucky*

2 pounds bulk pork sausage
1 large onion, chopped
2 cups cooked rice
3 cups crisp rice cereal
3 cups (12 ounces) shredded cheddar cheese
6 eggs
2 cans (10-3/4 ounces *each*) condensed cream of celery soup, undiluted
1/2 cup milk

In a skillet, cook sausage and onion over medium heat until meat is no longer pink; drain. Place in a lightly greased 13-in. x 9-in. x 2-in. baking dish. Layer with the rice, cereal and cheddar cheese. In a bowl, beat the eggs, soup and milk. Spread over top.

Bake, uncovered, at 350° for 55-60 minutes or until a knife inserted near the center comes out clean. Let stand for 5 minutes before cutting. Refrigerate any leftovers. **Yield:** 12 servings.

Sugar 'n' Spice Muffins

These sugar-and-spice treats are so tasty! The moist streusel-topped muffins are perfect for parties or nibbling with a hot cup of coffee, tea or hot chocolate. —*Monica Penner, Elma, Manitoba*

2 cups all-purpose flour
1 cup sugar
3/4 cup cold butter
1 teaspoon baking soda
1 teaspoon ground cinnamon
1 teaspoon ground cloves
1 cup buttermilk
1 egg, lightly beaten

In a bowl, combine flour and sugar; cut in butter until crumbly. Set aside 1/2 cup for topping. Add baking soda, cinnamon and cloves to remaining crumb mixture. Stir in buttermilk and egg just until moistened.

Fill greased or paper-lined muffin cups two-thirds full. Sprinkle with reserved topping. Bake at 375° for 18-20 minutes or until a toothpick comes out clean. Cool for 5 minutes before removing from pan to a wire rack to cool. Serve warm. **Yield:** 1 dozen.

Apricot Cream-Filled Waffles

You'll have more time to open gifts when you make these simply scrumptious waffles for breakfast. The rich mixture is easy to whip up and can quickly be doubled for unexpected company. —*Dorothy Smith, El Dorado, Arkansas*

1 package (3 ounces) cream cheese, softened
1 to 2 tablespoons honey
2/3 cup chopped canned apricots
8 frozen waffles, toasted
1/2 cup maple syrup, warmed

In a small bowl, combine cream cheese and honey; mix well. Stir in apricots. Spread cream cheese mixture on four waffles; top with remaining waffles. Serve with syrup. **Yield:** 4 servings.

Orange-Cream French Toast

My citrus-flavored toast adds a refreshingly fruity twist to standard brunch fare. —*Marilyn Lehman, Millersville, Pennsylvania*

6 eggs
1/2 cup orange juice
1/3 cup half-and-half cream
3 tablespoons sugar
1/2 teaspoon grated orange peel
1/4 teaspoon vanilla extract
Pinch salt
8 to 10 slices French bread (3/4 inch thick)
1/4 cup butter
ORANGE BUTTER:
1 cup butter, softened
1/3 cup orange marmalade
3 tablespoons chopped mandarin oranges

In a mixing bowl, beat eggs, orange juice, cream, sugar, orange peel, vanilla and salt. Dip the bread in egg mixture, coating each side. Place in a greased 13-in. x 9-in. x 2-in. baking dish. Pour remaining egg mixture over the bread. Cover and refrigerate overnight.

In a large skillet, melt butter; add bread. Cook for 5 minutes on each side or until golden brown. Meanwhile, combine orange butter ingredients in a small mixing bowl; beat until blended. Serve with French toast. **Yield:** 4-5 servings.

Breads, Rolls & Muffins

Frosted Caramel Nut Braid

(Pictured above)

It's become a Christmas-morning tradition for my husband, our two young children and me to munch on this scrumptious bread with its nutty filling while opening gifts. Since I make it ahead, I can also relax and enjoy the festivities. —*Paula Wiersma*
Eastampton, New Jersey

1 package (1/4 ounce) active dry yeast
1/4 cup warm water (110° to 115°)
1 cup warm milk (110° to 115°)
2 eggs
1/4 cup sugar
1/4 cup butter, softened
1-1/2 teaspoons salt
4-1/4 to 4-3/4 cups all-purpose flour

CARAMEL FILLING:
1 cup chopped pecans
2/3 cup packed brown sugar
1/3 cup butter, softened
2 tablespoons all-purpose flour

FROSTING:
1/3 cup butter
2 cups confectioners' sugar
1-1/2 teaspoons vanilla extract
3 to 4 teaspoons water
1/4 cup chopped pecans

In a mixing bowl, dissolve yeast in water. Add milk, eggs, sugar, butter, salt and 2 cups flour; beat until smooth. Add enough remaining flour to form a soft but sticky dough. Do not knead. Cover and let rise in a warm place until doubled, about 1-1/2 hours.

Beat 25 strokes with a spoon; turn onto a well-floured surface. Roll into a 16-in. x 12-in. rectangle. Combine filling ingredients with a fork; spread evenly over the dough. Cut dough lengthwise into three strips. Roll up jelly-roll style, beginning at a long end; pinch edges and ends to seal. Place three rolls diagonally, seam side down, on a foil-lined 15-in. x 10-in. x 1-in. baking pan. Braid ropes together gently (do not stretch); seal ends. Cover and let rise until doubled, about 1 hour. Bake at 350° for 25-30 minutes or until golden brown. Remove from pan and cool slightly on wire rack.

For frosting, heat butter in a saucepan over low heat until golden brown; cool slightly. Stir in sugar and vanilla. Stir in enough water to make a spreadable consistency. Frost top of braid; immediately sprinkle with pecans. **Yield:** 1 loaf.

Macadamia Nut Mini Loaves

While these loaves may be small, they have a big rich flavor. The macadamia nuts make them a special treat with tropical flair. Plus, they're so pretty with the toasted coconut topping. —*Kim Gilliland*
Simi Valley, California

1 jar (3-1/2 ounces) macadamia nuts, *divided*
1/3 cup flaked coconut
1-1/2 cups sugar, *divided*
3/4 cup butter, softened
2 eggs
3 cups all-purpose flour
1 teaspoon baking powder
1/2 cup milk
3 tablespoons lemon juice
2 teaspoons grated lemon peel
1-1/2 teaspoons vanilla extract

Finely chop enough of the macadamia nuts to measure 1/3 cup; set aside. Coarsely chop remaining nuts; toss with coconut and 1 tablespoon sugar. Set aside. In a mixing bowl, cream butter and remaining sugar on high until fluffy. Add eggs; mix well. Combine flour and baking powder; add alternately with milk

to creamed mixture. Stir in lemon juice and peel, vanilla and reserved finely chopped nuts. Spoon into six greased 4-1/2-in. x 2-1/2-in. x 1-1/2-in. loaf pans. Sprinkle with reserved coconut mixture.

Bake at 325° for 50 minutes or until a toothpick inserted near the center comes out clean. Cool in pans for 10 minutes; remove and cool on a wire rack. **Yield:** 6 loaves.

Soft Yeast Pan Rolls

Want to do something special for a good friend or neighbor? Bake them a pan of these melt-in-your-mouth rolls!
—Angie Price, Bradford, Tennessee

2 packages (1/4 ounce *each*) active dry yeast
1 teaspoon plus 2/3 cup sugar, *divided*
1 cup warm water (110° to 115°)
1/2 cup butter, softened
1/2 cup shortening
1 teaspoon salt
1 cup boiling water
2 eggs
7 to 7-1/2 cups all-purpose flour

In a bowl, dissolve yeast and 1 teaspoon sugar in warm water; let stand for 5 minutes. In a mixing bowl, cream butter, shortening, salt and remaining sugar. Add boiling water; cool to 110°-115°. Add yeast mixture and eggs; mix well. Stir in enough flour to form a soft dough.

Turn onto a floured surface; knead until smooth and elastic, about 6-8 minutes. Place in a greased bowl, turning once to grease top. Cover and let rise in a warm place until doubled, about 1 hour. Punch dough down.

Turn onto a lightly floured surface; divide into thirds. Divide each portion into nine pieces; shape into balls. Place in three greased 9-in. round baking pans. Cover and let rise until doubled, about 30 minutes. Bake at 350° for 20-25 minutes or until golden brown. Cool in pans on wire racks. **Yield:** 27 rolls.

Festive Brioches

(Pictured at right)

I love creating recipes, and these light and luscious rolls are among my holiday originals. Sometimes I'll substitute chocolate or butterscotch chips, raisins and cherries. *—Diane Halferty, Tucson, Arizona*

1 package (1/4 ounce) active dry yeast
1/4 cup warm water (110° to 115°)
1/2 cup butter, softened
1/3 cup plus 1 tablespoon sugar, *divided*
1 teaspoon salt
4 cups all-purpose flour
1/2 cup milk
4 eggs
1/2 cup dried cranberries
1/2 cup chopped candied pineapple
1/4 cup dried currants

In a small bowl, dissolve yeast in water; let stand for 5 minutes. In a mixing bowl, cream butter, 1/3 cup sugar and salt. Add 1 cup flour and milk. Separate one egg; refrigerate egg white. Add yolk and remaining eggs to the creamed mixture. Stir in the yeast mixture, fruit and remaining flour. Spoon into a greased bowl. Cover and let rise in a warm place until doubled, about 1-1/2 hours. Cover and refrigerate overnight.

Punch dough down; turn onto a floured surface. Divide into four portions. Divide three of the portions into eight pieces each. Shape into balls and place in well-greased muffin cups. Divide remaining dough into 24 small balls. Make a depression in the top of each large ball; place a small ball in each depression. Cover and let rise in a warm place until doubled, about 45 minutes.

Beat reserved egg white and remaining sugar; brush over rolls. Bake at 375° for 15-20 minutes or until golden brown. Remove from pans; cool on a wire rack. **Yield:** 2 dozen.

Poinsettia Coffee Cake

(Pictured below)

I often take this yeasty coffee cake to Christmas open houses or church functions. People ooh and aah over the fun poinsettia shape, but that doesn't stop them from cutting big pieces. —*Rowena Wilson, Jetmore, Kansas*

1 package (1/4 ounce) active dry yeast
1/4 cup warm water (110° to 115°)
3/4 cup warm milk (110° to 115°)
3 eggs, beaten
1/3 cup sugar
2 teaspoons grated lemon peel
1 teaspoon salt
5 to 5-1/2 cups all-purpose flour
3/4 cup chopped dates
1/2 cup chopped nuts
FROSTING:
1 tablespoon butter, softened
1 cup confectioners' sugar
3/4 teaspoon vanilla extract
3 to 4 teaspoons water
Yellow and red colored sugar

In a mixing bowl, dissolve yeast in warm water. Add milk, eggs, sugar, lemon peel, salt and 2-1/2 cups flour; beat until smooth. Stir in dates and nuts. Stir in enough remaining flour to form a soft dough. Turn onto a floured surface; knead until smooth and elastic, about 6-8 minutes. Place in a greased bowl, turning once to grease top. Cover and let rise in a warm place until doubled, about 1-1/2 hours.

Punch dough down. Turn onto a floured surface; divide into eight equal pieces. Shape one piece into eight smaller balls; mound in the center of a large greased baking sheet. Form remaining pieces into teardrop shapes by tapering one side of each ball. Place around smaller balls with wide end of petals touching the flower center. Cover and let rise until doubled, about 30 minutes.

Bake at 350° for 20-25 minutes or until golden brown. Cool slightly. Meanwhile, in a mixing bowl, combine butter, confectioners' sugar, vanilla and enough water to achieve desired frosting consistency. Spread over warm coffee cake. Sprinkle center with yellow sugar and petals with red sugar. **Yield:** 16-18 servings.

Editor's Note: This coffee cake dough contains no butter, shortening or oil.

Bran Refrigerator Rolls

These golden rolls are very soft and tender. They're a delightful addition to any meal and convenient since you start them the day before you want to serve them. —*Blanche Whytsell*
Arnoldsburg, West Virginia

1-3/4 cups boiling water
1 cup all-bran cereal
2 packages (1/4 ounce *each*) active dry yeast
1/4 cup warm water (110° to 115°)
1/2 cup shortening
1/2 cup sugar
1-1/2 teaspoons salt
2 eggs
5-1/2 to 6 cups all-purpose flour

In a small bowl, combine boiling water and bran; set aside to cool. In another bowl, dissolve yeast in warm water; set aside. In a mixing bowl, cream shortening, sugar and salt; add eggs. Add yeast mixture and mix well. Add bran mixture and 2 cups flour, mixing well after each addition. Gradually add enough remaining flour to form a soft dough. Turn onto a lightly floured surface; knead until smooth and elastic, about 6-8 minutes. Place in a greased bowl, turning once to grease top. Cover and refrigerate overnight.

Punch dough down; form into rolls. Place on greased baking sheets or in greased muffin cups. Cover and let rise until doubled, about 1 to 1-1/2 hours. Bake at 375° for 15 minutes or until light brown. Remove from pan and cool on wire racks. **Yield:** 3-1/2 dozen.

Confetti Bubble Ring

My daughters made this ring when they were in 4-H, and we've enjoyed it for years. Handy refrigerated biscuits get a holiday spin when combined with other colorful ingredients. —Virginia Krites, Cridersville, Ohio

1/2 pound sliced bacon, diced
1/4 cup chopped onion
1/4 cup grated Parmesan cheese
1/4 cup chopped green pepper
2 tubes (7-1/2 ounces *each*) refrigerated biscuits
1/3 cup butter, melted

In a skillet, cook bacon until crisp; drain. Place in a bowl; add onion, cheese and green pepper. Cut biscuits into quarters; add to bacon mixture. Add butter and toss to coat. Pour into a greased 10-in. tube pan. Bake at 350° for 30 minutes. **Yield:** 8-10 servings.

Swiss Cheese Bread

(Pictured above right)

Not only is this whole wheat loaf filled with plenty of wonderful garlic and Swiss cheese flavor, the holes that appear when baking make it look just like Swiss cheese! —Peggy Burdick, Burlington, Michigan

3 to 3-1/2 cups all-purpose flour, *divided*
2 cups whole wheat flour, *divided*
1/3 cup mashed potato flakes
2 packages (1/4 ounce *each*) active dry yeast
1-1/2 teaspoons salt
2 cups warm milk (120° to 130°)
1/4 cup butter, melted
2 eggs
4 to 6 garlic cloves, minced
1 block (6 ounces) Swiss cheese, cut into 1/4-inch cubes
1 egg yolk
1 tablespoon water

In a mixing bowl, combine 1 cup all-purpose flour, 1 cup whole wheat flour, potato flakes, yeast and salt. Add milk and butter; beat for 2 minutes. Add eggs and garlic; beat for 2 minutes. Stir in the remaining whole wheat flour and enough remaining all-purpose flour to form a soft dough.

Turn onto a floured surface; knead for 4 minutes. Sprinkle with cheese; knead 2 minutes longer or until smooth and elastic. Place in a greased bowl, turning once to grease top. Cover and let rise in a warm place until doubled, about 1 hour. Punch dough down. Divide in half; shape each half into a ball. Place on greased baking sheets; flatten to 7-in. diameter. With a sharp knife, make three parallel slashes about 1/2 in. deep on the top of each loaf.

Cover and let rise in a warm place until doubled, about 30 minutes. Beat egg yolk and water; brush over loaves. Bake at 375° for 30-35 minutes or until golden brown. Cool on wire racks. **Yield:** 2 loaves.

Orange-Chip Cranberry Bread

(Pictured above)

Tart berries, crunchy nuts and sweet chocolate are simply scrumptious when mixed together in this easy quick bread. Sometimes I'll top it off with an orange-flavored glaze. —*Donna Smith, Victor, New York*

2-1/2 cups all-purpose flour
1 cup sugar
1 teaspoon baking soda
1 teaspoon baking powder
1/4 teaspoon salt
2 eggs
3/4 cup vegetable oil
2 teaspoons grated orange peel
1 cup buttermilk
1-1/2 cups chopped fresh *or* frozen cranberries, thawed
1 cup miniature semisweet chocolate chips
1 cup chopped walnuts
3/4 cup confectioners' sugar, optional
2 tablespoons orange juice, optional

In a mixing bowl, combine first five ingredients. In another bowl, combine eggs, oil and orange peel; mix well. Add to dry ingredients alternately with buttermilk. Fold in cranberries, chocolate chips and walnuts. Pour into two greased 8-in. x 4-in. x 2-in. loaf pans.

Bake at 350° for 55-65 minutes or until a toothpick inserted near the center comes out clean. Cool for 10 minutes before removing from pans to wire racks. If glaze is desired, combine confectioners' sugar and orange juice until smooth; spread over cooled loaves. **Yield:** 2 loaves.

Butterscotch Crescents

(Pictured above)

When I was first married, I'd try all kinds of recipes to impress my husband. These crescents were such a hit I still make them! —*Phyllis Hofer, De Witt, Iowa*

1 can (12 ounces) evaporated milk, *divided*
1 package (3-1/2 ounces) cook-and-serve butterscotch pudding mix
1/2 cup butter
1 package (1/4 ounce) active dry yeast
1/4 cup warm water (110° to 115°)
2 eggs

2 teaspoons salt
5 to 5-1/2 cups all-purpose flour

FILLING:
2/3 cup packed brown sugar
2/3 cup flaked coconut
1/3 cup chopped pecans
1/4 cup butter, melted
2 tablespoons all-purpose flour

FROSTING:
1/4 cup packed brown sugar
2 tablespoons butter
1 cup confectioners' sugar
2 to 3 tablespoons hot water, optional

Set aside 2 tablespoons evaporated milk for frosting. In a saucepan, combine pudding mix and remaining evaporated milk until smooth. Bring to a boil over medium heat, stirring constantly. Remove from the heat; stir in butter until melted. Let stand until mixture cools to 110°-115°.

Meanwhile, in a mixing bowl, dissolve yeast in water. Beat in eggs, salt, 2 cups flour and pudding mixture until smooth. Stir in enough remaining flour to form a soft dough. Turn onto a floured surface; knead until smooth and elastic, about 6-8 minutes. Place in a greased bowl, turning once to grease top. Cover and let rise in a warm place until doubled, about 1 hour.

Punch dough down; divide into thirds. Roll each portion into a 15-in. circle. Combine filling ingredients; spread 1/2 cupful over each circle. Cut each into 12 wedges; roll each into a crescent shape, starting with wide end. Place point side down on greased baking sheets. Cover and let rise until doubled, about 45 minutes. Bake at 375° for 12-15 minutes or until golden brown. Cool on wire racks.

For frosting, combine brown sugar, butter and reserved evaporated milk in a saucepan. Cook and stir over low heat until smooth. Remove from the heat; stir in confectioners' sugar until smooth. Add water if needed to achieve desired consistency. Frost crescents. **Yield:** 3 dozen.

Cranberry Almond Sweet Rolls

(Pictured at right)

Perfect for a festive luncheon, these sweet rolls feature cranberries, almonds and vanilla chips. I don't save them just for special occasions, though.

—Marian Platt, Sequim, Washington

1 package (16 ounces) hot roll mix
2 tablespoons sugar
1/2 teaspoon ground cinnamon
1/2 teaspoon ground ginger
1/4 teaspoon ground nutmeg
1 cup warm water (110° to 115°)
2 tablespoons butter, softened
1 egg, beaten
1 cup finely chopped fresh *or* frozen cranberries
1 package (11 ounces) vanilla chips, *divided*
1 cup slivered almonds
1/4 cup confectioners' sugar
1/2 teaspoon lemon juice
3 to 4 teaspoons milk

In a large bowl, combine contents of hot roll mix, sugar, cinnamon, ginger and nutmeg; mix well. Stir in water, butter and egg to form a soft dough. Turn onto a floured surface; knead until smooth and elastic, about 6-8 minutes. Cover; let rest for 5 minutes.

Roll into a 15-in. x 10-in. rectangle; sprinkle with cranberries. Set aside 1/2 cup vanilla chips for glaze. Sprinkle almonds and remaining chips over cranberries. Roll up, starting with a long side; pinch edge to seal. Cut into 12 slices; place in a greased 13-in. x 9-in. x 2-in. baking pan. Cover and let rise in a warm place until doubled, about 30 minutes.

Bake at 375° for 18-20 minutes or until lightly browned. In a saucepan over low heat, melt reserved vanilla chips. Stir in confectioners' sugar, lemon juice and enough milk to achieve desired consistency. Drizzle over warm rolls. **Yield:** 1 dozen.

Cranberry Sticky Buns

(Pictured below)

The aroma of fresh bread baking reminds me of my childhood and the wonderful cinnamon rolls Mom used to make. This recipe is a variation of those treats with the seasonal addition of cranberries.
—Anne Frederick, New Hartford, New York

4 cups all-purpose flour
1 package (1/4 ounce) active dry yeast
1/4 cup sugar
1/4 cup butter
1 teaspoon salt
1 cup milk
2 eggs
TOPPING:
3/4 cup chopped fresh *or* frozen cranberries
2/3 cup packed brown sugar
1/2 cup butter
1/2 teaspoon ground cinnamon
3/4 cup chopped walnuts
2 tablespoons butter, melted
FILLING:
1/2 cup packed brown sugar
1/2 cup chopped walnuts
1/2 cup chopped fresh *or* frozen cranberries
1/2 teaspoon ground cinnamon

In a mixing bowl, combine 2 cups flour and yeast. In a saucepan, heat sugar, butter, salt and milk to 120°-130°. Add to dry ingredients; beat on low speed for 30 seconds. Add eggs; beat on high for 3 minutes. Beat in remaining flour. Turn onto a floured surface; knead until smooth and elastic, about 6-8 minutes. Place in a greased bowl, turning once to grease top. Cover and let rise in a warm place until doubled, about 1 hour.

In a saucepan, combine the first four topping ingredients; cook and stir over low heat until brown sugar is dissolved and butter is melted. Stir in walnuts. Spread into two greased 9-in. square baking pans; set aside.

Punch dough down; divide in half. Roll each portion into an 18-in. x 6-in. rectangle; brush with butter. Combine filling ingredients; sprinkle over dough to within 1/2 in. of edges. Roll up jelly-roll style, starting with a long side; pinch seam to seal. Cut each roll into nine slices; place cut side down over topping and flatten slightly. Cover and let rise until doubled, about 1 hour.

Bake at 375° for 10 minutes. Reduce heat to 350°; bake 15 minutes longer or until golden brown. Immediately invert onto serving plates. **Yield:** 1-1/2 dozen.

Swedish Cinnamon Twists

These tender twists are fantastic with fresh-brewed coffee. Although the recipe makes a big batch, the treats never seem to last long at our house.
—Cherie Baker, Whitetail, Montana

2 packages (1/4 ounce *each*) active dry yeast
1/2 cup warm water (110° to 115°)
2 cups warm buttermilk* (110° to 115°)
1/2 cup butter, softened
6 tablespoons sugar
2 eggs
2 teaspoons salt
1/2 teaspoon baking soda
7-1/2 cups all-purpose flour
FILLING:
1/4 cup butter, melted
1 cup packed brown sugar
1 teaspoon ground cinnamon
GLAZE:
1 cup confectioners' sugar
1 tablespoon butter, melted
1 tablespoon hot water

In a mixing bowl, dissolve yeast in warm water. Add buttermilk, butter, sugar, eggs, salt and

baking soda; mix well. Stir in flour to form a soft dough. Turn onto a floured surface; knead until smooth and elastic, about 6-8 minutes. Place in a greased bowl, turning once to grease top. Cover and let rise in a warm place until doubled, 1-1/2 hours.

Punch dough down. Turn onto a lightly floured surface; divide in half. Roll each into a 16-in. x 9-in. rectangle; brush with butter. Combine brown sugar and cinnamon; sprinkle over dough. Fold in half lengthwise, forming a 16-in. x 4-1/2-in. rectangle; pinch edges to seal. Cut into 4-1/2-in. x 1-in. strips; twist each strip two or three times. Place 2 in. apart on greased baking sheets. Cover and let rise until doubled, about 30 minutes.

Bake at 375° for 12-14 minutes or until golden brown. Remove from pans to wire racks to cool. Combine glaze ingredients; spoon over warm twists. **Yield:** 2-1/2 to 3 dozen.

***Editor's Note:** Warmed buttermilk will appear curdled.

Lemon-Twist Loaves

(Pictured above right)

Christmas at our house just wouldn't be the same without this mouth-watering tangy twist with its pretty glaze. —*Audrey Thibodeau, Mesa, Arizona*

2 cups water
3 cups sugar, ***divided***
1 cup butter, ***divided***
2 packages (1/4 ounce ***each*****) active dry yeast**
3/4 teaspoon salt
1 egg
1 egg yolk
7 cups all-purpose flour
1 cup sliced almonds, chopped
3 tablespoons grated lemon peel
GLAZE (optional):
3 cups confectioners' sugar
3 tablespoons grated lemon peel
3 to 4 tablespoons milk
1 teaspoon lemon extract
1 cup sliced almonds, toasted

In a saucepan, bring water and 1 cup sugar to a boil. Remove from heat; add 1/2 cup butter. Cool to 110°-115°; transfer to a mixing bowl. Beat in yeast, salt, egg and egg yolk. Add 4 cups flour; beat until smooth. Stir in enough remaining flour to form a soft dough. Turn onto a floured surface; knead until smooth and elastic. Place in a greased bowl, turning once to grease top. Refrigerate for 8 hours.

Punch dough down; divide into thirds. On a floured surface, roll each portion into a 16-in. x 10-in. rectangle. Melt remaining butter; spread over dough. Combine chopped almonds, lemon peel and remaining sugar; sprinkle over butter. Roll up jelly-roll style, starting with a long side; press edges and ends to seal.

Place on greased baking sheets. With a knife, cut loaves in half lengthwise to within 1 in. of one end. Holding the uncut end, loosely twist strips together. Cover and let rise until doubled, about 2 hours. Bake at 350° for 25-30 minutes. Combine first four glaze ingredients; spread over warm bread. Sprinkle with toasted almonds. **Yield:** 3 loaves.

Bread and Butter

For special occasions, try serving butter for your homemade bread in fun ways with little work.

To create butter cutouts, slice a chilled stick of butter 1/4 inch thick. Cut out shapes with small cookie cutters.

To make balls of butter, cut balls from a chilled 1-pound block of butter using a melon baller that's been dipped in hot water.

Arrange cutter cutouts or balls on crushed ice in a small decorative bowl or on individual bread-and-butter plates.

Herbed-Tomato Cheese Bread

(Pictured above)

This rustic-looking loaf is so versatile. Thick slices are great with Sunday breakfast omelets, a salad lunch, a pasta dinner or even as an appetizer for guests.
—Sheila Kimball, Simcoe, Ontario

3 cups all-purpose flour
1/2 cup grated Parmesan cheese
1/2 cup crumbled blue cheese
2 teaspoons baking powder
1 teaspoon baking soda
1 teaspoon *each* dried basil, thyme and rosemary, crushed
1/2 teaspoon salt
1/2 teaspoon pepper
1 egg
1-1/2 cups buttermilk
1/4 cup vegetable oil
3 tablespoons tomato paste

In a bowl, combine the flour, cheeses, baking powder, baking soda and seasonings. In another bowl, beat the egg, buttermilk, oil and tomato paste. Stir into dry ingredients just until moistened. Transfer to a greased 8-in. x 4-in. x 2-in. loaf pan.

Bake at 350° for 50-55 minutes or until a toothpick comes out clean. Cool for 10 minutes before removing from pan to a wire rack. **Yield:** 1 loaf.

Julekage

When we lived in California, a friend made these for us at Christmas. Once we moved here, I found myself missing those light, moist loaves dotted with candied fruit and blanketed with thick frosting. So I hunted up this recipe and started making them. The cardamom gives the bread a wonderfully distinctive flavor.
—Carol Mead, Los Alamos, New Mexico

2 packages (1/4 ounce *each*) active dry yeast
1 teaspoon plus 1/2 cup sugar, *divided*
1/2 cup warm water (110° to 115°)
3/4 cup warm milk (110° to 115°)
1/2 cup butter, softened
1 egg
1 teaspoon salt
1/2 teaspoon ground cardamom
5 to 5-1/2 cups all-purpose flour
1-1/2 cups chopped mixed candied fruit
1/2 cup golden raisins
FROSTING:
1 cup confectioners' sugar
2 tablespoons butter, melted
1 tablespoon milk
Red and green candied cherries

In a mixing bowl, dissolve yeast and 1 teaspoon sugar in water; let stand for 5 minutes. Add milk, butter, egg, salt, cardamom, 2-1/4 cups flour and remaining sugar. Beat until smooth. Stir in fruit, raisins and enough remaining flour to form a soft dough.

Turn onto a floured surface; knead until smooth and elastic, about 6-8 minutes. Place in a greased bowl, turning once to grease top. Cover and let rise in a warm place until doubled, about 1-1/2 hours. Punch dough down; shape into two loaves; place in two greased 8-in. x 4-in. x 2-in. loaf pans. Cover and let rise until doubled, about 45 minutes. Bake at 350° for 35-40 minutes or until golden brown. Remove from pans and cool on wire racks.

For frosting, combine sugar, butter and milk until smooth; spread over loaves. Decorate with cherries. **Yield:** 2 loaves.

Cran-Apple Muffins

(Pictured at right)

I pile these muffins on a plate when friends drop in for coffee. Even my grandkids enjoy the nice flavor combination.
—Millie Westland, Hayward, Minnesota

1/2 cup whole-berry cranberry sauce
1/2 teaspoon grated orange peel
1-1/2 cups all-purpose flour
1/2 cup sugar
1 teaspoon ground cinnamon
1/2 teaspoon baking soda
1/4 teaspoon baking powder
1/4 teaspoon salt
1 egg
1/3 cup milk
1/3 cup vegetable oil
1 cup shredded peeled tart apple
1/2 cup confectioners' sugar
1 tablespoon orange juice

In a small bowl, combine cranberry sauce and orange peel; set aside. In a large bowl, combine the flour, sugar, cinnamon, baking soda, baking powder and salt. Beat the egg, milk and oil; stir into dry ingredients just until moistened. Fold in apple. Fill greased or paper-lined muffin cups half full.

Make a well in the center of each muffin; fill with about 2 teaspoons of reserved cranberry mixture. Bake at 375° for 18-20 minutes or until a toothpick inserted in muffin comes out clean. Cool for 5 minutes before removing from pan to a wire rack. Combine confectioners' sugar and orange juice; drizzle over cooled muffins. **Yield**: about 1 dozen.

Spicy Pumpkin Bread

(Pictured at right)

I like anything made with pumpkin, but this tender loaf is irresistible. Sometimes, I'll top it with a spicy glaze that features nutmeg and cinnamon. —*Paula Cronk, Lander, Wyoming*

1 cup butter, softened
2 cups sugar
4 eggs
2 cups canned pumpkin
2 teaspoons vanilla extract
3-3/4 cups all-purpose flour
2 teaspoons baking soda
2 teaspoons ground cinnamon
1 teaspoon salt
1 teaspoon ground nutmeg
1/2 teaspoon ground cloves
1/2 teaspoon ground ginger
2 cups (12 ounces) semisweet chocolate chips
1 cup chopped walnuts

GLAZE (optional):
1 cup confectioners' sugar
2 tablespoons hot water
1/4 teaspoon ground nutmeg
1/4 teaspoon ground cinnamon
Dash ground cloves

In a large mixing bowl, cream butter and sugar. Add eggs, one at a time, beating well after each addition. Add pumpkin and vanilla; mix well. Combine the dry ingredients. Stir into pumpkin mixture just until moistened. Fold in chocolate chips and walnuts.

Spoon into two greased 8-in. x 4-in. x 2-in. loaf pans. Bake at 350° for 65-75 minutes or until a toothpick inserted near the center comes out clean. Cool for 10 minutes before removing from pans to wire racks. If desired, combine glaze ingredients; drizzle over cooled loaves. **Yield:** 2 loaves.

Cranberry Apricot Scones

(Pictured below)

Dried apricots and cranberries and a bit of grated orange peel give these golden scones plenty of fruity flavor. They're perfect served with a mug of hot coffee or tea. —Karin Bailey, Golden, Colorado

3 cups all-purpose flour
1/3 cup sugar
1 tablespoon baking powder
1/2 teaspoon baking soda
1/4 teaspoon salt
6 tablespoons cold butter
1/3 cup chopped dried apricots
1/3 cup dried cranberries
3/4 cup buttermilk
1 egg
1 egg white
2 teaspoons grated orange peel
Additional sugar

In a bowl, combine the dry ingredients. Cut in butter until mixture resembles fine crumbs. Stir in apricots and cranberries. In a bowl, combine the buttermilk, egg, egg white and orange peel; stir into crumb mixture just until blended.

Turn onto a floured surface; knead gently four times. Roll into a 12-in. x 6-in. rectangle. Cut into eight 3-in. squares. Cut each square into two triangles. Separate pieces and transfer to a greased baking sheet. Sprinkle with additional sugar. Bake at 400° for 12-15 minutes or until browned. Serve warm. **Yield:** 16 scones.

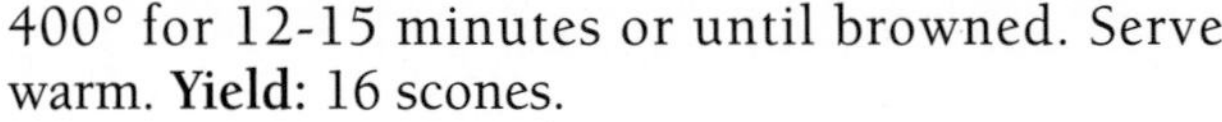

Caramel Orange Ring

It's tradition for me to set out this sweet ring at Christmas brunch. I'm glad to do it because it's so easy! The recipe relies on purchased marmalade, refrigerated biscuits and a few other simple ingredients. —Marjorie Poindexter, Coldwater, Mississippi

1/2 cup orange marmalade, warmed
1/2 cup chopped pecans
2 cups packed brown sugar
2 teaspoons ground cinnamon
2 tubes (12 ounces *each*) refrigerated buttermilk biscuits
1/2 cup butter, melted

Spoon marmalade into a greased and floured 10-in. fluted tube pan. Sprinkle with pecans. In a small bowl, combine brown sugar and cinnamon; set aside. Separate biscuits into 20 pieces. Dip in butter, then roll in the brown sugar mixture.

Arrange biscuits side by side in the pan with the narrow edge standing upright. Drizzle with remaining butter; sprinkle with remaining brown sugar mixture. Bake at 350° for 30-35 minutes or until lightly browned. Cool for 10 minutes; invert onto a serving platter. **Yield:** 10-14 servings.

Orange Cinnamon Bread

(Pictured above right)

This citrusy cinnamon bread is a hit with anyone who has a sweet tooth. You can also make a loaf that's terrific for toasting by eliminating the glaze. —Cindy Anderson, Delhi, New York

2 packages (1/4 ounce *each*) active dry yeast
1/4 cup warm water (110° to 115°)
1 cup milk
3/4 cup orange juice
1 cup sugar, *divided*
1 tablespoon grated orange peel

1-1/2 teaspoons salt
1 egg
6-1/2 to 7 cups all-purpose flour
Additional water
2 teaspoons ground cinnamon
GLAZE:
1 cup confectioners' sugar
2 tablespoons orange juice

In a mixing bowl, dissolve yeast in water; let stand for 5 minutes. In a saucepan, heat milk and orange juice to 110°; add to yeast mixture. Stir in 1/2 cup sugar, orange peel, salt, egg and 3 cups flour; beat until smooth. Add enough remaining flour to form a soft dough. Turn onto a floured surface; knead until smooth and elastic, about 6-8 minutes. Place in a greased bowl, turning once to grease top. Cover and let rise in a warm place until doubled, about 1 hour.

Punch dough down; divide in half. Roll each portion into a 15-in. x 7-in. rectangle. Brush with water. Combine cinnamon and remaining sugar; sprinkle over dough to within 1 in. of edge. Tightly roll up, jelly-roll style, starting with a short side; seal ends. Place seam side down in two greased 9-in. x 5-in. x 3-in. loaf pans. Cover and let rise in a warm place until doubled, about 1 hour.

Bake at 350° for 35-40 minutes or until golden brown. Remove from pans to cool on a wire rack. Combine glaze ingredients; drizzle over bread. **Yield:** 2 loaves.

Tomato Mini Muffins

(Pictured above)

It's delightful at Christmas to savor the big bite of summer baked into these scrumptious muffins. We munch on them warm from the oven. —*Retha Cobb*
Dothan, Alabama

1-3/4 cups all-purpose flour
1/3 cup grated Parmesan cheese
2 tablespoons sugar
2 teaspoons baking powder
1/4 to 1/2 teaspoon dried rosemary, crushed
1/4 teaspoon baking soda
1/8 teaspoon garlic powder
1/8 teaspoon pepper
1 egg
1/2 cup milk
1/2 cup tomato sauce
1/3 cup vegetable oil
Additional Parmesan cheese, optional

In a large bowl, combine first eight ingredients. In another bowl, beat egg. Add milk, tomato sauce and oil; mix well. Stir into dry ingredients just until moistened. Fill greased or paper-lined miniature muffin cups two-thirds full. Sprinkle with Parmesan cheese if desired. Bake at 375° for 10-12 minutes or until a toothpick comes out clean. **Yield:** 3 dozen.

Holiday Tree Bread

(Pictured above)

This recipe has been a hit at parties—guests just gobble it up. I learned to make bread as a child and do it all the time now. —*Meredith Love, San Angelo, Texas*

1 package (1/4 ounce) active dry yeast
2/3 cup warm water (110° to 115°)
2 eggs, beaten
1/3 cup butter, melted
1/4 cup packed brown sugar
1 teaspoon salt
4 to 4-1/2 cups all-purpose flour
FILLING:
5 teaspoons cold butter
3 tablespoons brown sugar
3/4 cup chopped nuts
2 teaspoons beaten egg
1/2 teaspoon ground cinnamon
1/2 teaspoon vanilla extract
GLAZE:
1 cup confectioners' sugar
1/2 teaspoon vanilla extract
Pinch salt
1 to 2 tablespoons milk
Candied red *and/or* green cherries

In a mixing bowl, dissolve yeast in water. Beat in eggs, butter, brown sugar, salt and 1-1/2 cups flour until smooth. Add enough remaining flour to form a soft dough. Turn onto a floured surface; knead until smooth and elastic, about 6-8 minutes. Place in a greased bowl, turning once to grease top. Cover; let rise in a warm place until doubled, about 1 hour. Meanwhile, in a bowl, cut butter into brown sugar until crumbly. Add nuts, egg, cinnamon and vanilla; stir well. Set aside.

Punch dough down. Roll to 3/8-in. thickness; let stand for 5 minutes. Cut out 15 circles with a 3-in. round cutter. Place a heaping teaspoon of filling in the center of each circle. Shape dough around filling to form a ball; pinch to seal. Line a baking sheet with foil; grease the foil.

To form a tree, place one ball seam side down in the center near the top of the baking sheet. Place two balls 1/4 in. apart in the second row. Repeat with remaining balls, adding one to each row until the tree has five rows. For trunk, shape dough scraps into a rectangle and center under the last row. Cover and let rise until doubled, about 45 minutes.

Bake at 350° for 20-25 minutes or until golden brown. Carefully remove from pan to a wire rack to cool. Combine confectioners' sugar, vanilla, salt and enough milk to achieve desired consistency; drizzle over tree, forming garland. Decorate with cherries. **Yield:** 15 servings.

Buttercup Squash Bread

We like this chewy, hearty bread as a substitute for white bread with holiday meals and at breakfast. My five children are grown but still live within "eating distance", so I often bake it in large quantities. —*Mary Merchant Barre, Vermont*

1 package (1/4 ounce) active dry yeast
1/2 cup warm water (110° to 115°)
2 tablespoons molasses
1 teaspoon salt
1/2 to 1 teaspoon caraway seeds
1 cup mashed cooked buttercup squash
3 cups all-purpose flour

In a large mixing bowl, dissolve yeast in water. Add molasses, salt, caraway, squash and 2 cups flour; mix well. Add enough remaining flour to form a soft dough. Turn onto a floured surface; knead until smooth and elastic, about 6-8 minutes. Place in a greased bowl, turning once to grease top. Cover and let rise in a warm place until doubled, about 1 hour.

Punch dough down; turn onto a floured surface and

shape into a loaf. Place in a greased 9-in. x 5-in. x 3-in. loaf pan. Cover and let rise until doubled, about 45 minutes. Bake at 400° for 25-30 minutes or until golden brown. Remove from pan to cool on a wire rack. **Yield:** 1 loaf.

Ginger Muffins

For fun, I give my friends this recipe along with a do-it-yourself muffin kit. It includes oven-ready batter in a decorative jar and a few finished muffins to nibble as a sample. —Erlene Cornelius, Spring City, Tennessee

1/2 cup shortening
1 cup sugar
2 eggs
1 cup molasses
3 cups all-purpose flour
2 teaspoons ground cinnamon
1 teaspoon ground ginger
1 teaspoon baking powder
1 teaspoon baking soda
1 teaspoon salt
1 cup sour milk*

In a mixing bowl, cream shortening and sugar. Add eggs and molasses; mix well. Combine dry ingredients; add to creamed mixture alternately with sour milk, mixing just until blended.

Fill greased muffin cups half full. Bake at 350° for 16-20 minutes or until a toothpick comes out clean. Cool for 10 minutes; remove from pans to wire racks to cool completely. **Yield:** 2-1/2 dozen.

***Editor's Note:** To sour milk, place 1 tablespoon white vinegar in measuring cup; add enough milk to measure 1 cup.

Cherry Lattice Coffee Cake

(Pictured at right)

This cheery coffee cake is an all-time favorite with my seven grandchildren. The latticed top showcases the cherries so beautifully that it's almost too pretty to eat. —Mrs. Otto Stank, Pound, Wisconsin

1 package (1/4 ounce) active dry yeast
1/4 cup warm water (110° to 115°)
1 cup (8 ounces) sour cream
1 egg
3 tablespoons sugar
2 tablespoons butter, softened
1 teaspoon salt
3 cups all-purpose flour

FILLING:

2-1/2 cups fresh *or* frozen pitted tart cherries, thawed, rinsed and drained
1/2 to 3/4 cup sugar
1/2 cup chopped almonds, toasted
2 tablespoons all-purpose flour
Dash salt

In a mixing bowl, dissolve yeast in water; let stand for 5 minutes. Add sour cream, egg, sugar, butter, salt and 2 cups flour; beat until smooth. Add enough remaining flour to form a soft dough. Turn onto a floured surface; knead until smooth and elastic, about 6-8 minutes. Place in a greased bowl, turning once to grease top. Cover and let rise in a warm place until doubled, about 1 hour.

Punch dough down. Reserve 1 cup dough. Divide remaining dough in half. Roll each portion into a 9-in. circle; place in greased 9-in. round baking pans. Combine filling ingredients; spread over dough to within 1/2 in. of edge. Roll out reserved dough to 1/4-in. thickness; cut into 1/2-in. strips. Make a lattice top over filling.

Cover and let rise until doubled, about 45 minutes. Bake at 375° for 15 minutes. Cover top with foil; bake 20 minutes longer or until browned. **Yield:** 2 coffee cakes.

Fruited Swedish Tea Ring

(Pictured below)

I entered this festive tea ring in our agricultural fair, and it won top honors. Every year, I make around 15 of the tasty wreaths to give as fresh-from-the-kitchen gifts.
—Betty Murray, Hamiota, Manitoba

FILLING:
1 cup chopped candied fruit
1/2 cup raisins
2/3 cup packed brown sugar
1/4 cup butter, melted
1 teaspoon grated orange peel
1/2 teaspoon ground cardamom
DOUGH:
1 package (1/4 ounce) active dry yeast
1-1/4 cups warm water (110° to 115°), ***divided***
1/3 cup sugar, ***divided***
2 eggs
1/4 cup shortening
1-1/2 teaspoons salt
4-1/4 to 4-3/4 cups all-purpose flour
ICING:
1 cup confectioners' sugar
1 tablespoon lemon juice
1 tablespoon milk
Candied cherries, optional

Combine filling ingredients in a bowl; cover and refrigerate. For dough, combine yeast, 1/4 cup water and 1 teaspoon sugar; let stand for 5 minutes. In a mixing bowl, combine remaining water and sugar; stir until dissolved. Add yeast mixture, eggs, shortening, salt and 3 cups flour; mix until smooth. Add enough remaining flour to form a soft dough. Turn onto a floured surface; knead until smooth and elastic, about 6-8 minutes. Place in a greased bowl, turning once to grease top. Cover and let rise in a warm place until doubled, about 1-1/2 hours.

Punch dough down; divide in half. Roll each portion into a 16-in. x 9-in. rectangle. Sprinkle filling over dough to within 1 in. of edge. Roll up, jelly-roll style, starting with a long side; seal ends. Place on greased baking sheets; pinch ends together to form a ring. With a scissors, cut from outside edge two-thirds of way toward center of ring at 1-in. intervals. Separate strips slightly; twist to allow filling to show. Cover; let rise until doubled, about 1 hour.

Bake at 350° for 20-25 minutes or until golden. Cool on wire racks for 20 minutes. In a small mixing bowl, beat confectioners' sugar, lemon juice and milk until smooth. Drizzle over warm tea rings. Decorate with cherries if desired. **Yield:** 2 tea rings.

Chocolate Nut Bread

You can't go wrong with my grandmother's chocolaty bread recipe. It tastes as yummy as it looks and is my most-requested special-occasion bread.
—Jennifer Reisinger, Sheboygan, Wisconsin

1 cup butter, softened
2 cups sugar
5 eggs
2 squares (1 ounce *each*) unsweetened chocolate, melted
1 teaspoon vanilla extract
2-1/2 cups cake flour
1 teaspoon baking soda
1/4 teaspoon salt
1 cup buttermilk
1 cup chopped walnuts, optional

In a mixing bowl, cream butter and sugar. Add eggs, chocolate and vanilla; mix well. Combine the flour, baking soda and salt; add to creamed mixture alternately with buttermilk, beating well after each addition. Stir in nuts if desired.

Pour into four greased 5-in. x 3-in. x 2-in. loaf pans. Bake at 350° for 35 minutes or until a toothpick inserted near the center comes out clean. Cool for 10 minutes; remove from pans to wire racks to cool completely. **Yield:** 4 mini loaves.

Pink Cherry Bread

Guests won't be able to overlook pieces of this delightful quick bread with its festive color. I bake it for all my Christmas parties, and it's always a big hit.
—Gail Graham, Laingsburg, Michigan

1 jar (10 ounces) maraschino cherries
3 cups all-purpose flour
2 cups sugar
3 teaspoons baking powder
1/2 teaspoon salt
4 eggs
1-1/2 cups coarsely chopped walnuts
1 cup flaked coconut

Drain cherries, reserving juice. Coarsely chop cherries; set cherries and juice aside. In a bowl, combine the dry ingredients. In another bowl, beat eggs and cherry juice. Stir into dry ingredients just until combined. Fold in the walnuts, coconut and cherries. Transfer to two greased 8-in. x 4-in. x 2-in. loaf pans.

Bake at 350° for 60-65 minutes or until a toothpick comes out clean. Cool for 10 minutes before removing from pans to wire racks. **Yield:** 2 loaves.

Cloverleaf Rolls

(Pictured above)

Tender and tasty, these rolls have been a favorite among our friends and family for more than 25 years. I'm the official holiday baker for our clan, so I bake dozens of these come Christmas. *—Pam Hays, Little Rock, Arkansas*

2 packages (1/4 ounce *each*) active dry yeast
1/2 cup warm water (110° to 115°)
1-1/2 cups warm milk (110° to 115°)
1/2 cup sugar
1 egg
1/4 cup shortening
2 teaspoons salt
5-1/2 to 6 cups all-purpose flour

In a mixing bowl, dissolve yeast in water. Beat in milk, sugar, egg, shortening, salt and 2 cups of flour until smooth. Stir in enough remaining flour to form a soft dough. Turn onto a floured surface; knead until smooth and elastic, about 6-8 minutes. Place in a greased bowl, turning once to grease top. Cover and let rise in a warm place until doubled, about 1 hour.

Punch dough down. Roll into 90 balls; place three balls each in greased muffin cups. Cover and let rise until doubled, about 45 minutes. Bake at 375° for 12-14 minutes or until golden brown. Cool on wire racks. **Yield:** 2-1/2 dozen.

Overnight Rolls

(Pictured above)

I'm pleased to share the recipe for these light and tender rolls, which I've made for over 25 years now. I once served them to a woman who'd been in the restaurant business. She said they were the best rolls she'd ever tasted.
—Dorothy Yagodich, Charleroi, Pennsylvania

1 package (1/4 ounce) active dry yeast
3/4 teaspoon plus 1/2 cup sugar, *divided*
1-1/3 cups plus 3 tablespoons warm water (110° to 115°), *divided*
1/3 cup vegetable oil
1 egg
1 teaspoon salt
4-3/4 to 5-1/4 cups all-purpose flour
Melted butter, optional

In a mixing bowl, dissolve yeast and 3/4 teaspoon sugar in 3 tablespoons water. Add remaining sugar and water, oil, egg, salt and 2 cups flour; mix well. Add enough remaining flour to form a soft dough. Turn onto a floured surface; knead until smooth and elastic, about 6-8 minutes. Place in a greased bowl, turning once to grease top. Cover and let rise in a warm place until doubled, about 1 hour.

Punch dough down. Shape into 20 rolls. Place on a greased baking sheet; cover and refrigerate overnight. Allow rolls to sit at room temperature for 15 minutes before baking. Bake at 375° for 12-15 minutes or until lightly browned. Brush with melted butter if desired. Remove to wire racks to cool. **Yield:** 20 rolls.

Coconut Banana Bread

White chocolate is the wonderfully different addition to this tropical-tasting bread. The moist slices are so scrumptious, they disappear as soon as I serve them.
—Elaine Kyle, Cleveland, Texas

1 cup butter, melted
1-1/2 cups sugar
2 eggs
1 teaspoon vanilla extract
1 teaspoon rum extract
2 cups mashed ripe bananas (about 4 medium)
2-3/4 cups all-purpose flour
1-1/4 teaspoons baking soda
1/2 teaspoon salt
6 squares (1 ounce *each*) white baking chocolate, coarsely chopped
1 cup flaked coconut
1 cup chopped pecans

In a mixing bowl, combine butter and sugar; mix well. Add eggs and extracts; beat on high speed until thickened. Stir in bananas. Combine the flour, baking soda and salt; gradually add to banana mixture. Fold in the chocolate, coconut and pecans.

Transfer to two greased 8-in. x 4-in. x 2-in. loaf pans. Bake at 350° for 70-75 minutes or until a toothpick comes out clean. Cool for 10 minutes before removing from pans to wire racks. **Yield:** 2 loaves.

Cranberry Sweet Potato Bread

We grow plenty of sweet potatoes, so I try to use them in different ways. Slices of this bread, studded with dried cranberries and nuts, are especially tasty served with the citrusy cream cheese spread. *—Margaret Pache*
Mesa, Arizona

1 cup orange juice
1/2 cup dried cranberries
1 package (8 ounces) cream cheese, softened
3 tablespoons confectioners' sugar
1 teaspoon lemon extract
DOUGH:
1/3 cup butter, softened
1-1/4 cups sugar

1 egg
1 cup cold mashed sweet potatoes
1-3/4 cups all-purpose flour
1 teaspoon ground cinnamon
1/2 teaspoon baking powder
1/2 teaspoon baking soda
1/2 teaspoon salt
1/2 cup dried cranberries
1/2 cup chopped macadamia nuts *or* almonds

In a saucepan, combine orange juice and cranberries; bring to a boil. Reduce heat. Simmer, uncovered, for 5 minutes or until cranberries are softened; drain. In a mixing bowl, beat cream cheese, confectioners' sugar and lemon extract until smooth. Fold in cranberry mixture. Cover and refrigerate for at least 1 hour.

Meanwhile, in a mixing bowl, cream butter and sugar. Beat in egg and sweet potatoes. Combine the dry ingredients; gradually add to creamed mixture. Fold in cranberries and nuts. Transfer to a greased 9-in. x 5-in. x 3-in. loaf pan. Bake at 350° for 55-65 minutes or until a toothpick comes out clean. Cover loosely with foil if top browns too quickly. Cool for 10 minutes before removing from pan to a wire rack. Serve with cream cheese spread. **Yield:** 1 loaf.

Glazed Lemon Muffins

Offer these at Christmas and watch folks come back for more! The topping and glaze complement the delicious lemony muffin. —Carol Stevison, Akron, Ohio

1-1/2 cups all-purpose flour
1-1/2 cups sugar
1/4 cup cold butter
MUFFINS:
1-1/2 cups butter, softened
3 cups sugar
6 eggs
1-1/2 cups (12 ounces) sour cream
3 tablespoons lemon juice
2 tablespoons grated lemon peel
4-1/2 cups all-purpose flour
1/2 teaspoon baking soda
1/2 teaspoon salt
GLAZE:
3/4 cup confectioners' sugar
1/3 cup lemon juice

In a bowl, combine flour and sugar. Cut in butter until crumbly; set aside. For muffins, cream butter and sugar in a mixing bowl. Beat in eggs, sour cream, lemon juice and peel. Combine flour, baking soda and salt; stir into creamed mixture just until moistened. Fill greased or paper-lined muffin cups two-thirds full. Sprinkle with reserved crumb topping.

Bake at 350° for 25-30 minutes or until a toothpick comes out clean. Cool in pans for 5 minutes before removing to wire racks. Combine glaze ingredients; drizzle over muffins. **Yield:** about 2 dozen.

Crispy Almond Strips

(Pictured below)

Remember sprinkling cinnamon and sugar on pieces of pastry dough and popping them in the oven along with the pie you just helped make? That's what these crisp strips taste like. —Darlene Markel, Roseburg, Oregon

1 cup cold butter
2 cups all-purpose flour
1/2 cup sour cream
2/3 cup sugar, *divided*
1 cup ground almonds
1 teaspoon ground cinnamon

In a bowl, cut butter into flour until mixture resembles coarse crumbs. With a fork, stir in sour cream until blended. Divide in half; shape each half into a ball and flatten. Wrap tightly; freeze for 20 minutes.

Sprinkle 1/3 cup sugar on a lightly floured surface; roll each portion of dough into a 12-in. square. Combine almonds, cinnamon and remaining sugar; sprinkle over dough. Using a rolling pin, press nut mixture into dough. Cut into 1-in. strips; cut each strip widthwise into thirds. Place 1 in. apart on greased baking sheets. Bake at 400° for 12-14 minutes or until golden brown. **Yield:** 6 dozen.

Onion French Bread

(Pictured below)

Holiday meals are even more memorable when I complement them with this chewy onion bread. Day-old slices taste great with soup and sandwich fillings, too.
—Sandi Pichon, Slidell, Louisiana

5 to 5-1/2 cups all-purpose flour
1 envelope onion soup mix
2 packages (1/4 ounce *each*) active dry yeast
3 tablespoons sugar
2 teaspoons salt
2 cups warm water (120° to 130°)
2 tablespoons shortening
1 egg white
1 tablespoon water

In a mixing bowl, combine 2 cups flour, soup mix, yeast, sugar and salt; add warm water and shortening. Beat on medium speed for 3 minutes. Add enough remaining flour to form a soft dough. Turn onto a floured surface; knead until smooth and elastic, about 3 minutes. Place in a greased bowl, turning once to grease top. Cover and let rise in a warm place until doubled, about 1 hour.

Punch dough down; knead 4-5 times. Divide in half. Roll each portion into a 14-in. x 6-in. rectangle. Roll up, jelly-roll style, starting with a long side; pinch edges and ends to seal. Place seam side down on a greased baking sheet. Beat egg white and water; brush over loaves. Cover with plastic wrap that has been sprayed with nonstick cooking spray; let rise until doubled, about 30-40 minutes.

With a sharp knife, make four shallow diagonal cuts across the top. Bake at 375° for 30-35 minutes or until golden brown. Cool on a wire rack. **Yield:** 2 loaves.

Evelyn's Sour Cream Twists

Evelyn is my mother-in-law, who always keeps some of these twists in her freezer to serve in a pinch. They go quickly around our house, especially during the holidays.
—Linda Welch, North Platte, Nebraska

1 package (1/4 ounce) active dry yeast
1/4 cup warm water (110° to 115°)
3 cups all-purpose flour
1-1/2 teaspoons salt
1/2 cup cold butter
1/2 cup shortening
2 eggs
1/2 cup sour cream
3 teaspoons vanilla extract, *divided*
1-1/2 cups sugar

In a small bowl, dissolve yeast in water; let stand for 5 minutes. In a mixing bowl, combine flour and salt. Cut in butter and shortening until the mixture resembles coarse crumbs. Stir in eggs, sour cream, 1 teaspoon vanilla and the yeast mixture; mix thoroughly. Cover and refrigerate overnight.

Combine sugar and remaining vanilla; lightly sprinkle 1/2 cup over a pastry cloth or countertop surface. On the sugared surface, roll half the dough into a 12-in. x 8-in. rectangle; refrigerate remaining dough. Sprinkle rolled dough with about 1 tablespoon of the sugar mixture. Fold rectangle into thirds. Give dough a quarter turn and repeat rolling, sugaring and folding two more times. Roll into a 12-in. x 8-in. rectangle. Cut into 4-in. x 1-in. strips; twist each strip two or three times.

Place on chilled ungreased baking sheets. Repeat with remaining sugar mixture and dough. Bake at 375° for 12-14 minutes or until lightly browned. Immediately remove from pan and cool on wire racks. **Yield:** 4 dozen.

Whole Wheat Butterhorns

These delicious whole wheat rolls go well with all types of dinner entrees. Be prepared, though! Their tempting buttery flavor is sure to have your guests asking for seconds. —*Mildred Sherrer, Bay City, Texas*

2-1/4 to 2-3/4 cups all-purpose flour, ***divided***
2 packages (1/4 ounce ***each*****) active dry yeast**
1-1/2 cups water
1/3 cup packed brown sugar
2 tablespoons honey
2 teaspoons salt
5 tablespoons butter, ***divided***
2 cups whole wheat flour

In a large mixing bowl, combine 1-1/2 cups all-purpose flour and yeast. In a small saucepan, heat water, brown sugar, honey, salt and 3 tablespoons butter until a thermometer reaches 120°-130° (butter does not need to melt). Add to yeast mixture; beat on low for 30 seconds. Beat on high for 3 minutes. Stir in whole wheat flour and enough remaining all-purpose flour to form a soft dough. Turn onto a floured surface; knead until smooth and elastic, about 6-8 minutes. Place in a greased bowl, turning once to grease top. Cover and let rise in a warm place until doubled, about 1-1/2 hours.

Punch dough down and divide into thirds. Shape each portion into a ball; cover and let rest for 10 minutes. On a lightly floured surface, roll each ball into a 12-in. circle. Cut each circle into six to eight pie-shaped wedges. Beginning at the wide end, roll up each wedge. Place rolls, point side down, 2 in. apart on greased baking sheets. Cover and let rise until doubled, about 1 hour. Melt remaining butter; brush over rolls. Bake at 400° for 10-15 minutes or until golden brown. Immediately remove from pans; cool on wire racks. **Yield:** 1-1/2 to 2 dozen.

Cherry Crescents

(Pictured above)

The festive cherry filling of these flaky pastries suits the holiday season, but you can substitute other flavors.
—*Leona Luecking, West Burlington, Iowa*

2 cups all-purpose flour
1/2 teaspoon salt
1 cup cold butter
1 egg yolk, lightly beaten
1 cup (8 ounces) sour cream
1 can (21 ounces) cherry pie filling
1/2 teaspoon almond extract
Confectioners' sugar

In a bowl, combine flour and salt. Cut in butter until mixture resembles coarse crumbs. Combine egg yolk and sour cream; add to crumb mixture and mix well. Refrigerate for several hours or overnight. Coarsely chop cherries in the pie filling; place in a small bowl. Stir in extract; set aside.

Divide dough into quarters. On a lightly floured surface, roll each portion into a 12-in. circle. Cut each circle into 12 wedges. Place 1 teaspoon filling at the wide end. Roll up from wide end and place point side down 1 in. apart on ungreased baking sheets. Curve ends to form crescent shape.

Bake at 375° for 20-24 minutes or until golden. Immediately remove from pans to wire racks to cool. Dust with confectioners' sugar. **Yield:** 4 dozen.

Danish Julekage

(Pictured above)

Cardamom and lots of fruit enliven this unique holiday bread. The recipe was handed down from my grandmother, who came to the United States from Denmark when she was 16 years old. —*Phyllis Levendusky*
Osage, Iowa

- 2 packages (1/4 ounce *each*) active dry yeast
- 1/4 cup warm water (110° to 115°)
- 2 cups warm milk (110° to 115°)
- 1 cup sugar
- 1/2 cup butter, softened
- 1 tablespoon shortening
- 2 teaspoons salt
- 1 teaspoon ground cardamom
- 3 eggs, beaten
- 8-1/2 to 9 cups all-purpose flour
- 1 cup raisins
- 1 cup chopped candied fruit

FILLING:

- 2 tablespoons butter, melted
- 1/4 cup sugar

TOPPING:

- 1/4 cup sugar
- 2 tablespoons all-purpose flour
- 1/2 teaspoon ground cardamom
- 2 tablespoons cold butter

In a mixing bowl, dissolve yeast in warm water. Add milk, sugar, butter, shortening, salt, cardamom, eggs and 4 cups flour; beat until smooth. Stir in raisins, candied fruit and enough remaining flour to form a soft dough.

Turn onto a floured surface; knead until smooth and elastic, about 6-8 minutes. Place in a greased bowl, turning once to grease top. Cover and let rise in a warm place until doubled, about 1-1/4 hours.

Punch dough down. Turn onto a lightly floured surface; divide in half. Roll each portion into a 12-in. x 9-in. rectangle. Brush with butter; sprinkle with sugar to within 1/2 in. of edges. Roll up, jelly-roll style, starting with a long side; pinch seams to seal and tuck ends under. Place, seam side down, in two greased 9-in. x 5-in. x 3-in. loaf pans. Cover and let rise until doubled, about 45 minutes.

For topping, combine the sugar, flour and cardamom; cut in butter until mixture resembles coarse crumbs. Sprinkle over loaves. Bake at 350° for 50-60 minutes or until golden brown. Remove from pans to cool on wire racks. **Yield:** 2 loaves.

Braided Egg Bread

(Pictured above left)

Since I first made this bread a few years ago, it's become a much-requested recipe. I'm sure I'll pass it down to future generations. —*Marlene Jeffrey*
Holland, Manitoba

- 3-1/4 to 3-3/4 cups all-purpose flour
- 1 tablespoon sugar
- 1 package (1/4 ounce) active dry yeast
- 3/4 teaspoon salt
- 3/4 cup water
- 3 tablespoons vegetable oil
- 2 eggs

TOPPING:
1 egg
1 teaspoon water
1/2 teaspoon poppy seeds

In a mixing bowl, combine 1-1/2 cups flour, sugar, yeast and salt. In a saucepan, heat water and oil to 120°-130°. Add to dry ingredients with eggs and blend well. Beat on medium speed for 3 minutes. Stir in enough remaining flour to form a soft dough. Turn onto a floured surface; knead until smooth and elastic, about 6-8 minutes. Place in a greased bowl, turning once to grease top. Cover and let rise in a warm place until doubled, about 1-1/2 hours.

Punch dough down. Set a third of the dough aside. Divide remaining dough into three pieces. Shape each portion into a 13-in. rope. Place ropes on a greased baking sheet and braid; pinch ends to seal and tuck under. Divide reserved dough into three equal pieces; shape each into a 14-in. rope. Braid ropes. Center 14-in. braid on top of the shorter braid. Pinch ends to seal and tuck under. Cover and let rise until doubled, about 30 minutes.

Beat egg and water; brush over dough. Sprinkle with poppy seeds. Bake at 375° for 25-30 minutes or until golden brown. Cover with foil during the last 15 minutes of baking. Remove from pan to cool on a wire rack. **Yield:** 1 loaf.

RAISIN ORANGE BREAD

(Pictured at right)

I've won many blue ribbons over the years with this recipe. No doubt my daughters will pass on the tradition and bake this bread for their own families.
—Eva Sue Jones, Shell Knob, Missouri

5 to 5-1/2 cups all-purpose flour
1/2 cup sugar
5 teaspoons grated orange peel
2 packages (1/4 ounce *each*) active dry yeast
1-1/2 teaspoons salt
1 teaspoon ground ginger
1 cup milk
1/2 cup butter, softened
1/4 cup water
2 eggs
1-1/2 cups raisins
WALNUT GLAZE:
1 cup confectioners' sugar
2 tablespoons orange juice
2 teaspoons butter, softened
1/2 cup finely chopped walnuts

In a mixing bowl, combine 2 cups flour, sugar, orange peel, yeast, salt and ginger. In a saucepan, heat milk, butter and water to 120°-130°. Add to dry ingredients; beat just until moistened. Add eggs; beat on low speed for 30 seconds. Beat on high for 3 minutes. Stir in raisins. Stir in enough remaining flour to form a soft dough. Turn onto a floured surface; knead until smooth and elastic, about 6-8 minutes. Place dough in a greased bowl, turning once to grease the top. Cover and let rise in a warm place until doubled, about 1-1/4 hours.

Punch dough down. Turn onto a floured surface; knead for 1 minute. Cover and let rest 15 minutes. Divide in half. Roll each portion into a 9-in. x 7-in. oval; fold in half lengthwise. Pinch edges to seal. Place in two greased 8-in. x 4-in. x 2-in. loaf pans. With a sharp knife, make three 1/4-in.-deep diagonal slashes across top of each loaf. Cover and let rise until doubled, about 45 minutes.

Bake at 375° for 45-50 minutes or until golden brown. Cover loosely with foil after 20 minutes to prevent overbrowning. Remove from pans to wire racks to cool. For glaze, combine confectioners' sugar, orange juice and butter until smooth. Stir in walnuts. Spread over loaves. **Yield:** 2 loaves.

Pineapple Banana Bread

(Pictured below)

This pretty loaf adds a tropical feel to any festive occasion. It's also a great way to use up your extra bananas. —*Stephanie Bates, Aiea, Hawaii*

1/2 cup butter, softened
1 cup sugar
2 eggs
1/2 cup mashed ripe banana
1/3 cup drained crushed pineapple
1/2 cup flaked coconut
2 cups all-purpose flour
1 teaspoon baking powder
1/2 teaspoon baking soda
1/2 teaspoon salt

In a mixing bowl, cream butter and sugar. Beat in eggs. Stir in banana, pineapple and coconut. Combine dry ingredients; stir into creamed mixture just until combined. Spoon into a greased 8-in. x 4-in. x 2-in. loaf pan. Bake at 350° for 65-70 minutes or until a toothpick inserted near center comes out clean. Cool in pan 10 minutes; remove to a wire rack. **Yield:** 1 loaf.

Pumpkin Coffee Ring

I make this delicious coffee cake, with its creamy pumpkin filling, for almost every holiday gathering, and everyone loves it. —*Carol McCartney, Danville, Ohio*

2-1/4 cups all-purpose flour
3/4 cup sugar, *divided*
1 package (1/4 ounce) active dry yeast
1/2 teaspoon salt
1/4 cup water
1/4 cup milk
3 tablespoons butter
1 egg
1 package (3 ounces) cream cheese, softened
1/2 cup canned pumpkin
1 teaspoon ground cinnamon
1/2 teaspoon salt
1/2 teaspoon ground ginger
1/2 teaspoon ground nutmeg
1/2 cup chopped walnuts
1/2 cup raisins
1 egg yolk, beaten

GLAZE:

1/2 cup confectioners' sugar
1/8 teaspoon vanilla extract

1 to 2 tablespoons milk
1/4 cup finely chopped walnuts

In a mixing bowl, combine 1-1/2 cups flour, 1/4 cup sugar, yeast and salt. In a saucepan, heat water, milk and butter to 120°-130°. Add to dry ingredients; beat just until moistened. Beat in egg. Stir in enough remaining flour to form a soft dough. Turn onto a floured surface; knead until smooth and elastic, about 6-8 minutes. Place in a greased bowl, turning once to grease top. Cover and let rise in a warm place until doubled, about 1 hour.

In a small mixing bowl, beat cream cheese and remaining sugar until smooth. Add the pumpkin, cinnamon, salt, ginger and nutmeg. Punch dough down; turn onto a floured surface. Roll into a 20-in. x 10-in. rectangle; spread pumpkin mixture to within 1/2 in. of edges. Sprinkle with nuts and raisins. Roll up jelly-roll style, starting with a long side; pinch ends together to form a ring. Place on a greased baking sheet. Cover and let rise until doubled, about 1 hour.

Brush dough with egg yolk. Bake at 350° for 20-25 minutes or until golden brown. Remove from pan to a wire rack. For glaze, combine the confectioners' sugar, vanilla and enough milk to achieve drizzling consistency. Drizzle over the warm ring, then sprinkle with nuts. **Yield:** 1 ring.

Mincemeat Coffee Cake

(Pictured above right)

For years my grandmother and I would have a contest to see whose mincemeat coffee cake was the best (our families voted). After years of losses, I modified my original recipe and finally won. —*Ed Layton*
Absecon, New Jersey

2 packages (1/4 ounce *each*) active dry yeast
1-1/4 cups warm milk (110° to 115°), *divided*
1/2 cup sugar
1/2 cup butter, softened
2 eggs
2 teaspoons salt
1 teaspoon ground cinnamon
1/8 teaspoon *each* ground allspice, cloves and mace
5 to 5-1/2 cups all-purpose flour
1-1/2 cups prepared mincemeat
Confectioners' sugar

In a large bowl, dissolve yeast in 1/2 cup milk. Add sugar, butter, eggs, salt, cinnamon, allspice, cloves, mace, 2-1/2 cups flour and the remaining milk; beat until smooth. Stir in enough remaining flour to form a soft dough. Turn onto a floured surface; knead until smooth and elastic, about 6-8 minutes. Place in a greased bowl, turning once to grease top. Cover and let rise in a warm place until doubled, about 1 hour.

Punch dough down; let rest 10 minutes. Turn onto a lightly floured surface. Roll into a 16-in. x 12-in. rectangle. Spread mincemeat to within 1 in. of edges. Roll up from one long side. Pinch seams; join and seal ends to form a circle. Place in a greased 10-in. fluted tube pan. Cover and let rise until nearly doubled, about 30 minutes.

Bake at 375° for 40-45 minutes or until golden brown. Cool 10 minutes in pan before removing to a wire rack. Just before serving, dust with confectioners' sugar. **Yield:** 12-16 servings.

Candy Cane Bread

(Pictured above)

A festive shape and Christmasy colors make this bread a hit at holiday time. Use cranberries for flavor, or substitute raisins or currants if you prefer.
—Marie Basinger, Connellsville, Pennsylvania

5-1/2 to 6 cups all-purpose flour, *divided*
2 packages (1/4 ounce *each***) active dry yeast**
1 teaspoon salt
1 cup milk
1/2 cup sugar
1/2 cup water
1/4 cup butter
2 eggs
2 tablespoons grated orange peel
1-1/2 cups dried cranberries, currants *or* **raisins**
FILLING:
6 tablespoons butter, softened, *divided*
3/4 cup packed brown sugar
1-1/2 teaspoons ground cinnamon
GLAZE:
1-1/2 cups confectioners' sugar
1 teaspoon vanilla extract
1 to 2 tablespoons milk

In a large mixing bowl, combine 2-1/2 cups flour, yeast and salt; mix well. In a small saucepan, heat milk, sugar, water and butter until a thermometer reads 120°-130° (butter does not need to be melted). Pour into yeast mixture; add eggs and orange peel. Beat for 30 seconds, scraping bowl often. Beat on high for 3 minutes. Stir in cranberries and enough remaining flour to form a firm dough. Turn onto a floured surface; knead until smooth and elastic, about 6-8 minutes. Place in a greased bowl, turning once to grease top. Cover and let rise in a warm place until doubled, about 1 hour.

Punch dough down. Divide into thirds. Roll one portion into a 12-in. x 9-in. rectangle. Spread with 2 tablespoons butter. Combine brown sugar and cinnamon; sprinkle a third over the butter. Roll up from a long end. Cut into 11 rolls; arrange in a candy cane shape on a large greased baking sheet. Repeat with remaining dough and filling.

Cover and let rise until nearly doubled, about 30 minutes. Bake at 350° for 18-23 minutes or until lightly browned. Cool on a wire rack. Combine glaze ingredients; drizzle over canes. **Yield:** 3 breads.

Cream Cheese Pinwheels

These eye-catching pinwheels always bake up beautifully. The sweetened cream cheese filling is rich and satisfying.
—Naticia Lethbridge, Eckville, Alberta

2-3/4 to 3-1/4 cups all-purpose flour
1/3 cup sugar
1 package (1/4 ounce) quick-rise yeast
1 teaspoon grated lemon peel
1/2 teaspoon salt
1/2 cup milk
1/3 cup butter, softened
1/4 cup water
1 egg
1 egg white
FILLING:
1 package (8 ounces) cream cheese, softened
1/4 cup sugar
1 tablespoon lemon juice
EGG WASH:
1 egg white
1 teaspoon water
1 tablespoon sugar

In a mixing bowl, combine 2 cups flour, sugar, yeast, lemon peel and salt. In a saucepan, heat milk, butter and water to 120°-130°. Add to dry ingredients; beat until moistened. Add egg and egg white; beat on medium speed for 2 minutes. Stir in enough

remaining flour to form a soft dough. Cover and let rest for 10 minutes. Turn onto a lightly floured surface. Roll into a 12-in. square; cut into sixteen 3-in. squares.

Combine filling ingredients; spoon onto center of each square. To form pinwheels, diagonally cut dough from each corner to within 3/4 in. of the center. Fold every other point toward the center, overlapping pieces. Moisten center edges with water; pinch to seal. Place 3 in. apart on greased baking sheets. Cover and let rise in a warm place until doubled, about 45 minutes.

Beat egg white and water; brush over pinwheels. Sprinkle with sugar. Bake at 350° for 15-20 minutes or until lightly browned. Remove from pans to cool on wire racks. **Yield:** 16 rolls.

Oatmeal Molasses Bread

You're sure to notice the distinctive taste of molasses in this pretty brown loaf. It's my favorite wholesome bread recipe. Try it toasted or serve slices with coffee for a quick snack during the busy holiday season.
—Carol Minogue, Buffalo, Minnesota

5 to 5-1/2 cups all-purpose flour
1 cup quick-cooking oats
1/2 cup all-bran cereal
1/3 cup toasted wheat germ
2 packages (1/4 ounce *each*) active dry yeast
1 tablespoon salt
2 cups water
1/2 cup molasses
2 tablespoons butter
Melted butter, optional

In a large mixing bowl, combine 3 cups flour, oats, cereal, wheat germ, yeast and salt. In a saucepan, heat the water, molasses and butter to 120°-130°. Add to dry ingredients; beat until smooth. Stir in enough remaining flour to form a soft dough.

Turn onto a floured surface; knead until smooth and elastic, about 6-8 minutes. Place in a greased bowl, turning once to grease top. Cover and let rise in a warm place until doubled, about 1 hour. Punch dough down. Turn onto a lightly floured surface; divide in half. Shape into loaves.

Place in two greased 9-in. x 5-in. x 3-in. loaf pans. Cover and let rise until doubled, about 45 minutes. Bake at 375° for 35-40 minutes or until golden brown. Remove from pans to wire racks to cool. Brush tops with butter if desired. **Yield:** 2 loaves.

Cornmeal Parker House Rolls

(Pictured below)

My mom deserves the credit for making this recipe a family tradition. These tender rolls have been on every holiday table at her house for as long as I can remember.
—Lisa Darnall Lapaseotes, Bridgeport, Nebraska

1/2 cup butter
1/2 cup sugar
1/3 cup cornmeal
1 teaspoon salt
2 cups milk
1 package (1/4 ounce) active dry yeast
1/2 cup warm water (110° to 115°)
2 eggs
4-1/2 to 5-1/2 cups all-purpose flour
Melted butter

In a saucepan, melt butter. Stir in the sugar, cornmeal and salt. Gradually add milk. Bring to a boil over medium-high heat, stirring constantly. Reduce heat; cook and stir for 5-10 minutes or until thickened. Cool to 110°-115°. In a mixing bowl, dissolve yeast in warm water. Add eggs and cornmeal mixture. Beat in enough flour to form a soft dough.

Turn onto a floured surface; knead until smooth and elastic, about 6-8 minutes. Place in a greased bowl, turning once to grease top. Cover and let rise in a warm place until doubled, about 1 hour.

Punch dough down. Turn onto a lightly floured surface; roll out to 1/2-in. thickness. Cut with a floured 2-1/2-in. biscuit cutter. Brush with melted butter; fold in half. Place 2 in. apart on greased baking sheets. Cover and let rise until nearly doubled, about 30 minutes. Bake at 375° for 15-20 minutes or until golden brown. Brush with butter. Remove from pans to cool on wire racks. **Yield:** 2-3 dozen.

Sugared Twists

(Pictured below)

Folks like these tender twists because they aren't rich or overly sweet. I usually double the recipe to feed our five eager eaters and fill holiday gift plates for friends.
—Shelley Blythe, Indianapolis, Indiana

1 package (1/4 ounce) active dry yeast
1/4 cup warm water (110° to 115°)
3-1/2 cups all-purpose flour
1-1/2 teaspoons salt
1/2 cup cold butter
1/2 cup shortening
2 eggs, lightly beaten
1/2 cup sour cream
2-1/2 teaspoons vanilla extract, *divided*
1 cup sugar
Red and green *or* multicolored nonpareils

In a small bowl, dissolve yeast in warm water; set aside. In a large bowl, combine flour and salt. Cut in butter and shortening until mixture resembles coarse crumbs. Add eggs, sour cream and 1 teaspoon vanilla; mix well. Add yeast mixture. Cover and refrigerate for 2 hours or overnight.

Punch dough down; divide in half. Combine sugar and remaining vanilla; sprinkle some over work surface. Roll each portion of dough into a 15-in. x 5-in. rectangle. Fold in thirds; sprinkle with additional sugar mixture. Repeat rolling and folding twice.

Cut into 5-in. x 1-in. strips. Twist and place on greased baking sheets. Sprinkle with nonpareils; press down lightly. Bake at 350° for 18-20 minutes or until golden brown. Remove from pans to wire racks to cool. **Yield:** 2-1/2 dozen.

Honey Whole Wheat Pan Rolls

(Pictured below)

With their pleasant wheat flavor and a honey of a glaze, these rolls always impress my dinner guests.
—Nancye Thompson, Paducah, Kentucky

4 to 5 cups bread flour
1/4 cup sugar
2 packages (1/4 ounce *each*) active dry yeast
1 teaspoon salt
1 cup milk
1 cup butter
1/2 cup water
2 eggs
2 cups whole wheat flour

HONEY BUTTER:

1 cup butter, softened
7 tablespoons honey

HONEY GLAZE:

2 tablespoons honey
1 tablespoon butter, melted

In a mixing bowl, combine 2 cups bread flour, sugar, yeast and salt. In a saucepan, heat milk, butter and water to 120°-130°. Add to dry ingredients; beat just until moistened. Add eggs; beat until smooth.

Stir in whole wheat flour and enough remaining bread flour to form a soft dough. Turn onto a floured surface; knead until smooth and elastic, about 10 minutes. Cover and let rest 15 minutes.

Divide dough into thirds. Roll each portion into a 20-in. rope. Cut each into 20 pieces; shape each into a ball. Grease three 9-in. round baking pans; arrange 20 balls in each pan. Cover and refrigerate overnight.

Let rise in a warm place until doubled, about 1-1/4 hours. Bake at 350° for 18-22 minutes or until golden brown. Meanwhile, in a small mixing bowl, cream butter. Add honey; beat until light and fluffy. Remove rolls from pans to wire racks. Combine glaze ingredients; brush over warm rolls. Serve with honey butter. **Yield:** 5 dozen (1-1/4 cups honey butter).

Cinnamon Swirl Bread

Here's a yummy recipe for yeast bread that doesn't require kneading! The swirled cinnamon filling looks and tastes so good. —*Betty Lou Wellman, Silverton, Oregon*

2 packages (1/4 ounce *each*) active dry yeast
1/2 cup warm water (110° to 115°)
1 cup warm milk (110° to 115°)
1/2 cup butter, softened
1 egg
1/2 cup uncooked Malt-O-Meal cereal
1/3 cup sugar
2 teaspoons salt
4 to 4-1/2 cups all-purpose flour

FILLING:

1 egg white, lightly beaten
1/2 cup sugar
1 tablespoon ground cinnamon

In a mixing bowl, dissolve yeast in water. Add milk, butter, egg, cereal, sugar, salt and 2 cups flour; mix until smooth. Stir in enough remaining flour to form a soft dough. Do not knead. Cover and let rise in a warm place until doubled, about 1-1/4 hours.

Punch dough down; divide in half. Roll each portion into a 12-in. x 7-in. rectangle. Brush with egg white. Combine sugar and cinnamon; sprinkle over rectangles. Starting with a short side, roll up tightly and seal edges. Place each in a greased 8-in. x 4-in. x 2-in. loaf pan. Cover and let rise until doubled, about 30 minutes. Bake at 375° for 40-45 minutes or until golden brown. Remove from pans to cool on wire racks. **Yield:** 2 loaves.

Cranberry Nut Muffins

(Pictured above)

This special holiday bread recipe combines two of my favorites—tangy dried cranberries and spicy cardamom. —*Marianne Clarke, Crystal Lake, Illinois*

2 cups all-purpose flour
1 cup sugar
1 teaspoon baking soda
1 teaspoon ground cardamom
1 teaspoon ground cloves
1 cup buttermilk
1 egg
1/2 cup butter, melted
1/2 cup dried cranberries
1/2 cup chopped walnuts

CARDAMOM BUTTER:

1/2 cup butter, softened
1/4 cup confectioners' sugar
1 teaspoon ground cardamom

In a bowl, combine the dry ingredients. Stir in buttermilk, egg, butter, cranberries and nuts just until moistened. Fill greased or paper-lined muffin cups three-fourths full. Bake at 400° for 20-25 minutes or until a toothpick comes out clean.

Cool in pans 10 minutes before removing to a wire rack. Beat cardamom butter ingredients until smooth; serve with muffins. **Yield:** 14 muffins and about 3/4 cup butter.

Orange-Hazelnut Breakfast Twists

(Pictured above)

These buttery spirals won a blue ribbon at Oregon's state fair. Friends always ask for more when I bring these to church gatherings. They add a merry note to Christmas morning! —*Loraine Meyer, Bend, Oregon*

3-3/4 to 4 cups all-purpose flour
1 cup mashed potato flakes
1/4 cup sugar
2 packages (1/4 ounce *each*) quick-rise yeast
2 teaspoons grated orange peel
1 teaspoon salt
1 cup milk
1/2 cup butter
1/2 cup sour cream
1/4 cup water
2 eggs
FILLING:
1/2 cup confectioners' sugar
1/4 cup butter, softened
1 cup ground hazelnuts *or* walnuts
ORANGE GLAZE:
1/4 cup sugar
1/4 cup orange juice
2 tablespoons butter
1/4 cup sour cream

In a large mixing bowl, combine 3 cups flour, potato flakes, sugar, yeast, orange peel and salt. In a saucepan, heat milk, butter, sour cream and water to 120°-130°. Add to dry ingredients; beat just until blended. Beat in eggs until smooth. Stir in enough remaining flour to form a soft dough. Turn onto a lightly floured surface; knead until smooth and elastic, about 3 minutes. Place in a greased bowl, turning once to grease top. Cover and let rise until doubled, about 25 minutes.

Meanwhile, for filling, combine confectioners' sugar and butter in a bowl. Stir in hazelnuts. For glaze, in a saucepan, bring sugar, orange juice and butter to a boil. Boil for 3 minutes. Remove from the heat; let stand for 10 minutes. Stir in sour cream; set aside.

Punch dough down; turn onto a lightly floured surface. With a long side facing you, roll into a 22-in. x 12-in. rectangle. Spread filling over bottom half of dough. Fold dough over filling; seal edges. Cut into 22 strips, 1 in. each. Twist each strip 4-5 times. Shape strips into a circle and pinch ends to seal. Place in greased 15-in. x 10-in. x 1-in. baking pans. Cover and let rise until doubled, about 25 minutes. Bake at 375° for 15-20 minutes or until golden brown. Cool for 5 minutes before removing from pans to wire racks. Immediately drizzle with glaze. **Yield:** 22 rolls.

Sweet Potato Biscuits

Moist and sweet, these biscuits are a delightful addition to any holiday meal, even breakfast. They don't need butter but they'll taste even better when you spread some on. —*Marjorie Webster*
Madison Heights, Virginia

3-1/2 cups all-purpose flour
4-1/2 teaspoons baking powder
1 teaspoon salt
1/2 teaspoon ground cinnamon
1-1/2 cups mashed cooked sweet potatoes (prepared without milk *or* butter)
1/2 cup butter, melted
1/2 cup sugar
2 tablespoons milk

In a large mixing bowl, combine the flour, baking powder, salt and cinnamon. In another bowl, combine sweet potatoes, butter, sugar and milk; add to

flour mixture and mix well. Turn onto a floured surface; knead 8-10 times. Roll to 1/2-in. thickness. Cut with a 2-1/2-in. biscuit cutter; place on greased baking sheet. Bake at 400° for 15-18 minutes or until golden brown. **Yield:** about 1-1/2 dozen.

Onion Potato Rolls

As a 4-H judge, I sampled these light, golden rolls with a touch of onion at our county fair. —Fancheon Resler Bluffton, Indiana

2 packages (1/4 ounce *each*) active dry yeast
1/2 cup warm water (110° to 115°)
1 cup warm milk (110° to 115°)
1 cup mashed potato flakes
1/2 cup butter, softened
1/2 cup packed brown sugar
2 eggs
1 envelope onion soup mix
1 teaspoon salt
2 cups whole wheat flour
2-1/2 to 3 cups all-purpose flour
TOPPING:
1 egg
1/4 cup dried minced onion

In a mixing bowl, dissolve yeast in warm water. Add the next eight ingredients; mix well. Stir in enough all-purpose flour to form a soft dough. Turn onto a floured surface; knead until smooth and elastic, about 6-8 minutes. Place in a greased bowl, turning once to grease top. Cover and let rise in a warm place until doubled, about 1 hour.

Punch the dough down; divide into 18 pieces. Shape each into a ball. Place 2 in. apart on greased baking sheets. Cover and let rise until doubled, about 30 minutes. Beat egg; brush over rolls. Sprinkle with dried onion. Bake at 350° for 15-18 minutes or until golden brown. Remove to wire racks to cool. **Yield:** 1-1/2 dozen.

Spiced Walnut Scones

(Pictured at right)

Yuletide visitors might stop by just for a taste of these moist and tender scones! Chock-full of walnuts and drizzled with orange-peel glaze, they are wonderful with a cup of coffee.—Kim Lueras, Eureka, California

3/4 cup milk
2 tablespoons lemon juice
3 cups all-purpose flour
3/4 cup sugar
1 tablespoon grated orange peel
1 teaspoon baking soda
1 teaspoon ground nutmeg
1/2 teaspoon baking powder
1/8 teaspoon ground cloves
1/8 teaspoon ground mace
1/2 cup cold butter
1/2 cup chopped walnuts
GLAZE:
1 cup confectioners' sugar
3 to 4 teaspoons orange juice
1/2 teaspoon grated orange peel
1/4 teaspoon almond extract

In a bowl, combine milk and lemon juice; let stand for 2 minutes. In a large bowl, combine the flour, sugar, orange peel, baking soda, nutmeg, baking powder, cloves and mace; cut in butter until mixture resembles coarse crumbs. Add walnuts and milk mixture; stir just until moistened.

Turn onto a floured surface; knead 10 times. Divide dough in half. Roll each portion into a 7-in. circle; cut each into six wedges. Separate wedges and place 1 in. apart on greased baking sheets. Bake at 400° for 18-20 minutes or until golden brown. Remove to wire racks. Combine glaze ingredients until smooth; drizzle over warm scones. **Yield:** 1 dozen.

Maple Nut Coffee Cake

(Pictured below)

Every time I make this coffee cake for the holidays or church functions, the pan is emptied in a hurry. People rave about it. —*Rosadene Herold, Lakeville, Indiana*

- 1 package (16 ounces) hot roll mix
- 3 tablespoons sugar
- 3/4 cup warm water (120° to 130°)
- 1 egg
- 1 teaspoon maple flavoring
- 1/2 cup butter, melted, *divided*

FILLING:

- 1/2 cup sugar
- 1 teaspoon ground cinnamon
- 1/2 teaspoon maple flavoring
- 1/3 cup chopped walnuts

GLAZE:

- 1-1/2 cups confectioners' sugar
- 1/4 teaspoon maple flavoring
- 1 to 2 tablespoons milk

In a large bowl, combine flour packet and yeast from hot roll mix. Add sugar. Stir in water, egg, flavoring and 6 tablespoons butter; mix well. Turn onto a floured surface; knead until smooth and elastic, 2-3 minutes. Place in a greased bowl; turn once to grease top. Cover and let rise in a warm place until doubled, 45-60 minutes. For filling, combine sugar, cinnamon and flavoring. Add nuts; set aside.

Divide dough into thirds. On a lightly floured surface, roll out one portion to a 12-in. circle; place on a greased 12-in. pizza pan. Brush with some of remaining butter. Sprinkle with a third of filling. Repeat, forming two more layers, ending with filling. Pinch dough around outer edge to seal. Mark a 2-in. circle in center of dough (do not cut through). Cut from outside edge just to the 2-in. circle, forming 16 wedges. Twist each wedge five to six times.

Cover and let rise until doubled, 30-45 minutes. Bake at 375° for 20-25 minutes or until golden brown. Cool on a wire rack. Combine glaze ingredients; drizzle over warm coffee cake. **Yield:** 16 servings.

Caramel Cinnamon Rolls

My husband and our four sons are delighted when I bake these sweetly satisfying cinnamon rolls with a terrific caramel glaze. They make any meal special.
—*Marjorie Miller, Haven, Kansas*

2 packages (1/4 ounce *each*) active dry yeast
1/4 cup warm water (110° to 115°)
2 cups warm milk (110° to 115°)
1 cup butter, softened
1 cup sugar
1 cup mashed potatoes (prepared without milk *or* butter)
2 eggs, beaten
1 teaspoon salt
1-1/2 cups whole wheat flour
7-1/4 cups all-purpose flour
FILLING:
1/4 cup butter, melted
1 cup packed brown sugar
3 tablespoons ground cinnamon
CARAMEL GLAZE:
1/2 cup heavy whipping cream
1/3 cup sugar
1/3 cup packed brown sugar
3 tablespoons butter
1 cup miniature marshmallows
2 cups confectioners' sugar
1 teaspoon vanilla extract

In a mixing bowl, dissolve yeast in warm water. Add the milk, butter, sugar, potatoes, eggs, salt and whole wheat flour; beat until smooth. Stir in enough all-purpose flour to form a soft dough. Turn onto a floured surface; knead until smooth and elastic, about 6-8 minutes. Place in a greased bowl, turning once to grease top. Cover and let rise in a warm place until doubled, about 45 minutes.

Punch dough down. Turn onto a floured surface; divide into thirds. Roll each portion into a 12-in. x 8-in. rectangle; spread with melted butter. Combine brown sugar and cinnamon; sprinkle over dough to within 1/2 in. of edges. Roll up jelly-roll style, starting with a long side; pinch seams to seal. Cut each into 12 slices; place cut side down in three greased 13-in. x 9-in. x 2-in. baking pans. Cover and let rise until doubled, about 45 minutes.

Bake at 350° for 27-30 minutes or until golden brown. Cool on wire racks. For glaze, combine the cream, sugars and butter in a saucepan. Bring to a boil; cook and stir for 2 minutes. Remove from the heat; stir in marshmallows until melted. Beat in confectioners' sugar and vanilla. Drizzle over rolls. **Yield:** 3 dozen.

Buttery Crescents

(Pictured above right)

I first learned this recipe when I was a new bride and my grandmother taught me how to make these homemade crescent rolls. They're crusty outside and tender inside.
—Lynne Peterson, Salt Lake City, Utah

2 packages (1/4 ounce *each*) active dry yeast
2 cups warm milk (110° to 115°)
6-1/2 to 7 cups all-purpose flour
2 eggs
1/4 cup butter, melted
3 tablespoons sugar
1 teaspoon salt
Additional melted butter, optional

In a large mixing bowl, dissolve yeast in milk. Add 4 cups flour, eggs, butter, sugar and salt; beat until smooth. Add enough remaining flour to form a soft dough. Turn onto a floured surface; knead until smooth and elastic, about 6-8 minutes. Place in a greased bowl, turning once to grease top. Cover and let rise in a warm place until doubled, about 1 hour.

Punch the dough down and divide in thirds. Roll each portion into a 12-in. circle; cut each circle into 12 wedges. Roll up wedges from the wide end and place with pointed end down on greased baking sheets. Cover and let rise until doubled, about 30 minutes. Bake at 400° for 12-14 minutes or until golden brown. Brush with butter if desired. **Yield:** 3 dozen.

Poteca Nut Roll

(Pictured above)

My mother-in-law brought this recipe from Yugoslavia in the early 1900s. It was a tradition in her family to serve it for holidays and special occasions. Now it's my tradition. Family members often help roll out the dough and add the filling. —*Mrs. Anthony Setta Saegertown, Pennsylvania*

1 package (1/4 ounce) active dry yeast
1/4 cup warm water (110° to 115°)
3/4 cup warm milk (110° to 115°)
1/4 cup sugar
1/4 cup shortening
1 teaspoon salt
1 egg, lightly beaten
3 to 3-1/2 cups all-purpose flour

FILLING:

4 cups ground *or* finely chopped walnuts
1 cup packed brown sugar
1/2 cup butter, softened
2 eggs, lightly beaten
1 teaspoon vanilla extract
1 teaspoon lemon extract, optional
Milk
1/2 cup confectioners' sugar, optional

In a mixing bowl, dissolve yeast in water. Add milk, sugar, shortening, salt, egg and 1-1/2 cups flour; beat until smooth. Add enough remaining flour to form a soft dough. Turn onto a floured surface; knead until smooth and elastic, about 6-8 minutes. Place in a greased bowl, turning once to grease top. Cover and let rise in a warm place until doubled, about 1 hour.

Combine nuts, brown sugar, butter, eggs, vanilla and lemon extract if desired. Add enough milk, about 1/2 cup, until mixture is of spreading consistency; set aside. Punch dough down. Roll into a 30-in. x 20-in. rectangle. Spread filling to within 1 in. of edges. Roll up from one long side; pinch seams and ends to seal.

Place on a greased baking sheet; shape into a tight spiral. Cover and let rise until nearly doubled, about 1 hour. Bake at 350° for 35 minutes or until golden brown. Cool on a wire rack. If desired, brush with a glaze of confectioners' sugar and milk. **Yield:** 1 coffee cake.

Jalapeno Cornmeal Muffins

My husband and I love anything spicy hot, but these zippy jalapeno-studded muffins also add color to our holiday table. Serve them with chili to warm up your caroling party! —*Molly Schultz, Hatley, Wisconsin*

2 tablespoons plus 3/4 cup cornmeal, *divided*
1-1/4 cups all-purpose flour
2 tablespoons sugar
3 teaspoons baking powder
1 teaspoon salt
1/4 teaspoon cayenne pepper
2 eggs, lightly beaten
1 cup milk
1/4 cup butter, melted
4 jalapeno peppers, seeded and chopped*

Grease 12 muffin cups and sprinkle with 2 tablespoons cornmeal; set aside. In a bowl, combine the flour, sugar, baking powder, salt, cayenne and remaining cornmeal. Combine the eggs, milk and butter; stir into dry ingredients just until moistened. Fold in jalapenos.

Fill prepared muffin cups two-thirds full. Bake at

400° for 20-25 minutes or until a toothpick comes out clean. Cool for 5 minutes before removing from pan to a wire rack. Serve warm. **Yield:** 1 dozen.

*__Editor's Note:__ When cutting or seeding hot peppers, use rubber or plastic gloves to protect your hands. Avoid touching your face.

Herbed Mozzarella Round

Served warm with soup or salad, this pretty bread is hearty enough to round out a quick meal during busy holidays. —June Brown, Veneta, Oregon

4-1/4 to 4-3/4 cups all-purpose flour
2 packages (1/4 ounce *each*) active dry yeast
1 tablespoon sugar
1 teaspoon salt
1 cup warm mashed potatoes (prepared with milk and butter)
1/2 cup butter, softened
1 cup warm milk (120° to 130°)
3 cups (12 ounces) shredded mozzarella cheese
1 to 3 teaspoons minced fresh thyme
1 teaspoon minced fresh rosemary
TOPPING:
1 egg
1 tablespoon milk
1 teaspoon poppy seeds

In a large mixing bowl, combine 3 cups flour, yeast, sugar and salt. Add potatoes and butter. Beat in warm milk until smooth. Stir in enough remaining flour to form a firm dough. Beat for 2 minutes. Turn onto a lightly floured surface; knead until smooth and elastic, about 5-7 minutes. Place dough in a greased bowl, turning once to grease top. Cover and let rise in a warm place until doubled, about 45 minutes.

Punch dough down; turn onto a lightly floured surface. Roll into an 18-in. circle. Transfer to a lightly greased 14-in. pizza pan. Sprinkle cheese over center of dough to within 5 in. of edge. Sprinkle with thyme and rosemary. Bring edges of dough to center; twist to form a knot. Cover and let rise until doubled, about 30 minutes.

In a small bowl, combine egg and milk; brush over top. Sprinkle with poppy seeds. Bake at 350° for 40-45 minutes or until golden brown. Cool for 20 minutes before slicing. Serve warm. **Yield:** 1 loaf.

Swedish Rye Bread

(Pictured below)

This recipe came from my mother, and it's long been a family favorite. You can make a meal of it with soup and a salad. —Mary Ann Ross, Crown Point, Indiana

1 package (1/4 ounce) active dry yeast
1-3/4 cups warm water (110° to 115°), *divided*
1/4 cup packed brown sugar
1/4 cup molasses
2 tablespoons shortening
2 teaspoons salt
2-1/2 cups rye flour
3-3/4 to 4-1/4 cups all-purpose flour
2 tablespoons butter, melted

In a mixing bowl, dissolve yeast in 1/4 cup water. Add sugar, molasses, shortening, salt and remaining water; stir well. Add rye flour; beat until smooth. Add enough all-purpose flour to form a soft dough. Turn onto a floured surface; knead until smooth and elastic, about 6-8 minutes. Place in a greased bowl, turning once to grease top. Cover and let rise in a warm place until doubled, about 1-1/2 hours.

Punch dough down. Shape into four round loaves. Place on greased baking sheets. Cover and let rise until doubled, about 45-60 minutes. Bake at 350° for 30-35 minutes or until golden brown. Brush with butter. **Yield:** 4 loaves.

Christmas Stollen

(Pictured below)

I like to make and share this festive delight with family and friends. The candied fruit and nuts add holiday color to a rich bread. A slice really brightens a snowy winter day. —Sharon Hasty, New London, Missouri

3/4 cup raisins
1/2 cup chopped mixed candied fruit
1/4 cup orange juice
1 package (1/4 ounce) active dry yeast
1/4 cup warm water (110° to 115°)
3/4 cup warm milk (110° to 115°)
1/2 cup butter, melted
1/4 cup sugar
2 eggs
2 tablespoons grated orange peel
1 tablespoon grated lemon peel
1 teaspoon salt
5-1/4 to 5-3/4 cups all-purpose flour
1/2 cup chopped almonds
Confectioners' sugar

Soak raisins and fruit in orange juice; set aside. In a mixing bowl, dissolve yeast in water. Add milk, butter, sugar, eggs, orange and lemon peel, salt and 3 cups flour; beat until smooth. Add raisin mixture and almonds. Add enough remaining flour to form a soft dough. Turn onto a floured surface; knead until smooth and elastic, about 6-8 minutes. Place in a greased bowl, turning once to grease top. Cover and let rise until doubled, about 1-1/2 hours.

Punch dough down; let rest for 10 minutes. Divide in half; roll each half into a 10-in. x 7-in. oval. Fold one of the long sides over to within 1 in. of the opposite side; press edges lightly to seal. Place on greased baking sheets. Cover; let rise until nearly doubled, about 1 hour.

Bake at 375° for 25-30 minutes or until golden brown. Cool on a wire rack. Just before serving, dust with confectioners' sugar. **Yield:** 2 loaves.

Herb Rolls

Because they start with convenient refrigerated biscuits, these buttery "homemade" treats couldn't be easier to make. —Julie Dykstra, Canyon Country, California

1/4 cup butter, melted
1 tablespoon grated Parmesan cheese
1/4 teaspoon dried minced onion
1/2 teaspoon garlic powder
1/2 teaspoon dried parsley flakes
1/2 teaspoon dill weed
1 tube (12 ounces) refrigerated buttermilk biscuits

In a bowl, combine the butter, Parmesan cheese, onion, garlic powder, parsley and dill. Spread in a 9-in. pie plate. Cut biscuits into quarters; place in plate and turn to evenly coat with herb mixture. Arrange biscuit pieces in a single layer. Bake at 400° for 10-12 minutes or until golden brown. **Yield:** 8-10 servings.

Sour Cream Crescents

My family insists I make these dinner rolls to complement our holiday feasts. They can be made ahead and frozen. —Judie Anglen, Riverton, Wyoming

3 teaspoons active dry yeast
1/3 cup warm water (110° to 115°)

1/2 cup sugar
1/2 teaspoon salt
1 cup butter, softened
1 cup (8 ounces) sour cream
2 eggs
4 cups all-purpose flour

In a large mixing bowl, dissolve yeast in warm water. Beat in sugar, salt, butter, sour cream and eggs until smooth. Add 3 cups flour; mix well. Stir in remaining flour. Cover; refrigerate 6 hours or overnight.

Punch dough down; turn onto a floured surface. Divide into four pieces. Roll each portion into a 10-in. circle; cut each into 12 wedges. Roll up wedges from the wide end; place pointed side down 3 in. apart on greased baking sheets. Curve ends down to form crescent shape. Cover and let rise in a warm place until doubled, about 1-1/2 hours. Bake at 375° for 15 minutes or until golden brown. Remove from pans to wire racks. **Yield:** 4 dozen.

Banana Nut Bread

Even Santa wouldn't guess grated potatoes are the secret ingredient that makes this quick bread so delightfully moist. —Dita Franklin, San Diego, California

1/2 cup butter, softened
1-1/2 cups sugar
2 eggs
3 medium ripe bananas, mashed
1/3 cup buttermilk
4 cups all-purpose flour
1 teaspoon baking powder
1 teaspoon baking soda
1 teaspoon salt
1-1/2 cups grated peeled uncooked potatoes
1 cup chopped walnuts

In a mixing bowl, cream butter and sugar. Add eggs; mix well. Combine bananas and buttermilk. Combine flour, baking powder, baking soda and salt; add to creamed mixture alternately with banana mixture. Stir in potatoes and walnuts.

Transfer to two greased 9-in. x 5-in. x 3-in. loaf pans. Bake at 350° for 45-55 minutes or until a toothpick inserted near center comes out clean. Cool for 10 minutes before removing from pans to wire racks. **Yield:** 2 loaves.

Orange Pan Rolls

(Pictured above)

A hint of orange in the dough makes these rolls refreshingly different. Similar in texture to a biscuit, they bake to a beautiful golden brown. I make them any time I want something warm from the oven to accompany a meal. —Jackie Riley, Holland, Michigan

1 tablespoon sugar
1/8 teaspoon ground nutmeg
1/2 cup all-purpose flour
3/4 teaspoon baking powder
1/8 teaspoon cream of tartar
1/8 teaspoon salt
1/2 teaspoon grated orange peel
2 tablespoons shortening
3 tablespoons milk
1 tablespoon butter, melted

In a small bowl, combine sugar and nutmeg; set aside. In a medium bowl, combine flour, baking powder, cream of tartar and salt. Add orange peel; cut in shortening until the mixture resembles coarse crumbs. Stir in milk just until moistened.

Divide dough into fourths. With floured hands, roll each piece of dough into a ball; dip in butter, then in sugar mixture. Evenly space in a greased 9-in. round baking pan. Bake at 450° for 10-12 minutes or until golden brown. **Yield:** 4 rolls.

Toasted Oatmeal Bread

I entered this special bread recipe in our state fair, and it won a blue ribbon. It's been a holiday favorite of mine ever since! —*Mrs. Wallace Anderson*
Colon, Nebraska

6 to 6-1/2 cups all-purpose flour, *divided*
1/4 cup sugar
2 packages (1/4 ounce *each*) active dry yeast
1-1/2 teaspoons salt
1-1/3 cups water
1/4 cup milk
1/4 cup molasses
1/4 cup butter
1 egg
1 cup old-fashioned oats, lightly toasted
2-1/2 cups chopped walnuts

In a mixing bowl, combine 1 cup flour, sugar, yeast and salt; mix well. In a small saucepan, heat water, milk, molasses and butter until a thermometer reads 120°-130° (butter does not need to melt). Add to yeast mixture; beat on medium speed for 2 minutes. Add egg, oats and 2 cups flour; beat on high for 2 minutes. Stir in nuts and enough remaining flour to form a soft dough.

Turn onto a floured surface; knead until smooth and elastic, about 6-8 minutes. Place in a greased bowl, turning once to grease top. Cover and let rise in a warm place until doubled, about 1-1/2 hours.

Punch dough down. Shape into two round loaves; place on greased baking sheets. With a sharp knife, cut four parallel slashes on top of each loaf. Cover and let rise until doubled, about 1 hour. Bake at 375° for 20-30 minutes or until golden brown. Remove from pans; cool on wire racks. **Yield:** 2 loaves.

Blueberry-Orange Coffee Cake

The orange peel and fre..h juice in this cake give it a delicious aroma and a moist texture, while the blueberries add color. —*Kathy Fannoun*
Robbinsdale, Minnesota

5 cups all-purpose flour
1 cup sugar
3/4 cup packed brown sugar, *divided*
2 tablespoons baking powder
1/2 teaspoon salt
2 to 3 teaspoons grated orange peel
3/4 cup butter
1 cup chopped walnuts
2 eggs plus 2 egg whites
2 cups milk
1 tablespoon orange juice
2 teaspoons vanilla extract
2-1/2 cups fresh *or* frozen blueberries
1-1/2 teaspoons ground cinnamon

In a bowl, combine flour, sugar, 1/2 cup brown sugar, baking powder, salt and orange peel. Cut in butter until mixture resembles coarse crumbs. Add nuts. Beat eggs, egg whites, milk, juice and vanilla; stir into dry ingredients just until moistened. Fold in blueberries.

Spoon half into a greased 10-in. fluted tube pan. Combine cinnamon and remaining brown sugar; sprinkle over batter. Top with remaining batter. Bake at 350° for 1 hour and 20 minutes or until a toothpick inserted near the center comes out clean. Cool in pan 10 minutes. Invert onto a serving plate. **Yield:** 16-20 servings.

Mini Poppy Seed Loaves

Each Christmas, I make plates of goodies for the neighbors. I try to include a few items that aren't as sweet as traditional cookies and candies. These mini loaves really fit the bill! —*Mrs. Richard Bridges*
Absarokee, Montana

2 cups all-purpose flour
1 cup sugar
1 tablespoon poppy seeds
1 teaspoon grated lemon peel
1/2 teaspoon baking soda
1 cup (8 ounces) plain yogurt
1/2 cup butter, melted
2 eggs, beaten
1 teaspoon vanilla extract
1/2 teaspoon almond extract

In a bowl, combine flour, sugar, poppy seeds, lemon peel and baking soda. Combine remaining ingredients; stir into flour mixture just until moistened. Spoon into three greased 5-in. x 2-1/2-in. mini loaf pans. Bake at 350° for 25-30 minutes or until a toothpick inserted near the center comes out clean. Cool on a wire rack. **Yield:** 3 loaves.

Candy

Brown Sugar Cashew Fudge

(Pictured above)

This creamy light-colored fudge, loaded with crunchy cashews, is a yummy variation on traditional chocolate fudge...and it disappears just as fast!
—Jennifer Adams, Plymouth, Massachusetts

1-1/2 teaspoons plus 1/4 cup butter, softened, *divided*
1 cup packed brown sugar
1/2 cup evaporated milk
2 tablespoons light corn syrup
2-1/2 cups confectioners' sugar
2 cups coarsely chopped salted cashews

Line a 9-in. square pan with foil and grease the foil with 1-1/2 teaspoons butter; set aside. In a heavy saucepan, combine the brown sugar, milk, corn syrup and remaining butter. Cook and stir over medium heat until the sugar is dissolved. Bring mixture to a rapid boil, stirring constantly for about 5 minutes.

Remove from the heat. Gradually add confectioners' sugar; mix well. Fold in cashews. Immediately spread into prepared pan. Cool. Using foil, lift fudge out of pan. Cut into 1-in. squares. Refrigerate in an airtight container. **Yield:** 3 dozen.

Truffle Cherries

(Pictured at left)

Chocolate is popular at our house, so these double-chocolate gems never last long!
—Anne Drouin, Dunnville, Ontario

1/3 cup heavy whipping cream
2 tablespoons butter
2 tablespoons sugar
4 squares (1 ounce *each*) semisweet chocolate
1 jar (8 ounces) maraschino cherries with stems, well drained

COATING:

6 squares (1 ounce *each*) semisweet chocolate
2 tablespoons shortening

In a saucepan, bring cream, butter and sugar to a boil, stirring constantly. Remove from the heat; stir in chocolate until melted. Cover and refrigerate for at least 4 hours or until easy to handle. Pat cherries with paper towel until very dry. Shape a teaspoonful of chocolate mixture around each cherry, forming a ball. Cover and refrigerate for 2-3 hours or until firm.

In a small saucepan, melt chocolate and shortening over low heat. Dip cherries until coated; shake off excess. Place on waxed paper to harden. **Yield:** about 2 dozen.

Old-Fashioned Molasses Candy

(Pictured above left)

This hard candy was always the first thing to sell out at fund-raisers we held back when I was in high school.
—Laurie Pester, Colstrip, Montana

3 tablespoons butter, softened, *divided*
1 cup sugar
3/4 cup light corn syrup
2 teaspoons cider vinegar
3/4 cup molasses
1/4 teaspoon baking soda

Grease a 15-in. x 10-in. x 1-in. pan with 1 tablespoon butter; set aside. In a heavy saucepan, combine sug-

ar, corn syrup and vinegar. Cook over low heat until sugar is dissolved, stirring frequently. Increase heat to medium; cook until a candy thermometer reads 245° (firm-ball stage), stirring occasionally. Add molasses and remaining butter. Cook, uncovered, until a candy thermometer reads 260° (hard-ball stage), stirring occasionally. Remove from heat. Add baking soda; beat well.

Pour into prepared pan. Let stand for 5 minutes or until cool enough to handle. Butter fingers; quickly pull candy until firm but pliable (color will be light tan). When candy is ready for cutting, pull into a 1/2-in. rope. Cut into 1-in. pieces. Wrap each in waxed paper or colored candy wrappers. **Yield:** 1-1/2 pounds.

Editor's Note: We recommend that you test your candy thermometer before each use by bringing water to a boil; the temperature should read 212°. Adjust your recipe temperature up or down based on your test.

Create-a-Bark

With a little imagination and varied ingredients, you can create a custom candy with this recipe that you'll love. —*Sharon Skildem, Maple Grove, Minnesota*

1 package (24 ounces) white candy coating
2 cups of one *or* more of the following: dessert mints, jelly beans, M&M's, sugar-coated cereal, miniature sandwich cookies, etc.

Melt the coating in a double boiler over simmering water or in a microwave-safe bowl. Stir in candy, cereal and/or cookies. Spread on a foil-lined baking sheet. Cool. Break into pieces. **Yield:** about 2 pounds.

Sesame Toffee

(Pictured below)

I make more cakes and cookies than candy, but I love to stir up a batch of this toffee for Christmas because it's so easy! —*Janet Owen, Kalamazoo, Michigan*

2 teaspoons plus 3/4 cup butter, softened, *divided*
1/3 cup light corn syrup
2/3 cup sugar
1/2 cup sesame seeds, toasted

Line a 15-in. x 10-in. x 1-in. baking pan with foil and grease the foil with nonstick cooking spray; set aside. Grease the sides of a large heavy saucepan with 2 teaspoons butter. Add the corn syrup and remaining butter; cook over medium heat until butter is melted.

Add sugar and sesame seeds; cook and stir until mixture comes to a boil. Cook and stir until mixture turns golden brown and a candy thermometer reads 300° (hard-crack stage). Pour into prepared pan (do not scrape sides of saucepan). Spread evenly. Cool; break into pieces. **Yield:** about 3/4 pound.

Editor's Note: We recommend that you test your candy thermometer before each use by bringing water to a boil; the temperature should read 212°. Adjust your recipe temperature up or down based on your test.

Nutty Sandwich Treats

(Pictured below)

The ingredients in my layered snacks provide plenty of texture and flavor. Plus, kids can help out by spreading the filling on the graham crackers.
—Kim Rehfeldt, Bellingham, Washington

2/3 cup chunky peanut butter
2 tablespoons butter
1 cup miniature marshmallows
1/2 cup chopped pecans
8 whole graham crackers (4-3/4 inches x 2-1/2 inches)
6 ounces white candy coating, melted

In a saucepan over low heat, cook and stir peanut butter and butter until blended. Stir in marshmallows until melted. Remove from the heat; fold in pecans.

Break or cut each graham cracker into four pieces. Spread with peanut butter mixture; top with remaining crackers. Spread candy coating over both sides. Place crackers on lightly greased waxed paper and chill until firm. **Yield:** 16 treats.

Grandma's Butterscotch Candy

The recipe for this wonderfully buttery candy was handed down from my grandma. My brothers, sisters and I love it now as much as we did when we were little...and so do our families. It's become a cherished tradition.
—Catherine Rothermel, Columbus, Ohio

2 cups sugar
2/3 cup water
1/4 teaspoon cream of tartar
2 tablespoons butter
1 teaspoon vanilla extract

Butter a 13-in. x 9-in. x 2-in. pan; set aside. In a heavy saucepan, combine the sugar, water and cream of tartar. Bring to a boil, without stirring, over medium heat until a candy thermometer reads 300° (hard-crack stage). Syrup will turn a golden color.

Remove from the heat; stir in butter and vanilla. Return to heat. Cook and stir until thermometer returns to 300°. Pour into prepared pan. Cool. Break into pieces. **Yield:** about 3/4 pound.

Editor's Note: We recommend that you test your candy thermometer before each use by bringing water to a boil; the temperature should read 212°. Adjust your recipe temperature up or down based on your test.

Ice Cream Sundae Caramels

These soft caramels are a hit at holiday time. I came up with the recipe using ingredients I commonly have on hand. It's a favorite!
—Arlinda Petersen, Swanton, Nebraska

2 cups sugar
2 cups (16 ounces) dark corn syrup
2 cups (1 pint) vanilla ice cream, melted, *divided*
1 cup butter
8 ounces chocolate candy coating
1/2 cup peanuts, finely chopped

In a heavy 4-qt. saucepan, combine sugar, corn syrup, 1 cup ice cream and butter. Cook and stir over low heat until mixture boils. Increase heat to medium; cook and stir until can-

dy thermometer reads 242° (nearly firm-ball stage). Remove from the heat; gradually stir in remaining ice cream. Return to the heat; cook without stirring to 244° (firm-ball stage). Immediately pour, without stirring, into a buttered 13-in. x 9-in. x 2-in. baking pan. Let cool until firm. Invert candy onto a baking sheet.

Melt candy coating in a microwave-safe bowl or in a double boiler over simmering water. Spread over candy; sprinkle with nuts. Score top into 1-in. squares. Allow chocolate to harden. Cut into 1-in. squares, following score marks. Wrap individually in waxed paper or plastic wrap. **Yield:** about 3-1/2 pounds.

Editor's Note: We recommend that you test your candy thermometer before each use by bringing water to a boil; the temperature should read 212°. Adjust your recipe temperature up or down based on your test.

Candied Grapefruit Peel

My mother always made this fruity holiday sweet, and so do I. It takes time, but the house is filled with a "Christmasy" aroma while the grapefruit cools—and the candied sticks are simply delicious!

—Edna Everitt, Melbourne, Florida

3 medium grapefruit
1 teaspoon salt
2 cups sugar, ***divided***
1 cup water

With a sharp knife, score grapefruit peel into 8 to 10 wedge-shaped sections. Loosen peel with a tablespoon. With a small sharp knife, carefully remove white pith from peel. (Save fruit for another use.) In a large saucepan, combine peel and salt; cover with water. Bring to a boil. Reduce heat; simmer, uncovered, for 20 minutes. Drain. Repeat process twice (only covering with water and not adding more salt). Cool for 10 minutes. Cut peel into 1/4- to 1/2-in. strips; set aside.

In the same pan, combine 1-1/2 cups sugar and 1 cup water. Cook and stir until sugar is dissolved and mixture comes to a boil. Cook and stir 2 minutes. Add grapefruit peel. Return to a boil. Reduce heat; simmer, uncovered, 35-38 minutes or until syrup is almost absorbed and peel is transparent, stirring occasionally (watch carefully to prevent scorching).

Drain any remaining syrup. Cool peel in a single layer on a foil-lined baking sheet for at least 2-1/2 hours. Sprinkle with the remaining sugar if needed. **Yield:** about 1-1/2 cups.

Chocolate Peanut Clusters

(Pictured above)

There are a few recipes I absolutely have to pull out every Christmas, and this is one of them. The nutty clusters are so smooth and chocolaty.

—Darlyne Shoemaker, Byron Center, Michigan

2 pounds white candy coating
1 package (12 ounces) semisweet chocolate chips
1 package (11-1/2 ounces) milk chocolate chips
5 cups salted dry roasted peanuts

In a heavy saucepan over low heat, cook and stir candy coating and chips until melted and smooth. Cool for 10 minutes; stir in peanuts. Drop by rounded tablespoonfuls onto waxed paper-lined baking sheets. Refrigerate until firm, about 45 minutes. **Yield:** 10 dozen.

Raspberry Truffles

(Pictured above)

Although they look fussy, these melt-in-your-mouth delights are actually a cinch to make. What's more, they're a hit everywhere I take them. —*J. Hill*
Sacramento, California

1/2 cup evaporated milk
1/4 cup sugar
1 package (11-1/2 ounces) milk chocolate chips
1/4 cup seedless raspberry preserves
1/2 teaspoon instant coffee granules
3/4 cup finely chopped almonds, toasted

In a heavy saucepan, combine milk and sugar. Bring to a rolling boil over medium heat; boil and stir for 3 minutes. Remove from the heat; stir in chocolate chips, preserves and coffee until mixture is smooth. Chill for 1 hour. Roll into 1-in. balls; roll in almonds. Place on waxed paper-lined baking sheets. Chill until firm. Cover and store in the refrigerator. **Yield:** 2-1/2 dozen.

Date Nut Candy

Even though my two grown sons aren't big "sweets eaters", they think these candies are exceptional. The big peanut butter flavor is a hit combined with holiday staples like walnuts and dates. —*Pauline Block*
Aurora, Indiana

1 cup creamy peanut butter
1 cup confectioners' sugar
1 cup chopped dates
1 cup chopped walnuts
1 tablespoon butter, softened
1 teaspoon vanilla extract
1 pound white candy coating

In a mixing bowl, combine the first six ingredients; mix well. Shape into 3/4-in. balls; place on a waxed paper-lined baking sheet. Refrigerate for 1-2 hours or until firm. In a microwave or double boiler, melt candy coating; stir until smooth. Dip balls in coating and place on waxed paper to harden. **Yield:** about 4 dozen.

Chocolate Chip Nougat

This sweet, chewy nougat adds a pretty holiday blush to Yuletide gatherings. It takes a little extra effort to make, but candy this festive is worth it! —*Sandi Friest*
Paynesville, Minnesota

1 teaspoon plus 1/4 cup butter, softened, *divided*
3 cups sugar, *divided*
2/3 cup plus 1-1/4 cups light corn syrup, *divided*
2 tablespoons water
2 egg whites
2 cups chopped walnuts
2 teaspoons vanilla extract
1 cup miniature semisweet chocolate chips
2 to 3 drops red food coloring, optional

Line a 9-in. square pan with foil and grease the foil with 1 teaspoon butter; set aside. In a small heavy saucepan, combine 1 cup sugar, 2/3 cup corn syrup and water. Bring to a boil over medium heat, stirring constantly. Reduce the heat to medium-low. Cook, without stirring, until a candy thermometer reads 238°.

Meanwhile, beat egg whites in a heat-proof mixing bowl until stiff peaks form. When the syrup reaches 238°, add it in a thin stream to egg whites, beating constantly at high speed until thick; cover and set aside.

In a large heavy saucepan, combine remaining sugar and corn syrup. Bring to a boil over medium heat, stirring constantly. Reduce heat to medium-low; cook, without stirring, until a candy thermometer

reads 275° (soft-crack stage). Meanwhile, melt remaining butter. Pour hot syrup all at once into reserved egg white mixture; mix with a wooden spoon. Stir in the walnuts, melted butter and vanilla.

Pour half of the nougat mixture into prepared pan; press evenly. Sprinkle with chocolate chips. If desired, stir food coloring into remaining nougat mixture; turn into pan over chocolate chips. Press down evenly with buttered fingers. Let stand for several hours until set. Using foil, lift nougat out of pan. Discard foil; cut nougat into 1-in. squares. Wrap individually in waxed paper or foil; twist ends. **Yield:** 3 pounds.

Editor's Note: We recommend that you test your candy thermometer before each use by bringing water to a boil; the temperature should read 212°. Adjust your recipe temperature up or down based on your test.

Chocolate Peanut Butter Cups

(Pictured below)

I developed this recipe by combining some dessert recipes in my collection. The smooth peanut butter flavor earns rave reviews. —Joanne Banko, Eastlake, Ohio

2 cups (12 ounces) semisweet chocolate chips
2 tablespoons shortening
36 paper *or* foil bonbon-size baking cups
1 cup peanut butter
1/2 cup nonfat dry milk powder
1/2 cup light corn syrup
1 teaspoon vanilla extract

In a double boiler over simmering water, or in a microwave-safe bowl, melt chocolate chips and shortening; mix well. Place a scant teaspoonful inside each paper or foil cup and rotate it gently in the palm of your hand to coat the sides and bottom. (Use a spoon to help coat the sides if necessary.) Place cups in miniature muffin pans; chill until firm. Set remaining chocolate aside.

In a medium bowl or food processor, combine peanut butter, milk powder, corn syrup and vanilla. Stir with a wooden spoon or process until well blended. Shape into 1-in. balls; press one ball into each chocolate cup. Top with remaining melted chocolate. Chill until set. Store in the refrigerator. **Yield:** 3 dozen.

Sugarless Licorice Stars

You can enjoy this candy even if you are on a restricted diet since it's sugar-free. Use small seasonal cutters to make shapes everyone will be sweet on.
—Margaret Richardson, Spring Grove, Illinois

2 envelopes unflavored gelatin
4 cups diet cherry soda, *divided*
3 packages (.3 ounce *each*) sugar-free cherry gelatin
2 teaspoons anise flavoring

In a large bowl, soften gelatin in 1/2 cup soda. In a small saucepan, bring remaining soda to a boil. Remove from the heat; add to gelatin mixture and mix well. Stir in flavored gelatin until dissolved. Add anise; mix well. If necessary, skim foam.

Pour into a 13-in. x 9-in. x 2-in. pan. Chill until firm. Use small star-shaped or other holiday cutters or cut into 1-in. squares. Store in the refrigerator. **Yield:** 7-9 dozen.

Sugarplums

(Pictured below)

When our kids read about sugarplums in a holiday tale, they were intrigued, and so was I! In short order, I figured out a no-bake way to make the sweets from dried fruits and nuts. —Suzanne McKinley, Lyons, Georgia

1 package (15 ounces) raisins
1 package (12 ounces) pitted prunes
1 package (8 ounces) dried mixed fruit
1-1/2 cups chopped pecans
Sugar

In a food processor, coarsely chop raisins, prunes, mixed fruit and pecans. Transfer to a bowl; mix well. Roll into 1-in. balls, then roll in sugar. Place on waxed paper and let stand at room temperature for 4 hours. Store in an airtight container. Roll in additional sugar before serving if desired. **Yield:** about 8 dozen.

Coconut Bonbons

My family and friends never fail to include these chocolates on their Christmas wish list. Luckily, this recipe makes a big batch, so my supply meets the candy demand. —Beverly Cray, Epping, New Hampshire

1/2 cup butter, softened
2 pounds confectioners' sugar
1 can (14 ounces) sweetened condensed milk
4 cups chopped pecans
1 package (10 ounces) flaked coconut
1 teaspoon vanilla extract
2 cups (12 ounces) semisweet chocolate chips
1 tablespoon shortening

In a mixing bowl, cream butter and sugar. Add the milk, pecans, coconut and vanilla; mix well. Shape into 1-in. balls. Refrigerate for 30-45 minutes or until firm. In a microwave or heavy saucepan, melt the chips and shortening; stir until smooth. Dip balls and place on waxed paper to harden. Store in an airtight container at room temperature. **Yield:** about 21 dozen.

Editor's Note: Candies can be frozen for up to 3 months before dipping in chocolate. Thaw in refrigerator before dipping.

Mixed Nut Brittle

Peanut brittle is done one better when prepared with mixed nuts instead. This impressive candy is simply delicious. I like to pack some in pretty plastic bags to give as gifts. —Mrs. James Merriman, Preble, Indiana

4 cups mixed nuts
1-1/2 cups sugar
1 cup light corn syrup

1/3 cup water
2 tablespoons butter
1 teaspoon vanilla extract
1/2 teaspoon salt

Place nuts in two greased 15-in. x 10-in. x 1-in. baking pans. Bake at 350° for 10 minutes or until warm. Set aside and keep warm.

Meanwhile, in a large heavy saucepan, combine sugar, corn syrup and water. Cover and bring to a boil over medium heat. Uncover and cook until a candy thermometer reads 290° (soft-crack stage). Remove from the heat; stir in nuts, butter, vanilla and salt. Quickly spread into a thin layer on baking pans. Cool completely; break into pieces. **Yield:** 2-1/2 pounds.

Editor's Note: We recommend that you test your candy thermometer before each use by bringing water to a boil; the temperature should read 212°. Adjust your recipe temperature up or down based on your test.

Chocolate Zebra Clusters

Just one bite and chocolate lovers will melt over these yummy clusters filled with salted nuts, rice cereal and marshmallows! And they're so pretty, no one can believe how easy they are. —*Paige Scott*
Murfreesboro, Tennessee

2 cups (12 ounces) semisweet chocolate chips
12 ounces white candy coating, *divided*
1-1/4 cups salted peanuts
1-1/4 cups crisp rice cereal
2-1/4 cups miniature marshmallows
1 teaspoon shortening

Line two baking sheets with waxed paper; set aside. In a large microwave-safe bowl, melt chips and 7 ounces white candy coating at 70% power; stir until smooth. Stir in peanuts and cereal. Cool slightly; fold in marshmallows. Drop by rounded tablespoonfuls onto prepared baking sheets.

In another microwave-safe bowl, melt shortening and remaining candy coating; stir until smooth. Transfer to a pastry or plastic bag; cut a small hole in the corner of bag. Drizzle over clusters. Refrigerate for 5 minutes or until set. Store in an airtight container. **Yield:** 2-1/2 dozen.

Editor's Note: This recipe was tested in an 850-watt microwave.

Chocolate Caramel Wafers

(Pictured above)

To keep my holiday cooking quick, I've come to rely on fast recipes like this one. The crunchy-chewy tidbits are our youngsters' favorite. —*Susan Laubach*
Vida, Montana

1 package (14 ounces) caramels
1/4 cup evaporated milk
1 package (12 ounces) vanilla wafers
8 plain milk chocolate candy bars (1.55 ounces *each*), broken into squares
Chopped pecans, optional

Place caramels and milk in a microwave-safe bowl; microwave, uncovered, on high for 3 minutes or until melted. Stir until smooth. Spread over vanilla wafers; place on ungreased baking sheets. Top each with a square of chocolate. Place in a 225° oven for 1-2 minutes or until chocolate is melted. Spread with an icing knife. Top with pecans if desired. **Yield:** about 7 dozen.

Editor's Note: This recipe was tested in an 850-watt microwave and with Hershey's caramels.

Candy Cane Popcorn Balls

(Pictured above)

When I was a little girl, my mother and I made these popcorn balls for family and friends at Christmas. Now my husband and I carry on the tradition.
—Rebecca Gove, Cape Neddick, Maine

4 quarts popped popcorn
2 teaspoons water
1 teaspoon baking soda
1/2 teaspoon vanilla extract
1 cup light corn syrup
1/4 cup butter
2 cups sugar
24 miniature candy canes

Place popcorn in a large greased bowl or roasting pan; set aside. In a small bowl, combine the water, baking soda and vanilla; set aside. In a heavy saucepan, combine corn syrup and butter; heat over medium heat until butter is melted. Add sugar; cook and stir until sugar is dissolved and mixture comes to a boil. Cook and stir until a candy thermometer reaches 230° (thread stage), about 2 minutes.

Remove from the heat. Stir in vanilla mixture (mixture will foam) until blended. Immediately pour over popcorn, stirring to coat evenly. Cool for about 5 minutes, stirring several times. When cool enough to handle, firmly shape with buttered hands into 2-in. balls. Insert straight end of candy cane in the center of each ball. **Yield:** 2 dozen.

Editor's Note: We recommend that you test your candy thermometer before each use by bringing water to a boil; the temperature should read 212°. Adjust your recipe temperature up or down based on your test.

Chocolate Cream Bonbons

My grandmother gave me this tasty recipe when I was a girl. Some of my fondest childhood memories are of her huge kitchen and all the delicious treats she made.
—Joan Lewis, Reno, Nevada

4 cups (1 pound) confectioners' sugar
1 cup ground pecans *or* walnuts
1/2 cup plus 2 tablespoons sweetened condensed milk
1/4 cup butter, softened
3 cups semisweet chocolate chips
2 tablespoons shortening

In a mixing bowl, combine the first four ingredients; mix well. Form into 1-in. balls. Place on baking sheets. Cover and refrigerate overnight.

Melt the chocolate chips and shortening in a microwave-safe bowl or in a double boiler over simmering water. Dip balls and place on waxed paper to harden. (If balls are too soft to dip, place in the freezer for a few minutes first.) **Yield:** about 6 dozen.

Toffee Chip Fudge

I combined two recipes to come up with this yummy fudge dotted with crisp toffee bits. *—Maxine Smith*
Owanka, South Dakota

1-1/2 teaspoons plus 1/4 cup butter, *divided*
1-1/2 cups sugar
1 can (5 ounces) evaporated milk
1/4 teaspoon salt
2 cups (12 ounces) semisweet chocolate chips
2 cups miniature marshmallows
1/2 cup plus 2 tablespoons English toffee bits *or* almond brickle chips, *divided*
1 teaspoon vanilla extract

Line a 9-in. square baking pan with foil. Grease the foil with 1-1/2 teaspoons butter; set aside. In a large heavy saucepan, combine the sugar, milk, salt and remaining butter. Cook and stir over medium heat until sugar is dissolved. Bring to a rapid boil; boil for 5 minutes, stirring constantly.

Remove from the heat; stir in chocolate chips and marshmallows until melted. Fold in 1/2 cup toffee bits and vanilla; mix well. Pour into prepared pan. Sprinkle with remaining toffee bits. Chill until firm. Remove from pan and cut into 1-in. squares. Store in the refrigerator. **Yield:** 2 pounds.

Glazed Almonds

These glossy candy-coated almonds are almost like brittle but much easier to make. With the sweet and salty combination, it's hard to stop munching these delicious nuts. —*Katie Koziolek, Hartland, Minnesota*

4 tablespoons butter, ***divided***
2 cups blanched whole almonds
3/4 cup sugar
1 teaspoon vanilla extract
1/2 teaspoon salt

Line a baking sheet with foil. Grease the foil with 1 tablespoon butter; set aside. In a large heavy skillet, combine the almonds, sugar and remaining butter. Cook and stir over medium heat for 6-8 minutes or until sugar is golden brown.

Remove from the heat; carefully stir in vanilla. Spread onto prepared baking sheet; immediately sprinkle with salt. Cool before breaking into pieces. Store in an airtight container. **Yield:** about 1 pound.

Layered Mint Candies

(Pictured below)

These incredible melt-in-your-mouth candies have the perfect amount of mint nestled between layers of mild chocolate. Even when I make a double batch for everyone to enjoy, the supply never lasts long at Christmas!
—*Rhonda Vauble, Sac City, Iowa*

1 tablespoon butter
1-1/2 pounds white candy coating, ***divided***
1 cup (6 ounces) semisweet chocolate chips
1 teaspoon peppermint extract
4 drops green food coloring, optional
3 tablespoons heavy whipping cream

Line a 13-in. x 9-in. x 2-in. baking pan with foil. Grease foil with the butter; set aside. In a microwave or heavy saucepan, melt 1 pound candy coating and chocolate chips. Spread half into prepared pan; set remaining mixture aside. Melt remaining candy coating; stir in extract and food coloring if desired. Stir in cream until smooth (mixture will be stiff). Spread over first layer; refrigerate for 10 minutes or until firm.

Warm reserved chocolate mixture if necessary; spread over mint layer. Refrigerate for 1 hour or until firm. Lift out of the pan with foil and remove the foil. Cut into 1-in. squares. Store in an airtight container in the refrigerator. **Yield:** about 2 pounds (about 9-1/2 dozen).

Chocolate Peppermint Candies

The cool mint filling in these patties makes them especially delicious. Friends often request that I bring them to parties. —Jeanne Fry, Greensburg, Indiana

3/4 cup sweetened condensed milk
1-1/2 teaspoons peppermint extract
4 to 4-1/2 cups confectioners' sugar
3 cups (18 ounces) semisweet chocolate chips
2 teaspoons shortening

In a bowl, combine milk and extract. Stir in 3-1/2 to 4 cups confectioners' sugar to form a stiff dough. Turn onto a surface sprinkled lightly with confectioners' sugar. Knead in enough remaining sugar to form a dough that is very stiff and no longer sticky. Shape into 1-in. balls. Place on a waxed paper-lined baking sheet. Flatten into 1-1/2-in. circles. Let dry 1 hour.

Turn and let dry 1 hour longer. Melt chocolate chips and shortening in a double boiler or microwave-safe bowl; cool slightly. Dip patties in chocolate mixture. Place on waxed paper to harden. **Yield:** 3 dozen.

Snowballs

(Pictured below)

I've been making these popular treats for over 40 years, much to my family's delight. They look impressive with chocolate and coconut wrapped around a chewy marshmallow center, yet they're surprisingly simple to assemble. —Muriel White, Brampton, Ontario

1/2 cup butter
1 can (14 ounces) sweetened condensed milk
3 tablespoons baking cocoa
1 teaspoon vanilla extract
2 cups graham cracker crumbs (about 32 squares)
3-1/2 cups flaked coconut, *divided*
32 to 36 large marshmallows

Line a baking sheet with waxed paper; set aside. In a saucepan, combine the butter, milk, cocoa and vanilla. Cook and stir over medium heat until butter is melted and mixture is smooth. Remove from the heat; stir in cracker crumbs and 1-1/2 cups coconut. Let stand until cool enough to handle.

Using moistened hands, wrap about 1 tablespoon of mixture around each marshmallow (dip hands in water often to prevent sticking). Roll in remaining coconut; place on prepared baking sheet. Cover and freeze until firm. Store in an airtight container in the refrigerator or freezer. May be frozen for up to 2 months. **Yield:** about 3 dozen.

Pecan Divinity

The table at our Sunday school Christmas party has a spot reserved for my divinity. —Carolyn Weber, Vicksburg, Mississippi

2 cups sugar
1 cup water
1 jar (7 ounces) marshmallow creme
1 teaspoon vanilla extract
1-1/2 cups chopped pecans

In a large heavy saucepan, combine sugar and water. Cook over medium heat, without stirring, until a candy thermometer reads 250° (hard-ball stage). Remove from the heat; stir in marshmallow creme, vanilla and pecans.

Continue stirring until candy cools and begins to hold its shape when dropped from a spoon. Quickly drop by heaping teaspoonfuls onto waxed paper-lined baking sheets. Store in an airtight container at room temperature. **Yield:** 4 dozen.

Editor's Note: We recommend that you test your candy thermometer before each use by bringing water to a boil; the temperature should read 212°. Adjust your recipe temperature up or down based on your test.

Popcorn Almond Brittle

With popcorn, almonds and candied cherries tossed together in a sweet crisp coating, this is a festive favorite.
—Ruth Peterson, Jenison, Michigan

6 cups popped popcorn
1 cup slivered almonds
1/2 cup *each* red and green candied cherries, chopped
1-1/2 cups sugar
1/2 cup corn syrup
1/2 cup water
1/2 teaspoon salt
2 tablespoons butter
1 teaspoon vanilla extract

In a greased 13-in. x 9-in. x 2-in. baking pan, combine popcorn, almonds and cherries. Bake at 350° for 10 minutes. Turn oven off; keep mixture warm in oven.

Meanwhile, in a large heavy saucepan, combine the sugar, corn syrup, water and salt; cook and stir over low heat until sugar is dissolved. Cook over medium heat, without stirring, until a candy thermometer reads 305°-310° (hard-crack stage).

Remove from heat; stir in butter and vanilla. Immediately pour over popcorn mixture; toss gently. Spread onto a greased baking sheet. Cool; break into small pieces. **Yield:** about 1-1/2 pounds.

Editor's Note: We recommend that you test your candy thermometer before each use by bringing water to a boil; the temperature should read 212°. Adjust your recipe temperature up or down based on your test.

Chocolate-Covered Cherries

(Pictured above)

Each year, I have to plan on producing even more of these simple-to-make candies. They're the ones my husband likes best, and they're the first to disappear.
—Lori O'Brien, Milbank, South Dakota

1/2 cup butter, softened
2 cups marshmallow creme
Pinch salt
1 teaspoon almond extract
4 cups confectioners' sugar
1 jar (16 ounces) maraschino cherries, well drained
2 cups (12 ounces) semisweet chocolate chips
2 tablespoons shortening

In a mixing bowl, cream butter. Add marshmallow creme, salt, extract and sugar; mix well. Knead into a large ball; chill for 1 hour. Roll into 1-in. balls and flatten into 2-in. circles. Wrap circles around cherries and carefully shape into balls. Place on a waxed paper-lined baking sheet. Cover loosely; refrigerate for 4 hours or overnight.

Melt chocolate chips and shortening in a double boiler or microwave-safe bowl. Dip cherries into chocolate; place on waxed paper to harden. Refrigerate in a covered container 1-2 weeks before serving. **Yield:** about 4-1/2 dozen.

Chocolate Toffee Crunchies

(Pictured above)

From the buttery crust to the golden toffee, melted chocolate and chopped pecans, these bars are filled with Noel flavor. —*Joni Crans, Woodhull, New York*

2 cups vanilla wafer crumbs
1/4 cup packed brown sugar
1/2 cup butter, melted
TOPPING:
1/2 cup butter
1/2 cup packed brown sugar
1 cup (6 ounces) semisweet chocolate chips
1/2 cup finely chopped pecans

Combine crumbs, brown sugar and butter. Press into an ungreased 13-in. x 9-in. x 2-in. baking pan. Bake at 350° for 8-10 minutes or until lightly browned. In a saucepan, bring butter and brown sugar to a boil over medium heat; boil and stir for 1 minute. Pour evenly over crust.

Bake at 350° for 10 minutes. Remove from oven; let stand for 2 minutes. Sprinkle with chocolate chips; let stand until chocolate is melted. Spread evenly over top; sprinkle with pecans. Cool completely before cutting. **Yield:** 4 dozen.

Cinnamon Walnuts

Sampling just one of these taste-bud tempters almost always leads to another. That's why I package a big batch in gift tins for happy holiday snackers.
—*Betty Rogers, Walnut Creek, California*

1 cup sugar
1/3 cup evaporated milk
1 teaspoon ground cinnamon
1/4 teaspoon salt
1/4 teaspoon vanilla extract
3 cups walnut halves

In a heavy saucepan, combine the sugar, milk, cinnamon and salt. Cook over medium heat, without stirring, until a candy thermometer reads 238° (soft-ball stage). Remove from the heat; stir in vanilla and walnuts. Spread onto waxed paper to harden. Break into pieces. Store in an airtight container at room temperature. **Yield:** about 1 pound.

Editor's Note: We recommend that you test your candy thermometer before each use by bringing water to a boil; the temperature should read 212°. Adjust your recipe temperature up or down based on your test.

Buttermilk Pralines

Years ago, I received this candy recipe from a dear friend in Texas. The creamy texture and sumptuous sweetness has earned me rave reviews each time I've made it.
—*Dorothy Purdy, Fontanelle, Iowa*

2 cups sugar
1 cup buttermilk
1 teaspoon baking soda
1 tablespoon butter
1-1/2 cups pecan halves
1 teaspoon vanilla extract

In a heavy 3-qt. saucepan, combine sugar, buttermilk and baking soda. Cook and stir over medium heat until a candy thermometer reads 210°. Stir in butter and pecans; cook until thermometer reads 230°.

Remove from the heat; add vanilla. Beat with a wooden spoon until mixture loses its gloss and begins to set, about 8 minutes. Quickly drop by teaspoonfuls onto foil-lined baking sheets. Cool. **Yield:** 1-1/2 pounds.

Editor's Note: We recommend that you test your candy thermometer before each use by bringing wa-

ter to a boil; the temperature should read 212°. Adjust your recipe temperature up or down based on your test.

Chewy Walnut Apricot Candies

A bit old-fashioned, these fruit-and-nut confections are both different and delicious. —*Edie Sword* *Weslaco, Texas*

4 cups apricot nectar *or* apple juice
4-3/4 cups sugar, ***divided***
4 envelopes unflavored gelatin
1 cup cold water
3 cups finely chopped walnuts
1-1/2 teaspoons orange extract
Pinch salt

Line a 13-in. x 9-in. x 2-in. pan with foil. Butter the foil; set aside. In a heavy saucepan, combine apricot nectar and 4 cups of sugar. Bring to a boil over medium heat until a candy thermometer reads 238° (soft-ball stage), stirring occasionally. Remove from heat and set aside. In a bowl, soften gelatin in water; let stand for 1 minute. Stir into apricot mixture until gelatin is dissolved. Stir in walnuts, orange extract and salt. Pour into prepared pan. Cover and let stand at room temperature overnight.

Place remaining sugar in a shallow bowl. Cut candy into 1-in. squares; roll in sugar. Place on baking sheets. Let stand for 1 hour. Roll candies in additional sugar if desired. Store in an airtight container at room temperature. **Yield:** about 8 dozen.

Editor's Note: We recommend that you test your candy thermometer before each use by bringing water to a boil; the temperature should read 212°. Adjust your recipe temperature up or down based on your test.

Pulled Taffy Candy Canes

(Pictured at right)

My grandmother always made these at Christmastime. The soft and chewy canes have a great minty flavor. —*Sheryl O'Danne, Port Townsend, Washington*

2 cups sugar
1/2 cup light corn syrup
1/2 cup water
1/4 teaspoon cream of tartar
3/4 teaspoon peppermint extract
1 teaspoon red food coloring

In a large heavy saucepan over low heat, cook sugar, corn syrup, water and cream of tartar until sugar dissolves, stirring frequently. Increase heat to medium and cook until candy thermometer reads 265° (hard-ball stage), stirring occasionally. Remove from the heat; add extract. Pour half into a buttered 15-in. x 10-in. x 1-in. pan. Add food coloring to remaining mixture; mix well. Pour into another buttered 15-in. x 10-in. x 1-in. pan. Cool 5 minutes or until cool enough to handle.

Butter fingers; quickly pull half of the white or red at a time until firm but pliable (the white portion will have a milky color). When taffy is ready for cutting, pull into a 1/4-in. rope. Cut into 6-in. pieces. Twist red and white pieces together; form into canes. Place on waxed paper-lined baking sheets. Cool. **Yield:** 1 to 1-1/2 dozen.

Editor's Note: We recommend that you test your candy thermometer before each use by bringing water to a boil; the temperature should read 212°. Adjust your recipe temperature up or down based on your test.

Butter Mints

(Pictured below)

These creamy mints are smooth as silk and melt in your mouth! As a wife and mother of three youngsters, I treasure treats like these that come together quickly but taste terrific. —*Bev Schloneger, Dalton, Ohio*

1/2 cup butter, softened
1 package (1 pound) confectioners' sugar
1 tablespoon half-and-half cream *or* milk
1 teaspoon vanilla extract
1/4 teaspoon peppermint extract
Red and green paste *or* liquid food coloring, optional

In a mixing bowl, cream the butter. Gradually add sugar, cream and extracts; beat on medium speed for 3-4 minutes. If desired, divide dough into portions and knead in food coloring.

Form into balls by teaspoonfuls; flatten into patties, or roll between two pieces of waxed paper to 1/8-in. thickness and cut into desired shapes. Cover and refrigerate for several hours or overnight. Store in the refrigerator. **Yield:** about 8 dozen.

Coconut Cashew Brittle

This rich buttery brittle has always been part of our Christmas candy collection. Lots of coconut and cashews ensure it's extra scrumptious.
—*Darlene Markel, Mount Hood, Oregon*

2 cups cashew halves
2 cups flaked coconut
2 cups sugar
1 cup light corn syrup
1/2 cup plus 1 teaspoon water, *divided*
1 cup butter, cubed
2 teaspoons vanilla extract
1-1/2 teaspoons baking soda

Combine cashews and coconut on a 15-in. x 10-in. x 1-in. baking pan. Bake at 350° for 8-10 minutes or until golden brown, stirring occasionally. Butter two baking sheets and warm in a 200° oven.

In a large heavy saucepan, combine sugar, corn syrup and 1/2 cup water. Cook and stir over medium heat until mixture comes to a boil. Add butter; cook and stir until butter is melted. Continue cooking, without stirring, until a candy thermometer reads 300° (hard-crack stage).

Meanwhile, combine the vanilla, baking soda and remaining water. Remove saucepan from the heat; add cashews and coconut. Stir in baking soda mixture. Quickly pour onto prepared baking sheets. Spread with a buttered metal spatula to 1/4-in. thickness. Cool before breaking into pieces. Store in an airtight container. **Yield:** about 3 pounds.

Editor's Note: We recommend that you test your candy thermometer before each use by bringing water to a boil; the temperature should read 212°. Adjust your recipe temperature up or down based on your test.

Nutty Chocolate Nuggets

My family can't get enough of these chewy, chocolaty drop candies. They're so quick and easy to fix that I can whip up several batches, even during the busy holiday season. —*Joann Wolfe*
Toledo, Washington

1/4 cup butter, softened
1/2 cup sugar
1 egg
1-1/2 teaspoons vanilla extract
1-1/2 squares (1-1/2 ounces) unsweetened chocolate, melted and cooled
1/2 cup all-purpose flour
1/4 teaspoon baking powder
1/2 teaspoon salt
2 cups chopped walnuts *or* pecans

In a mixing bowl, cream the butter and sugar. Beat in the egg and vanilla. Stir in the melted chocolate. Combine the flour, baking powder and salt; gradually add to the chocolate mixture. Stir in the walnuts.

Drop by rounded teaspoonfuls 2 in. apart onto ungreased baking sheets. Bake at 350° for 10-11 minutes or until the edges are firm. Remove to wire racks to cool completely. **Yield:** about 3-1/2 dozen.

Microwave Mint Fudge

(Pictured above right)

My family loves both chocolate and mint, so I decided to combine those two favorite flavors in this one quick-to-fix fudge recipe. —*Helen Brust*
Union Mills, Indiana

1-1/2 cups sugar
1 can (5 ounces) evaporated milk
1/4 cup butter
5 cups miniature marshmallows
1 package (10 ounces) mint chocolate chips
1 packet (1 ounce) pre-melted baking chocolate
1/2 cup chopped walnuts
1 teaspoon vanilla extract
1/2 teaspoon peppermint extract

In a 2-qt. microwave-safe bowl, combine sugar, milk and butter. Microwave on high until mixture comes to a full rolling boil, stirring after 2-1/2 minutes. Cook 5 minutes more, stirring after 3 minutes.

Add marshmallows; stir until melted. Stir in chips and chocolate until smooth. Stir in nuts and extracts. Immediately pour into a greased 11-in. x 7-in. x 2-in. pan. Chill until firm. Cut into squares. Store in the refrigerator. **Yield:** 2-1/4 pounds.

Editor's Note: This recipe was tested using a 700-watt microwave.

Coconut Apricot Balls

These zesty confections are filled with fresh fruity flavor. They are a nice change from the usual chocolate candy and make a nice addition to any candy tray.
—*Geraldine Seney, Grand Rapids, Michigan*

2 cups dried apricots
1 cup flaked coconut
1 tablespoon grated lemon peel
1 tablespoon grated orange peel
1/4 cup sugar, *divided*
1 to 2 teaspoons orange juice, optional

In a food processor, combine the apricots, coconut, lemon peel and orange peel. Cover and process for 1-2 minutes or until blended.

Sprinkle work surface with 1 tablespoon of sugar. Knead apricot mixture until smooth, about 15-20 times. Add orange juice if necessary to moisten mixture. Shape into 1-in. balls and roll in remaining sugar. Store in an airtight container. **Yield:** about 4 dozen.

Walnut Caramel Treats

(Pictured above)

Better than visions of sugarplums, these triple-decker treats feature creamy caramel and nuts sandwiched between milk chocolate layers—a candy lover's dream come true! —Machelle Wall, Rosamond, California

2 teaspoons plus 1/3 cup butter, ***divided***
2 packages (11-1/2 ounces ***each*****) milk chocolate chips,** ***divided***
4 tablespoons shortening, ***divided***
2 packages (14 ounces ***each*****) caramels***
1/4 cup water
3 cups chopped walnuts

Line an ungreased 9-in. square pan with foil and grease the foil with 2 teaspoons butter; set aside. In a microwave or heavy saucepan, melt one package of chips and 2 tablespoons shortening; stir until smooth. Pour into prepared pan. Refrigerate for 20 minutes.

Meanwhile, in a heavy saucepan over medium-low heat, combine the caramels, water and remaining butter. Cook and stir until caramels are melted and mixture is smooth. Stir in walnuts. Pour over chocolate layer. Refrigerate for 45 minutes.

In a microwave or heavy saucepan, melt remaining chips and shortening. Spread over caramel layer. Cover and refrigerate for at least 2 hours or until firm. Using foil, lift candy out of pan. Discard foil; cut candy into squares. Store in the refrigerator. **Yield:** about 4 pounds.

***Editor's Note:** This recipe was tested with Hershey caramels.

Coconut Surprise Candy

What's the secret ingredient in these dipped balls? Mashed potatoes! The spuds create the creamy texture, while coconut and chocolate chips figure big in the flavor. —Irene Smith, Lidgerwood, North Dakota

2-1/2 cups flaked coconut
2-1/2 cups confectioners' sugar
1/3 cup mashed potatoes (prepared without milk and butter)
1 cup (6 ounces) semisweet chocolate chips
1 tablespoon shortening
Chopped walnuts, optional

In a large bowl, combine coconut, sugar and mashed potatoes; mix well. Roll into 1-in. balls; place on waxed paper-lined baking sheets. In a microwave or double boiler, melt chocolate chips and shortening; stir until smooth. Dip the balls into chocolate and then walnuts if desired. Return to waxed paper until chocolate is set. **Yield:** about 4 dozen.

Penuche

My mom used to make this brown sugar fudge every year during the holidays, both for our family and to give as gifts. It has such wonderful old-fashioned flavor. —Rosemarie Anderson, Great Valley, New York

2 cups packed brown sugar
1 cup sugar
1 cup half-and-half cream

2 tablespoons light corn syrup
1 teaspoon lemon juice
Pinch salt
2 tablespoons butter
1 teaspoon vanilla extract
1/2 cup chopped pecans

In a large heavy saucepan, combine sugars, cream, corn syrup, lemon juice and salt. Bring to a boil over medium heat, stirring occasionally. Cook, without stirring, until a candy thermometer reads 238° (soft-ball stage). Hold at soft-ball stage for 5-6 minutes. Remove from the heat. Add butter; do not stir.

Cool to 110°. Stir in vanilla; beat vigorously by hand until mixture is very thick and slightly lighter in color, about 20 minutes. Quickly stir in pecans, then pour into a greased 8-in. square pan. Cool. Cut into 1-in. squares. **Yield:** 1-3/4 pounds.

Editor's Note: We recommend that you test your candy thermometer before each use by bringing water to a boil; the temperature should read 212°. Adjust your recipe temperature up or down based on your test.

Peppermint Hard Candy

This easy-to-make clear hard candy has a mint flavor from the combination of peppermint and vanilla extracts. Plus, the eye-catching sweets won't stick to your teeth. —Lois Ostenson, Aneta, North Dakota

1 tablespoon butter
2 cups sugar
1 cup light corn syrup
1 to 1-1/2 teaspoons peppermint extract
1 teaspoon vanilla extract
6 to 8 drops green food coloring, optional

Line a 13-in. x 9-in. x 2-in. baking pan with foil. Grease the foil with the butter; set aside. In a large heavy saucepan, combine sugar and corn syrup. Bring to a boil over medium heat, stirring occasionally. Cover and cook for 3 minutes to dissolve sugar crystals. Uncover; cook over medium-high heat, without stirring, until a candy thermometer reads 300° (hard-crack stage).

Remove from the heat; stir in extracts and food coloring. Pour into prepared pan. Cool; break into pieces. Store in airtight containers. **Yield:** about 1-1/4 pounds.

Editor's Note: We recommend that you test your candy thermometer before each use by bringing water to a boil; the temperature should read 212°. Adjust your recipe temperature up or down based on your test.

Peanut Candy Popcorn Balls

(Pictured below)

Kids love these colorful novelties, made from popcorn, nuts, M&M's and marshmallows, so they make great stocking stuffers. —Alida Jaeger, Ixonia, Wisconsin

4 quarts popped popcorn
1-1/2 cups salted peanuts
1-1/2 cups chopped pecans
1 package (16 ounces) green and red milk chocolate M&M's
1/2 cup butter
1/2 cup vegetable oil
1 package (16 ounces) miniature marshmallows

In a large bowl, combine the first four ingredients; mix well and set aside. In a large saucepan, combine the butter, oil and marshmallows; cook and stir until smooth. Pour over popcorn mixture; mix well.

When cool enough to handle, shape into popcorn balls. Let stand at room temperature until firm before wrapping in plastic wrap or stacking. **Yield:** about 20 popcorn balls.

Dandy Caramel Candies

(Pictured below)

I've made these morsels almost every Christmas for over 40 years. Everyone enjoys the chewy treats.
—Marlene Pierce, Welch, Texas

1 cup sugar
1 cup packed brown sugar
1 cup dark corn syrup
1 cup butter
2 cups heavy whipping cream
3-3/4 cups chopped pecans (about 1 pound)
1 teaspoon vanilla extract
Dark *or* milk chocolate candy coating, melted

In a heavy saucepan, combine sugars, corn syrup, butter and cream. Bring to a boil over medium-high heat, stirring constantly. Cook over medium heat until a candy thermometer reads 248° (firm-ball stage). Remove from the heat; stir in pecans and vanilla.

Quickly spread into a buttered 13-in. x 9-in. x 2-in. baking pan. Cool. Cut into 1-in. squares. Place squares on waxed paper-lined baking sheets; chill thoroughly. Dip each candy into melted candy coating. Return to refrigerator to harden. **Yield:** about 8 dozen.

Editor's Note: We recommend that you test your candy thermometer before each use by bringing water to a boil; the temperature should read 212°. Adjust your recipe temperature up or down based on your test.

Dipped Peanut Butter Logs

Nibbling on my nutty confections has long been a Christmas tradition. Even after our seven children moved away, they'd still ask me to send batches to them each December.
—Paddy Schwemlein
Sandwich, Illinois

1 cup butter, melted
1/2 cup chunky peanut butter
3-3/4 cups confectioners' sugar
3-3/4 cups (10 ounces) flaked coconut
1 cup chopped pecans
1/2 cup graham cracker crumbs (about 8 squares)
2 teaspoons vanilla extract
2 cups (12 ounces) semisweet chocolate chips
2 tablespoons shortening

In a mixing bowl, combine the first seven ingredients; mix well. Chill for 1 hour or until firm enough to shape. Shape into 2-in. logs; place on a waxed paper-lined baking sheet.

In a microwave or double boiler, melt chocolate chips and shortening. Dip one end of each log into chocolate or drizzle chocolate over logs. Return to waxed paper-lined sheet; chill until chocolate is set. **Yield:** about 4 dozen.

Homemade Marshmallows

(Pictured above right)

My husband Dale's grandmother fixed these fluffy marshmallows only for special occasions. Since she had no electric mixer, beating the ingredients by hand for 30 minutes was a labor of love. Now, Dale makes them. They're delicious!
—Nancy Shields, Hillsdale, Michigan

2 cups cold water, *divided*
4 envelopes unflavored gelatin
4 cups sugar
1/8 teaspoon salt
2 teaspoons vanilla extract
Confectioners' sugar
Toasted flaked coconut *or* ground pecans, optional

In a large mixing bowl, combine 3/4 cup of water and gelatin; set aside. In a large heavy

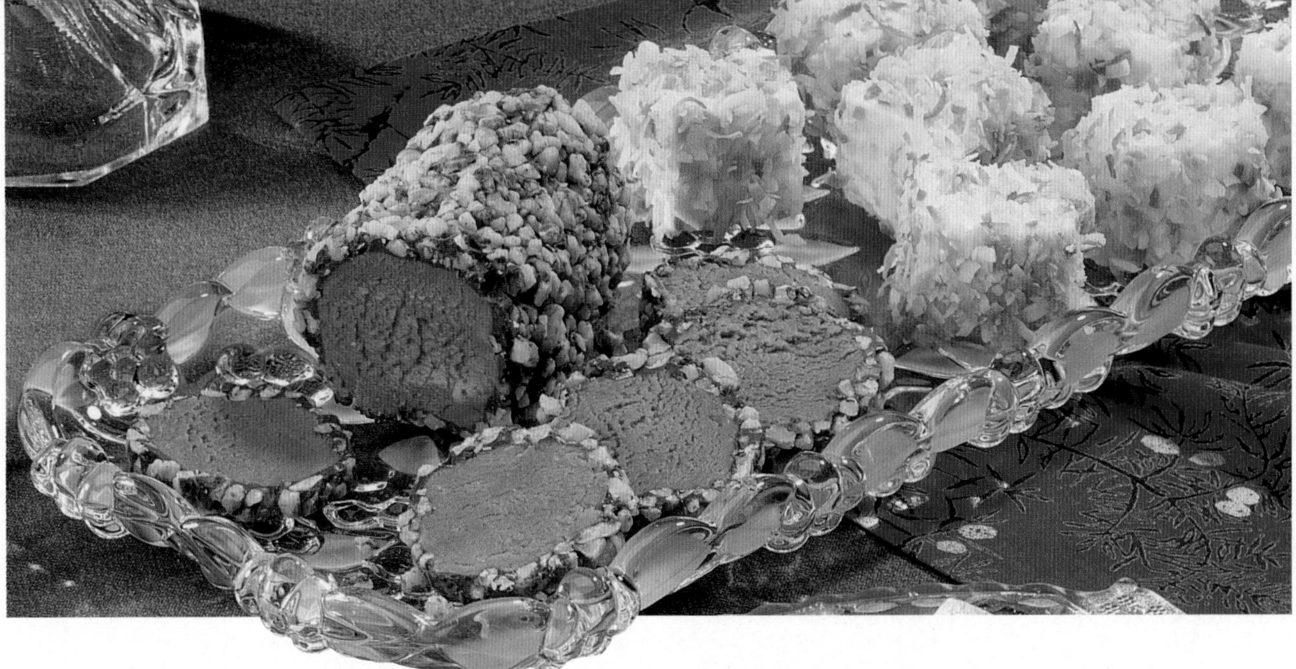

saucepan over medium heat, combine sugar, salt and remaining water. Bring to a boil, stirring occasionally. Cover and continue cooking for 3 minutes to dissolve any sugar crystals. Uncover and cook on medium-high heat, without stirring, until a candy thermometer reads 270° (soft-crack stage).

Remove from the heat and gradually add to gelatin. Beat on low speed for 3 minutes. Add vanilla; beat on medium for 10 minutes. Spread mixture into a 13-in. x 9-in. x 2-in. pan sprinkled with confectioners' sugar. Cover and cool at room temperature for 6 hours or overnight. Cut into 1-in. squares; roll in coconut or nuts if desired. Store in airtight containers in a cool dry place. **Yield:** about 8 dozen.

Editor's Note: We recommend that you test your candy thermometer before each use by bringing water to a boil; the temperature should read 212°. Adjust your recipe temperature up or down based on your test.

Chocolate Nut Fudge Rolls

(Pictured above)

The recipe for these rich chocolaty nut rolls comes from a handwritten cookbook full of memorable holiday treats. My mother compiled it for me the last Christmas I lived at home.—Connie Korbel, Lakeport, California

2 tablespoons butter
1 square (1 ounce) unsweetened chocolate
3 cups sugar
1 cup milk
1/4 cup honey
1/8 teaspoon salt
1 teaspoon vinegar
1 teaspoon vanilla extract
2 cups (12 ounces) semisweet chocolate chips
1 tablespoon shortening
3 cups chopped walnuts

In a large heavy saucepan, melt butter and chocolate over low heat. Add sugar, milk, honey and salt. Bring to a boil over medium heat, stirring occasionally. Cover and continue to boil for 2 minutes. Uncover and cook, without stirring, until a candy thermometer reads 240° (soft-ball stage). Remove from the heat; stir in vinegar. Let cool to 110°. Add vanilla; beat vigorously by hand until mixture thickens and loses its gloss, about 8-10 minutes.

Turn onto a buttered baking sheet. Let stand until cool enough to handle. Knead for 2-3 minutes. Shape into 4-in. x 1-1/2-in. rolls. Place on waxed paper-lined baking sheets; chill for 3-4 hours.

Melt chocolate chips and shortening in a double boiler or microwave-safe bowl. Dip rolls in chocolate; roll in nuts. Place on waxed paper-lined baking sheets and chill until firm. Cut into 1/4-in. slices. **Yield:** about 2-1/4 pounds.

Editor's Note: We recommend that you test your candy thermometer before each use by bringing water to a boil; the temperature should read 212°. Adjust your recipe temperature up or down based on your test.

Deluxe Caramel Corn

(Pictured above)

A batch of this colorful, crunchy snack mix is perfect for gift-giving or serving at a holiday party.
—Lisa Claas, Watertown, Wisconsin

4 quarts plain popped popcorn
5 cups mini pretzel twists
2 cups packed brown sugar
1 cup butter
1/2 cup dark corn syrup
1/2 teaspoon salt
1/2 teaspoon baking soda
1 cup salted peanuts
2 cups non-chocolate candy (gumdrops, Skittles, etc.)

Place popcorn and pretzels in a large bowl; set aside. In a large heavy saucepan, combine sugar, butter, corn syrup and salt; cook over medium heat, stirring occasionally, until mixture comes to a rolling boil. Cook and stir until candy thermometer reads 238° (soft-ball stage). Remove from the heat; stir in baking soda. Quickly pour over popcorn and mix thoroughly; stir in peanuts.

Turn into two greased 13-in. x 9-in. x 2-in. baking pans. Bake at 200° for 20 minutes; stir. Bake 25 minutes more. Remove from the oven; add the candy and mix well. Remove from pans and place on waxed paper to cool. Break into clusters. Store in airtight containers or plastic bags. **Yield:** 6-1/2 quarts.

Editor's Note: We recommend that you test your candy thermometer before each use by bringing water to a boil; the temperature should read 212°. Adjust your recipe temperature up or down based on your test.

Caramel Marshmallow Buttons

Kids of all ages dive into these sweet, fluffy treats. The chewy marshmallow, gooey caramel and crisp coating set off an appetizing explosion of textures.
—Mrs. Terry Dorale, Cody, Wyoming

50 to 54 large marshmallows
1 package (14 ounces) caramels*
1 can (14 ounces) sweetened condensed milk
1 cup butter
5 to 6 cups crisp rice cereal

Place a toothpick in each marshmallow. Place on waxed paper-lined baking sheets. Freeze until firm, 1 hour. In a heavy saucepan over medium-low heat, combine the caramels, milk and butter. Cook and stir until caramels are melted and mixture is smooth.

Dip marshmallows in caramel mixture; roll in cereal. Freeze until firm, at least 1 hour. Remove from the freezer 45 minutes before serving; discard toothpicks. **Yield:** 50-54 pieces.

***Editor's Note:** This recipe was tested with Hershey caramels.

Chocolate Crunch Patties

This candy's so fast and easy to make that I turn out hundreds of pieces each Christmas. People are always

surprised to learn that one of the ingredients is potato chips! —*Nancy Currie, Schaller, Iowa*

2 cups (12 ounces) butterscotch chips
1 cup (6 ounces) milk chocolate chips
1-1/2 cups dry roasted peanuts
1 cup crushed thick ripple-cut potato chips

In a medium microwave-safe bowl, combine butterscotch and chocolate chips. Microwave at 50% power for 2-4 minutes or until softened, stirring after each minute. Stir until smooth. Add peanuts and potato chips; mix well. Drop by teaspoonfuls onto waxed paper-lined baking sheets. Allow to harden. **Yield:** about 4 dozen.

Editor's Note: This recipe was tested using a 700-watt microwave.

Festive Popcorn Bars

For a popcorn ball taste but with less fuss, try these bars. Adding peanut butter and M&M's makes them fun. They're a hit with all ages. —*Ella Scheller, Odessa, Washington*

4 cups popped popcorn
3 cups puffed rice cereal
2 cups peanut M&M's
1 cup light corn syrup
1 cup sugar
1/4 cup butter
3/4 cup peanut butter

In a large greased bowl, combine the popcorn, cereal and M&M's; set aside. In a heavy saucepan, combine the corn syrup, sugar and butter. Cook and stir over low heat until sugar is dissolved. Add peanut butter; stir until blended.

Pour over popcorn mixture; toss gently to coat. Spread into a greased 15-in. x 10-in. x 1-in. baking pan. Cool before cutting. **Yield:** about 3 dozen.

Cinnamon Hard Candy

(Pictured at right)

My Amish aunt made dozens of these spicy red squares for holiday gatherings when I was a tot. I'd always look for them glowing among the other candies she'd carry in on a pretty tray! —*Mary Ellen Geigley, Willcox, Arizona*

2 cups sugar
1 cup water
1/2 cup light corn syrup
1/4 to 1/2 teaspoon cinnamon oil
1/2 teaspoon red food coloring

In a large heavy saucepan, combine sugar, water and corn syrup. Bring to a boil over medium heat, stirring occasionally. Cover and cook for 3 minutes. Uncover and cook over medium-high heat, without stirring, until a candy thermometer reads 310° (hard-crack stage).

Remove from heat; stir in cinnamon oil and food coloring, keeping face away from mixture as the odor will be very strong. Immediately pour onto a greased baking sheet. Quickly spread into a 13-in. x 9-in. rectangle.

Using a sharp knife, score into 1-in. squares. Recut rectangle along scored lines until candy is cut into squares. Let stand at room temperature until dry. Separate into squares, using a knife if necessary. **Yield:** 1 pound.

Editor's Note: We recommend that you test your candy thermometer before each use by bringing water to a boil; the temperature should read 212°. Adjust your recipe temperature up or down based on your test.

Christmas Eve Mice

(Pictured below)

Assembling these merry mice is so much fun that the kids will definitely want to help. My daughter gave me the recipe, along with a warning...your guests just might think these treats are too cute to eat!
—Margene Pons, West Valley City, Utah

24 double-stuffed cream-filled chocolate sandwich cookies
1 cup (6 ounces) semisweet chocolate chips
2 teaspoons shortening
24 red maraschino cherries with stems, well drained
24 milk chocolate kisses
48 sliced almonds
1 small tube green decorative icing gel
1 small tube red decorative icing gel

Carefully twist cookies apart; set aside the halves with cream filling. Save plain halves for another use. In a microwave or heavy saucepan, melt chocolate chips and shortening; stir until smooth. Holding each cherry by the stem, dip in melted chocolate, then press onto the bottom of a chocolate kiss. Place on the cream filling of cookie, with cherry stem extending beyond cookie edge.

For ears, place slivered almonds between the cherry and kiss. Refrigerate until set. With green gel, pipe holly leaves on the cream. With red gel, pipe holly berries between leaves and pipe eyes on each chocolate kiss. Store in an airtight container at room temperature. **Yield:** 2 dozen.

Licorice Caramel Candy

These delicious treats are a fun cross between caramels and licorice. I always get compliments on them, especially from those who enjoy black licorice.
—Paula Fischer, Rapid City, South Dakota

1-1/2 teaspoons butter
2 cups sugar
3 cups heavy whipping cream, *divided*
1-1/3 cups light corn syrup
2 teaspoons anise extract
1/4 to 1/2 teaspoon red *or* black paste food coloring

Line an 8-in. square pan with foil. Grease the foil with the butter; set aside. In a heavy Dutch oven, combine the sugar, 1-1/2 cups cream and corn syrup. Bring to a boil over medium heat, stirring constantly. Cook and stir until a candy thermometer reads 234° (soft-ball stage). Gradually add remaining cream; return to a boil, stirring constantly, until a candy thermometer reads 248° (firm-ball stage).

Remove from heat; stir in extract and food coloring if desired (keep face away from mixture as odor is strong). Pour into prepared pan (do not scrape pan). Cool completely before cutting. Store in an airtight container in refrigerator. **Yield:** about 4 dozen.

Editor's Note: We recommend that you test your candy thermometer before each use by bringing water to a boil; the temperature should read 212°. Adjust your recipe temperature up or down based on your test.

Chocolate Nut Candies

I've been making these yummy candies for many years. With their three rich gooey layers, a little goes a long way. —*Mary Parker, Copperas Cove, Texas*

3 cups (18 ounces) semisweet chocolate chips
2 cups creamy peanut butter
1 cup butter
1/2 cup evaporated milk
1/4 cup instant vanilla pudding mix
1 teaspoon vanilla extract
2 pounds confectioners' sugar
3 cups salted peanuts

In a heavy saucepan over low heat, melt chocolate chips and peanut butter, stirring frequently. Pour half into a greased 15-in. x 10-in. x 1-in. baking pan; chill. Set remaining chocolate mixture aside.

In another saucepan, bring butter, milk and pudding mix to a boil; boil for 1 minute, stirring constantly. Remove from heat; pour into a large bowl; add vanilla. Gradually stir in sugar. Spread over chocolate layer in baking pan; chill. Add peanuts to reserved chocolate mixture; spread over filling. Chill. Cut into 1-in. x 1/2-in. pieces. **Yield:** 25 dozen.

Butterscotch Coconut Squares

My former boss used to prepare these sweet morsels. I was thrilled to discover they're not hard to make. —*Eve Campbell, Crysler, Ontario*

1-1/2 teaspoons plus 1/2 cup butter, *divided*
1 package (11 ounces) butterscotch chips
1 cup peanut butter
1 cup miniature marshmallows
1/2 cup flaked coconut

Grease a 9-in. square pan with 1-1/2 teaspoons butter; set aside. In a microwave or heavy saucepan, melt the butterscotch chips, peanut butter and remaining butter until smooth. Cool for 20 minutes. Stir in marshmallows just until combined (do not melt marshmallows). Pour into prepared pan; sprinkle with coconut. Refrigerate, uncovered, for 2 hours or until firm. Cut into 1-in. pieces. Store in an airtight container. **Yield:** about 6-1/2 dozen.

Marbled Almond Roca

(Pictured above)

My easy recipe is an old favorite that we keep in steady use from mid-November until the New Year. —*Niki-Jeanne Rooke, Pollockville, Alberta*

1/2 cup slivered almonds
1 cup butter
1 cup sugar
3 tablespoons boiling water
2 tablespoons light corn syrup
1/2 cup semisweet chocolate chips
1/2 cup vanilla *or* white chips

Sprinkle almonds on a greased 15-in. x 10-in. x 1-in. baking pan. Bake at 300° for 15 minutes or until toasted and golden; remove from oven and set aside.

In a saucepan over low heat, cook butter and sugar for 5 minutes. Add water and corn syrup. Bring to a boil over medium heat; cook, stirring occasionally, until a candy thermometer reads 300° (hard-crack stage). Quickly pour over almonds. Sprinkle chips on top; let stand for 1-2 minutes or until melted. Spread and swirl chocolate over candy. Cool completely; break into pieces. **Yield:** 1-1/2 pounds.

Editor's Note: We recommend that you test your candy thermometer before each use by bringing water to a boil; the temperature should read 212°. Adjust your recipe temperature up or down based on your test.

Holiday Wreath

(Pictured above)

My mom gave me this recipe. I look forward to crafting and sharing the wreath every Christmas. It's crisp and chewy, and a real eye-catcher on the table.
—Denise Glisson, Kingshill, U.S. Virgin Islands

30 large marshmallows
1/2 cup butter
1 tablespoon vanilla extract
20 to 22 drops green food coloring
3-1/2 cups cornflakes
Red-hot candies
Red shoestring licorice and one red Dot candy, optional

In a heavy saucepan, combine marshmallows, butter, vanilla and food coloring; cook and stir over low heat until smooth. Remove from the heat; add cornflakes and mix well. Drop by spoonfuls onto greased foil, forming a 9-in. wreath. Decorate with red-hots. If desired, form a bow with licorice and place on wreath; add Dot on top of bow. **Yield:** 10-12 servings.

Nut 'n' Corn Clusters

I can tell this recipe has served me faithfully for a long time by the old dog-eared recipe card. These crisp caramel corn clusters are a holiday treat my family enjoys munching.
—Maryeileen Jahnke
South Milwaukee, Wisconsin

5 quarts popped popcorn
2 cups mixed nuts
1-1/2 teaspoons butter
1 cup sugar
1/2 cup honey
1/2 cup corn syrup
1 cup peanut butter
1 teaspoon vanilla extract
1 teaspoon molasses

Line baking sheets with waxed paper; set aside. Combine popcorn and nuts in a large roasting pan; place in a 250° oven. Meanwhile, grease the sides of a heavy saucepan with the butter. Combine the sugar, honey and corn syrup in saucepan. Bring to a

boil over medium heat, stirring constantly. Boil for 2 minutes without stirring.

Remove from the heat; stir in peanut butter, vanilla and molasses. Pour over warm popcorn mixture and stir to coat. Working quickly, use buttered hands to form mixture into 1-1/2-in. clusters. Place on prepared baking sheets to dry. Store in an airtight container at room temperature. **Yield:** about 12 dozen.

Editor's Note: If mixture becomes too firm to form into clusters, rewarm in a 250° oven for a few minutes.

Chewy Chocolate Logs

When I made these for our church Christmas bazaar, folks would snap them up within minutes. They're nice and soft like chocolate caramels but not sticky.
—Pat Walter, Pine Island, Minnesota

2 squares (1 ounce *each*) unsweetened baking chocolate
2 tablespoons butter
1/2 cup light corn syrup
1 teaspoon vanilla extract
3 cups confectioners' sugar, *divided*
3/4 cup instant nonfat dry milk powder

In a saucepan over low heat, melt chocolate and butter. Transfer to a mixing bowl; add corn syrup, vanilla, 2 cups sugar and milk powder. Mix well.

Place remaining sugar on a clean surface; place dough on the surface and knead sugar into the dough until all of it is absorbed. Shape teaspoonfuls into 2-in. logs; wrap in waxed paper and twist ends. Refrigerate until firm. **Yield:** about 6 dozen.

Sugary Orange Peel

(Pictured at right)

These sugar-coated citrus strips attract lots of compliments whenever I set them out at parties.
—Alice Schmidlin, Banks, Oregon

4 medium navel oranges
2 to 3 cups sugar, *divided*
1 cup water
1/2 teaspoon salt
1/2 cup semisweet chocolate chips, optional
2 teaspoons shortening, optional

With a knife, score the peel from each orange into quarters. With fingers, remove peel with white pith attached. Place peel in a saucepan; cover with water. Bring to a boil. Boil, uncovered, for 30 minutes. Drain and repeat twice.

Meanwhile, in another saucepan, combine 1 cup of sugar, water and salt. Bring to a boil; boil and stir for 2 minutes or until sugar is dissolved. Drain peel and add to syrup. Bring to a boil; reduce heat. Simmer, uncovered, for 50-60 minutes or until syrup is almost all absorbed, stirring occasionally. (Watch carefully to prevent scorching.) Drain any remaining syrup.

Cool orange peel in a single layer on a foil-lined baking sheet for 1 hour. Cut into 1/8-in. to 1/4-in. strips. Sprinkle remaining sugar on an ungreased 15-in. x 10-in. x 1-in. baking pan. Sprinkle the strips over sugar and toss to coat. Let stand for 8 hours or overnight, tossing occasionally.

If desired, melt chocolate chips and shortening. Dip one end of each orange strip into chocolate; let stand on waxed paper until chocolate hardens. Store in an airtight container for up to 3 weeks. **Yield:** 5 cups.

Old-Fashioned Caramels

(Pictured below)

Before I was married, my future father-in-law would fix these creamy caramels at Christmas and send me some. The recipe has been in my husband's family for decades. —*Jan Batman, Oskaloosa, Iowa*

2 cups sugar
1-3/4 cups light corn syrup
1 cup butter, cubed
2 cups half-and-half cream
1 teaspoon vanilla extract
1 cup chopped pecans, optional

Line an 11-in. x 7-in. x 2-in. pan with foil; butter the foil and set aside. In a large heavy saucepan over medium heat, combine sugar, corn syrup and butter. Bring to a boil, stirring constantly; boil gently for 4 minutes without stirring.

Remove from heat; stir in cream. Reduce heat to medium-low and cook until a candy thermometer reads 238° (soft-ball stage), stirring constantly. Remove from heat; stir in vanilla and pecans if desired. Pour into prepared pan; cool. Remove from pan and cut into 1-in. squares. Wrap individually in waxed paper; twist ends. **Yield:** about 6 dozen.

Editor's Note: We recommend that you test your candy thermometer before each use by bringing water to a boil; the temperature should read 212°. Adjust your recipe temperature up or down based on your test.

Hard Candy

Every evening for a week in December, my husband and I mix up several batches of this candy. When we finish, we have all our favorite flavors and a rainbow of colors. —*Virginia Sue Barlow, Farmer City, Illinois*

5 to 6 cups confectioners' sugar
2 cups sugar
3/4 cup light corn syrup
1/2 cup water
1 to 2 teaspoons anise, lemon *or* orange extract
Red, yellow *or* orange liquid food coloring, optional

Fill a 15-in. x 10-in. x 1-in. baking pan with confectioners' sugar to a depth of 1/2 in. Using the handle of a wooden spoon, make a continuous curved-line indentation in the sugar; set pan aside.

In a large heavy saucepan, combine sugar, corn syrup and water. Bring to a boil over medium heat, stirring occasionally. Cover and continue cooking for 3 minutes to dissolve any sugar crystals. Uncover and cook on medium-high heat, without stirring, until a candy thermometer reads 300° (hard-crack stage). Remove from the heat; stir in extract and food coloring if desired (keep face away from mixture because aroma is very strong).

Carefully pour into a glass measuring cup. Working quickly, pour into prepared indentation in pan. Cover candy with confectioners' sugar. When candy is cool enough to handle, cut into pieces with a scissors. Store in a covered container. **Yield:** 3/4 pound.

Editor's Note: We recommend that you test your candy thermometer before each use by bringing water to a boil; the temperature should read 212°. Adjust your recipe temperature up or down based on your test.

Spearmint Crunch

I love getting food ready for the holidays, so I start planning early. This is one of my favorite recipes, and it's so easy to make. Kids can have fun crushing the spearmint candies. —*Rose Randall, Derry, Pennsylvania*

1 pound white candy coating, coarsely chopped
3/4 cup crushed spearmint candy (4 ounces)

In a microwave-safe bowl, melt coating at 70% power for 1 minute; stir. Microwave at additional 30-second intervals, stirring until smooth. Stir in spearmint

candy. Spread onto a waxed paper-lined baking sheet. Chill for 8-10 minutes. Break into small pieces; store in airtight containers. **Yield:** 1-1/4 pounds.

Napoleon Cremes

(Pictured above)

For the annual Christmas open house we host, I set out a buffet with lots of food and candies like these lovely layered treats. They're so creamy, and with a green pistachio layer of pudding peeking out, they're very merry.
—Gloria Jesswein, Niles, Michigan

1 cup butter, softened, ***divided***
1/4 cup sugar
1/4 cup baking cocoa
1 teaspoon vanilla extract
1 egg, lightly beaten
2 cups finely crushed graham cracker crumbs (about 32 squares)
1 cup flaked coconut
3 tablespoons milk
1 package (3.4 ounces) instant pistachio ***or*** **lemon pudding mix**
2 cups confectioners' sugar
TOPPING:
1 cup (6 ounces) semisweet chocolate chips
3 tablespoons butter

In a double boiler, combine 1/2 cup butter, sugar, cocoa and vanilla; cook and stir until butter is melted. Add egg; cook and stir until mixture thickens, about 5 minutes. Stir in crumbs and coconut. Press into a greased 9-in. square baking pan.

In a mixing bowl, cream remaining butter. Add milk, pudding mix and confectioners' sugar; beat until fluffy. Spread over crust. Refrigerate until firm, about 1-1/2 to 2 hours. Melt chocolate chips and butter; cool. Spread over pudding layer. Refrigerate. Cut into bars. **Yield:** 4 dozen.

Truffle Cups

(Pictured above)

When I serve this elegant confection for the holidays, it never fails to draw compliments. Delightfully tempting, the cups are a fun, fluffy variation on traditional truffles.
—Katie Dowler, Birch Tree, Missouri

1 package (11-1/2 ounces) milk chocolate chips
2 tablespoons shortening
1 pound white candy coating, cut into 1/2-inch pieces
1/2 cup heavy whipping cream

In a double boiler or microwave, melt chips and shortening. Stir until smooth; cool for 5 minutes. With a narrow pastry brush, "paint" the chocolate mixture on the inside of 1-in. foil candy cups. Place on a tray and refrigerate until firm, about 45 minutes. Remove about 12 cups at a time from the refrigerator; remove and discard foil cups. Return chocolate cups to refrigerator.

For filling, melt candy coating and cream; stir until smooth. Transfer to a mixing bowl; cover and refrigerate for 30 minutes or until mixture begins to thicken. Beat filling for 1-2 minutes or until light and fluffy. Use a pastry star tube or spoon to fill the chocolate cups. Store in refrigerator. **Yield:** 5 dozen.

ORANGE TAFFY

(Pictured above)

This taffy has a satisfying tangy sweetness. It takes time to wrap all the little candies, but the kids can help.
—Christine Olson, Horse Creek, California

2 cups sugar
2 cups light corn syrup
1 can (6 ounces) frozen orange juice concentrate
1 cup half-and-half cream
1/2 cup butter

In a heavy saucepan, combine first three ingredients. Cook and stir over medium heat until sugar is dissolved. Bring to a boil and cook until a candy thermometer reads 245° (firm-ball stage). Add cream and butter; cook and stir until mixture reaches 245° again. Pour into a greased 15-in. x 10-in. x 1-in. pan; cool. Roll into 1-1/2-in. logs. Wrap individually in foil or waxed paper; twist ends. **Yield:** about 6 dozen.

Editor's Note: We recommend testing your candy thermometer before each use by bringing water to a boil; the thermometer should read 212°. Adjust your recipe temperature up or down based on your test.

TUTTI-FRUTTI

Red and green cherries make these treats look festive. Substitute any fruit in the amount that pleases your palate. *—Florence Munger, Malone, New York*

3 tablespoons butter, melted
1/4 cup evaporated milk
1 teaspoon almond extract
1/4 teaspoon salt
4-1/4 to 4-3/4 cups confectioners' sugar
1/4 cup *each* chopped citron, candied pineapple, and green and red candied cherries
3/4 cup finely chopped almonds

In a large bowl, combine the butter, milk, almond extract and salt. Gradually stir in confectioners' sugar until a stiff dough is formed.

Turn onto a surface lightly dusted with confectioners' sugar. Knead 15-20 times or until mixture forms a smooth ball. Knead in candied fruit. Shape into 1-in. balls, then roll in almonds. Cover and refrigerate for 1 hour. Store in an airtight container in the refrigerator. **Yield:** about 3 dozen.

PEANUT BUTTER COCOA BONBONS

I'm a minister's wife and also have a candy-making business. This yummy pairing of peanut butter and chocolate produced terrific treats for a recent fellowship. Everyone commented on the flavor and quickly emptied my tray. *—Debbie Downs, Steens, Mississippi*

2 packages (3 ounces *each*) cream cheese, softened
4 cups confectioners' sugar
1/3 cup baking cocoa
1 teaspoon vanilla extract
1 cup chopped peanuts
1 package (10 ounces) peanut butter chips
1 tablespoon shortening

In a large mixing bowl, beat cream cheese, confectioners' sugar, cocoa and vanilla until smooth. Stir in peanuts. Cover and refrigerate for 2 hours or until firm. Drop by heaping teaspoonfuls onto a waxed paper-lined baking sheet. Refrigerate, uncovered, for 1 hour. Shape into 1-in. balls; return to baking sheet. Refrigerate, uncovered, for 3 hours or until firm.

In a microwave or heavy saucepan, melt peanut butter chips and shortening; stir until smooth and blended. Dip balls and place on waxed paper-lined baking sheets. Chill until firm. Store in an airtight container in the refrigerator. **Yield:** about 3 dozen.

Coconut Chocolate Creams

My mom gave me the recipe for these tempting truffle-like candies. They make any occasion special for my family. I love to impress dinner guests by setting out a pretty plate of these treats at the end of the meal.
—Kelly-Ann Gibbons
Prince George, British Columbia

2-1/2 cups flaked coconut
1 cup (6 ounces) semisweet chocolate chips
1/2 cup evaporated milk
2-1/2 cups confectioners' sugar
1/3 cup chopped pecans
1/3 cup chopped maraschino cherries

Place coconut in a blender or food processor; cover and process until finely chopped. In a microwave or heavy saucepan, melt chocolate chips and milk. Remove from the heat; stir in confectioners' sugar, 1-1/4 cups coconut, pecans and cherries. Cover and refrigerate for 2 hours or until firm. Set remaining coconut aside.

Shape chocolate mixture into 1-in. balls; roll in reserved coconut. Place on waxed paper-lined baking sheets. Refrigerate for 2 hours or until firm. Store in an airtight container in the refrigerator. **Yield:** about 3 dozen.

Double Chocolate Fudge

Anyone who's fond of chocolate will like this smooth, nutty fudge twice as much. I enjoy making several batches when Christmas rolls around. It doesn't last long at our house during December festivities!
—Florence Hasty, Louisiana, Missouri

1 package (12 ounces) semisweet chocolate chips
1 can (14 ounces) sweetened condensed milk, *divided*
2 teaspoons vanilla extract, *divided*
1 cup chopped walnuts, *divided*
1 package (11-1/2 ounces) milk chocolate chips

Line a 9-in. square pan with foil and butter the foil; set aside. In a heavy saucepan, melt semisweet chocolate chips with 1/2 cup plus 3 tablespoons milk over low heat. Remove from heat; stir in 1 teaspoon vanilla and 1/2 cup walnuts. Spread into prepared pan.

In a saucepan, melt milk chocolate chips with remaining milk. Remove from the heat; stir in remaining vanilla and walnuts. Spread over first layer. Cover and refrigerate until firm. Remove from pan and cut into 1-in. squares. Store at room temperature. **Yield:** 6-1/2 dozen.

Chocolate-Covered Chips

(Pictured below)

Whenever I give these candies as gifts or serve them to guests, they're conversation starters! The savory-sweet combination makes a tempting treat.
—Marcille Meyer, Battle Creek, Nebraska

1 package (24 ounces) white candy coating
1 package (14 ounces) thick ripple-cut potato chips
1 package (24 ounces) milk *or* dark chocolate candy coating

In a double boiler over simmering water, or in a microwave-safe bowl, melt white coating. Dip chips halfway in coating; shake off excess. Place on waxed paper-lined baking sheets to harden. When hardened, melt chocolate coating and dip other half of chips. Allow to harden. **Yield:** about 4 pounds.

Angel Food Candy

(Pictured below)

Dipped in both white and dark candy coating, this two-toned candy really stands out on the goody tray.
—Carrol Holloway, Hindsville, Arkansas

1 cup sugar
1 cup dark corn syrup
1 tablespoon white vinegar
1 tablespoon baking soda
1/2 pound white candy coating
1/2 pound dark chocolate candy coating

In a large heavy saucepan, combine sugar, corn syrup and vinegar. Cook and stir over medium heat until sugar is dissolved. Cook, without stirring, until a candy thermometer reads 290° (soft-crack stage). Remove from the heat; stir in baking soda. Pour into a buttered 13-in. x 9-in. x 2-in. pan. Cool. Break into pieces.

Melt white candy coating; dip the candies halfway, shaking off excess. Place on waxed paper-lined baking sheets to harden. Melt dark chocolate coating; dip uncoated portion of candies. Return to waxed paper to harden. **Yield:** 1-1/2 pounds.

Editor's Note: We recommend that you test your candy thermometer before each use by bringing water to a boil; the temperature should read 212°. Adjust your recipe temperature up or down based on your test.

Chocolate Almond Bars

Loaded with almond flavor, these chewy bars are one of my husband's favorite sweet treats.
—Jackie Hannahs, Fountain, Wisconsin

1-1/2 cups all-purpose flour
2/3 cup sugar
3/4 cup cold butter
1 can (14 ounces) sweetened condensed milk
1-1/2 cups semisweet chocolate chips, *divided*
1 egg, beaten
2 cups chopped almonds, toasted
1/4 teaspoon almond extract
1 teaspoon shortening

In a bowl, combine the flour and sugar; cut in butter until crumbly. Press into a greased 13-in. x 9-in. x 2-in. baking pan. Bake at 350° for 18-20 minutes or until lightly browned. Cool on a wire rack.

In a saucepan, combine the milk and 1 cup chocolate chips. Cook and stir over low heat until chips are melted. Remove from the heat; cool slightly. Stir in egg, almonds and extract. Spread over crust. Bake at 350° for 20-25 minutes or until a toothpick inserted near the center comes out clean. Cool on a wire rack. In a microwave, melt shortening and remaining chips; drizzle over top. Cut into bars. **Yield:** 4 dozen.

Maple Pralines

This recipe rekindles memories of my grandfather and his love for making maple syrup. When I was in college, my mother would send me a package of her pralines during sugaring season. They were so popular with my friends, I barely managed to tuck away a few for myself.
—Mary Beth Cool, Canajoharie, New York

1 cup sugar
2/3 cup milk
1/2 cup maple syrup
2 tablespoons butter
3/4 cup coarsely chopped pecans, toasted

In a heavy 1-qt. saucepan, combine sugar, milk and syrup. Cook and stir over medium heat until mixture boils. Reduce heat to medium-low. Cook, uncovered, until a candy thermometer reads 234° (soft-ball stage), stirring occasionally.

Remove from the heat. Add butter; do not stir. Cool, without stirring, to 160°. Stir in pecans. Beat vigorously with a wooden spoon until mixture just begins

to thicken but is still glossy. Quickly drop by spoonfuls onto waxed paper. Cool. Store in an airtight container. **Yield:** about 1 pound.

Editor's Note: We recommend that you test your candy thermometer before each use by bringing water to a boil; the temperature should read 212°. Adjust your recipe temperature up or down based on your test.

Butterscotch Taffy

It's a good thing that this recipe isn't a lot of fuss—the soft tempting taffy goes so fast I sometimes don't even get to wrap the pieces!
—Teri Lindquist, Wildwood, Illinois

1/2 cup butter
48 large marshmallows
1 tablespoon water
1/2 teaspoon salt
2 cups (12 ounces) butterscotch chips

In a heavy saucepan, combine butter, marshmallows, water and salt; cook and stir over low heat until smooth. Add chips; stir until melted. Pour into a buttered 8-in. square baking pan; cool. Cut into 1-in. squares. Wrap individually in waxed paper; twist ends. **Yield:** about 5 dozen.

Cranberry Gumdrops

(Pictured above right)

This unique treat combines two holiday favorites—the tangy flavor of cranberry and a sweet chewy candy. I've made them for years. They're popular with all ages.
—Elaine Thu, Graettinger, Iowa

2 envelopes unflavored gelatin
1/2 cup cold water
1 can (16 ounces) jellied cranberry sauce
2 cups sugar, ***divided***
3 packages (3 ounces ***each*****) raspberry gelatin**
Additional sugar, optional

In a saucepan, sprinkle unflavored gelatin over water; let stand for 2 minutes to soften. Add cranberry sauce and 1 cup of sugar; cook over low heat until sauce is melted and sugar is dissolved, about 10 minutes. Whisk until smooth. Remove from the heat and add raspberry gelatin; stir until completely dissolved, about 3 minutes. Pour into an 8-in. square baking pan coated with nonstick cooking spray. Cover and let stand at room temperature for 12 hours or overnight (do not refrigerate).

Cut into 1-in. squares; roll in remaining sugar. Place on baking sheets; let stand at room temperature for 3 hours. Turn pieces over and let stand 3 hours longer. Roll in additional sugar if desired. Store in an airtight container at room temperature. **Yield:** about 5 dozen.

Candy Making Tips

Measure and assemble all of the ingredients for a candy recipe before beginning. Do not substitute or alter the basic ingredients.

Use heavy-gauge saucepans that are deep enough to allow candy mixtures to boil freely without boiling over.

For safe stirring when preparing recipes with hot boiling sugar, use wooden spoons with long handles.

Chewy Apple Candies

(Pictured above)

This chewy fruity candy is a refreshing change of pace from traditional chocolates and fudge. It keeps well in the refrigerator if you have any left over!
—Roberta Dillinger, Topeka, Kansas

1-1/4 cups raspberry- ***or*** **cinnamon-flavored applesauce,** ***divided***
2 envelopes unflavored gelatin
2 cups sugar
2 teaspoons vanilla extract
1 cup coarsely chopped walnuts
1/2 cup confectioners' sugar

In a bowl, combine 1/2 cup applesauce and gelatin; set aside to soften. In a 2-qt. saucepan, bring sugar and remaining applesauce to a boil. Add gelatin mixture; return to boiling. Boil for 15 minutes, stirring constantly. Remove from the heat; stir in vanilla and nuts. Pour into a buttered 8-in. square pan. Cover and chill overnight.

Cut into 1-1/2-in. x 1/2-in. pieces; roll in confectioners' sugar. Chill several hours. Store in an airtight container in refrigerator. **Yield:** about 7 dozen.

Old-Time Butter Crunch Candy

Both my children and my grandchildren say the season wouldn't be the same without the big tray of candies and cookies I prepare. This one's a popular part of that collection.
—Mildred Duffy, Bella Vista, Arkansas

1 cup butter
1-1/4 cups sugar
2 tablespoons light corn syrup
2 tablespoons water
2 cups finely chopped toasted almonds
8 milk chocolate candy bars (1.55 ounces ***each*****)**

Line a 13-in. x 9-in. x 2-in. baking pan with foil; set aside. Using part of the butter, grease sides of a large heavy saucepan. Add remaining butter to saucepan; melt over low heat. Add sugar, corn syrup and water. Cook and stir over medium heat until a candy thermometer reads 300° (hard-crack stage). Remove from heat and stir in almonds. Quickly pour into prepared pan, spreading to cover bottom of pan. Cool completely. Carefully invert pan to remove candy in one piece; remove foil.

Melt half of the chocolate in a double boiler or microwave-safe bowl; spread over top of candy. Let cool. Turn candy over and repeat with remaining chocolate; cool. Break into 2-in. pieces. Store in an airtight container. **Yield:** about 2 pounds.

Editor's Note: We recommend that you test your candy thermometer before each use by bringing water to a boil; the temperature should read 212°. Adjust your recipe temperature up or down based on your test.

Double-Decker Fudge

Everyone loves peanut butter and chocolate, so this layered fudge is always a hit with family and friends. I found the recipe about 15 years ago and have been making it for the holidays ever since. *—Jennifer Russell*
Mount Ulla, North Carolina

1 tablespoon plus 1/2 cup butter, ***divided***
4-1/2 cups sugar

1 can (12 ounces) evaporated milk
1 jar (7 ounces) marshmallow creme
2 cups peanut butter chips, *divided*
1/2 cup baking cocoa
1 teaspoon vanilla extract

Line a 9-in. square pan with foil and grease the foil with 1 tablespoon butter and set aside. In a heavy saucepan, combine the sugar, milk, marshmallow creme and 1/4 cup butter. Cook and stir over medium heat until sugar is dissolved. Bring to a rapid boil; boil for 5 minutes, stirring constantly. Remove from the heat.

Pour 3 cups of hot mixture into a bowl; add 1 cup peanut butter chips. Stir until chips are melted and mixture is smooth. Pour into prepared pan. To the remaining hot mixture, add cocoa, vanilla, and remaining chips and butter; stir until chips and butter are melted and mixture is smooth. Pour evenly over peanut butter layer in pan. Cool. Using foil, lift fudge out of pan. Cut into 1-in. squares. Refrigerate in airtight containers. **Yield:** 3-1/2 pounds.

Coconut Peaks

I found this gem on a slip of paper in a cookbook I got at a yard sale. The candies get great flavor from browned butter. I've received many requests for this recipe over the years. —Patricia Shinn, Fruitland Park, Florida

1/4 cup butter
3 cups flaked coconut
2 cups confectioners' sugar
1/4 cup half-and-half cream
1 cup (6 ounces) semisweet chocolate chips
2 teaspoons shortening

Line a baking sheet with waxed paper; set aside. In a saucepan, cook butter over medium-low heat until golden brown, about 5 minutes. Remove from the heat; stir in the coconut, sugar and cream. Drop by rounded teaspoonfuls onto prepared baking sheet. Refrigerate until easy to handle, about 25 minutes.

Roll mixture into balls, then shape each into a cone. Return to baking sheet; refrigerate for 15 minutes. In a microwave or heavy saucepan, melt chocolate chips and shortening. Dip bottoms of cones into chocolate. Return to waxed paper to harden. Store in an airtight container in the refrigerator. **Yield:** about 3 dozen.

Orange-Sugared Pecans

(Pictured below)

*I regularly cook up these candied pecans for Christmas gift-giving and family munching. The citrusy-sweet flavor is different and delicious. —Nancy Johnson
Laverne, Oklahoma*

1-1/2 cups sugar
1/4 cup water
3 tablespoons orange juice concentrate
2 cups pecan halves
1/2 teaspoon grated orange peel

In a heavy saucepan, combine sugar, water and orange juice concentrate. Cook over medium-high heat, without stirring, until a candy thermometer reads 238° (soft-ball stage).

Remove from the heat; stir in pecans and orange peel. Beat with a spoon until mixture thickens and loses its gloss, about 2 minutes. Drop by teaspoonfuls onto waxed paper to harden. Store in an airtight container. **Yield:** 2-1/2 dozen.

Editor's Note: We recommend that you test your candy thermometer before each use by bringing water to a boil; the temperature should read 212°. Adjust your recipe temperature up or down based on your test.

Mint Chocolate Cookie Crunch

(Pictured below)

I usually give a different homemade treat to my nieces and nephews every Christmas. This rich no-bake candy was a hit. With just four ingredients, it's easy enough for kids to make. —*Kathy Kelzer*
St. Louis Park, Minnesota

3 packages (12 ounces *each*) semisweet chocolate chips
1 to 1-1/2 teaspoons peppermint extract
1 package (20 ounces) cream-filled chocolate sandwich cookies, coarsely crushed
4 cups crisp rice cereal

Line baking sheets with waxed paper; set aside. In a microwave or heavy saucepan, melt chocolate chips. Stir in extract. Combine cookies and cereal in a large bowl. Add chocolate mixture and stir to coat. Drop by tablespoonfuls onto prepared baking sheets; cool. Store in airtight containers at room temperature. **Yield:** about 8 dozen.

Marshmallow Fudge

My mom has made this fast-to-fix fudge every year for Christmas for as long as I can remember. Pretty pastel marshmallows add a colorful and fun twist to the scrumptious candy. —*Mary Peltz*
Glen Ullin, North Dakota

1 tablespoon plus 2 cups butter, *divided*
1 package (10-1/2 ounces) pastel miniature marshmallows
1 package (12 ounces) semisweet chocolate chips
1 package (11 ounces) butterscotch chips
1 cup peanut butter

Line a 13-in. x 9-in. x 2-in. pan with foil; grease the foil with 1 tablespoon butter. Place the marshmallows in prepared pan.

In a saucepan over low heat, melt chocolate and butterscotch chips, peanut butter and remaining butter, stirring constantly. Pour over marshmallows. Tap pan lightly on work surface. Refrigerate. Using foil, lift fudge out of pan. Cut into squares. Store in an airtight container in the refrigerator. **Yield:** 5 dozen.

Nutty Citrus Candy

A friend shared the recipe for these refreshing tangy-sweet goodies. Whenever I need a guaranteed crowd-pleaser, I roll them out by the dozens.
—Betty Hostetler, Ocean Park, Washington

1 package (1 pound) confectioners' sugar
1 package (12 ounces) vanilla wafers, crushed
1 can (6 ounces) frozen orange juice concentrate, thawed
1/2 cup butter, melted
1-1/2 to 2 cups ground walnuts

In a bowl, combine the confectioners' sugar, wafer crumbs, orange juice and butter; mix well. Shape into 3/4-in. balls, then roll in walnuts. Cover and refrigerate for at least 24 hours before serving. Store in an airtight container in the refrigerator. **Yield:** 8 dozen.

Orange Cappuccino Creams

(Pictured at right)

As holiday gifts, these mocha-orange morsels are sure to be a sweet success. The delighted response they get is well worth the kitchen time it takes to make them.
—Lucile Cline, Wichita, Kansas

12 squares (1 ounce *each*) white baking chocolate, chopped
6 tablespoons heavy whipping cream, *divided*
1-1/2 teaspoons orange juice
1/2 teaspoon orange extract
1-1/2 teaspoons finely grated orange peel
1/4 cup finely chopped walnuts
2 teaspoons instant coffee granules
4 squares (1 ounce *each*) semisweet chocolate, chopped

In a heavy saucepan over low heat, melt white chocolate with 1/4 cup cream, orange juice, extract and peel. Stir until chocolate is melted. Remove from the heat; stir in walnuts. Cool for 10-12 minutes. Using a small spoon, fill 1-in. foil or paper candy cups about two-thirds full. Chill for 30 minutes.

Meanwhile, combine coffee granules and remaining cream in a saucepan. Cook and stir over low heat until coffee is dissolved. Add semisweet chocolate; cook and stir until chocolate is melted. Spoon about 1/2 teaspoon over white chocolate in each cup. Store in an airtight container at room temperature. **Yield:** about 4 dozen.

Great Gift Idea

Don't let guests leave empty-handed this holiday season. Put homemade goodies such as fudge or seasoned nuts into inexpensive mugs, decorative tins or small canisters.

Wrap the containers with clear or colored plastic and place in a pretty box. Place the gifts on a tray near the door, and let everybody choose one as they leave your house.

S'more Clusters

Our two sons love to help me break up the chocolate and graham crackers for these tasty treats—that way, they can tell their friends they made them! The chocolaty clusters taste just like s'mores, but without the gooey mess. —*Kathy Schmittler, Sterling Heights, Michigan*

6 milk chocolate candy bars (1.55 ounces *each*), broken into pieces
1-1/2 teaspoons vegetable oil
2 cups miniature marshmallows
8 whole graham crackers, broken into bite-size pieces

In a large microwave-safe bowl, toss chocolate and oil. Microwave, uncovered, at 50% power for 1-1/2 to 2 minutes or until chocolate is melted, stirring once. Stir in marshmallows and graham crackers. Spoon into paper-lined muffin cups (about 1/3 cup each). Refrigerate for 1 hour or until firm. **Yield:** 1 dozen.

Editor's Note: This recipe was tested in an 850-watt microwave.

Pecan Delights

A relative visiting from Oklahoma brought these and the recipe with her. Who can resist rich chewy caramel over crunchy pecans drizzled with sweet chocolate? These candies have become a favorite to both make and eat!
—*Linda Jonsson, Marion, Ohio*

2-1/4 cups packed brown sugar
1 cup butter
1 cup light corn syrup
1/8 teaspoon salt
1 can (14 ounces) sweetened condensed milk
1 teaspoon vanilla extract
1-1/2 pounds whole pecans
1 cup (6 ounces) semisweet chocolate chips
1 cup (6 ounces) milk chocolate chips
2 tablespoons shortening

In a large saucepan, combine first four ingredients. Cook over medium heat until sugar is dissolved. Gradually add milk; mix well. Continue cooking until candy thermometer reads 248° (firm-ball stage).

Remove from the heat; stir in vanilla until blended. Fold in the pecans. Drop by tablespoonfuls onto a greased or parchment-lined baking sheet. Chill until firm. Melt chocolate chips and shortening in a microwave-safe bowl or double boiler. Drizzle over each cluster. Cool. **Yield:** about 4 dozen.

Editor's Note: We recommend that you test your candy thermometer before each use by bringing water to a boil; the temperature should read 212°. Adjust your recipe temperature up or down based on your test.

Cookies 'n' Cream Fudge

I invented this confection for a bake sale at our children's school. Boy, was it a hit! The crunchy chunks of sandwich cookie soften a bit as the mixture mellows.
—*Laura Lane, Richmond, Virginia*

16 chocolate cream-filled sandwich cookies, broken into chunks, *divided*
1 can (14 ounces) sweetened condensed milk
2 tablespoons butter
2-2/3 cups vanilla chips
1 teaspoon vanilla extract

Line an 8-in. square baking pan with aluminum foil; coat with nonstick cooking spray. Place half of the broken cookies in pan. In a heavy saucepan, combine the milk, butter and chips; cook and stir over low heat until chips are melted. Remove from the heat; stir in vanilla. Pour over cookies in pan. Sprinkle with remaining cookies. Cover and refrigerate for at least 1 hour. Cut into squares. **Yield:** 3 dozen.

Sweet Tooth Treats

I frequently stir up these homemade treats for my husband and two daughters. They love the blend of peanut butter and chocolate, and I love that they don't keep me in the kitchen all day. —*Tina Jacobs, Wantage, New Jersey*

1 cup peanut butter
1/2 cup light corn syrup
1/2 cup confectioners' sugar
1/4 cup flaked coconut
2 cups Cheerios
1 cup (6 ounces) semisweet chocolate chips
1 tablespoon shortening

In a bowl, combine peanut butter, corn syrup, sugar and coconut until blended. Stir in cereal. Shape into 1-1/2-in. balls. In a small saucepan over medium heat, melt chocolate chips and shortening. Dip balls halfway into chocolate; place on waxed paper-lined baking sheets to harden. **Yield:** 2-1/2 dozen.

Cookies & Bars

Reindeer Cookies

(Pictured above)

This is one cookie recipe I especially enjoy making. My grandchildren love the graham cracker taste and the cute reindeer shape. I like that they're so quick and easy to assemble! —*Flo Burtnett, Gage, Oklahoma*

1 cup confectioners' sugar
1 teaspoon vanilla extract
3 to 4 tablespoons heavy whipping cream
12 graham cracker halves
24 chocolate chips
12 red-hot candies
12 mini pretzel twists

In a small bowl, combine sugar, vanilla and enough cream to reach a spreading consistency; cover and set aside. Using a serrated knife and a gentle sawing motion, cut graham crackers diagonally in half, forming two triangles. Frost one triangle. With frosted triangle on bottom, overlap triangles so the shortest side of unfrosted triangle runs along the longest cut edge of frosted triangle; match smallest points of crackers to form the nose. The remaining narrow points of both crackers form the ears.

Frost top cracker. Gently press on chocolate chips for eyes and a red-hot for nose. Using the serrated knife and a gentle sawing motion, cut pretzels in half to form antlers; press onto ears. Place on wire rack until set. **Yield:** 1 dozen.

Editor's Note: It is a good idea to have a few extra graham crackers and pretzels on hand because they break easily when cut.

Eggnog Snickerdoodles

It simply wouldn't be Christmas without these melt-in-your-mouth cookies on my platter! They have a lovely eggnog flavor and look great with their crunchy tops. —*Darlene Markel, Salem, Oregon*

1/2 cup butter, softened
1/2 cup shortening
1-3/4 cups sugar, *divided*
2 eggs
1/4 to 1/2 teaspoon rum extract
2-3/4 cups all-purpose flour
2 teaspoons cream of tartar
1 teaspoon baking soda
1/4 teaspoon salt
2 teaspoons ground nutmeg

In a mixing bowl, cream butter, shortening and 1-1/2 cups sugar. Beat in eggs and extract. Combine the flour, cream of tartar, baking soda and salt; gradually add to creamed mixture.

In a shallow bowl, combine the nutmeg and remaining sugar. Roll dough into 1-in. balls; roll in sugar mixture. Place 2 in. apart on ungreased baking sheets. Bake at 400° for 10-12 minutes or until lightly browned. Remove to wire racks to cool. **Yield:** 6-1/2 dozen.

Meringue Kisses

There's a nice surprise of chocolate inside these frothy kisses. They're my husband's top choice each Christmas. —*Tami Henke, Lockport, Illinois*

3 egg whites
1/4 teaspoon cream of tartar
Pinch salt
1 cup sugar
1 teaspoon vanilla extract
Red and green food coloring, optional
44 chocolate kisses

In a mixing bowl, beat egg whites until foamy. Sprinkle with cream of tartar and salt; beat until soft peaks form. Gradually add sugar and vanilla, beating until stiff peaks form, about 5-8 minutes. If desired, divide batter in half and fold in red and green food coloring.

Drop by rounded tablespoonfuls 1-1/2 in. apart onto lightly greased baking sheets. Press a chocolate kiss into the center of each cookie and cover it with meringue using a knife. Bake at 275° for 30-35 minutes or until firm to the touch. Immediately remove to a wire rack to cool. Store in an airtight container. **Yield:** 44 cookies.

Chocolate-Mint Sandwich Cookies

Refreshing mint filling sandwiched between two chocolate cookies makes for some tasty Noel nibbling.
—*Monica Kneuer, Peconic, New York*

3/4 cup butter, softened
1 cup sugar
1 egg
1/2 teaspoon vanilla extract
2 cups all-purpose flour
3/4 cup baking cocoa
1 teaspoon baking powder
1/2 teaspoon baking soda
1/2 teaspoon salt
1/4 cup milk
FILLING:
3 tablespoons butter, softened
1-1/2 cups confectioners' sugar
1 tablespoon milk
1/4 teaspoon peppermint extract
2 to 3 drops green food coloring, optional

In a mixing bowl, cream butter and sugar. Add egg and vanilla; mix well. Combine the flour, cocoa, baking powder, baking soda and salt; add to creamed mixture alternately with milk. Shape into two 10-1/2-in. rolls; wrap each in plastic wrap. Refrigerate overnight.

Unwrap dough and cut into 1/8-in. slices. Place 2 in. apart on lightly greased baking sheets. Bake at 325° for 9-11 minutes or until edges are set. Remove to wire racks to cool. Combine first four filling ingredients; beat until smooth. Add food coloring if desired. Spread on bottom of half of the cookies; top with remaining cookies. **Yield:** 5 dozen.

Christmas Candy Cookies

(Pictured below)

These delightful cookies hold up well in care packages I send to friends and relatives. They're also the first to go at Christmas parties.
—*Joan Graham*
Angel Fire, New Mexico

1 cup butter, softened
1 cup sugar
1 cup confectioners' sugar
1 cup vegetable oil
2 eggs
1 teaspoon almond extract
3-1/2 cups all-purpose flour
1 cup whole wheat flour
1 teaspoon baking soda
1 teaspoon salt
1 teaspoon cream of tartar
1 cup chopped almonds
1 package (8 ounces) mini red and green M&M's *or* Heath baking bits
Additional sugar

In a mixing bowl, cream butter, sugars and oil. Add eggs and extract; mix well. Combine flours, baking soda, salt and cream of tartar; gradually add to creamed mixture. Mix well. Stir in almonds and candy. Chill for 1 hour or until firm enough to handle.

Shape into 1-in. balls; roll in sugar. Place on ungreased baking sheets. Flatten with a flat-bottomed glass. Bake at 350° for 15-18 minutes or until lightly browned. Cool on wire racks. **Yield:** about 8 dozen.

Gingerbread Rings

(Pictured below)

This recipe yields quite a bit, so I end up with plenty of cookies for my family and friends. —*Donna Hinton*
Lincoln, Nebraska

1 cup shortening
2 cups sugar
2 egg yolks
1 cup water
1 cup light molasses
8 cups all-purpose flour
2 teaspoons baking soda
1-1/2 teaspoons ground ginger
1 teaspoon ground cinnamon
1 teaspoon ground allspice
3/4 teaspoon salt
FROSTING:
2-1/2 cups sugar
1/2 cup water
1/2 teaspoon light corn syrup
2 egg whites
1 teaspoon vanilla extract
Red and green decorating gel, optional

In a mixing bowl, cream shortening and sugar. Beat in egg yolks, water and molasses. Combine dry ingredients; gradually add to the creamed mixture. Cover and refrigerate for 2 hours or until easy to handle.

On a lightly floured surface, roll out to 1/4-in. thickness. Cut with a 2-3/4-in. doughnut cutter. Remove and discard centers. Place 2 in. apart on ungreased baking sheets. Bake at 350° for 10 minutes or until set. Remove to wire racks.

In a heavy saucepan, combine the sugar, water and corn syrup. Bring to a boil; cook until a candy thermometer reads 238° (soft-ball stage), about 5 minutes. Remove from the heat. In a mixing bowl, beat egg whites and vanilla until soft peaks form. Gradually add sugar mixture, beating on high for 7-8 minutes or until thickened. Frost cookies. Decorate if desired. **Yield:** about 5 dozen.

Editor's Note: We recommend that you test your candy thermometer before each use by bringing water to a boil; the temperature should read 212°. Adjust your recipe temperature up or down based on your test.

Merry Cherry Bars

These luscious bars, filled with cherries and almonds, really suit the Christmas season. —*Judith Dial*
Hampton, Virginia

2 cups all-purpose flour
1/2 cup confectioners' sugar
1 cup cold butter
FILLING:
1-1/2 cups packed brown sugar
2 eggs
1/4 cup all-purpose flour
1/2 teaspoon baking powder
1/2 teaspoon salt
1 cup finely chopped almonds
1/2 cup finely chopped maraschino cherries, drained
CHERRY ICING:
2 cups confectioners' sugar
1/4 cup cherry juice
3 tablespoons butter, softened
1/2 teaspoon almond extract

In a bowl, combine flour and confectioners' sugar; cut in butter until crumbly. Press into a greased 13-in. x 9-in. x 2-in. baking pan. Bake at 350° for 12-15 minutes or until lightly browned.

Meanwhile, in a mixing bowl, combine brown sugar and eggs; mix well. Combine flour, baking powder and salt; gradually add to egg mixture. Stir in almonds and cherries. Spread over crust. Bake at 350° for 30-35 minutes or until bars begin to pull away from sides of pan. Cool on a wire rack. In a small mixing bowl, beat icing ingredients until smooth. Frost bars. **Yield:** 3 dozen.

Spumoni Slices

(Pictured at right)

My sweet rectangles get their name from the old-fashioned tri-colored ice cream. Our whole family loves them. —Mary Chupp, Chattanooga, Tennessee

1 cup butter, softened
1-1/2 cups confectioners' sugar
1 egg
1 teaspoon vanilla extract
2-1/2 cups all-purpose flour
2 squares (1 ounce *each*) semisweet chocolate, melted
1/2 cup chopped pecans
3 to 5 drops green food coloring
1/4 cup finely chopped candied red cherries
1/2 teaspoon almond extract
3 to 5 drops red food coloring

In a mixing bowl, cream the butter and sugar. Beat in the egg and vanilla. Gradually add the flour and mix well. Divide dough into three portions. Stir chocolate into one portion; mix well. Add the pecans and green food coloring to the second portion. Add the cherries, almond extract and red food coloring to the third.

Roll each portion between two pieces of waxed paper into an 8-in. x 6-in. rectangle. Remove paper. Place chocolate rectangle on a piece of plastic wrap. Top with green and pink rectangles; press together lightly. Wrap with plastic wrap; chill overnight.

Cut chilled dough in half lengthwise. Return one rectangle to refrigerator. Cut remaining rectangle into 1/8-in. slices. Place 1 in. apart on ungreased baking sheets. Bake at 375° for 5-7 minutes or until set. Cool for 2 minutes before removing to wire racks. Repeat with remaining dough. **Yield:** about 7 dozen.

Italian Holiday Cookies

Many of our holiday traditions center on the foods my mother made while I was growing up. These cookies, which we called "Strufoli", bring back wonderful memories. —Sue Seymour, Valatie, New York

1 tablespoon sugar
1 teaspoon grated lemon peel
1 teaspoon vanilla extract
1/2 teaspoon salt
4 eggs
2-1/2 cups all-purpose flour
Oil for deep-fat frying
1 cup honey
Candy sprinkles

In a mixing bowl, combine the sugar, lemon peel, vanilla and salt. Add eggs and 2 cups flour; mix well. Turn onto a floured surface and knead in remaining flour (dough will be soft). With a floured knife or scissors, cut into 20 pieces. With hands, roll each piece into pencil shapes. Cut "pencils" into 1/2-in. pieces.

In an electric skillet or deep-fat fryer, heat oil to 350°. Fry pieces, a few at a time, for 2 minutes per side or until golden brown. Drain on paper towels. Place in a large bowl. Heat the honey to boiling; pour over cookies and mix well. With a slotted spoon, spoon onto a serving platter and slowly mound into a tree shape if desired. Decorate with candy sprinkles. Cool completely. **Yield:** about 15 dozen.

Rich Chocolate Cream Bars

(Pictured above)

Thick and fudgy, these treats only look fussy. The truth is, they're layered bars that don't require any baking time at all! —*Michele Paul, Fort Collins, Colorado*

1/2 cup butter
5 tablespoons baking cocoa
1/4 cup sugar
1 egg, beaten
1 teaspoon vanilla extract
1-1/2 cups graham cracker crumbs (about 24 squares)
1 cup flaked coconut
1/2 cup chopped walnuts

FILLING:

1/4 cup butter, softened
3 tablespoons milk
2 tablespoons instant vanilla pudding mix
2 cups confectioners' sugar
1 teaspoon vanilla extract

GLAZE:

4 squares (1 ounce *each*) semisweet chocolate
1 tablespoon butter

In the top of a double boiler, combine butter, cocoa, sugar, egg and vanilla. Cook and stir over simmering water until mixture reaches 160° and is thickened. In a large bowl, combine graham cracker crumbs, coconut and walnuts. Stir in cocoa mixture; blend well. Press into a greased 9-in. square baking pan; set aside.

For filling, combine butter, milk and pudding mix in a mixing bowl. Gradually beat in confectioners' sugar and vanilla until smooth; spread over crust. For glaze, melt chocolate and butter; spread over filling. Cover and refrigerate until set. Cut into bars. **Yield:** about 3 dozen.

Chewy Pecan Drops

(Pictured at left)

The cherry center gives a festive look to my nutty cookies. They're easy to make and take to holiday gatherings. —*Violet Klause, Onoway, Alberta*

2 cups ground pecans
1/2 cup all-purpose flour
1-1/4 cups sugar, *divided*
4 egg whites
1/2 teaspoon vanilla extract
5 to 6 maraschino cherries, coarsely chopped

In a large bowl, combine pecans, flour and 1 cup sugar; set aside. In a small mixing bowl, beat egg whites until foamy. Gradually add remaining sugar, beating until stiff peaks form. Fold in vanilla and half of the flour mixture. Fold in remaining flour mixture.

Drop by rounded teaspoonfuls 2 in. apart onto ungreased foil-lined baking sheets. Top each with a cherry piece. Bake at 325° for 20-25 minutes or until edges are lightly browned. Cool completely before removing from pans. **Yield:** about 5 dozen.

Anise Sugar Cookies

As much as I love giving away my baking, a few goodies, like these cookies, are "keepers". The light anise flavor makes them a perfect after-dinner treat.
—*Paula Marchesi, Rocky Point, New York*

1 cup butter, softened
1-1/2 cups sugar
2 eggs
1/4 to 1/2 teaspoon anise extract
3 cups all-purpose flour
1 to 1-1/2 teaspoons aniseed

1 teaspoon baking powder
1 teaspoon baking soda
1 teaspoon salt
Frosting and colored sugar, optional

In a mixing bowl, cream butter and sugar. Add eggs and extract; mix well. Combine flour, aniseed, baking powder, baking soda and salt; gradually add to creamed mixture and mix well.

Shape into 1-in. balls; place on greased baking sheets. Flatten with a glass dipped in sugar. Bake at 375° for 6-7 minutes. Cool on wire racks. If desired, frost cookies and sprinkle with colored sugar. **Yield:** 9 dozen.

Lime Spritz Cookies

The refreshing citrus flavor in these cookies comes from lime gelatin. They're easy, festive and delightfully different. —*Lori Daniels, Elkins, West Virginia*

1-1/2 cups butter, softened
1 cup sugar
1 package (3 ounces) lime gelatin
1 egg
1 teaspoon vanilla extract
4 cups all-purpose flour
1 teaspoon baking powder
Red and green colored sugar, optional

In a mixing bowl, cream butter, sugar and gelatin. Beat in egg and vanilla. Combine flour and baking powder; gradually add to the creamed mixture.

Using a cookie press fitted with disk of your choice, press dough into desired shapes 2 in. apart onto ungreased baking sheets. Sprinkle with colored sugar if desired. Bake at 350° for 8-10 minutes or until set. Remove to wire racks to cool. **Yield:** 14 dozen.

Roly-Poly Santas

(Pictured at right)

I tuck one of these fanciful Santas into every gift cookie tray I make. They're a guaranteed hit with kids, young and old. And I like that they're not too difficult to assemble. —*Mrs. Andrew Seyer, Oak Ridge, Missouri*

1 cup butter, softened
1/2 cup sugar
1 tablespoon milk
1 teaspoon vanilla extract
2-1/4 cups all-purpose flour
Red paste food coloring
Miniature chocolate chips
FROSTING:
1/2 cup shortening
1/2 teaspoon vanilla extract
2-1/3 cups confectioners' sugar, ***divided***
2 tablespoons milk, ***divided***

In a mixing bowl, cream butter and sugar. Add milk and vanilla; mix well. Add flour and mix well. Remove 1 cup dough; add red food coloring. Shape white dough into 12 balls, 3/4 in. each, and 48 balls, 1/4 in. each. Shape red dough into 12 balls, 1 in. each, and 60 balls, 1/2 in. each.

Place the 1-in. red balls on two ungreased baking sheets for the body of 12 Santas; flatten to 1/2-in. thickness. Attach 3/4-in. white balls for heads; flatten to 1/2-in. thickness. Attach four 1/2-in. red balls to each Santa for arms and legs. Attach 1/4-in. white balls to ends of arms and legs for hands and feet. Shape remaining 1/2-in. red balls into hats. Add chocolate chip eyes and buttons. Bake at 325° for 12-15 minutes or until set. Cool for 10 minutes; carefully remove from pans to wire racks (cookies will be fragile).

For frosting, combine shortening and vanilla in a small mixing bowl; mix well. Gradually add 1-1/3 cups confectioners' sugar; add 1 tablespoon milk. Gradually add remaining sugar and milk. Fill a pastry bag with frosting. With a round decorator's tip, add a band of icing on hat, cuffs at hands and feet, and down the front and at bottom of jacket. Use a small star tip to pipe beard and pom-pom on hat. **Yield:** 1 dozen.

Editor's Note: Remaining dough may be shaped into balls and baked.

Sour Cream Cutouts

(Pictured below)

As a city kid, I was always eager to visit my grandparents on their farmstead. There I acquired my taste for country food, like these tender cookies with buttery icing.
—Bobbie Hanks, Tulsa, Oklahoma

1 cup butter, softened
2 cups sugar
3 eggs
6 cups all-purpose flour
2 teaspoons baking soda
1/2 teaspoon salt
1 cup (8 ounces) sour cream
FROSTING:
1/2 cup butter, softened
4 cups confectioners' sugar
3 tablespoons milk
Food coloring, optional

In a mixing bowl, cream butter and sugar. Add eggs, one at a time, beating well after each. Combine dry ingredients; add to the creamed mixture alternately with sour cream (dough will be sticky). Cover and refrigerate for 2 hours or until easy to handle.

On a floured surface, roll out dough to 1/4-in. thickness. Cut into desired shapes with cookie cutters dipped in flour. Place 1 in. apart on greased baking sheets. Bake at 375° for 8-12 minutes or until lightly browned. Cool for 1-2 minutes before removing to wire racks.

For frosting, in a mixing bowl, beat the butter, confectioners' sugar and milk until smooth. Add food coloring if desired. Frost cookies. **Yield:** about 9 dozen.

Sweetheart Cookies

(Pictured below)

These rounds filled with fruit preserves were blue-ribbon winners at the county fair two years running. A family favorite, they never last past December 25!
—Pamela Esposito, Smithville, New Jersey

3/4 cup butter, softened
1/2 cup sugar
1 egg yolk
1-1/2 cups all-purpose flour
2 tablespoons raspberry *or* strawberry preserves
Confectioners' sugar, optional

In a mixing bowl, cream butter and sugar. Add egg yolk; mix well. Stir in the flour by hand. On a lightly floured surface, gently knead dough for 2-3 minutes or until thoroughly combined. Roll into 1-in. balls. Place 2 in. apart on greased baking sheets.

Using the end of a wooden spoon handle, make an indention in the center of each. Fill each with 1/4 teaspoon preserves. Bake at 350° for 13-15 minutes or until edges are lightly browned. Remove to wire racks. Dust warm cookies with confectioners' sugar if desired. Cool. **Yield:** about 2 dozen.

Holiday Melting Moments

The name of these cookies says it all—they melt in your mouth. Adding candied cherries to the dough makes them merry. —Lorraine Sheeley, Waynesboro, Pennsylvania

1 cup butter, softened
3/4 cup packed brown sugar
1 egg
3/4 teaspoon vanilla extract
1-3/4 cups cake flour
1/2 teaspoon baking soda
1/2 teaspoon cream of tartar
1/8 teaspoon salt
1/2 cup quartered red *and/or* green candied cherries
1/2 cup chopped pecans

In a mixing bowl, cream butter and brown sugar. Beat in the egg and vanilla. Combine the dry ingredients; gradually add to the creamed mixture. Stir in cherries and pecans. Drop by teaspoonfuls 2 in. apart onto well-greased baking sheets. Bake at 350° for 8-10 minutes or until golden brown. Remove to wire racks to cool. **Yield:** 5 dozen.

Pecan-Topped Sugar Cookies

This recipe dresses up refrigerated cookie dough with cream cheese and coconut. Folks love the almond flavor. —Betty Lech, St. Charles, Illinois

1 can (8 ounces) almond paste
1 package (3 ounces) cream cheese, softened
1/4 cup flaked coconut
1 tube (18 ounces) refrigerated sugar cookie dough
1 cup pecan halves

In a mixing bowl, beat paste and cream cheese. Add coconut; mix well. Cut cookie dough into 1/2-in. slices; divide each slice into four portions. Roll into balls. Place 2 in. apart on greased baking sheets.

Shape 1/2 teaspoonfuls of almond mixture into balls; place one on each ball of dough. Lightly press pecans into tops. Bake at 350° for 10-12 minutes or until lightly browned. Remove to wire racks to cool. **Yield:** about 3-1/2 dozen.

Soft Sugar Cookie Puffs

(Pictured above)

My husband's Aunt Laurel always made these cake-like cookies with her own farm-fresh eggs, cream and butter. Now I prepare batches for Christmas each year. —D. Elaine Rutschke, Spruce View, Alberta

3 eggs
1 cup heavy whipping cream
1 cup sugar
2 teaspoons butter, melted
1 teaspoon almond extract
4 cups all-purpose flour
4 teaspoons baking powder
Assorted colored sugars, optional

In a mixing bowl, beat eggs; add cream and beat well. Beat in the sugar, butter and almond extract. Combine flour and baking powder; gradually add to sugar mixture. Cover and refrigerate for 1 hour or until easy to handle.

On a lightly floured surface, roll out dough to 1/4-in. thickness. Cut with 2-1/2-in. cookie cutters dipped in flour. Place 1 in. apart on greased baking sheets. Sprinkle with colored sugars if desired. Bake at 375° for 10-12 minutes or until edges are lightly browned. Remove to wire racks to cool. **Yield:** about 6 dozen.

Pineapple Star Cookies

(Pictured above)

I'm grateful my neighbor gave me this special recipe. When you see the cookies' pretty shape and savor the pineapple filling and sweet frosting, you'll know they're worth the effort. —*Sarah Lukaszewicz Batavia, New York*

1 cup butter, softened
1 package (8 ounces) cream cheese, softened
2 cups all-purpose flour
FILLING:
3/4 cup sugar
4-1/2 teaspoons all-purpose flour
1 can (8 ounces) crushed pineapple, drained
FROSTING:
1 cup confectioners' sugar
2 tablespoons butter, melted
2 tablespoons milk
1/2 teaspoon vanilla extract
1/2 cup chopped walnuts

In a mixing bowl, cream the butter and cream cheese. Add flour and mix well. Cover and refrigerate for 2 hours or until easy to handle. Meanwhile, in a saucepan, combine sugar and flour; add pineapple. Cook over low heat until mixture is thickened, stirring frequently. Cover and refrigerate.

Divide dough in half. On a lightly floured surface, roll out each portion to 1/8-in. thickness. Cut into 3-in. squares. Place 1 in. apart on ungreased baking sheets. To form star, make a 1-1/4-in. cut from each corner toward center (do not cut through center). Place 1/4 teaspoon of pineapple filling in the center of each. Fold every other point toward the center, overlapping pieces; press lightly to seal.

Bake at 375° for 8-10 minutes or until set. Remove to wire racks to cool. For frosting, combine the confectioners' sugar, butter, milk and vanilla until smooth. Drizzle over cookies; sprinkle with walnuts. **Yield:** 5 dozen.

Painted Holiday Delights

These soft sandwich cookies are eye-catching, thanks to the holiday designs you paint on with food coloring. Orange juice and strawberry preserves add a light fruity flavor. —*Judy Degenstein, Ottawa, Kansas*

2 cups all-purpose flour
1/2 cup sugar
1/2 cup confectioners' sugar
2 teaspoons ground cinnamon
3/4 teaspoon baking powder
1/4 teaspoon salt
1/2 cup cold butter
1 egg
1/4 cup orange juice
FILLING:
1 package (8 ounces) cream cheese, softened
3 tablespoons confectioners' sugar
3 tablespoons strawberry preserves
GLAZE:
1 cup confectioners' sugar
1/4 teaspoon vanilla extract
1 to 2 tablespoons milk
Assorted food coloring

In a bowl, combine the first six ingredients. Cut in butter until mixture resembles coarse crumbs. Combine egg and orange juice; stir into crumb mixture just until moistened. Shape into a ball; cover and chill for 1-2 hours or until easy to handle. On a floured surface, roll out dough to 1/8-in. thickness. Cut with a 2-in. round cookie cutter. Place 1 in. apart on ungreased

baking sheets. Bake at 375° for 8-10 minutes or until lightly browned. Remove to wire racks to cool.

Combine filling ingredients; spread on the bottom of half of the cookies. Top with remaining cookies. For glaze, combine sugar, vanilla and enough milk to achieve desired consistency. Spread over tops of cookies; dry. Using a small new paintbrush and food coloring, paint holiday designs on cookie tops. Store in the refrigerator. **Yield:** about 2 dozen.

Cashew Tassie Cups

These little treats are packed with plenty of flavor. The nutty filling sits in rich-tasting mini pastry shells. Delicious! —Lois Zimmerman, Plymouth, Nebraska

1/2 cup butter, softened
1 package (3 ounces) cream cheese, softened
1 cup all-purpose flour

FILLING:

2/3 cup coarsely chopped cashews
1/2 cup packed brown sugar
1 egg
1 teaspoon vanilla extract

In a mixing bowl, beat butter and cream cheese until smooth; stir in flour. Shape into 1-in. balls. Press dough onto the bottom and up the sides of ungreased miniature muffin cups. Spoon cashews into shells; set aside.

In another mixing bowl, beat the brown sugar, egg and vanilla until combined; spoon over nuts. Bake at 350° for 20-25 minutes or until filling is set and pastry is golden brown. Cool for 1 minute before removing from pans to wire racks. **Yield:** 2 dozen.

Mocha Cherry Cookies

(Pictured below)

*Flecked with cherries and glistening with sugar, these dainty cookies always go over big. They're rich and tender, much like shortbread, and have a pleasant chocolate-coffee flavor. —Diane Molbert
Emerald Park, Saskatchewan*

1 cup butter, softened
1/2 cup sugar
1 teaspoon vanilla extract
1 teaspoon instant coffee granules
1 teaspoon hot water
1/4 cup baking cocoa
2 cups all-purpose flour
1/2 cup chopped maraschino cherries
1/2 cup chopped walnuts
Additional sugar
Melted semisweet chocolate, optional

In a mixing bowl, cream butter and sugar until fluffy. Add vanilla. Dissolve coffee granules in water; add to creamed mixture with cocoa. Add flour and mix well. Stir in cherries and walnuts. Shape into 1-1/4-in. balls; roll in sugar. Place on ungreased baking sheets. Bake at 325° for 20-22 minutes. Cool on wire racks. Drizzle with chocolate if desired. **Yield:** about 3 dozen.

Macaroon Kisses

(Pictured below)

These cookies are a holiday favorite around our house. You can top them off with cherries or chocolate, or some of each! —*Alice McTarnaghan, Castleton, New York*

1/3 cup butter, softened
1 package (3 ounces) cream cheese, softened
3/4 cup sugar
1 egg yolk
1-1/2 teaspoons almond extract
2 teaspoons orange juice
1-1/4 cups all-purpose flour
2 teaspoons baking powder
1/4 teaspoon salt
5 cups flaked coconut, *divided*
Candied cherries *and/or* chocolate kisses

In a mixing bowl, cream butter, cream cheese and sugar until light and fluffy. Combine egg yolk, extract and juice; add to creamed mixture and mix well. Combine flour, baking powder and salt; gradually add to creamed mixture and mix well. Stir in 3 cups of coconut. Cover and chill for at least 1 hour.

Shape into 1-in. balls; roll in remaining coconut. Place 2 in. apart on ungreased baking sheets. Bake at 350° for 10-12 minutes or until lightly browned. Immediately place a cherry or chocolate kiss on top of each cookie. Cool 5 minutes; remove to a wire rack to cool completely. **Yield:** about 4 dozen.

Cathedral Cookies

Children love the colorful marshmallows in these festive confections, which look just like stained glass when they're sliced. —*Carol Shaffer*
Cape Girardeau, Missouri

1 cup (6 ounces) semisweet chocolate chips
2 tablespoons butter
1 egg, beaten
3 cups pastel miniature marshmallows
1/2 cup chopped pecans *or* walnuts
1 cup flaked coconut

In a heavy saucepan, melt chocolate chips and butter over low heat, stirring occasionally. Stir a small amount into the egg, then return all to pan. Cook and stir over low heat for 2 minutes. Pour into a bowl; let cool for 15 minutes. Gently stir in marshmallows and nuts. Chill for 30 minutes.

Turn onto a sheet of waxed paper. Form into a roll about 1-1/2 in. in diameter. Gently roll onto another sheet of waxed paper sprinkled with coconut. Using the waxed paper, cover the outside of the roll with the coconut. Wrap roll tightly, twisting ends to seal. Freeze for 4 hours or overnight. Remove waxed paper. Cut into 1/4-in. slices. Store in an airtight container in the refrigerator. **Yield:** about 5 dozen.

Candy Cane Cookies

These festive cookies have a rich almond flavor and a pretty sprinkling of peppermint. Their candy cane shape makes them especially appealing. It would not be Christmas at my house without them!
—*Tammy Schenk, Harlowton, Montana*

1 cup butter, softened
1 cup confectioners' sugar
1 egg
1-1/2 teaspoons almond extract
2-1/2 cups all-purpose flour
1 teaspoon salt
Red food coloring
1/2 cup crushed peppermint candy canes
1/2 cup sugar

In a mixing bowl, cream butter and confectioners' sugar. Add egg and extract; mix well. Add flour and salt; mix well. Divide dough in half; add 6-7 drops of food coloring to one half.

Shape tablespoonfuls of each color of dough into 4-in. ropes. Place ropes side by side; lightly press ends together and twist. Place on ungreased

baking sheets; curve top of cane down. Bake at 375° for 9-12 minutes or until lightly browned. Combine crushed candy canes and sugar; immediately sprinkle over cookies. Cool for 2 minutes; remove to wire racks to cool completely. **Yield:** 3 dozen.

Crispy Norwegian Bows

I've been fixing these cookies for so long, I don't recall where the recipe came from. They're a must at our house for Christmas and throughout the year.
—Janie Norwood, Albany, Georgia

3 egg yolks
3 tablespoons sugar
3 tablespoons heavy whipping cream
1/2 teaspoon ground cardamom
1 to 1-1/4 cups all-purpose flour
Oil for deep-fat frying
Confectioners' sugar

In a mixing bowl, beat egg yolks and sugar until light and lemon-colored. Add cream and cardamom; mix well. Gradually add flour until dough is firm enough to roll. On a lightly floured surface, roll into a 15-in. square. Using a pastry wheel or knife, cut into 15-in. x 1-1/2-in. strips; cut diagonally at 2-1/2-in. intervals. In the center of each diamond, make a 1-in. slit; pull one end through slit.

In an electric skillet or deep-fat fryer, heat oil to 375°. Fry bows, a few at a time, for 20-40 seconds or until golden brown on both sides. Drain on paper towels. Dust with confectioners' sugar. **Yield:** 4 dozen.

Mint Swirl Bars

(Pictured above right)

My folks love these cake-like bars, so I always make them for the holidays. The chocolaty mint squares look simply scrumptious and taste even better.
—Debbie Devore, Fremont, Nebraska

1 package (3 ounces) cream cheese, softened
1/4 cup butter, softened
3/4 cup sugar
2 eggs
2/3 cup all-purpose flour
1/2 teaspoon baking powder
1/2 teaspoon salt
1/3 cup chopped walnuts
1 square (1 ounce) semisweet chocolate, melted
1/2 teaspoon peppermint extract
2 to 3 drops green *or* red food coloring, optional

GLAZE:

1 square (1 ounce) semisweet chocolate
1 tablespoon butter
1 cup confectioners' sugar
1/2 teaspoon vanilla extract
2 to 3 tablespoons boiling water

In a mixing bowl, beat cream cheese, butter and sugar. Add eggs, one at a time, beating well after each addition. Combine the flour, baking powder and salt; add to creamed mixture and mix well. Transfer half of the batter to another bowl; stir in nuts and chocolate. Spread into a greased 9-in. square baking pan.

Stir peppermint extract and food coloring if desired into remaining batter. Spoon over chocolate layer; cut through batter with a knife to swirl. Bake at 350° for 15-20 minutes or until a toothpick inserted near the center comes out clean. Cool on a wire rack.

In a saucepan, melt chocolate and butter. Remove from the heat; stir in confectioners' sugar, vanilla and enough water to achieve glaze consistency. Pour over brownies and spread evenly. Cut into bars. **Yield:** 2 dozen.

Orange Cookies

(Pictured above)

Dozens of these citrusy delights travel along with me to the school and church functions I attend during the holidays. The abundant orange flavor is refreshing.
—Diane Myers, Meridian, Idaho

1 cup shortening
1-1/2 cups sugar
1 cup buttermilk
3 eggs
2/3 cup orange juice
4-1/2 teaspoons grated orange peel
3 to 3-1/2 cups all-purpose flour
1 teaspoon baking soda
1 teaspoon baking powder
ICING:
4-1/4 cups confectioners' sugar
1/4 teaspoon orange extract
1/3 to 1/2 cup orange juice

In a mixing bowl, cream shortening and sugar. Add buttermilk, eggs, orange juice and peel. Combine dry ingredients; gradually add to creamed mixture. Drop by teaspoonfuls 2 in. apart onto ungreased baking sheets. Bake at 375° for 10 minutes or until lightly browned. Remove to wire racks to cool.

For icing, combine the confectioners' sugar, orange extract and enough orange juice to achieve desired consistency. Spread over cooled cookies. **Yield:** about 12 dozen.

Angel Wings

I knew I'd hit on a winner with these crispy roll-ups when my sister first sampled them. After one taste, she was so impressed she asked me to bake her wedding cake! —R. Lane, Tenafly, New Jersey

1 cup cold butter, cubed
1-1/2 cups all-purpose flour
1/2 cup sour cream
10 tablespoons sugar, ***divided***
1 tablespoon ground cinnamon, ***divided***

In a bowl, cut butter into flour until the mixture resembles coarse crumbs. Stir in the sour cream. Turn onto a lightly floured surface; knead 6-8 times or until mixture holds together. Shape into four balls; flatten slightly. Wrap in plastic wrap; refrigerate for 4 hours or overnight.

Unwrap one ball. Sprinkle 2 tablespoons sugar on waxed paper; coat all sides of ball with sugar. Roll into a 12-in. x 5-in. rectangle between two sheets of waxed paper. Remove top sheet of waxed paper. Sprinkle dough with 3/4 teaspoon cinnamon. Lightly mark a line down the center of the dough, making two 6-in. x 5-in. rectangles. Starting with a short side, roll up, jelly-roll style, to the center mark; peel waxed paper away while rolling. Repeat with other short side. Wrap in plastic wrap; freeze for 30 minutes. Repeat three times.

Place remaining sugar on waxed paper. Unwrap one roll. Cut into 1/2-in. slices; dip each side into sugar. Place 2 in. apart on ungreased baking sheets. Bake at 375° for 12 minutes or until golden brown. Turn cookies; bake 5-8 minutes longer. Remove to wire racks to cool. **Yield:** about 3 dozen.

Cherry-Filled Cookies

The luscious cherry filling peeking out of these rounds is just a hint of how scrumptious they are. Using a doughnut cutter to shape each cookie top really speeds up the process. —Mrs. Delbert Benton, Guthrie Center, Iowa

1/2 cup shortening
1 cup packed brown sugar
1/2 cup sugar
2 eggs
1/4 cup buttermilk
1 teaspoon vanilla extract

3-1/2 cups all-purpose flour
1/2 teaspoon salt
1/2 teaspoon baking soda
1 can (21 ounces) cherry pie filling

In a mixing bowl, cream shortening and sugars. Add eggs, buttermilk and vanilla; mix well. Combine flour, salt and baking soda; gradually add to creamed mixture and mix well. Cover and chill for 1 hour.

Divide dough in half. On a floured surface, roll each portion to 1/8-in. thickness. Cut with a 2-3/4-in. round cutter. Place half of the circles 2 in. apart on greased baking sheets; top each with a heaping teaspoon of pie filling. Cut holes in the center of remaining circles with a 1-in. round cutter; place over filled circles. Seal edges. Bake at 375° for 10 minutes or until golden brown. Cool on wire racks. **Yield:** about 3 dozen.

Cardamom Almond Biscotti

These crunchy slices are requested often during the holidays, particularly by my husband. He likes to dunk them in coffee. —*Verna Eberhart Watertown, South Dakota*

1 cup butter, softened
1-3/4 cups sugar
2 eggs
2 teaspoons almond extract
5-1/4 cups all-purpose flour
1 teaspoon salt
1 teaspoon baking soda
1 teaspoon ground cardamom
1 cup (8 ounces) sour cream
1 cup chopped almonds

In a mixing bowl, cream butter and sugar. Add eggs, one at a time, beating well after each addition. Beat in extract. Combine the flour, salt, baking soda and cardamom; add to the creamed mixture alternately with sour cream. Fold in almonds.

Divide dough into fourths; shape each portion into a ball. On two greased baking sheets, roll each ball into a 15-in. log (two logs per pan). Bake at 350° for 30 minutes or until lightly browned and firm to the touch. Transfer to a cutting board; cut diagonally with a sharp knife into 1/2-in. slices. Place with cut side down on greased baking sheets.

Bake for 10-12 minutes or until lightly browned. Remove to wire racks to cool. Store in airtight containers. **Yield:** about 7 dozen.

Frosted Spice Cutouts

(Pictured below)

The spicy taste of these cutouts is a festive change of pace from ordinary sugar cookies. Everyone in our house favors them. —*Pamela Drake, Ventura, California*

1/2 cup butter, softened
1 cup vegetable oil
3/4 cup sugar
4 cups all-purpose flour
2 teaspoons baking powder
1 teaspoon ground cinnamon
1/2 teaspoon ground cloves
1/2 teaspoon ground nutmeg
1/3 cup milk
FROSTING:
2 cups confectioners' sugar
2 tablespoons plus 2 teaspoons water
Red and green paste food coloring, optional

In a mixing bowl, cream butter, oil and sugar. Combine flour, baking powder, cinnamon, cloves and nutmeg; gradually add to the creamed mixture. Beat in milk. Divide dough in half. Cover and refrigerate for 8 hours or overnight (dough will be soft).

On a lightly floured surface, roll out one portion at a time to 1/4-in. thickness. Cut into desired shapes. Place 2 in. apart on ungreased baking sheets. Bake at 350° for 12-15 minutes or until edges begin to brown. Remove to wire racks. For frosting, beat confectioners' sugar and water in a mixing bowl. Add food coloring if desired. Frost cooled cookies. **Yield:** about 4 dozen.

Chocolate Reindeer

(Pictured below)

These cute cutout reindeer really fly off the plate when my brother's around. They're his favorite! The subtle chocolate color and taste make them a nice alternative to plain vanilla sugar cookies. —*Lisa Rupple*
Keenesburg, Colorado

1 cup butter, softened
1 cup sugar
1/2 cup packed brown sugar
1 egg
1 teaspoon vanilla extract
2-3/4 cups all-purpose flour
1/2 cup baking cocoa
1 teaspoon baking soda
44 red-hot candies
ICING (optional):
1-1/2 cups confectioners' sugar
2 to 3 tablespoons milk

In a mixing bowl, cream butter and sugars until fluffy. Beat in egg and vanilla. Combine flour, cocoa and baking soda; add to creamed mixture and mix well. Cover and refrigerate for at least 2 hours.

On a lightly floured surface, roll dough to 1/8-in. thickness. Cut with a reindeer-shaped cookie cutter. Place on greased baking sheets. Bake at 375° for 8-9 minutes. Immediately press a red-hot onto each nose. Cool for 2-3 minutes; remove from pans to wire racks. If desired, combine confectioners' sugar and milk until smooth. Cut a small hole in the corner of a heavy-duty resealable plastic bag; fill with icing. Pipe around edges of cookies and add a dot for eye. **Yield:** about 3-1/2 dozen.

Frosted Pumpkin Cookies

These family favorites taste so good, it's hard to eat just one! They freeze and travel well, especially if you let the icing completely dry, then layer the cookies between sheets of waxed paper. —*Leona Luttrell*
Sarasota, Florida

1 cup shortening
2 cups packed brown sugar
2 cups canned pumpkin
4 cups all-purpose flour
2 teaspoons baking powder
2 teaspoons baking soda
2 teaspoons ground cinnamon
1/8 teaspoon salt
1 cup chopped pecans
1 cup chopped dates
CARAMEL FROSTING:
1/2 cup butter
1-1/2 cups packed brown sugar
1/4 cup milk

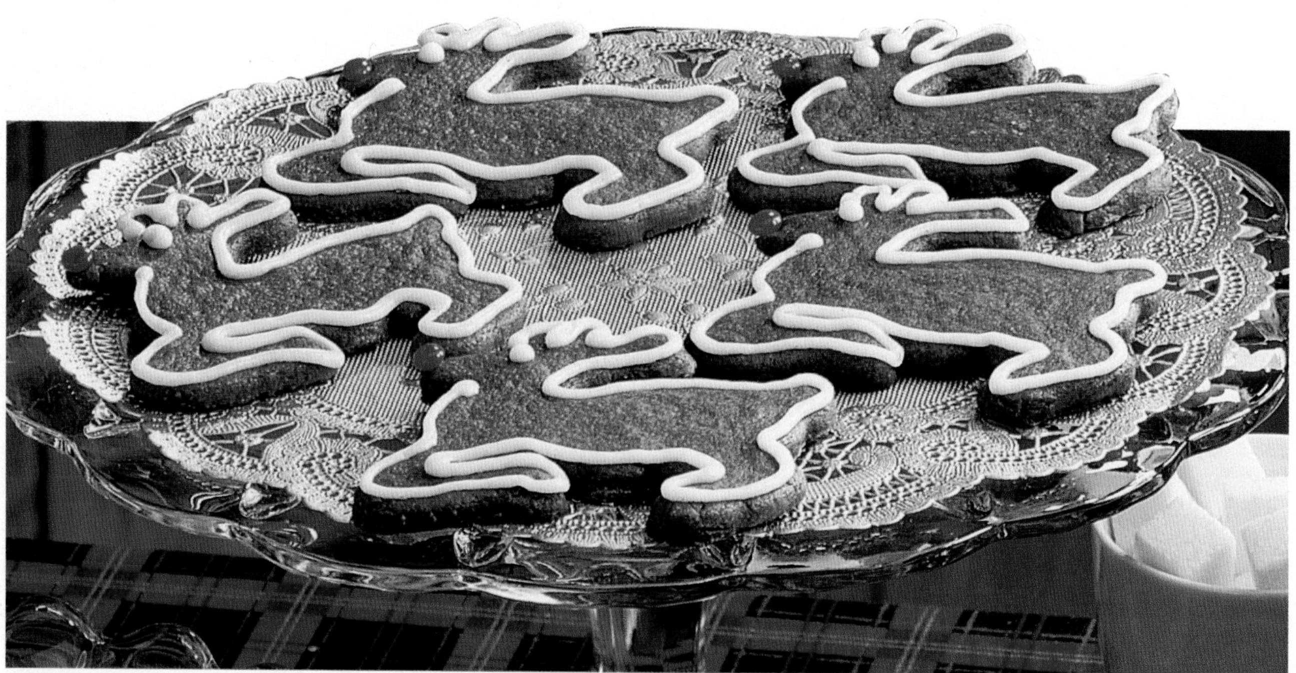

1 teaspoon maple flavoring
1/2 teaspoon vanilla extract
2 to 2-1/2 cups confectioners' sugar

In a mixing bowl, cream shortening and brown sugar. Add pumpkin; mix well. Combine flour, baking powder, baking soda, cinnamon and salt; gradually add to pumpkin mixture. Stir in pecans and dates. Drop by rounded teaspoonfuls 2 in. apart onto ungreased baking sheets. Bake at 375° for 13-15 minutes or until firm.

Meanwhile, for frosting, combine the butter, brown sugar and milk in a saucepan. Bring to a boil over medium heat, stirring constantly; boil for 3 minutes. Remove from the heat; stir in maple flavoring and vanilla. Cool slightly; beat in enough confectioners' sugar to achieve spreading consistency. Remove cookies to wire racks; frost while warm. **Yield:** 6-1/2 dozen.

Date Swirl Cookies

Deliciously old-fashioned, these chewy treats have been a tradition in our family for 60 years. The recipe earned me a ribbon at the county fair and is a full-flavored winner anytime. —Linda Nilsen, Anoka, Minnesota

1-1/2 cups pitted dates, chopped
3/4 cup sugar, *divided*
1/3 cup water
1/4 cup chopped walnuts
Pinch salt
1/2 cup butter, softened
1/2 cup packed brown sugar
1 egg
2 cups all-purpose flour
1/2 teaspoon baking soda
1/4 teaspoon salt

In a saucepan, combine dates, 1/4 cup sugar, water, nuts and salt. Cook over medium heat, stirring constantly, until thick, about 5 minutes. Set aside to cool. In a mixing bowl, beat butter, brown sugar, egg and remaining sugar. Combine flour, baking soda and salt; gradually stir into butter mixture. Chill for 30 minutes.

Roll dough on a lightly floured surface to a 1/4-in.-thick rectangle. Spread with date mixture; roll up jelly-roll style, starting at a long end. Wrap with waxed paper. Chill for at least 4 hours. Remove paper. Cut into 1/8-in. to 1/4-in. slices. Place 2 in. apart on greased baking sheets. Bake at 375° for 8 minutes. Cool on a wire rack. **Yield:** about 4 dozen.

Fudgy Macaroon Bars

(Pictured above)

Sweet tooths make a beeline for my dessert tray whenever these rich squares show up. They're attractive on the platter and delectable with fudge and coconut. —Beverly Zdurne, East Lansing, Michigan

4 squares (1 ounce *each*) unsweetened chocolate
1 cup butter
2 cups sugar
1 cup all-purpose flour
1/4 teaspoon salt
1 teaspoon vanilla extract
3 eggs, lightly beaten

FILLING:
3 cups flaked coconut
1 can (14 ounces) sweetened condensed milk
1 teaspoon vanilla extract
1/2 teaspoon almond extract

TOPPING:
1 cup (6 ounces) semisweet chocolate chips
1/2 cup chopped walnuts

In a saucepan over low heat, melt chocolate and butter. Remove from heat; cool slightly. Stir in sugar, flour, salt, vanilla and eggs; mix well. Spread half of the batter into a greased 13-in. x 9-in. x 2-in. baking pan. In a bowl, combine filling ingredients. Spoon over chocolate layer. Carefully spread remaining chocolate mixture over filling.

Bake at 350° for 35-40 minutes or until sides pull away from pan. Immediately sprinkle with chocolate chips. Allow chips to soften for a few minutes, then spread over bars. Sprinkle with walnuts. Cool completely before cutting. **Yield:** 3 dozen.

Chocolate Fruit 'n' Nut Cookies

(Pictured above)

Filled with fruit, nuts and chocolate, these traditional Italian treats hit the spot. We enjoy them at Christmas.
—Valerie Putsey, Winamac, Indiana

- **6 tablespoons butter**
- **1/3 cup milk**
- **1/4 cup sugar**
- **2 tablespoons honey**
- **1 cup sliced almonds**
- **1/2 cup mixed candied fruit, finely chopped**
- **1/4 cup all-purpose flour**
- **3/4 cup semisweet chocolate chips**
- **2 tablespoons shortening**

In a saucepan, combine butter, milk, sugar and honey. Bring to a boil. Remove from heat; stir in almonds and fruit. Stir in flour until blended. Drop by tablespoonfuls 3 in. apart onto greased and floured baking sheets. Spread with a spoon to form 2-1/2-in. circles. Bake at 350° for 6-9 minutes or until edges are lightly browned. Cool on pans for 1 minute before carefully removing to waxed paper to cool completely.

For coating, combine chocolate chips and shortening in a small saucepan. Cook over low heat until melted. Spread 1 teaspoonful over the bottom of each cookie. When chocolate is almost set, draw wavy lines with a fork or cake decorating comb. Store in the refrigerator. **Yield:** about 2 dozen.

Coconut Raspberry Bars

While mixing a batch of plain bars, I was inspired to add raspberry preserves and flaked coconut to the dough and wound up with these yummy treats.
—Amanda Denton, Barre, Vermont

- **3/4 cup butter, softened**
- **1 cup sugar**
- **1 egg**
- **1/2 teaspoon vanilla extract**
- **2 cups all-purpose flour**
- **1/4 teaspoon baking powder**
- **2 cups flaked coconut, *divided***
- **1/2 cup chopped walnuts**
- **1 jar (12 ounces) raspberry preserves**
- **1 cup vanilla *or* white chips**

In a mixing bowl, cream butter and sugar. Beat in egg and vanilla. Combine flour and baking powder; gradually add to the creamed mixture. Stir in 1-1/4 cups coconut and the walnuts.

Press three-fourths of the dough into a greased 13-in. x 9-in. x 2-in. baking pan. Spread with preserves. Sprinkle with chips and remaining coconut. Crumble remaining dough over the top; press lightly. Bake at 350° for 30-35 minutes or until golden brown. Cool on a wire rack. Cut into squares. **Yield:** 3 dozen.

Marzipan Bars

My husband's grandmother made these lovely layered bars for us as our newlywed Christmas present.
—Jeanne Koniuszy, Nome, Texas

- **1/2 cup butter, softened**
- **1/2 cup packed brown sugar**
- **1 egg yolk**
- **1 teaspoon vanilla extract**
- **2 cups all-purpose flour**
- **1/2 teaspoon baking soda**
- **1/4 teaspoon salt**
- **1/4 cup milk**
- **1 jar (10 ounces) raspberry jelly**

FILLING:

- **1 can (8 ounces) almond paste, cubed**
- **3 tablespoons butter, softened**
- **1/2 cup sugar**
- **1 egg white**
- **1 teaspoon vanilla extract**
- **3 eggs**

6 drops green food coloring
ICING:
2 squares (1 ounce *each*) unsweetened chocolate
1 tablespoon butter
2 cups confectioners' sugar
4 to 5 tablespoons milk
1 teaspoon vanilla extract

In a mixing bowl, cream butter and brown sugar. Add egg yolk and vanilla; mix well. Combine flour, baking soda and salt; add to creamed mixture alternately with milk. Press into a greased 15-in. x 10-in. x 1-in. baking pan. Spread with jelly. For filling, combine almond paste, butter, sugar, egg white and vanilla in a mixing bowl. Beat in eggs. Add food coloring; mix well. Pour over jelly layer. Bake at 350° for 35 minutes or until set. Cool on a wire rack.

For icing, heat chocolate and butter in a small saucepan on low until melted. Add confectioners' sugar and enough milk to make a smooth icing. Stir in vanilla. Immediately spread over bars. Cover and store overnight at room temperature before cutting. **Yield:** about 6-1/2 dozen.

Chocolate Hazelnut Thumbprints

Since we live in hazelnut country, I love making these special cookies for festive occasions. I usually bake two or three batches for parties and homemade gifts.
—Ethel Garrison, Tacoma, Washington

2/3 cup butter, softened
1/2 cup sugar
1 egg plus 1 egg yolk
1/2 teaspoon vanilla extract
1-1/2 cups all-purpose flour
1/4 cup baking cocoa
1/2 teaspoon salt
2/3 cup ground hazelnuts *or* filberts
1/2 cup raspberry preserves
Confectioners' sugar

In a mixing bowl, cream butter and sugar. Add egg, yolk and vanilla; mix well. Combine flour, cocoa and salt; add a third at a time to creamed mixture, beating well after each addition. Stir in nuts. Roll into 1-in. balls; place on ungreased baking sheets.

With thumb, make indentation in center of cookies; fill with 1/4 teaspoon of preserves. Bake at 350° for 10-12 minutes. Cool on wire racks. Lightly dust with confectioners' sugar. **Yield:** about 6 dozen.

Peppermint Cookies

(Pictured below)

Some 40 years ago, I whipped up these minty morsels as a way to use leftover candy canes, and my daughter has enthusiastically anticipated the cookies for Christmas ever since! —Mrs. Robert Nelson, Des Moines, Iowa

1 cup shortening
1/2 cup sugar
1/2 cup packed brown sugar
2 eggs
1-1/2 teaspoons vanilla extract
2-3/4 cups all-purpose flour
1 teaspoon salt
1/2 teaspoon baking soda
1/2 cup crushed peppermint candies

In a mixing bowl, cream shortening and sugars. Add the eggs, one at time, beating well after each addition. Beat in vanilla. Combine the dry ingredients; gradually add to the creamed mixture. Stir in crushed candies. Shape into a 15-in. roll; wrap in plastic wrap. Refrigerate for 4 hours or until firm.

Unwrap and cut into 1/8-in. slices. Place 2 in. apart on ungreased baking sheets. Bake at 375° for 6-8 minutes or until edges begin to brown. Remove to wire racks to cool. **Yield:** about 6 dozen.

Molasses Sugar Cookies

(Pictured below)

There's nothing really fancy about these cookies, but they're my husband's all-time favorite. He enjoys their chewy, comforting flavor and the childhood memories they bring back. —*Kay Curtis, Guthrie, Oklahoma*

3/4 cup vegetable oil
1 cup sugar
1/4 cup molasses
1 egg
2 cups all-purpose flour
2 teaspoons baking soda
1 teaspoon ground cinnamon
1/2 teaspoon salt
1/2 teaspoon ground cloves
1/2 teaspoon ground ginger
Additional sugar

In a large mixing bowl, combine the oil, sugar and molasses. Add egg; mix well. Combine the flour, baking soda, cinnamon, salt, cloves and ginger; add to sugar mixture and mix well. Cover and refrigerate for 4 hours or until easy to handle.

Shape dough into 1-in. balls; roll in sugar. Place 3 in. apart on greased baking sheets. Bake at 375° for 7-9 minutes or until tops are cracked and edges are set. Cool for 2-3 minutes before removing from pans to wire racks. **Yield:** about 4 dozen.

Dutch Spice Cookies

My sister gave me the recipe for these cookies, which have become a holiday tradition at our house. My kids tear into the spicy, crisp cookies right out of the oven. I prefer them cooled, but it's risky waiting. I might not get any! —*Mary Peterson, Charleston, Rhode Island*

3/4 cup butter, softened
1 cup packed brown sugar
2-1/4 cups all-purpose flour
2 teaspoons ground cinnamon
1/2 teaspoon ground mace
1/2 teaspoon crushed aniseed
1/4 teaspoon *each* ground ginger, nutmeg and cloves
1/4 teaspoon baking powder
1/8 teaspoon salt
3 tablespoons milk
1 cup finely chopped slivered almonds

In a mixing bowl, cream butter and brown sugar. Combine the flour, spices, baking powder and salt; gradually add to creamed mixture. Stir in milk and almonds. Roll dough into a 16-in. x 10-in. rectangle between two sheets of waxed paper. Cut into 2-in. squares. Cover with waxed paper and refrigerate for 30 minutes.

Place squares 1 in. apart on ungreased baking sheets. Bake at 375° for 8-10 minutes or until firm. Remove to wire racks to cool. **Yield:** 40 cookies.

Apricot Cream Cheese Drops

This treasured recipe is from a favorite aunt. Her soft, rich cookies have a yummy apricot flavor, but you could substitute strawberry, pineapple or raspberry preserves if you prefer. —*Melinda Leonowitz, Birdsboro, Pennsylvania*

1/2 cup butter, softened
1 package (3 ounces) cream cheese, softened
1/2 cup apricot preserves
1/4 cup packed brown sugar
1 tablespoon milk
1-1/4 cups all-purpose flour

1-1/2 teaspoons baking powder
1-1/2 teaspoons ground cinnamon
1/4 teaspoon salt
FROSTING:
1 cup confectioners' sugar
1/4 cup apricot preserves
1 tablespoon butter, softened
1 to 2 teaspoons milk
Ground nuts *or* flaked coconut

In a mixing bowl, cream the butter, cream cheese, apricot preserves, brown sugar and milk. Combine the flour, baking powder, cinnamon and salt; gradually add to creamed mixture. Drop by teaspoonfuls onto ungreased baking sheets. Bake at 350° for 8-10 minutes or until lightly browned. Remove to wire racks to cool.

For frosting, in a bowl, combine the confectioners' sugar, apricot preserves, butter and enough milk to achieve desired consistency. Frost cookies. Sprinkle with nuts or coconut. **Yield:** 3 dozen.

Celestial Bars

(Pictured above)

My aunt gave me the recipe for these wonderfully nutty bars. With their marbled base, fluffy icing and pretty chocolate glaze, they're the stars of bake sales, cookie gift packs and parties. —*Maribeth Gregg*
Cable, Ohio

1/2 cup butter, softened
2 cups packed brown sugar
1 teaspoon vanilla extract
1/2 teaspoon almond extract
3 eggs
2 cups all-purpose flour
1/2 teaspoon salt
1-1/2 cups chopped pecans
2 squares (1 ounce *each*) unsweetened chocolate, melted
ICING:
1/2 cup butter, softened
3 cups confectioners' sugar
3 to 4 tablespoons milk
1 teaspoon vanilla extract
GLAZE:
1/2 cup semisweet chocolate chips
2 teaspoons shortening

In a mixing bowl, cream butter and brown sugar. Add extracts. Add eggs, one at a time, beating well after each addition. Combine flour and salt; add to creamed mixture and mix well. Stir in pecans.

Divide batter in half; stir chocolate into one portion. Alternately spoon plain and chocolate batters into a greased 13-in. x 9-in. x 2-in. baking pan. Swirl with a knife (batter will be thick). Bake at 350° for 16-20 minutes or until a toothpick inserted near the center comes out clean. Cool completely.

For icing, cream butter and confectioners' sugar in a mixing bowl. Add milk and vanilla; mix until smooth. Spread over bars. For glaze, melt chocolate chips and shortening in a microwave or double boiler. Drizzle over bars. Let stand until chocolate is completely set before cutting. **Yield:** 4 dozen.

Eggnog Cutout Cookies

(Pictured above)

I created this cookie recipe because my sons liked eggnog so much. After frosting the cookies, you can add to their festive flair by sprinkling them with colored sugar.
—Glenna Tooman, Boise, Idaho

1/2 cup butter, softened
1 cup sugar
2 eggs
2 tablespoons plus 1 teaspoon eggnog*
2-1/2 cups all-purpose flour
1/2 teaspoon salt
1/4 teaspoon baking soda
1/4 teaspoon ground nutmeg
ICING:
2 cups confectioners' sugar
1/4 teaspoon ground nutmeg, optional
4 to 5 tablespoons eggnog*
Liquid *or* paste food coloring, optional

In a mixing bowl, cream the butter and sugar. Beat in eggs. Stir in the eggnog. Combine the flour, salt, baking soda and nutmeg; gradually add to creamed mixture. Cover and refrigerate for 1 hour or until dough is easy to handle.

On a lightly floured surface, roll out dough to 1/8-in. thickness. Cut with 2-1/2-in. cookie cutters dipped in flour. Place 2 in. apart on greased baking sheets. Bake at 375° for 8-10 minutes or until edges begin to brown. Remove to wire racks to cool. In a mixing bowl, beat confectioners' sugar, nutmeg if desired and enough eggnog to achieve icing consistency. Add food coloring if desired. Spread over cooled cookies; let dry. **Yield:** about 4 dozen.

***Editor's Note:** This recipe was tested with commercially prepared eggnog.

Pecan Chocolate Puddles

Since my grandchildren like frosted cookies, I came up with this chocolate-topped version that satisfies them and is almost fuss-free for me. I have used the recipe for years and now make them for my great-grandchildren, too. *—Joyce Kutzler, Clinton, Minnesota*

1/2 cup butter, softened
1 cup packed brown sugar
1 egg
1 teaspoon vanilla extract
1 cup all-purpose flour
1/2 cup quick-cooking oats
1/2 teaspoon salt
1/2 teaspoon baking powder
1 cup chopped pecans
1 cup (6 ounces) miniature semisweet chocolate chips
FILLING:
1 cup (6 ounces) semisweet chocolate chips
1/2 cup sweetened condensed milk
48 pecan halves

In a mixing bowl, cream butter and brown sugar. Beat in egg and vanilla. Combine the flour, oats, salt and baking powder; gradually add to creamed mixture. Stir in chopped pecans and miniature chocolate chips. In a saucepan, melt chocolate chips with milk; stir until smooth. Roll dough into 1-in. balls. Place 2 in. apart on ungreased baking sheets.

Using the end of a wooden spoon handle, make an indentation in the center of each ball. Fill with a rounded teaspoonful of melted chocolate; top with a pecan half. Bake at 350° for 14-16 minutes or until the edges are lightly browned. Remove to wire racks to cool. **Yield:** 4 dozen.

Lemon Coconut Bars

When I pull these bars from the oven, everyone gathers to catch a citrusy whiff. The lemony filling, with its chewy coconut texture, squeezes a welcome hint of sunshine into each satisfying bite. —Doris Jean Armstrong
Santa Fe, New Mexico

- 1/2 cup butter, softened
- 1 cup sugar
- 1 egg
- 1/4 cup molasses
- 2-1/4 cups all-purpose flour
- 1 teaspoon cinnamon
- 1/2 teaspoon baking soda
- 1/4 teaspoon salt

FILLING:

- 1/2 cup sugar
- 1/4 cup lemon juice
- 1 tablespoon grated lemon peel
- 1 tablespoon butter
- 2 eggs
- 1/8 teaspoon salt
- 1 cup flaked coconut

In a mixing bowl, cream butter and sugar. Beat in egg and molasses. Combine flour, cinnamon, baking soda and salt; gradually add to creamed mixture and mix well. Refrigerate for 2 hours or overnight.

For filling, in a saucepan, combine sugar, lemon juice, peel, butter, eggs and salt. Cook and stir over low heat until thickened, about 10 minutes. Remove from heat; stir in coconut. Cool slightly; chill.

Divide dough into fourths. Roll each portion into a 15-in. x 3-1/2-in. rectangle. Spread 1/4 cup filling off-center down each rectangle. Bring long edges together over filling; seal edges. Cut into 1-1/2-in. bars; place on ungreased baking sheets. Bake at 350° for 12-15 minutes or until edges are lightly browned. Cool for 2 minutes; remove to a wire rack to cool completely. **Yield:** about 3-1/2 dozen.

Gingerbread Cookies with Buttercream Icing

(Pictured at right)

These holiday spiced cookies are the first ones I make in December. The recipe came from my mother-in-law. If you like, tint the buttery icing a cheery pink or green and pipe it on with a decorating tip. —Ann Scherzer
Anacortes, Washington

- 2/3 cup shortening
- 1 cup sugar
- 1 egg
- 1/4 cup molasses
- 2 cups all-purpose flour
- 1 teaspoon baking soda
- 1 teaspoon salt
- 1 teaspoon *each* ground cinnamon, cloves and ginger

ICING:

- 3 cups confectioners' sugar
- 1/3 cup butter, softened
- 1 teaspoon vanilla extract
- 1/4 teaspoon lemon extract
- 1/4 teaspoon butter flavoring
- 3 to 4 tablespoons milk

In a mixing bowl, cream shortening and sugar. Beat in egg and molasses. Combine flour, baking soda, salt and spices; gradually add to the creamed mixture and mix well. Refrigerate for 2 hours or overnight.

On a lightly floured surface, roll dough to 1/4-in. thickness. Cut into desired shapes. Place on ungreased baking sheets. Bake at 350° for 8-10 minutes or until edges begin to brown. Cool on a wire rack. For icing, beat sugar, butter and flavorings in a mixing bowl. Gradually stir in milk until smooth and thick. Frost cookies. **Yield:** about 3-1/2 dozen (2-1/2-inch cookies).

Raspberry Kisses

These light and airy drops, bursting with bits of chocolate, have long been a holiday favorite at our house.
—Ruth Vanderberg, Liberty, Missouri

3 egg whites
1/8 teaspoon salt
3/4 cup sugar
3 tablespoons plus 2 teaspoons raspberry gelatin powder
1 tablespoon vinegar
1 cup miniature chocolate chips

In a mixing bowl, beat egg whites and salt until foamy. Combine sugar and gelatin powder; gradually add to egg whites, beating until stiff peaks form and sugar is dissolved. Beat in vinegar. Fold in the chocolate chips. Drop by teaspoonfuls 2 in. apart onto parchment paper-lined baking sheets.

Bake at 250° for 25 minutes. Turn oven off, leaving kisses in the oven 20 minutes longer. Remove to wire racks to cool. **Yield:** about 6 dozen.

Orange Crispies

When I want to drop a little sunshine into my cookie jar, I bake up a double batch of these citrusy and sweet treats. *—Ruth Gladstone, Brunswick, Maryland*

1 cup shortening
1 cup sugar
1 egg
1-1/2 teaspoons orange extract
1/2 teaspoon salt
1-1/2 cups flour
Sugar *or* orange-colored sugar

In a mixing bowl, cream shortening and sugar until fluffy. Beat in egg, extract and salt. Add flour; mix well. Drop rounded tablespoonfuls of dough 2 in. apart onto ungreased baking sheets. Bake at 375° for 10 minutes or until edges begin to brown. Cool for 1-2 minutes; remove from pans to wire racks. Sprinkle with sugar while warm. **Yield:** 3-1/2 dozen.

Coconut Fruitcake Cookies

(Pictured below)

Brimming with candied fruit, coconut and pecans, these sweet morsels my grandma used to bake resemble fruitcake. *—Jolene Davis, Minden, Nevada*

3 cups chopped pecans
2-1/2 cups flaked coconut
1-1/4 cups chopped candied cherries
1-1/4 cups chopped candied pineapple
1 cup chopped dates
2 cups sweetened condensed milk

In a bowl, combine first five ingredients. Stir in milk. Fill paper-lined miniature muffin cups two-thirds full. Bake at 300° for 20-25 minutes or until gold-

en brown. Cool for 10 minutes before removing from pans to waxed paper to cool completely. Let stand for 24 hours in an airtight container at room temperature before serving. **Yield:** 8 dozen.

Fruitcake Squares

My family prefers these scrumptious squares to the larger, more traditional fruitcake. They're so quick and simple to make. —Nora Seaton, McLean, Virginia

6 tablespoons butter, melted
4 cups vanilla wafer crumbs
1 cup pecan halves
3/4 cup chopped dates
3/4 cup chopped mixed candied fruit
1/2 cup chopped candied pineapple
1 can (14 ounces) sweetened condensed milk
1 teaspoon vanilla extract

Pour butter into a 15-in. x 10-in. x 1-in. baking pan. Sprinkle with wafer crumbs. Arrange pecans and fruit over crumbs; press down gently. Combine milk and vanilla; pour evenly over fruit. Bake at 350° for 20-25 minutes or until lightly browned. Cool on a wire rack. **Yield:** about 3 dozen.

Simple Sesames

My kitchen counter is covered with these crispy crowd-pleasers at Christmastime. I make them for friends and family. —Jennifer Lynn, Kamiah, Idaho

1 cup butter, softened
3/4 cup sugar
1-1/2 cups all-purpose flour
1 cup flaked coconut
1/2 cup sesame seeds
1/4 cup finely chopped almonds

In a mixing bowl, cream butter and sugar. Add flour; mix just until combined. Stir in coconut, sesame seeds and almonds. Chill for 15 minutes. Divide dough in half. Shape each half into a 2-in.-diameter roll. Wrap each roll in waxed paper, twisting ends to seal. Refrigerate for 2 hours or overnight.

Remove waxed paper. Cut into 1/4-in. slices; place on ungreased baking sheets. Bake at 300° for 20-25 minutes or until lightly browned. Cool for 2 minutes; remove to a wire rack to cool completely. **Yield:** about 3-1/2 dozen.

Christmas Cutouts

(Pictured above)

Making and decorating these tender sugar cookies left a lasting impression on our four children. Now that they're grown, they've all asked for my recipe so they can bake them with their own children. —Shirley Kidd, New London, Minnesota

1 cup butter, softened
1-1/2 cups confectioners' sugar
1 egg
1 teaspoon vanilla extract
1/2 teaspoon almond extract
2-1/2 cups all-purpose flour
1 teaspoon baking soda
1 teaspoon cream of tartar
FROSTING:
4 cups confectioners' sugar
3 tablespoons butter, softened
1 teaspoon vanilla extract
2-1/2 to 3 tablespoons milk
Liquid *or* paste food coloring, optional

In a mixing bowl, cream butter and sugar. Add egg and extracts. Combine flour, baking soda and cream of tartar; gradually add to the creamed mixture and mix well. Chill for 2-3 hours. On a lightly floured surface, roll dough to 1/8-in. thickness. Cut into desired shapes. Place on ungreased baking sheets. Bake at 375° for 7-8 minutes or until edges begin to brown. Cool on a wire rack.

For frosting, beat sugar, butter and vanilla in a mixing bowl. Gradually stir in milk until smooth and thick; add food coloring if desired. Frost cookies. **Yield:** 5 dozen (2-inch cookies).

Strawberry Oatmeal Bars

(Pictured above)

Their fruity filling and fluffy coconut topping make these bars truly one of a kind. They really dress up my trays of Christmas goodies. —*Flo Burtnett Gage, Oklahoma*

1-1/4 cups all-purpose flour
1-1/4 cups quick-cooking oats
1/2 cup sugar
1/2 teaspoon baking powder
1/4 teaspoon salt
3/4 cup butter, melted
2 teaspoons vanilla extract
1 cup strawberry preserves
1/2 cup flaked coconut

In a bowl, combine dry ingredients. Add butter and vanilla; stir until crumbly. Set aside 1 cup. Press remaining crumb mixture into an ungreased 13-in. x 9-in. x 2-in. baking pan. Spread preserves over crust.

Combine coconut and reserved crumb mixture; sprinkle over preserves. Bake at 350° for 25-30 minutes or until coconut is lightly browned. Cool. **Yield:** 3 dozen.

Peanut Butter Pinwheels

These doubly delightful pinwheel cookies are easy to prepare but look impressive. They feature the classic combination of creamy peanut butter and chocolate in an attractive swirl. —*Kandy Dick, Junction, Texas*

1/2 cup shortening
1/2 cup creamy peanut butter
1 cup sugar
1 egg
2 tablespoons milk
1-1/4 cups all-purpose flour
1/2 teaspoon baking soda
1/2 teaspoon salt
1 cup (6 ounces) semisweet chocolate chips

In a mixing bowl, cream shortening, peanut butter and sugar. Beat in the egg and milk. Combine the flour, baking soda and salt; gradually add to the creamed mixture.

Roll out between waxed paper into a 12-in. x 10-in. rectangle. Melt chocolate chips; cool slightly. Spread over dough to within 1/2 in. of edges. Roll up tightly, jelly-roll style, starting with a long side; wrap in plastic wrap. Refrigerate for 20-30 minutes or until easy to handle.

Unwrap dough and cut into 1/4-in. slices. Place 1 in. apart on greased baking sheets. Bake at 375° for 10-12 minutes or until the edges are lightly browned. Remove to wire racks to cool. **Yield:** about 4 dozen.

Peppermint Brownies

My grandmother encouraged me to enter these mint brownies in the county fair some years ago, and they earned top honors! They're a great chewy treat to serve during the holidays. —*Marcy Greenblatt Redding, California*

3/4 cup vegetable oil
2 cups sugar
2 teaspoons vanilla extract
4 eggs
1-1/3 cups all-purpose flour
1 cup baking cocoa
1 teaspoon baking powder
1 teaspoon salt
3/4 cup crushed peppermint candy, *divided*

GLAZE:
1 cup (6 ounces) semisweet chocolate chips
1 tablespoon shortening

Line a 13-in. x 9-in. x 2-in. baking pan with foil; grease the foil and set aside. In a mixing bowl, beat oil and sugar. Stir in vanilla. Add eggs, one at a time, beating well after each addition. Combine the flour, cocoa, baking powder and salt; gradually add to creamed mixture. Set aside 2 tablespoons peppermint candy for garnish; stir remaining candy into creamed mixture. Spread into prepared pan.

Bake at 350° for 35-40 minutes or until a toothpick inserted near the center comes out clean. Cool on a wire rack. For glaze, melt chocolate chips and shortening in a microwave or heavy saucepan; stir until smooth. Spread over brownies; sprinkle with reserved candy. **Yield:** 2 dozen.

Chocolate-Dipped Peanut Logs

A cookie exchange introduced me to these fancy peanut butter treats. They're eye-catching for the holidays and bake sales. —Patricia Grall, Hortonville, Wisconsin

1 cup creamy peanut butter
1/2 cup butter, softened
1/2 cup shortening
1 cup sugar
1 cup packed brown sugar
2 eggs
2-1/2 cups all-purpose flour
1-1/2 teaspoons baking soda
1 teaspoon baking powder
1/4 teaspoon salt
8 ounces dark chocolate candy coating
2/3 cup ground salted peanuts

In a mixing bowl, cream the peanut butter, butter, shortening and sugars. Add eggs, one at a time, beating well after each addition. Combine the dry ingredients; gradually add to the creamed mixture. Shape into 2-in. logs. Place 2 in. apart on ungreased baking sheets. Bake at 350° for 8-10 minutes or until lightly browned. Remove to wire racks to cool.

In a microwave or heavy saucepan, melt candy coating; stir until smooth. Dip one end of each cookie into coating; shake off excess. Dip into peanuts. Place on waxed paper to harden. **Yield:** about 8-1/2 dozen.

Walnut-Filled Pillows

(Pictured below)

These tender cookie pillows, filled with a delicious walnut mixture, are my husband's favorite. He says it wouldn't be Christmas without them.
—Nancy Kostrej, Canonsburg, Pennsylvania

1/2 cup cold butter
1 package (3 ounces) cold cream cheese
1-1/4 cups all-purpose flour
3/4 cup ground walnuts
1/4 cup sugar
2 tablespoons milk
1/2 teaspoon vanilla *or* almond extract
1 egg, lightly beaten
Confectioners' sugar

In a large bowl, cut butter and cream cheese into flour until mixture resembles coarse crumbs. Using your hands, blend mixture together until a smooth dough forms, about 3 minutes. Pat into a rectangle; wrap in plastic wrap. Refrigerate for 1 hour or until firm. For filling, combine the walnuts, sugar, milk and vanilla.

Unwrap dough and place on a lightly floured surface. Roll into a 17-1/2-in. x 10-in. rectangle; cut into 2-1/2-in. squares. Place a level teaspoonful of filling in the center of each square. Moisten edges with water; fold in half and seal with a fork. Place 1 in. apart on ungreased baking sheets. Brush with egg. Bake at 375° for 10-12 minutes or until edges are golden brown. Remove to wire racks to cool. Dust with confectioners' sugar. **Yield:** 28 cookies.

Chocolate Mint Creams

(Pictured below)

This recipe came from an old family friend and is always high on everyone's cookie request list. I make at least six batches for Noel nibbling and give some away as gifts.
—Beverly Fehner, Gladstone, Missouri

1 cup butter, softened
1-1/2 cups confectioners' sugar
2 squares (1 ounce *each*) unsweetened chocolate, melted and cooled
1 egg
1 teaspoon vanilla extract
2-1/2 cups all-purpose flour
1 teaspoon baking soda
1 teaspoon cream of tartar
1/4 teaspoon salt
FROSTING:
1/4 cup butter, softened
2 cups confectioners' sugar
2 tablespoons milk
1/2 teaspoon peppermint extract
Green food coloring, optional

In a large mixing bowl, cream butter and confectioners' sugar. Add chocolate, egg and vanilla; mix well. Combine dry ingredients; gradually add to creamed mixture, beating well. Shape dough into a 2-in.-diameter roll; wrap in plastic wrap. Refrigerate for 1 hour or until firm.

Unwrap dough and cut into 1/8-in. slices. Place 2 in. apart on ungreased baking sheets. Bake at 400° for 7-8 minutes or until edges are firm. Remove to wire racks to cool. In a small mixing bowl, combine frosting ingredients. Frost cookies. Store in airtight containers. **Yield:** about 6 dozen.

Caramel Pecan Shortbread

My grandchildren look for Grandma's "candy bar cookies" every Christmas. I recommend doubling the recipe for these sweet treats because they go so fast.
—Dorothy Buiter, Worth, Illinois

3/4 cup butter, softened
3/4 cup confectioners' sugar
2 tablespoons evaporated milk
1 teaspoon vanilla extract
2 cups all-purpose flour
1/4 teaspoon salt
FILLING:
28 caramels*
2 tablespoons evaporated milk
2 tablespoons butter
1 cup confectioners' sugar
3/4 cup finely chopped pecans
ICING:
1 cup (6 ounces) semisweet chocolate chips
3 tablespoons evaporated milk
2 tablespoons butter
1/2 cup confectioners' sugar
1/2 teaspoon vanilla extract
Pecan halves

In a mixing bowl, cream butter and confectioners' sugar. Beat in milk and vanilla. Combine flour and salt; gradually add to creamed mixture. Cover and refrigerate for 1 hour or until easy to handle. On a lightly floured surface, roll out the dough to 1/4-in. thickness. Cut into 2-in. x 1-in. strips. Place 1 in. apart on greased baking sheets. Bake at 325° for 12-14 minutes or until lightly browned. Remove to wire racks to cool.

For filling, combine caramels and milk in a saucepan. Cook and stir over medium-low heat until caramels are melted and smooth. Remove from the heat; stir in butter, sugar and pecans. Cool for 5 minutes. Spread 1 teaspoon over each cookie.

For icing, combine chocolate chips and milk in a saucepan. Cook and stir over medium-low heat until chips are melted and smooth. Remove from the heat; stir in butter, sugar and vanilla. Cool for 5 minutes. Spread over filling; top each with a pecan half. Store in an airtight container. **Yield:** about 4 dozen.

***Editor's Note:** This recipe was tested with Hershey caramels.

Two-Tone Christmas Cookies

I dreamed up this recipe using two of my favorite flavors, pistachio and raspberry. These pink and green cookies are tasty and eye-catching, too. They're perfect for formal or informal gatherings, and everybody likes them. —*Marie Capobianco*
Portsmouth, Rhode Island

1 cup butter, softened
1-1/2 cups sugar
2 egg yolks
2 teaspoons vanilla extract
1 teaspoon almond extract
3-1/2 cups all-purpose flour
1 teaspoon salt
1 teaspoon baking powder
1/2 teaspoon baking soda
9 drops green food coloring
1 tablespoon milk
1/3 cup chopped pistachios
9 drops red food coloring
3 tablespoons seedless raspberry jam
2 cups (12 ounces) semisweet chocolate chips, melted
Additional chopped pistachios

In a mixing bowl, cream the butter and sugar. Beat in egg yolks and extracts. Combine the flour, salt, baking powder and baking soda; gradually add to creamed mixture. Divide dough in half. Stir green food coloring, milk and nuts into one portion; mix well. Add red food coloring and jam to the other half.

Shape each portion between two pieces of waxed paper into an 8-in. x 6-in. rectangle. Cut in half lengthwise. Place one green rectangle on a piece of plastic wrap. Top with pink rectangle; press together lightly. Repeat. Wrap each in plastic wrap and refrigerate overnight.

Unwrap the dough and cut in half lengthwise. Return one of the rectangles to the refrigerator. Cut the remaining rectangle into 1/8-in. slices. Place 1 in. apart on ungreased baking sheets. Bake at 375° for 7-9 minutes or until set. Remove to wire racks to cool. Repeat with the remaining dough. Drizzle cooled cookies with melted chocolate. Sprinkle with additional pistachios. **Yield:** 6-1/2 dozen.

Crisp Sand Stars

(Pictured above)

With a subtle almond flavoring and a whole almond in the center, these thin crispy cookies should play a starring role on your Christmas cookie platter.
—*Gladys Scharrer, Allenton, Wisconsin*

1/2 cup butter, softened
1 cup sugar
2 egg yolks
1 tablespoon milk
1/2 teaspoon vanilla extract
1/4 teaspoon almond extract
1-1/2 cups all-purpose flour
1 teaspoon baking powder
1/2 teaspoon baking soda
1/2 teaspoon salt
Unblanched whole almonds
2 egg whites, lightly beaten
Additional sugar

In a mixing bowl, cream the butter and sugar. Beat in the egg yolks, milk and extracts. Combine the flour, baking powder, baking soda and salt; gradually add to creamed mixture. Cover and refrigerate dough for 1 hour or until easy to handle.

On a lightly floured surface, roll out dough to 1/8-in. thickness. Cut with a floured 3-in. star cutter. Place 1 in. apart on ungreased baking sheets. Press an almond in the center of each. Brush with egg white; sprinkle with sugar. Bake at 350° for 8-10 minutes or until lightly browned. Remove to wire racks to cool. **Yield:** about 5 dozen.

Peanut Butter Cutout Cookies

(Pictured above)

Here's a nice change of pace from the more traditional sugar cutout cookies. And children will find that these peanut butter versions are just as much fun to roll, cut out and decorate with frosting, sprinkles and a dash of Yuletide imagination. —*Cindi Bauer Marshfield, Wisconsin*

1 cup creamy peanut butter
3/4 cup sugar
3/4 cup packed brown sugar
2 eggs
1/3 cup milk
1 teaspoon vanilla extract
2-1/2 cups all-purpose flour
1/2 teaspoon baking powder
1/2 teaspoon baking soda
Vanilla frosting
Red, green, yellow and blue gel food coloring
Assorted colored sprinkles

In a large mixing bowl, cream peanut butter and sugars. Beat in the eggs, milk and vanilla. Combine the flour, baking powder and baking soda; add to creamed mixture and mix well. Cover and refrigerate for 2 hours or until easy to handle.

On a lightly floured surface, roll out dough to 1/4-in. thickness. Cut with 2-in. to 4-in. cookie cutters. Place 2 in. apart on ungreased baking sheets. Bake at 375° for 7-9 minutes or until edges are browned. Cool for 1 minute before removing from pans to wire racks to cool completely. Frost and decorate as desired. **Yield:** about 4-1/2 dozen.

Minty Chocolate Crackles

Each December, I whip up big batches of these chewy mint morsels, then watch them disappear in a flash! —*Pat Habiger, Spearville, Kansas*

1 cup (6 ounces) semisweet chocolate chips
1/2 cup plus 4-1/2 teaspoons shortening
3/4 cup sugar
1 egg
1/4 cup light corn syrup
1 teaspoon peppermint extract
1 teaspoon vanilla extract
2 cups all-purpose flour
1/2 teaspoon baking soda
1/4 teaspoon salt
1/4 cup crushed peppermint candy
Additional sugar

In a microwave or double boiler, melt chocolate chips; cool slightly. In a mixing bowl, cream shortening and sugar. Beat in egg, corn syrup, extracts and melted chocolate. Combine flour, baking soda and salt; gradually add to the creamed mixture. Fold in candy. Roll into 1-in. balls; roll in sugar.

Place 2 in. apart on ungreased baking sheets. Bake at 350° for 12-14 minutes or until edges are firm and surface cracks (center will be soft). Cool 5 minutes; remove to wire racks. **Yield:** about 4 dozen.

Triple Layered Bars

We created these chocolaty bars in our food science class at school. They're really pretty drizzled in white and taste great! —*Sarah Nut, Rachel Wallace and Maranda Abercrombie, Little Rock, Arkansas*

1 cup butter, softened
1 cup sugar
1 egg
1/4 teaspoon lemon extract
2 cups all-purpose flour
FILLING:
1/2 cup butter, cubed
2 squares (1 ounce *each*) unsweetened chocolate
2 eggs
1 cup sugar
1 teaspoon vanilla extract
1/2 cup all-purpose flour
1/2 teaspoon salt
4 ounces white candy coating, melted

In a large mixing bowl, cream butter and sugar. Beat in egg and lemon extract. Gradually add flour. Press into a greased 15-in. x 10-in. x 1-in. baking pan; set aside. In a heavy saucepan, melt butter and chocolate until smooth. Remove from heat; cool slightly. In a mixing bowl, beat eggs, sugar and vanilla. Beat in cooled chocolate mixture, flour and salt. Pour over crust.

Bake at 350° for 20-22 minutes or until a toothpick inserted near the center comes out clean. Cool completely on a wire rack. Drizzle candy coating over bars. Cool for 20 minutes before cutting. **Yield:** 32 bars.

Fennel Tea Cookies

These tender buttery tea cookies have a lovely fennel flavor and add a touch of elegance to any holiday cookie tray. Rolled in confectioners' sugar, they look like snowballs! —*Susan Beck, Napa, California*

1 tablespoon fennel seed, crushed
2 tablespoons boiling water
3/4 cup butter, softened
2/3 cup packed brown sugar
1 egg
2 cups all-purpose flour
1/2 teaspoon baking soda
Confectioners' sugar

In a small bowl, soak fennel seed in boiling water; set aside. In a mixing bowl, cream butter and brown sugar. Beat in egg. Drain fennel seed. Combine the flour, baking soda and fennel seed; gradually add to creamed mixture. Roll into 1-in. balls; place 2 in. apart on ungreased baking sheets. Bake at 350° for 10-12 minutes or until lightly browned. Roll warm cookies in confectioners' sugar. Cool on wire racks. **Yield:** 3 dozen.

Crispy Christmas Trees

(Pictured below)

These holiday novelties from our Taste of Home Test Kitchen will draw admiring comments wherever you serve them. A sprinkle of sugar supplies a Yuletide touch to each fanciful hand-shaped creation.

2 tablespoons butter
2 cups pastel miniature marshmallows
3 cups crisp rice cereal
1/4 cup finely chopped pecans
Green decorator's sugar
Confectioners' sugar

In a heavy saucepan, melt butter. Stir in marshmallows; cook and stir over low heat until melted. Remove from the heat; stir in cereal and pecans. Let cool just enough to handle. With greased hands, shape into trees. (Work quickly as the cereal hardens quickly and becomes difficult to form.) Roll in green sugar. Place on a serving tray; dust with confectioners' sugar. **Yield:** about 1-1/2 dozen.

Cream Cheese Spritz

(Pictured below)

A hint of orange and cinnamon highlights these Christmastime classics. I like to add colorful sprinkles before baking them. The recipe is from a booklet that came with a cookie press in the 1950s, and I still have the press!
—Sarah Bedia, Lake Jackson, Texas

1 cup shortening
1 package (3 ounces) cream cheese, softened
1 cup sugar
1 egg yolk
1 teaspoon vanilla extract
1 teaspoon grated orange peel
2-1/2 cups all-purpose flour
1/2 teaspoon salt
1/4 teaspoon ground cinnamon
Green food coloring, decorator candies and colored sugar, optional

In a mixing bowl, beat shortening and cream cheese until blended. Add sugar; beat until creamy. Beat in egg yolk, vanilla and orange peel. Combine the flour, salt and cinnamon; gradually add to creamed mixture. Add food coloring if desired.

Using a cookie press fitted with the disk of your choice, press dough 1 in. apart onto ungreased baking sheets. Decorate if desired. Bake at 350° for 9-12 minutes or until set (do not brown). Remove to wire racks to cool. **Yield:** about 9 dozen.

Gumdrop Cookies

These fun cookies are chock-full of chewy gumdrops. I use red and green ones at Christmas, black and orange for Halloween and pastel shades for Easter. I've made this recipe for years and find that kids really get a kick out of the cookies with a candy surprise inside!
—Carolyn Stromberg, Wever, Iowa

3/4 cup shortening
1 cup sugar, *divided*
1/2 teaspoon almond extract
1-3/4 cups all-purpose flour
1/2 teaspoon baking soda
1/4 teaspoon salt
1 cup chopped fruit-flavored *or* spiced gumdrops
2 egg whites

In a mixing bowl, cream shortening and 3/4 cup sugar. Beat in extract. Combine flour, baking soda and salt; gradually add to creamed mixture. Stir in gumdrops. In a small mixing bowl, beat egg whites until soft peaks form. Gradually add remaining sugar, beating until stiff peaks form. Fold into dough.

Drop by heaping teaspoonfuls 2 in. apart onto ungreased baking sheets. Bake at 350° for 12-15 minutes or until golden brown. Cool for 1 minute before removing from pans to wire racks to cool completely. **Yield:** 3-1/2 dozen.

Chocolate-Drizzled Cherry Bars

I've been making bars since I was in third grade, but these are special. I bake them for the church Christmas party every year, and folks always rave about them and ask for a copy of the recipe. —Janice Heikkila Deer Creek, Minnesota

2 cups all-purpose flour
2 cups quick-cooking oats
1-1/2 cups sugar
1-1/4 cups butter, softened
1 can (21 ounces) cherry pie filling
1 teaspoon almond extract
1/4 cup semisweet chocolate chips
3/4 teaspoon shortening

In a mixing bowl, combine flour, oats, sugar and butter until crumbly. Set aside 1-1/2 cups for topping. Press remaining crumb mixture into an ungreased 13-in. x 9-in. x 2-in. baking dish. Bake at 350° for 15-18 minutes or until edges begin to brown.

In a bowl, combine pie filling and extract; carefully spread over crust. Sprinkle with reserved crumb mixture. Bake 20-25 minutes longer or until edges and topping are lightly browned. In a microwave or heavy saucepan, melt chocolate chips and shortening; stir until smooth. Drizzle over warm bars. Cool completely on a wire rack. **Yield:** 3 dozen.

Holiday Cheesecake Bars

(Pictured above right)

Christmas officially arrives at our house when I make these melt-in-your-mouth bars. Red and green maraschino cherries add a jolly finish to each light and creamy morsel. —Kathy Dorman, Snover, Michigan

2 cups all-purpose flour
2/3 cup packed brown sugar
2/3 cup cold butter
1 cup chopped walnuts
FILLING:
2 packages (8 ounces *each*) cream cheese, softened
1/2 cup sugar
2 eggs
1/4 cup milk
2 tablespoons lemon juice
1 teaspoon vanilla extract
Sliced red and green maraschino cherries, optional

In a bowl, combine flour and brown sugar; cut in butter until mixture resembles coarse crumbs. Stir in walnuts. Reserve 1 cup. Press remaining crumbs onto the bottom of an ungreased 13-in. x 9-in. x 2-in. baking pan. Bake at 350° for 12 minutes.

Meanwhile, in a mixing bowl, beat cream cheese and sugar until light and fluffy. Add eggs, one at a time, beating well after each addition. Beat in milk, lemon juice and vanilla; pour over crust. Sprinkle with reserved crumbs. Bake 25-30 minutes longer or until edges are lightly browned and filling is almost set. Cool in pan on a wire rack. Cut into squares. Garnish with cherries if desired. Store in the refrigerator. **Yield:** 2 dozen.

Making Pressed Cookies

Be sure your butter or cream cheese is softened to room temperature before beginning.

If the dough is too soft and not making a sharp design, refrigerate briefly. If the dough is too stiff and won't move through the press, let the dough stand at room temperature briefly until it is the right consistency.

Chocolate-Tipped Butter Cookies

(Pictured above)

My husband and I enjoy these buttery cookies so much that we have a hard time saving them for guests!
—*Thara Baker-Alley, Columbia, Missouri*

1 cup plus 3 tablespoons butter, softened, *divided*
1/2 cup confectioners' sugar
2 cups all-purpose flour
1 teaspoon vanilla extract
1 cup (6 ounces) semisweet chocolate chips
1/2 cup finely chopped pecans *or* walnuts

In a mixing bowl, cream 1 cup butter and sugar. Add flour and vanilla; mix well. Cover and refrigerate for 1 hour. Shape 1/2 cupfuls of dough into 1/2-in.-thick logs. Cut logs into 2-1/2-in. pieces; place on ungreased baking sheets. Bake at 350° for 12-14 minutes or until lightly browned. Cool on wire racks.

In a microwave or double boiler, melt chocolate and remaining butter. Dip one end of each cookie into chocolate and then into nuts; place on waxed paper until chocolate is set. **Yield:** about 5 dozen.

Gingerbread Boys

(Pictured on front cover)

These lightly spiced festive fellows are great to munch on. And if I punch a hole in the cutout shapes before baking, I can use the sturdy cookies as tree ornaments, too.
—*Doré Merrick Grabski, Utica, New York*

2/3 cup shortening
1/2 cup sugar
1/2 cup molasses
1 egg
3 cups all-purpose flour
1 teaspoon baking soda
1 teaspoon *each* ground cinnamon, ginger and cloves
1/2 teaspoon salt
1/2 teaspoon ground nutmeg
Confectioners' sugar icing, red-hot candies and miniature chocolate chips, optional

In a mixing bowl, cream shortening and sugar. Add molasses and egg; mix well. Combine the flour, baking soda, cinnamon, ginger, cloves, salt and nutmeg; gradually add to creamed mixture and mix well. Divide dough in half. Refrigerate for at least 2 hours.

On a lightly floured surface, roll out each portion to 1/8-in. thickness. Cut with a floured 4-in. cookie cutter. Place 2 in. apart on greased baking sheets. Bake at 350° for 9-11 minutes or until edges are firm. Remove to wire racks to cool. Decorate as desired. **Yield:** about 2 dozen.

Chocolate Snowballs

These dainty cookies just melt in your mouth. I enjoy making them for get-togethers when there are lots of people around to enjoy them.
—*Mary Lou Welsh, Hinsdale, Illinois*

3/4 cup butter, softened
3/4 cup packed brown sugar
1 egg
1/4 cup milk
1 teaspoon vanilla extract
2 cups all-purpose flour
1/2 cup baking cocoa
1 teaspoon baking powder
1/2 teaspoon salt
1/4 teaspoon baking soda
Confectioners' sugar

In a mixing bowl, cream butter and brown sugar. Add egg, milk and vanilla; mix well. Combine flour, cocoa, baking powder, salt and baking soda; gradually add to creamed mixture. Cover and refrigerate overnight. Shape into 1-in. balls; place 2 in. apart on ungreased baking sheets.

Bake at 350° for 7-8 minutes or until tops are crackled. Remove from baking sheets; immediately roll in confectioners' sugar. Cool completely. Roll again in confectioners' sugar. **Yield:** 6 dozen.

Frosted Cashew Cookies

(Pictured below right)

Some "dairy" merry snacking is guaranteed when you pass out these cashew-packed goodies! I found the recipe in a flyer promoting dairy products years ago. It's been this farm wife's standby ever since.
—June Lindquist, Hammond, Wisconsin

1/2 cup butter, softened
1 cup packed brown sugar
1 egg
1/2 teaspoon vanilla extract
2 cups all-purpose flour
3/4 teaspoon baking powder
3/4 teaspoon baking soda
1/4 teaspoon salt
1/3 cup sour cream
1-3/4 cups chopped cashews
FROSTING:
1/2 cup butter
3 tablespoons half-and-half cream
1/4 teaspoon vanilla extract
2 cups confectioners' sugar
Cashew halves, optional

In a mixing bowl, cream butter and brown sugar. Beat in egg and vanilla. Combine dry ingredients; add alternately with sour cream to creamed mixture. Stir in cashews. Drop by tablespoonfuls onto greased baking sheets. Bake at 375° for 8-10 minutes or until lightly browned. Cool on a wire rack.

For frosting, lightly brown butter in a small saucepan. Remove from heat and cool slightly. Add cream and vanilla. Beat in confectioners' sugar until smooth and thick. Frost cookies; top each with a cashew half if desired. **Yield:** about 5 dozen.

Cream Cheese Macadamia Cookies

With their soft cake-like texture and subtle orange flavor, these tender drop cookies are sure to liven up holiday tea parties and luncheons. They also make great gifts for loved ones and tasty treats to have on hand throughout the season. *—Lillie Grove, Beaver, Oklahoma*

1/2 cup butter, softened
1 package (8 ounces) cream cheese, softened
3/4 cup packed brown sugar
4 teaspoons grated orange peel
2 teaspoons vanilla extract
1-1/2 cups all-purpose flour
2 teaspoons baking powder
3/4 cup coarsely chopped salted macadamia nuts *or* almonds

In a mixing bowl, cream the butter, cream cheese, brown sugar, orange peel and vanilla. Combine flour and baking powder. Gradually add to creamed mixture; mix well. Fold in nuts. Cover and refrigerate for 1 hour or until firm.

Drop by rounded teaspoonfuls 2 in. apart onto ungreased baking sheets; flatten slightly. Bake at 400° for 9-11 minutes or until lightly browned. Remove to wire racks to cool. **Yield:** about 3-1/2 dozen.

Editor's Note: If using unsalted macadamia nuts, add 1/4 teaspoon salt to the dough. This recipe does not use eggs.

Roll-Out Cookies

(Pictured below)

I collect cookie cutters, so a good cutout recipe is a must. These cookies are crisp and buttery with a hint of lemon.
—Bonnie Price, Yelm, Washington

1 cup butter, softened
1 cup sugar
1 egg
1 teaspoon vanilla extract
1/2 teaspoon lemon extract
3 cups all-purpose flour
2 teaspoons baking powder
GLAZE:
1 cup confectioners' sugar
2 tablespoons water
1 tablespoon light corn syrup
Food coloring, optional

In a mixing bowl, cream butter and sugar. Add egg and extracts. Combine flour and baking powder; gradually add to creamed mixture and mix well. (Dough will be very stiff. If necessary, stir in the last cup of flour mixture by hand. Do not chill.)

On a lightly floured surface, roll dough to 1/8-in. thickness. Cut out cookies into desired shapes. Place 2 in. apart on ungreased baking sheets. Bake at 400° for 6-7 minutes or until edges are lightly browned. Cool 2 minutes before removing to wire racks; cool completely.

For glaze, combine the sugar, water and corn syrup until smooth. Tint with food coloring if desired. Using a small brush and stirring glaze often, brush on cookies, decorating as desired. **Yield:** about 6 dozen (2-1/4-inch cookies).

Split-Second Cookies

(Pictured below)

I love baking cookies, and this is a recipe I've used for many Christmases over the years. Raspberry jam makes these cookies flavorful and colorful.
—Mrs. Richard Foust, Stoneboro, Pennsylvania

3/4 cup butter, softened
2/3 cup sugar
1 egg
1 teaspoon vanilla extract
2 cups all-purpose flour
1/2 teaspoon baking powder
1/2 teaspoon salt
1/3 cup raspberry jam

In a mixing bowl, cream butter and sugar. Add egg and vanilla; mix well. Combine flour, baking powder and salt; gradually add to creamed mixture. Mix well.

Divide dough into four equal portions; shape each into a 12-in. x 3/4-in. log. Place 4 in. apart on greased baking sheets. Make a 1/2-in. depression down center of logs; fill with jam. Bake at 350° for 15-20 minutes or until lightly browned. Cool for 2 minutes; cut

diagonally into 3/4-in. slices. Remove to wire racks to cool completely. **Yield:** about 5 dozen.

Chocolate-Filled Spritz

I found this delicious cookie recipe years ago. Over time, I decided to liven them up with a chocolate filling.
—Theresa Ryan, White River Junction, Vermont

1 cup butter, softened
2/3 cup sugar
1 egg
1/2 teaspoon vanilla extract
1/2 teaspoon lemon *or* orange extract
2-1/4 cups all-purpose flour
1/4 teaspoon baking powder
1/4 teaspoon salt
4 squares (1 ounce *each*) semisweet chocolate

In a mixing bowl, cream butter and sugar. Beat in the egg and extracts. Combine the dry ingredients; gradually add to the creamed mixture. Using a cookie press fitted with the disk of your choice, press dough 2 in. apart onto ungreased baking sheets.

Bake at 350° for 10-12 minutes or until set (do not brown). Remove to wire racks to cool. Melt chocolate; spread over bottom of half of the cookies. Top with remaining cookies. **Yield:** about 3 dozen.

Cranberry Oat Cookies

These cookies call to mind ones my mother used to bake. Instead of stirring in raisins like she did, I add bright red cranberries. *—Marjorie Goertzen, Chase, Kansas*

2/3 cup butter, softened
2/3 cup packed brown sugar
2 eggs
1-1/2 cups all-purpose flour
1-1/2 cups old-fashioned oats
1 teaspoon baking soda
1 teaspoon ground cinnamon
1/2 teaspoon salt
1-1/4 cups dried cranberries
1 cup chopped pecans, toasted
2/3 cup vanilla *or* white chips

In a mixing bowl, cream butter and brown sugar. Add eggs; mix well. Combine the dry ingredients; gradually add to the creamed mixture. Stir in the cranberries, pecans and chips. Drop by tablespoonfuls 3 in. apart onto ungreased baking sheets. Bake at 375° for 10-12 minutes or until golden brown. Remove to wire racks to cool. **Yield:** about 4 dozen.

Italian Horn Cookies

(Pictured above)

My family has been making these fruit-filled cookies for generations. Light and flaky, they have the look of an elegant pastry. *—Gloria Siddiqui, Houston, Texas*

1 cup cold butter
4 cups all-purpose flour
2 cups vanilla ice cream, softened
1 can (12-1/2 ounces) cherry filling*
Sugar

In a large bowl, cut butter into flour until mixture resembles coarse crumbs. Stir in ice cream. Divide into four portions. Cover and refrigerate for 2 hours.

On a lightly floured surface, roll each portion to 1/8-in. thickness. With a fluted pastry cutter, cut into 2-in. squares. Place about 1/2 teaspoon filling in the center of each square. Overlap two opposite corners of dough over the filling and seal. Sprinkle lightly with sugar. Place on ungreased baking sheets. Bake at 350° for 10-12 minutes or until bottoms are light brown. Cool on wire racks. **Yield:** about 5 dozen.

***Editor's Note:** This recipe was tested using Solo brand cherry filling, found in the baking aisle of most grocery stores. Poppy seed filling may also be used.

Raspberry Nut Pinwheels

I won first prize in a recipe contest with these yummy swirl cookies a number of years ago. The taste of raspberry and walnuts really comes through in each bite, and they're so much fun to make! —*Pat Habiger Spearville, Kansas*

1/2 cup butter, softened
1 cup sugar
1 egg
1 teaspoon vanilla extract
2 cups all-purpose flour
1 teaspoon baking powder
1/4 cup seedless raspberry jam
3/4 cup finely chopped walnuts

In a mixing bowl, cream butter and sugar. Beat in egg and vanilla. Combine the flour and baking powder; gradually add to creamed mixture. Roll out dough between waxed paper into a 12-in. square. Remove top piece of waxed paper. Spread dough with jam and sprinkle with nuts. Roll up tightly jelly-roll style, starting with a long side; wrap in plastic wrap. Refrigerate for 2 hours or until firm.

Unwrap dough and cut into 1/4-in. slices. Place 2 in. apart on ungreased baking sheets. Bake at 375° for 9-12 minutes or until edges are lightly browned. Remove to wire racks to cool completely. **Yield:** about 3-1/2 dozen.

Black Forest Oatmeal Crisps

Although the recipe for my hearty chocolate-cherry novelties is sized right for a bake sale or cookie exchange, it can be cut in half for smaller gatherings. —*Paula Smith, Naperville, Illinois*

1 cup butter-flavored shortening
1 cup sugar
1 cup packed brown sugar
2 eggs
2 tablespoons milk
1 teaspoon almond extract
1-2/3 cups all-purpose flour
1 teaspoon baking soda
3/4 teaspoon salt
1/2 teaspoon baking powder
2-1/2 cups quick-cooking oats
6 squares (1 ounce *each*) white baking chocolate, chopped *or* 1 cup vanilla *or* white chips
1-1/2 cups chopped red candied cherries
1 cup (6 ounces) semisweet chocolate chips
3/4 cup slivered almonds

In a mixing bowl, cream shortening and sugars. Add the eggs, one at a time, beating well after each. Beat in milk and extract. Combine flour, baking soda, salt and baking powder; gradually add to the creamed mixture. Stir in the remaining ingredients.

Drop by heaping teaspoonfuls 2 in. apart onto ungreased baking sheets. Bake at 375° for 8-10 minutes or until golden brown. Remove to wire racks to cool. **Yield:** about 14 dozen.

Butterscotch Meringue Bars

These fast and easy bars are unlike any others I've eaten. They're irresistibly rich and always draw oohs, aahs and requests for the recipe after the very first bite! —*Betty Behnken, Beverly Hills, Florida*

1 cup butter-flavored shortening
1/2 cup sugar
1/2 cup packed brown sugar
3 egg yolks
1 tablespoon water
3 teaspoons vanilla extract
2 cups all-purpose flour
1/4 teaspoon baking soda
1/4 teaspoon salt
1 cup butterscotch chips
MERINGUE:
3 egg whites
1 cup packed brown sugar
1 cup chopped walnuts

In a mixing bowl, cream shortening and sugars. Beat in egg yolks, water and vanilla. Combine flour, baking soda and salt; gradually add to creamed mixture. Spread into a greased 13-in. x 9-in. x 2-in. baking pan. Sprinkle with butterscotch chips and pat lightly.

For meringue, in a small mixing bowl, beat egg whites until stiff peaks form. Gradually add brown sugar, beating well. Spread over chips. Sprinkle with walnuts and gently press into meringue. Bake at 350° for 25-30 minutes or until golden brown. Cool on a wire rack. Cut into bars. Refrigerate leftovers. **Yield:** 3 dozen.

Desserts

Eggnog Pound Cake

(Pictured above)

A flavorful blend of eggnog and nutmeg makes this cake a natural holiday favorite. It uses a convenient boxed mix base. —*Theresa Koetter, Borden, Indiana*

1 package (18-1/4 ounces) yellow cake mix
1 cup eggnog*
3 eggs
1/2 cup butter, softened
1/2 to 1 teaspoon ground nutmeg
CUSTARD SAUCE:
1/4 cup sugar
1 tablespoon cornstarch
1/4 teaspoon salt
1 cup milk
1 egg yolk, lightly beaten
1 teaspoon butter
1 teaspoon vanilla extract
1/2 cup heavy whipping cream, whipped

In a mixing bowl, combine the first five ingredients. Beat on low speed until moistened, scraping bowl occasionally. Beat on medium for 2 minutes. Pour into a greased and floured 12-cup fluted tube pan. Bake at 350° for 40-45 minutes or until a toothpick inserted near the center comes out clean. Cool in pan for 10 minutes; invert onto a wire rack. Remove from pan; cool completely.

For sauce, combine sugar, cornstarch and salt in a saucepan; gradually stir in milk until smooth. Cook and stir over medium-high heat until thickened and bubbly. Reduce heat; cook and stir 2 minutes longer. Remove from heat. Blend a small amount into egg yolk. Return all to the pan; mix well. Bring to a gentle boil; cook and stir for 2 minutes. Remove from the heat; stir in butter and vanilla. Cool quickly by placing pan in ice water. Fold in whipped cream. Store in the refrigerator. Serve with the cake. **Yield:** 16-20 servings.

*__Editor's Note:__ This recipe was tested with commercially prepared eggnog.

Strawberry Dessert

I like to garnish this dessert with strawberry slices arranged to look like poinsettias. It's pretty, festive and feeds a crowd! —*Delores Romyn, Stratton, Ontario*

1 package (3 ounces) ladyfingers, split
1 package (4-3/4 ounces) strawberry Junket Danish Dessert*
1-3/4 cups cold water
2 pints fresh strawberries, sliced
1 carton (8 ounces) frozen whipped topping, thawed
Additional sliced strawberries, optional

Place ladyfingers in a single layer in a 13-in. x 9-in. x 2-in. dish; set aside. In a saucepan, bring dessert mix and water to a boil. Cook and stir for 1 minute. Cool for 4-5 minutes; fold in strawberries. Spread gently over ladyfingers. Cover; refrigerate for 3-4 hours. Spread with whipped topping. Garnish with additional strawberries if desired. **Yield:** 12-15 servings.

*__Editor's Note:__ Look for Strawberry Junket Danish Dessert in the gelatin section of your grocery store.

Cranberry Cream

This delightful gelatin cream brings Christmas meals to a happy ending. It's not heavy, and I relish its zesty goodness. —*Sharlene Atkinson, Tacoma, Washington*

2-1/2 cups orange juice, *divided*
1 can (16 ounces) jellied cranberry sauce
1 package (6 ounces) raspberry gelatin
1-1/2 cups heavy whipping cream
1 to 2 medium oranges, peeled and sectioned

1/4 cup fresh *or* frozen cranberries, thawed
Corn syrup and sugar

In a saucepan, combine 3/4 cup orange juice, cranberry sauce and gelatin. Mash and cook over medium-low heat until gelatin is dissolved. Stir in remaining orange juice. Chill until mixture begins to thicken, about 2-1/2 hours.

Beat cream until soft peaks form; fold into gelatin mixture. Pour into an 8-cup serving bowl; refrigerate until firm. Garnish with oranges. Brush cranberries with corn syrup; sprinkle with sugar. Place over oranges. **Yield:** 8-10 servings.

Banbury Tarts

Deliciously old-fashioned, these tempting tarts our Taste of Home Test Kitchen came up with are a "must" for Santa's Christmas Eve cookie plate.

1 cup chopped raisins
1 cup sugar
1/4 cup graham cracker crumbs
1 egg
2 tablespoons lemon juice
2 teaspoons grated lemon peel
1/4 cup finely chopped walnuts, optional
Pastry for two double-crust pies (9 inches)
1 cup confectioners' sugar
4 teaspoons milk

In a bowl, combine the first six ingredients. Stir in walnuts if desired. Roll out pastry to 1/8-in. thickness; cut into forty-eight 3-in. circles; moisten edges with water. Put 1-1/2 teaspoons filling on half of each circle. Fold other half over the filling; press edges together with a fork to seal.

Cut a slit in top of each tart. Place on a lightly greased baking sheet. Bake at 375° for 13-15 minutes or until lightly browned. Remove to wire racks to cool. Combine sugar and milk; drizzle over cooled tarts. **Yield:** 4 dozen.

Almond Rice with Raspberry Sauce

(Pictured at right)

It simply wouldn't be Christmas in our family without this old-fashioned dessert. Cool and creamy, it looks beautiful drizzled with the tart raspberry sauce.
—Bonnie Wehrman, Ambrose, North Dakota

5 cups water, *divided*
2 cups uncooked long grain rice
2 teaspoons salt
2-1/2 cups milk
1 cup sugar
1 cup slivered almonds, toasted
1/4 teaspoon almond extract
3 tablespoons cornstarch
2 packages (10 ounces *each*) frozen sweetened raspberries, thawed
2 tablespoons lemon juice
2 cups heavy whipping cream
Fresh mint, optional

In a large saucepan over medium heat, bring 4 cups of water, rice and salt to a boil. Reduce heat; cover and simmer for 15 minutes or until rice is tender and liquid is absorbed. Stir in milk and sugar. Bring to a boil over medium heat; reduce heat and simmer, uncovered, until milk is absorbed and rice is creamy. Remove from the heat; stir in almonds and extract. Cool slightly; cover and chill.

Meanwhile, in another saucepan, combine cornstarch and remaining water; add raspberries. Bring to a boil over medium heat; boil and stir for 2 minutes or until thickened. Remove from the heat; stir in lemon juice. Cover and chill. Just before serving, whip cream until soft peaks form; fold into rice mixture. Spoon into individual serving dishes and top with raspberry sauce. Garnish with mint if desired. **Yield:** 8-10 servings.

Strawberry Angel Trifle

(Pictured below)

I always get compliments when I bring this attractive and tasty trifle out of the refrigerator. Not only does it serve a big group nicely, I can make it ahead of time, too.
—Lucille Belsham, Fort Fraser, British Columbia

1 package (16 ounces) angel food cake mix
2 packages (3 ounces *each*) strawberry gelatin
3/4 cup plus 1/3 cup sugar, *divided*
2 cups boiling water
5 cups fresh *or* frozen unsweetened strawberries, thawed and drained
2 cups heavy whipping cream

Prepare and bake cake mix according to package directions; cool completely. In a large bowl, dissolve gelatin and 3/4 cup sugar in boiling water. Mash half of the strawberries; add to gelatin mixture. Refrigerate until slightly thickened, about 1 hour. Slice remaining strawberries; stir into the gelatin.

Cut cake into 1-in. cubes. Place half in a 2-1/2-qt. trifle or glass bowl. Top with half of the gelatin mixture. Repeat. Cover and refrigerate until set, about 4 hours. In a mixing bowl, beat cream until soft peaks form. Gradually add remaining sugar, beating until stiff peaks form. Spoon over gelatin. **Yield:** 12-16 servings.

Creamy Citrus Mousse

Light and fluffy, this marvelous mousse is the perfect ending to a holiday meal. Guests always save room for it.
—Phy Bresse, Lumberton, North Carolina

2 tablespoons lime juice
2 tablespoons sugar
1 package (3 ounces) lime gelatin
1 cup boiling water
1/3 cup cold water
2 cups whipped topping
1/2 cup sweetened condensed milk
1 tablespoon grated lime peel, optional
2 teaspoons orange extract
Maraschino cherries, optional
Additional grated lime peel, optional

Dip the rims of six individual dessert dishes in lime juice, then in sugar; set aside. In a bowl, dissolve gelatin in boiling water. Stir in cold water. Refrigerate until slightly thickened, about 30 minutes.

Meanwhile, combine the whipped topping, milk, lime peel if desired and orange extract. Fold into gelatin. Spoon into dessert dishes. Refrigerate for 1 hour or until firm. Just before serving, garnish with cherries and lime peel if desired. **Yield:** 6 servings.

Walnut Apple Cake

Loaded with tart apples and crunchy walnuts, this cake is fun to take to potlucks or family gatherings. The sweet buttery sauce tops off pieces just right.
—Dorothy Anderson, Ottawa, Kansas

1/2 cup butter, softened
2 cups sugar
2 eggs
2 cups all-purpose flour
1 teaspoon baking powder
3/4 teaspoon baking soda
1/2 teaspoon salt
1/2 teaspoon ground cinnamon
1/2 teaspoon ground nutmeg
3 cups chopped peeled tart apples (about 3)
1-1/2 cups chopped walnuts
SAUCE:
1 cup sugar
1/2 cup butter

1/2 cup half-and-half cream
1/2 teaspoon rum extract

In a mixing bowl, cream butter and sugar. Add eggs, one at a time, beating well after each addition. Combine flour, baking powder, baking soda, salt, cinnamon and nutmeg; gradually add to the creamed mixture. Stir in apples and walnuts. Spoon into a greased 13-in. x 9-in. x 2-in. baking pan. Bake at 325° for 45-50 minutes or until a toothpick inserted near the center comes out clean.

In a saucepan, combine the sugar, butter and cream; mix well. Cook over low heat until heated through. Remove from the heat; stir in rum extract. Serve sauce warm with the cake. **Yield:** 12-16 servings.

Raspberry Walnut Torte

I get lots of compliments on this sweet treat filled with nuts and fruity flavor. It was a favorite at the tearoom I once operated. —*Helen Schmidt, Moline, Illinois*

1/2 cup butter, softened
1/3 cup sugar
1 egg
1-1/4 cups all-purpose flour
1 cup ground walnuts
1 jar (12 ounces) raspberry preserves, *divided*

FILLING:

4 eggs
3/4 cup packed brown sugar
2 cups flaked coconut
2 cups chopped walnuts
2 tablespoons all-purpose flour
1/4 teaspoon baking powder
2 to 3 tablespoons water

In a mixing bowl, cream butter and sugar. Add egg; mix well. Add flour; mix until blended. Stir in walnuts. Press onto the bottom and 1-1/2 in. up the sides of a greased 9-in. springform pan. Refrigerate for 1 hour. Spread 1/4 cup preserves over crust.

In a mixing bowl, beat eggs and brown sugar until light and fluffy. Combine coconut, walnuts, flour and baking powder; fold into egg mixture. Pour into crust. Bake at 350° for 1 hour. Cool; remove sides of pan. Thin remaining preserves with water. Spread over torte. **Yield:** 10-12 servings.

Cherry Date Fruitcake

(Pictured above)

It's a Christmas tradition for me to serve this fruitcake at parties and give it to friends and family. Jam-packed with nuts and cherries, it puts a new spin on a holiday mainstay. —*Judy Schultz, Jamestown, New York*

1-1/2 cups all-purpose flour
1-1/2 cups sugar
1 teaspoon baking powder
1 teaspoon salt
5-1/2 cups pecan halves
2 jars (16 ounces *each*) maraschino cherries, drained and halved
1 pound diced candied pineapple
2 packages (8 ounces *each*) chopped pitted dates
6 eggs
1/2 cup apple juice
1/4 cup light corn syrup

In a large bowl, combine the first four ingredients. Add pecans, cherries, pineapple and dates; toss to coat. Beat eggs and apple juice; add to fruit mixture and mix well. Grease two foil-lined 9-in. x 5-in. x 3-in. loaf pans. Press half of the mixture into each pan.

Bake at 300° for 1-3/4 to 2 hours or until a toothpick inserted near center comes out clean. Cool in pans on a wire rack for 10 minutes. Remove from pans; remove foil. Brush each loaf with corn syrup. Cool completely. **Yield:** 2 fruitcakes.

Chocolate Peanut Butter Cheesecake

(Pictured above)

Family and friends always ooh and aah when I bring out this tempting cheesecake after holiday dinners! It's a showstopper. —*Mrs. H.L. Sosnowski*
Grand Island, New York

BROWNIE CRUST:
1/4 cup butter
3 squares (1 ounce *each*) unsweetened chocolate
1 cup packed brown sugar
2 eggs
1-1/2 teaspoons vanilla extract
2/3 cup all-purpose flour
1/8 teaspoon baking powder
1 square (1 ounce) semisweet chocolate, chopped
FILLING:
1 jar (12 ounces) creamy peanut butter
2 packages (one 8 ounces, one 3 ounces) cream cheese, softened
1 cup packed brown sugar
3 eggs
1/2 cup sour cream
TOPPING:
3/4 cup sour cream
2 teaspoons sugar
Melted semisweet chocolate, optional

In a microwave, melt butter and unsweetened chocolate; set aside. In a mixing bowl, beat brown sugar and eggs until light and fluffy, about 4 minutes. Add chocolate mixture and vanilla; mix well. Combine flour and baking powder; add to batter. Stir in chopped chocolate.

Spread 1 cup batter into a greased 9-in. springform pan. Cover and refrigerate remaining batter. Place pan on a baking sheet. Bake at 350° for 17-19 minutes or until a toothpick inserted near the center comes out clean. Cool on a wire rack for 5 minutes; place in freezer for 15 minutes.

For filling, in a mixing bowl, beat peanut butter, cream cheese and brown sugar until smooth. Add eggs and sour cream; beat on low speed just until combined. Spread remaining brownie batter about 1-1/2 in. high around sides of pan, sealing to baked crust. Pour filling into center. Bake at 350° for 45 minutes or until center is almost set.

For topping, combine sour cream and sugar; spread over filling to within 3/4 in. of edges. Return cheesecake to the oven; turn oven off and let stand for 5 minutes. Cool on a wire rack for 10 minutes. Carefully run a knife around pan to loosen; cool 1 hour longer. Chill overnight. Remove sides of pan. Drizzle top with melted chocolate if desired. Refrigerate leftovers. **Yield:** 12 servings.

Pistachio Cherry Squares

This dessert's Christmas colors really add to the festivity of a buffet table, but it's the creamy, cool taste that keeps people coming back for more. —*Kathy Zielicke*
Fond du Lac, Wisconsin

2 cups graham cracker crumbs
1/2 cup butter, melted
1/4 cup sugar
CREAM CHEESE LAYER:
1 package (8 ounces) cream cheese, softened
2/3 cup confectioners' sugar
1 carton (8 ounces) frozen whipped topping, thawed
PUDDING LAYER:
2-1/2 cups cold milk
2 packages (3.4 ounces *each*) instant pistachio pudding mix
TOPPING:
1 carton (8 ounces) frozen whipped topping, thawed
2 cans (21 ounces *each*) cherry pie filling

Combine the cracker crumbs, butter and sugar; press into an ungreased 13-in. x 9-in. x 2-in. dish. Refrigerate. In a mixing bowl, beat cream cheese and confectioners' sugar; fold in whipped topping. Spread over crust. In a mixing bowl, beat milk and pudding mixes on low speed for 2 minutes. Spread over cream cheese layer; chill until firm, about 1 hour.

Spread whipped topping over pudding layer. Top with pie filling. Refrigerate overnight. Cut into squares. **Yield:** 12-15 servings.

Festive Mint Cream Dessert

(Pictured at right)

Mint ice cream and colorful sprinkles make this cool concoction perfect for holiday parties or meals. For a chocolaty dessert, use rocky road or chocolate ice cream instead. —*Sally Hook, Houston, Texas*

3/4 cup butter, *divided*
1 package (14 ounces) chocolate cream-filled sandwich cookies, crushed
2 quarts mint ice cream
1-1/2 cups milk chocolate chips
1 cup confectioners' sugar
3/4 cup evaporated milk
1 carton (16 ounces) frozen whipped topping, thawed
Chocolate syrup and red and green sprinkles, optional

In a saucepan or microwave, melt 1/2 cup butter. Stir in cookie crumbs; mix well. Press into an ungreased 13-in. x 9-in. x 2-in. dish. Freeze for 30 minutes or until firm. Meanwhile, remove ice cream from freezer to soften. Spread ice cream over crust; return to the freezer until firm.

In a saucepan, combine chocolate chips, confectioners' sugar, milk and remaining butter. Bring to a boil, stirring frequently. Cook and stir for 3-5 minutes or until thickened. Cool to room temperature. When cool, spread over ice cream; return to freezer.

When chocolate layer has hardened, spread with whipped topping (dish will be full). Cover and freeze. Remove from the freezer 20-30 minutes before serving. If desired, drizzle with chocolate syrup and top with sprinkles. **Yield:** 24 servings.

Eggnog Cream Pie

I discovered this easy recipe on the back of an eggnog carton, then modified it slightly to simplify things. I can whip up the pie and still have time to devote to guests.
—Susan Williams, Reno, Nevada

1 package (5.1 ounces) cook-and-serve vanilla pudding mix
1/8 to 1/4 teaspoon ground nutmeg
1-1/2 cups eggnog*
2 cups heavy whipping cream, whipped
1 pastry shell (9 inches), baked
Additional whipped cream and ground nutmeg, optional

In a saucepan, combine the pudding mix, nutmeg and eggnog. Cook and stir over medium heat until mixture comes to a boil. Cook and stir 1-2 minutes longer or until thickened. Remove from the heat. Cool. Fold in whipped cream. Pour into crust. Garnish with whipped cream and nutmeg if desired. **Yield:** 6-8 servings.

***Editor's Note:** This recipe was tested with commercially prepared eggnog.

Baked Fudge Pudding

(Pictured below)

This easy-to-make pudding is a true chocolate lover's delight. I always look forward to that first dishful warm from the oven. You can top it with whipped cream, spoon it over ice cream or enjoy the fudgy flavor all by itself!
—Sue Ann Chapman, Tulsa, Oklahoma

2 cups sugar
1/2 cup all-purpose flour
1/2 cup baking cocoa
4 eggs
2 teaspoons vanilla extract
1 cup butter, melted
1 cup chopped pecans
Mint chocolate chip ice cream, whipped cream, chopped pecans *and/or* chocolate sauce, optional

In a mixing bowl, combine sugar, flour and cocoa. Add eggs; mix well. Beat in vanilla and butter; stir in pecans. Pour into a greased 8-in. square baking pan. Place in a larger pan filled with 1 in. of hot water.

Bake at 300° for 65 minutes or until set. Serve warm or at room temperature; top with ice cream, whipped cream, pecans and/or chocolate sauce if desired. **Yield:** 9 servings.

Sweet Potato Cake Roll

Smooth cream cheese filling is all rolled up in the cinnamony sweet potato flavor of a sponge cake. This tantalizing change-of-pace dessert makes an attractive conclusion to a holiday meal. *—Bernice Taylor*
Wilson, North Carolina

2 eggs
1 cup sugar
2/3 cup mashed cooked sweet potatoes
1 cup self-rising flour*
1 teaspoon ground cinnamon
2 tablespoons confectioners' sugar
CREAM CHEESE FILLING:
1 package (8 ounces) cream cheese, softened
1 cup confectioners' sugar
1 tablespoon butter, melted
1 teaspoon vanilla extract
1/3 cup chopped pecans
Additional confectioners' sugar, optional

Line a greased 15-in. x 10-in. x 1-in. baking pan with waxed paper and grease the paper; set aside. In a mixing bowl, beat eggs on high speed for 5 minutes. Gradually beat in sugar until thick and lemon-colored. Add sweet potatoes; mix well. Combine flour and cinnamon; fold into sweet potato mixture. Spread into prepared pan.

Bake at 350° for 10-15 minutes or until cake springs back when lightly touched. Cool for 5 minutes; invert cake onto a kitchen towel dusted with confectioners' sugar. Gently peel off waxed paper. Roll up cake in the towel jelly-roll style, starting with a short side. Cool on a wire rack.

For filling, in a mixing bowl, beat cream cheese, confectioners' sugar, butter and vanilla until fluffy. Fold in nuts. Unroll cake; spread filling evenly over cake to within 1/2 in. of edges. Roll up again. Cover and refrigerate until serving. Dust with confectioners' sugar if desired. **Yield:** 8-10 servings.

*__Editor's Note:__ As a substitute for 1 cup self-rising flour, place 1-1/2 teaspoons baking powder and 1/2 teaspoon salt in a measuring cup. Add all-purpose flour to measure 1 cup.

Old-Fashioned Chocolate Pie

Preparing this old-fashioned pie brings back memories. When I was a girl, we cranked homemade ice cream to serve with it. —*Betsey Sue Halcott*
Lebanon, Connecticut

1/2 cup water
1-1/2 squares (1-1/2 ounces) unsweetened baking chocolate
1/4 cup butter
2/3 cup sugar
1-1/2 teaspoons vanilla extract
FILLING:
1/4 cup shortening
3/4 cup sugar
1 egg
1 cup all-purpose flour
1 teaspoon baking powder
1/2 teaspoon salt
1/2 cup milk
1 unbaked pastry shell (9 inches)
2 tablespoons chopped nuts, optional

In a saucepan, bring water, chocolate and butter to a boil; boil for 1 minute. Remove from the heat; add sugar and vanilla. Set aside. In a mixing bowl, cream shortening and sugar until light and fluffy. Add egg; beat well. Combine flour, baking powder and salt; add to creamed mixture alternately with milk.

Pour into pastry shell. Carefully pour reserved chocolate mixture over filling. Sprinkle with nuts if desired. Cover edges of pastry with foil. Bake at 350° for 55-60 minutes or until a toothpick inserted near the center comes out clean. **Yield:** 8 servings.

Jeweled Sherbet Mold

(Pictured above)

Besides being a colorful addition to any holiday buffet table, this frozen dessert keeps well and is deliciously different. —*Mary Gaylord, Balsam Lake, Wisconsin*

1 pint lime sherbet, softened
1 pint lemon sherbet, softened
1 can (8 ounces) crushed pineapple, drained
1/3 cup chopped mixed candied fruit
1/4 teaspoon rum extract, optional

Line a 1-1/2-qt. metal or glass bowl with plastic wrap or foil. Pack lime sherbet into the bottom of the bowl; smooth top. Freeze for 15 minutes. In another bowl, combine lemon sherbet, pineapple, candied fruit and extract if desired. Spoon over lime sherbet; smooth top. Cover and freeze for 2 hours or until firm.

Remove from the freezer 15 minutes before serving. Uncover and invert onto a serving platter. Remove bowl and plastic wrap; smooth sides. **Yield:** 12-14 servings.

Cranberry-Pear Apple Crisp

(Pictured above)

With its crunchy golden topping and flavorful blend of tart cranberries and sweet apples and pears, this dessert makes a refreshing finish to heavy winter meals.
—Louis Gelzer, Oak Bluffs, Massachusetts

8 medium pears, peeled and sliced
4 medium tart apples, peeled and sliced
2 cups fresh *or* frozen cranberries, thawed
1 cup sugar
3/4 cup all-purpose flour
TOPPING:
1 cup packed brown sugar
3/4 cup all-purpose flour
3/4 cup quick-cooking oats
1/4 teaspoon ground cinnamon
1/2 cup cold butter
Ice cream, optional

In a large bowl, toss the fruit, sugar and flour. Pour into a greased 13-in. x 9-in. x 2-in. baking dish. For topping, in a bowl, combine the brown sugar, flour, oats and cinnamon. Cut in butter until mixture resembles coarse crumbs. Sprinkle over fruit mixture.

Bake, uncovered, at 350° for 60-65 minutes or until fruit is tender and topping is golden brown. Serve with ice cream if desired. **Yield:** 12-14 servings.

Peppermint Charlotte

My guests always save room for this pretty pink peppermint dessert. You'll know why after just one cool and fluffy bite. —Lucille Watters, Palmyra, Missouri

2 envelopes unflavored gelatin
3-1/2 cups milk
1/2 cup sugar
1/8 teaspoon salt
5 egg yolks, beaten
1/2 cup finely crushed peppermint candy
8 drops red food coloring
1-1/2 cups heavy whipping cream, whipped
12 ladyfingers, split

In a saucepan, soften gelatin in milk for 1 minute. Stir in sugar and salt. Cook and stir over medium-low heat for 5 minutes or until gelatin is dissolved. Remove from the heat. Stir a small amount of hot mixture into egg yolks. Return all to the pan.

Cook and stir over low heat until the mixture thickens slightly and coats the back of a metal spoon or reaches 160° (do not boil). Remove from the heat. Add candy and food coloring; stir until candy is dissolved. Refrigerate, stirring occasionally, until mixture begins to thicken, about 30 minutes. Fold in whipped cream.

Place ladyfinger halves around a greased 9-in. springform pan. Pour mixture into center of pan. Cover and chill for 4 hours or overnight. Just before serving, run a knife around edge of pan to loosen; remove sides. **Yield:** 10-12 servings.

Plum Ice Cream

(Pictured at right)

Here's a pretty ice cream that is such a light refreshing finale to a holiday meal, it melts any resistance to dessert! —Jo Baker, Litchfield, Illinois

2 cans (30 ounces *each*) whole plums
6 cups milk
4 cups heavy whipping cream
2 cups sugar
1/3 cup lemon juice
Red food coloring, optional

Drain plums, reserving 1 cup syrup. Peel plums and remove pits. In a food processor or blender, cover and process plums until smooth. In a bowl, combine milk,

cream, sugar, lemon juice, plums, reserved syrup and food coloring if desired. Stir until sugar is dissolved.

Fill cylinder of ice cream freezer two-thirds full; freeze according to manufacturer's directions. Refrigerate remaining mixture until ready to freeze. Allow to ripen in ice cream freezer or firm up in refrigerator freezer for 2-4 hours before serving. **Yield:** 4 quarts.

Caramel Pecan Cheesecake

(Pictured below)

I created this creamy cheesecake using two favorites—caramel and pecans. It's a stunning cake and rivals any I've tasted. —*Deidre Sizer, Kettering, Ohio*

- **2 cups crushed shortbread cookies**
- **3 tablespoons butter, melted**
- **1/4 cup plus 2 tablespoons all-purpose flour, *divided***
- **1 jar (12-1/4 ounces) caramel ice cream topping**
- **1 cup chopped pecans, *divided***
- **5 packages (8 ounces *each*) cream cheese, softened**
- **1-3/4 cups sugar**
- **1-1/2 teaspoons vanilla extract**
- **4 eggs**
- **2 egg yolks**
- **1/3 cup heavy whipping cream**

SOUR CREAM TOPPING:

- **2 cups (16 ounces) sour cream**
- **1/3 cup sugar**

In a bowl, combine cookie crumbs and butter; mix well. Press onto the bottom and 1 in. up the sides of a greased 10-in. springform pan. Place pan on a baking sheet. Bake at 350° for 8-10 minutes or until set. Cool on a wire rack.

In a small bowl, stir 1/4 cup flour into the caramel topping. Set aside 1/3 cup caramel mixture and 2 tablespoons pecans for garnish. Drizzle remaining caramel mixture over crust; sprinkle with remaining pecans. In a mixing bowl, beat the cream cheese, sugar, vanilla and remaining flour until smooth. Add eggs and yolks; beat on low speed just until combined. Stir in cream. Pour over crust. Bake at 325° for 65-70 minutes or until center is almost set.

Combine sour cream and sugar; carefully spread over warm filling. Bake 10-12 minutes longer or until topping is set. Cool on a wire rack for 10 minutes. Carefully run a knife around edge of pan to loosen; cool 1 hour longer. Chill for 8 hours or overnight. Remove sides of pan. Drizzle with reserved caramel mixture and sprinkle with reserved pecans. Refrigerate leftovers. **Yield:** 12 servings.

Frozen Cranberry Cups

It's just not Christmas at our house without this lighter-than-air whipped dessert. It couldn't be easier to make and looks so festive in foil cups. —*Marilyn Huntley*
St. Augustine, Florida

3/4 cup whole-berry cranberry sauce
3 tablespoons orange juice concentrate
2 tablespoons chopped pecans
1/2 cup heavy whipping cream
2 tablespoons sugar

Place the cranberry sauce in a bowl; chop the cranberries. Stir in the orange juice concentrate and pecans; set aside. In a mixing bowl, beat cream until soft peaks form. Gradually add sugar, beating until stiff peaks form. Fold into the cranberry mixture.

Fill foil-lined muffin cups two-thirds full. Cover and freeze until firm. Remove from the freezer 15 minutes before serving. **Yield:** 8 servings.

Ice Cream Balls

(Pictured below)

This is a fun and easy dessert to fix for Christmas gatherings—even the kids can help. The cereal adds a crunchy texture to the ice cream and makes an everyday treat something special. —*Ann Marie Woodhull*
Cedar Springs, Michigan

1-1/2 cups Corn Chex cereal, crushed
1/4 cup packed brown sugar
2 tablespoons butter, melted
1/4 cup finely chopped walnuts
1 pint vanilla ice cream, softened
Hot fudge *or* caramel ice cream topping, optional

In a shallow bowl, combine cereal, sugar and butter; mix well. Add nuts. Shape ice cream into 1-in. balls; roll in cereal mixture until well coated. Freeze for at least 1 hour. If desired, serve with fudge or caramel ice cream topping. **Yield:** 12-16 balls.

Nutcracker Sweet

My mother baked this chocolate-almond dessert for family gatherings and her bridge club meetings when I was growing up. Continuing the tradition, I take the cake to potlucks, neighborhood parties and Christmas celebrations. —*Patty Webb, Calgary, Alberta*

1 cup graham cracker crumbs (about 16 squares)
1 cup finely chopped almonds
1 square (1 ounce) unsweetened chocolate, grated
6 eggs, *separated*
1 cup sugar, *divided*
1/4 cup all-purpose flour
1-1/4 teaspoons baking powder
1-1/4 teaspoons ground cinnamon
1/4 teaspoon ground cloves
2 tablespoons vegetable oil
1 teaspoon almond extract
ALMOND CREAM:
2 cups heavy whipping cream
1/2 cup confectioners' sugar
1/2 teaspoon almond extract
Grated semisweet chocolate, optional

Combine crumbs, almonds and chocolate; set aside. In a small mixing bowl, beat egg whites until foamy. Gradually beat in 1/2 cup sugar until stiff peaks form; set aside. In a large mixing bowl, combine flour, baking powder, cinnamon, cloves and remaining sugar. In another bowl, beat egg yolks, oil and extract. Add to dry ingredients; beat on medium for 1 minute. Stir in crumb mixture. Fold in egg whites.

Pour into two greased 9-in. round baking pans lined with greased waxed paper. Bake at 350° for 30-35 minutes or until a toothpick inserted near the center comes out clean. Cool for 10 minutes; remove from pans to wire racks. Carefully remove waxed paper; cool completely. In a mixing bowl, beat cream and confectioners' sugar until soft peaks form. Add extract;

beat until stiff peaks form. Split cake layers in half horizontally; spread almond cream over each layer. Stack on a serving plate. (Do not frost sides of cake.) Garnish with grated semisweet chocolate if desired. Cover and refrigerate overnight. **Yield:** 12-16 servings.

Cherry Almond Pie

I love trying new recipes for Christmas, but my husband can't get enough of traditional classics like this cherry pie. —*Johanna Gerow, Raytown, Missouri*

2 cans (14 ounces *each*) pitted tart cherries
1 cup sugar
1/4 cup cornstarch
1/8 teaspoon salt
2 tablespoons butter
1/2 teaspoon almond extract
1/2 teaspoon vanilla extract
1/4 teaspoon red food coloring, optional
Pastry for double-crust pie (9 inches)
1 egg yolk, beaten
Additional sugar

Drain cherries, reserving 1 cup juice. In a saucepan, combine the sugar, cornstarch and salt; gradually stir in reserved cherry juice until smooth. Bring to a boil; cook and stir for 2 minutes or until thickened. Remove from the heat; stir in butter, extracts and food coloring if desired. Fold in cherries. Cool slightly.

Line a 9-in. pie plate with bottom crust; trim pastry to 1 in. beyond edge of plate. Pour filling into crust. Roll out remaining pastry; make a lattice crust. Trim, seal and flute edges. Brush lattice top with egg yolk. Sprinkle with additional sugar. Cover edges loosely with foil. Bake at 425° for 15 minutes. Remove foil. Bake 20-25 minutes longer or until crust is golden brown and filling is bubbly. Cool on a wire rack. **Yield:** 6-8 servings.

Stuffed Apples with Custard Sauce

(Pictured above right)

Chock-full of old-fashioned goodness, this baked apple recipe is yummy to the core. Its sauce drizzles on so smooth and creamy, it rivals the fanciest desserts.
—*Nancy Snyder, Albuquerque, New Mexico*

1 cup chopped walnuts
1 cup raisins
1/2 cup sugar
1/4 cup butter, melted
8 medium unpeeled tart apples
1/2 cup water
CUSTARD SAUCE:
1/2 cup sugar
1 tablespoon all-purpose flour
1/8 teaspoon salt
1 cup milk
1 cup heavy whipping cream
4 egg yolks, lightly beaten
1/4 teaspoon vanilla extract

In a blender or food processor, combine walnuts, raisins and sugar; cover and process until ground. Stir in butter; set aside. Core apples and remove enough pulp to leave a 1-in. shell. Fill each apple with 1/4 cup nut mixture. Place in a greased shallow 3-qt. baking dish. Pour water around apples. Bake, uncovered, at 375° for 30-40 minutes or until tender.

Meanwhile, for custard sauce, combine the sugar, flour and salt in a saucepan. Gradually stir in the milk and cream until smooth. Bring to a boil over medium heat; cook and stir for 2 minutes or until thickened. Remove from the heat. Stir a small amount of hot milk mixture into egg yolks; return all to the pan, stirring constantly. Bring to a gentle boil; cook and stir for 2 minutes. Remove from the heat; stir in vanilla. Cool. Serve over warm apples. Refrigerate any leftovers. **Yield:** 8 servings.

Miniature Almond Tarts

(Pictured above)

My family requests these adorable little tarts each Christmas. I always enjoy making them since the almond paste in the filling reflects our Dutch heritage. They're also popular at special gatherings.
—Karen Van Den Berge, Holland, Michigan

1 cup butter, softened
2 packages (3 ounces *each*) cream cheese, softened
2 cups all-purpose flour
FILLING:
6 ounces almond paste, crumbled
2 eggs, beaten
1/2 cup sugar
FROSTING:
1-1/2 cups confectioners' sugar
3 tablespoons butter, softened
4 to 5 teaspoons milk
Maraschino cherry halves (about 48)

In a mixing bowl, cream the butter and cream cheese. Add flour; mix well. Refrigerate for 1 hour. Shape into 1-in. balls. Place in ungreased miniature muffin cups; press into the bottom and up the sides to form a shell. For filling, combine almond paste, eggs and sugar in a mixing bowl. Beat on low speed until blended. Fill each shell with about 1-1/2 teaspoons filling.

Bake at 325° for 25-30 minutes or until edges are golden brown. Cool for 10 minutes before removing to wire racks to cool completely. For frosting, combine the confectioners' sugar, butter and enough milk to achieve desired consistency. Pipe or spread over tarts. Top each with a cherry half. **Yield:** about 4 dozen.

Linzertorte

My Austrian grandmother made this nutty jam-filled dessert only at Christmastime and so did my mother. Now I'm proud to carry on the tasty tradition. It's a great way to end a holiday meal. *—Jeanne Siebert*
Salt Lake City, Utah

2 cups all-purpose flour
2 cups ground hazelnuts *or* walnuts
1/2 cup sugar
1/2 cup packed brown sugar
1 teaspoon ground cinnamon
1/8 teaspoon salt
Dash ground cloves
1 cup cold butter
2 eggs, lightly beaten
1 teaspoon grated lemon peel
1-1/3 cups raspberry jam
Confectioners' sugar, optional

In a bowl, combine the first seven ingredients. Cut in butter until mixture resembles coarse crumbs. Add eggs and lemon peel; stir until mixture forms a ball. Divide into fourths. Cover and refrigerate for 3-4 hours or until chilled. Remove two portions of dough from refrigerator; press each into an ungreased 9-in. fluted tart pan with removable bottom. Spread 2/3 cup jam over each.

Between two sheets of lightly floured waxed paper, roll one portion of the remaining dough into a 10-in. x 6-in. rectangle. Cut six 1-in.-wide strips; arrange in a lattice design over the jam. Repeat with the remaining dough (return dough to the refrigerator if needed). Bake at 350° for 40-45 minutes or until bubbly and the crust is browned. Cool completely. Dust with confectioners' sugar if desired. **Yield:** 2 tortes (8 servings each).

Chocolate Mint Cream Pie

This light, refreshing pie is an ideal way to give your holiday guests a treat without going to a lot of fuss. What's more, it cuts nicely, making it a cinch to serve.
—Donna Christopher, Crestwood, Missouri

2 cups crushed chocolate-covered mint cookies
3 to 4 tablespoons hot water
1 graham cracker crust (8 inches)
1 package (3 ounces) cream cheese, softened
1/3 cup sugar
2 tablespoons milk
1/4 teaspoon peppermint extract
1 carton (8 ounces) frozen whipped topping, thawed
6 to 10 drops green food coloring, optional

Set aside 2 tablespoons cookie crumbs for garnish. In a bowl, combine remaining crumbs with enough hot water to make crumbs spreadable. Spoon over the graham cracker crust; spread out evenly; set aside. In a mixing bowl, beat cream cheese until fluffy. Add the sugar, milk and extract; beat until smooth. Fold in whipped topping.

If food coloring is desired, divide mixture in half and add coloring to one half. Alternately spoon mounds of plain and colored mixture into crust; swirl with a knife. Sprinkle with reserved cookie crumbs. Cover and refrigerate for 3 hours or until firm. **Yield:** 8-10 servings.

Christmas Cheesecake

(Pictured below)

With a cheery cherry topping and mint green garnish, this is the perfect dessert to top off a holiday dinner.
—Verna Arthur, Perkins, Oklahoma

1-1/2 cups graham cracker crumbs (about 24 squares)
6 tablespoons butter, melted
1 envelope unflavored gelatin
1/4 cup cold water
1/4 cup milk
1 package (8 ounces) cream cheese, softened
1/2 cup confectioners' sugar
2 teaspoons grated lemon peel
1 carton (8 ounces) frozen whipped topping, thawed, *divided*
1 can (21 ounces) cherry pie filling

Combine crumbs and butter; press onto the bottom of a greased 9-in. springform pan. Chill 15 minutes. In a saucepan, combine gelatin and water; let stand for 1 minute. Add milk; cook and stir over low heat until gelatin is dissolved. Beat cream cheese and sugar until light and fluffy. Add gelatin mixture and lemon peel; mix well. Chill until partially set.

Fold in 2 cups whipped topping. Pour over crust. Chill until firm, at least 3 hours. Spread pie filling over gelatin layer. Top with remaining whipped topping. **Yield:** 10-12 servings.

Holiday Cranberry Cobbler

(Pictured below)

For a change of pace from pumpkin pie, I prepare this merry berry cobbler at Christmas. Our children, grandchildren and great-grandchild all enjoy it.
—Helen Weissinger, Caribou, Maine

- **1 can (21 ounces) peach pie filling**
- **1 can (16 ounces) whole-berry cranberry sauce**
- **1 package (18-1/4 ounces) yellow cake mix**
- **1 teaspoon ground cinnamon**
- **1/4 teaspoon ground nutmeg**
- **1 cup cold butter**
- **1 cup chopped nuts**
- **Vanilla ice cream**

Combine pie filling and cranberry sauce. Spread in an ungreased 13-in. x 9-in. x 2-in. baking dish. In a bowl, combine dry cake mix, cinnamon and nutmeg; cut in butter until crumbly. Stir in nuts; sprinkle over fruit. Bake at 350° for 35-40 minutes or until a toothpick inserted near the center of cake comes out clean. Serve warm with ice cream. **Yield:** 12-15 servings.

Salted Peanut Cake

My mother-in-law shared this treasured family recipe with me. We adore the nutty cake with its smooth frosting. *—Kay Beauchamp, Marquette, Michigan*

- **1/2 cup shortening**
- **1 cup sugar**

- **1 egg**
- **1-1/2 cups all-purpose flour**
- **1 teaspoon baking soda**
- **1 teaspoon baking powder**
- **1 cup buttermilk**
- **1 pound salted peanuts, ground**

FROSTING:

- **1/2 cup all-purpose flour**
- **1 cup milk**
- **1 cup butter, softened**
- **1 cup confectioners' sugar**
- **1 teaspoon vanilla extract**

In a mixing bowl, cream shortening and sugar. Add egg; beat well. Combine the flour, baking soda and baking powder; add to creamed mixture alternately with buttermilk. Set aside 3/4 cup peanuts for topping. Stir remaining peanuts into batter. Spread into a greased 13-in. x 9-in. x 2-in. baking pan. Bake at 350° for 40-45 minutes or until a toothpick inserted near the center comes out clean. Cool on a wire rack.

Meanwhile, for the frosting, combine the flour and the milk in a saucepan until smooth. Bring to a boil over medium heat, stirring frequently. Cook and stir for 2 minutes or until thickened. Remove from the heat; cool completely.

In a mixing bowl, cream the butter and the confectioners' sugar until fluffy. Add the cooled flour mixture and the vanilla; beat until fluffy, about 4 minutes. Spread over the cake; sprinkle with the reserved peanuts. **Yield:** 16-20 servings.

Gingersnap Ice Cream Torte

My husband and I developed this sweet frozen treat featuring gingersnaps, caramel and ice cream. Since a little of this rich cake goes a long way, it'll easily feed a crowd. *—Cary Schulte, Broadway, Virginia*

- **2 cups finely crushed gingersnaps (about 40 cookies)**
- **1/2 cup packed brown sugar**
- **1/2 cup butter, melted**
- **1 package (14 ounces) caramels***
- **1/3 cup half-and-half cream *or* milk**
- **1-1/2 cups cold milk**
- **2 packages (3.4 ounces *each*) instant vanilla pudding mix**
- **1/2 gallon vanilla ice cream, softened**
- **1/2 cup chopped pecans**

In a bowl, combine the gingersnaps, brown sugar and butter; set half aside. Press remaining mixture onto the bottom of a greased 9-in. springform pan. Bake at 350° for 10 minutes. Cool completely. In a microwave or heavy saucepan, melt caramels. Stir in cream until smooth; set aside.

In a mixing bowl, beat milk and pudding mixes on low speed for 2 minutes. Stir in ice cream until blended. Spoon half into the crust. Top with half of the reserved gingersnap mixture. Drizzle with half of the caramel sauce; sprinkle with half of the pecans. Repeat layers. Cover and freeze for at least 4 hours or until firm. Remove from the freezer 15 minutes before serving. **Yield:** 16-20 servings.

***Editor's Note:** This recipe was tested with Hershey caramels.

Marbled Peppermint Angel Cake

Although it doesn't puff up as much as other angel food cakes during baking, the refreshing minty flavor and festive red swirls raise this version above ordinary desserts!
—Kathy Kittell, Lenexa, Kansas

1-1/2 cups egg whites (about 12)
1-1/2 teaspoons cream of tartar
1-1/2 teaspoons vanilla extract
1 teaspoon peppermint extract
1/4 teaspoon salt
1-1/2 cups sugar, *divided*
3/4 cup all-purpose flour
6 drops red food coloring, optional
GLAZE:
2 cups confectioners' sugar
1/4 cup milk
1/4 teaspoon peppermint extract
6 drops red food coloring, optional
1/4 cup crushed peppermint candies

In a mixing bowl, beat egg whites, cream of tartar, extracts and salt on high speed. Gradually add 3/4 cup of sugar, beating until stiff peaks form and sugar is dissolved. Combine flour and remaining sugar; gradually fold into the batter, 1/4 cup at a time.

Divide batter in half; tint half with red food coloring. Alternately spoon plain and pink batters into an ungreased 10-in. tube pan. Cut through batter with a knife to remove air pockets. Bake at 350° for 30-40 minutes or until cake springs back when lightly touched. Immediately invert pan; cool completely.

Run a knife around sides of cake. Remove from the pan. For glaze, combine confectioners' sugar, milk, extract and food coloring if desired. Drizzle over cake. Sprinkle with crushed candies. **Yield:** 12-16 servings.

Cranberry Dream Pie

(Pictured above)

Plenty of cranberries are grown in this area, so the tart and tangy fruit finds its way into my cooking quite often. This luscious pie is one I regularly prepare.
—Lila Scheer, Ocean Park, Washington

3/4 cup sugar
2 teaspoons cornstarch
1/4 cup cold water
2 cups fresh *or* frozen cranberries
2 packages (3 ounces *each*) cream cheese, softened
1 cup confectioners' sugar
1 teaspoon vanilla extract
1 cup heavy whipping cream, whipped
1 pastry shell, baked *or* graham cracker crust (9 inches)

In a saucepan, combine sugar, cornstarch and water until smooth. Add cranberries. Bring to a boil; boil and stir for 2 minutes. Reduce heat; cook until berries pop, 5 minutes. Set aside. In a mixing bowl, beat cream cheese, confectioners' sugar and vanilla until fluffy. Fold in whipped cream. Spread into pie shell. Top with cranberry mixture. Chill for at least 4 hours. Store in the refrigerator. **Yield:** 6-8 servings.

Butterscotch Brownie Pinwheels

(Pictured above)

A neighbor gave the recipe for these rich chewy treats to my mother when I was still in grade school, and I've been preparing them each Christmas for over 30 years.
—Virginia Nicky, Bloomingdale, Illinois

1 cup semisweet chocolate chips
4 tablespoons butter, ***divided***
1 can (14 ounces) sweetened condensed milk
1 cup all-purpose flour
1 teaspoon vanilla extract
Confectioners' sugar
1 cup butterscotch chips
1/2 cup chopped walnuts

Grease a 15-in. x 10-in. x 1-in. baking pan; line with waxed paper and spray the paper with nonstick cooking spray. Set aside. In a microwave or heavy saucepan, melt the chocolate chips and 2 tablespoons of butter; stir until smooth. Stir in milk, flour and vanilla; mix well. Spread into prepared pan. Bake at 325° for 12-14 minutes or until a toothpick inserted 2 in. from the edges comes out clean. Cool in pan on a wire rack for 3 minutes.

Turn onto a kitchen towel dusted with confectioners' sugar. Gently peel off waxed paper. Roll up brownie in the towel, jelly-roll style, starting with a long side. Cool for 12 minutes on a wire rack. Melt butterscotch chips and remaining butter. Unroll brownie; spread filling to within 1/2 in. of edges. Sprinkle with walnuts. Reroll; wrap in foil. Refrigerate for 2 hours or until firm. Unwrap and dust with confectioners' sugar. With a sharp thin knife, cut into 1/4-in. slices. **Yield:** 5 dozen.

Editor's Note: If brownie cracks while rolling, press together with fingers and continue rolling.

Caramel Custard

Although my husband isn't a fan of egg-custard desserts, he finds this one irresistible. It's rich and velvety—a perfect dish to serve warm on a wintry day.
—Yvonne Wyble, Port Allen, Louisiana

2 cups heavy whipping cream
4 egg yolks
1 teaspoon vanilla extract
1/4 cup sugar
1/8 teaspoon salt
Brown sugar

In a saucepan over medium-low heat, bring cream almost to a simmer. Remove from the heat. In a mixing bowl, beat egg yolks, vanilla, sugar and salt until thick and lemon-colored, about 3 minutes. Gradually beat in cream. Pour into an ungreased 1-qt. baking dish. Place baking dish into a 13-in. x 9-in. x 2-in. baking pan. Pour hot water into baking pan to a depth of 1 in.

Bake at 350° for 55-60 minutes or until a knife inserted near center comes out clean. Cool on a wire rack for 15 minutes. Refrigerate until chilled. Remove from refrigerator 30 minutes before serving. Sprinkle with enough brown sugar to cover the top. Broil 6 in. from heat for 2 minutes or until sugar is melted. Serve immediately. **Yield:** 6 servings.

Spice Cake Bars

Whenever I went to Grandmother's, she served these flavorful bars, topped with creamy frosting. Today, I do the same for our grandchildren, who like the little treats just as much.
—Dena Hayden, Vassar, Michigan

1 cup butter, softened
1 cup sugar
1 cup molasses

1 cup hot water
1 egg
3 cups all-purpose flour
2 teaspoons ground ginger
2 teaspoons ground allspice
1 teaspoon baking soda
1 teaspoon ground cloves

FROSTING:

1/2 cup shortening
1/2 cup butter, softened
2 to 3 teaspoons lemon juice
4 cups confectioners' sugar

In a mixing bowl, cream butter and sugar. Beat in molasses, water and egg. Combine flour, ginger, allspice, baking soda and cloves; gradually add to the creamed mixture. Pour into a greased 15-in. x 10-in. x 1-in. baking pan. Bake at 375° for 18-22 minutes or until a toothpick inserted near the center comes out clean.

Cool on wire rack. In a mixing bowl, cream shortening, butter and lemon juice. Beat in sugar until fluffy. Frost bars. **Yield:** about 2 dozen.

Cherry Cheese Cupcakes

Our church Christmas party always includes these pretty cupcakes as my home-baked contribution. The holidays were the sweet inspiration for their cheery garnish of cherries and mint leaves. —*Leanne Beagley Rochester, New York*

3 packages (8 ounces *each*) cream cheese, softened
1-1/2 cups sugar, *divided*
1-1/2 teaspoons vanilla extract, *divided*
5 eggs
1 cup (8 ounces) sour cream
1-1/2 cups cherry pie filling
Mint leaves

In a mixing bowl, combine cream cheese, 1 cup sugar and 1 teaspoon vanilla; beat until smooth. Add eggs, one at a time, beating well after each addition. Spoon into foil-lined muffin cups. Bake at 300° for 25-30 minutes or until set. Cool 5 minutes.

In a small bowl, combine sour cream and remaining sugar and vanilla until smooth. Spoon onto cupcakes. Return to oven for 6-8 minutes or until set. Cool completely. Top with pie filling. Garnish with mint leaves. Chill. **Yield:** 22-24 servings.

Chocolate Mousse Loaf

(Pictured below)

This showstopping loaf would make a tempting centerpiece for the most sumptuous holiday table.
—*Daphene Miller, Princeton, Missouri*

2 cups heavy whipping cream, *divided*
3 egg yolks
16 squares (1 ounce *each*) semisweet chocolate
1/2 cup butter
1/2 cup light corn syrup
1/4 cup confectioners' sugar
1 teaspoon vanilla extract

RASPBERRY SAUCE:

1 package (10 ounces) frozen sweetened raspberries, thawed
1/4 cup light corn syrup

In a bowl, whisk 1/2 cup cream and egg yolks; set aside. In a 3-qt. saucepan, heat chocolate, butter and corn syrup over low heat until chocolate and butter are melted. Remove from heat. Stir about 1 cup into the egg yolk mixture; return all to pan. Cook and stir over low heat until mixture coats back of a metal spoon or reaches 160°. Remove from heat; cool.

In a mixing bowl, beat remaining cream with confectioners' sugar and vanilla until soft peaks form. Fold into chocolate mixture until well blended. Pour into a 9-in. x 5-in. x 3-in. loaf pan that has been lined with plastic wrap. Refrigerate for 8-10 hours.

For sauce, place raspberries in a blender; cover and puree. Strain and discard seeds. Stir corn syrup into raspberry puree; refrigerate. Unmold mousse onto a serving platter; serve with raspberry sauce. **Yield:** 12-14 servings.

Eggnog Cake Roll

(Pictured below)

This festive dessert is on the menu for lots of special occasions at our house, especially Christmas. The eggnog flavor really comes through. —*Lee Herzog*
Salt Lake City, Utah

4 eggs, ***separated***
3/4 cup sugar, ***divided***
1-1/2 teaspoons vanilla extract, ***divided***
3/4 cup sifted cake flour
3/4 teaspoon baking powder
1/4 teaspoon salt
1/4 teaspoon ground nutmeg
4 tablespoons confectioners' sugar, ***divided***
4 teaspoons cornstarch
1-1/2 cups eggnog*
1 can (8 ounces) crushed pineapple, well drained
2/3 cup quartered maraschino cherries
1/4 cup flaked coconut
1 cup heavy whipping cream
Green food coloring

In a large mixing bowl, beat egg yolks until thick and lemon-colored, about 3 minutes. Add 1/2 cup of sugar; beat 2 minutes. Add 1 teaspoon vanilla; mix well. In another mixing bowl, beat egg whites until foamy; gradually add remaining sugar, beating until soft peaks form. Fold into yolk mixture.

Combine cake flour, baking powder, salt and nutmeg. Fold into egg mixture until no flour streaks remain. Spread batter evenly in a greased and floured 15-in. x 10-in. x 1-in. baking pan. Bake at 375° for 13-15 minutes or until a toothpick comes out clean. Turn out onto a linen towel dusted with 2 tablespoons confectioners' sugar. Roll cake up in towel, starting with a short end. Cool on wire rack.

Meanwhile, for filling, combine cornstarch and a small amount of eggnog in a saucepan; mix until smooth. Stir in remaining eggnog; bring to a boil, stirring constantly. Cook and stir 2 minutes more. Remove from heat; stir in remaining vanilla. Cool.

Unroll cake; spread with filling. Sprinkle with pineapple, cherries and coconut; roll up again. Whip cream with remaining confectioners' sugar; tint green. Spread over outside of cake roll. Chill 3-4 hours. **Yield:** 10-12 servings.

***Editor's Note:** This recipe was tested with commercially prepared eggnog.

Elizabeth's Pumpkin Pie

In my ice cream-loving husband's opinion, traditional pumpkin pie can't compare with this melt-in-your-mouth version. —*Elizabeth Montgomery*
Taylorville, Illinois

1 quart vanilla ice cream, softened
1 pastry shell (9 inches), baked
1 cup canned pumpkin
3/4 cup sugar
1/2 teaspoon ground cinnamon
1/2 teaspoon salt
Dash ground nutmeg
1 cup heavy whipping cream, whipped

SYRUP:

1/2 cup packed brown sugar
1/4 cup water
1/4 cup dark corn syrup
1/4 teaspoon vanilla extract
1/8 teaspoon almond extract

Spread ice cream into pastry shell. Cover and freeze until firm. In a bowl, combine pumpkin, sugar, cinnamon, salt and nutmeg; fold in whipped cream. Pour evenly over ice cream; cover and freeze until firm.

For syrup, combine brown sugar, water and corn syrup in a saucepan; bring to a boil. Boil for 4-5 minutes, stirring often. Cool; stir in extracts. Drizzle over pie. **Yield:** 6-8 servings.

Festive Cranberry Dessert Squares

From Thanksgiving through Christmas, you'll find these tart and tasty treats at our house. Although the recipe uses a convenient mix, it's made-from-scratch scrumptious! —*Bev Batty, Minneapolis, Minnesota*

1 cup fresh *or* frozen cranberries
2 tablespoons sugar
2/3 cup butter, melted
1 package (15.6 ounces) cranberry quick bread mix
1 cup quick-cooking oats
2 tablespoons brown sugar
1 cup butterscotch caramel fudge ice cream topping*
1/3 cup all-purpose flour
1-1/2 cups chopped dates
1 cup chopped walnuts

In a bowl, combine cranberries and sugar; set aside. In a large bowl, combine butter, quick bread mix, oats and brown sugar; set aside 1 cup for topping. Press remaining crumb mixture into a greased 13-in. x 9-in. x 2-in. baking dish. Bake at 350° for 10 minutes.

Meanwhile, combine ice cream topping and flour; set aside. Sprinkle the cranberry mixture, dates and nuts over crust; drizzle with ice cream topping. Sprinkle with reserved crumb mixture. Bake for 25-30 minutes or until golden brown and bubbly. Cool in pan on a wire rack. Serve warm or cold. Store in the refrigerator. **Yield:** 15-18 servings.

***Editor's Note:** This recipe was tested with Mrs. Richardson's Butterscotch Caramel Fudge Topping.

Almond Cream Parfaits

(Pictured above)

Cooking is one of my favorite hobbies, particularly during the Christmas season. These parfaits have a sweet almond flavor but aren't too heavy or filling.
—*Lynn McAllister, Mt. Ulla, North Carolina*

1 cup sugar, *divided*
1/4 cup cornstarch
3 cups milk
4 egg yolks
1 tablespoon butter
1/2 teaspoon almond extract
3/4 cup chopped toasted almonds
1/2 cup shortbread cookie crumbs
1 cup heavy whipping cream
6 to 8 maraschino cherries

In a medium saucepan, combine 3/4 cup sugar and cornstarch. Gradually add milk; cook and stir over medium heat until thickened and bubbly. Reduce heat; cook and stir 2 minutes longer. Remove from the heat. In a small bowl, beat egg yolks; gradually add 1 cup of hot milk mixture. Return all to pan. Bring to a boil; cook and stir for 1-2 minutes longer. Add butter and extract; mix well. Chill for 1 hour or until cool. Add almonds.

Pour into six to eight parfait glasses; sprinkle with cookie crumbs. In a mixing bowl, beat cream and remaining sugar until soft peaks form. Spoon over parfaits. Chill. Just before serving, garnish with cherries. **Yield:** 6-8 servings.

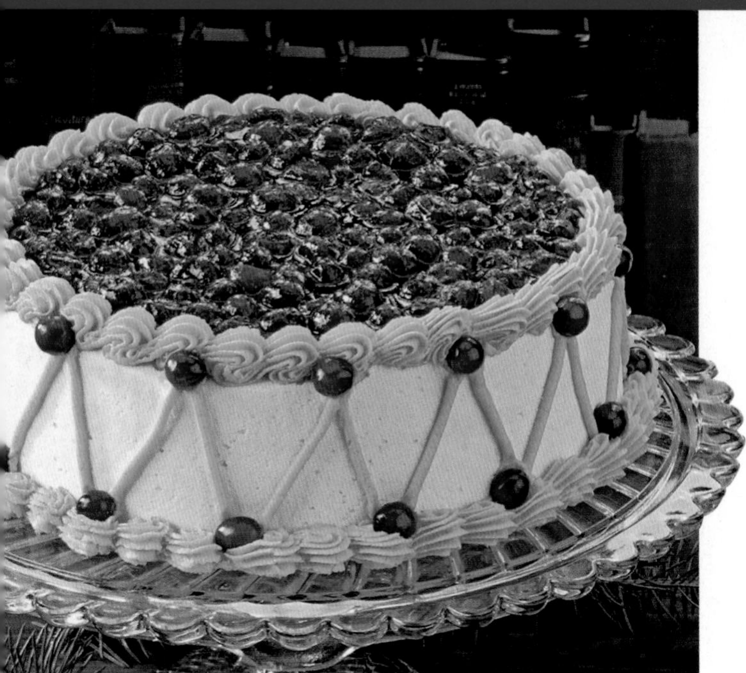

Drummer Boy Cake

(Pictured above)

Looking for an impressive finale to your holiday dinner? This spectacular dessert, drummed up by our Taste of Home Test Kitchen, features a sweet-tart cranberry topping paired with a tangy orange cake and filling.

- 1 envelope unflavored gelatin
- 1/4 cup cold water
- 3 cups fresh *or* frozen cranberries
- 1 cup sugar
- 1/2 cup red currant jelly

CAKE/FILLING:

- 1 medium navel orange, unpeeled and quartered
- 1 package (18-1/4 ounces) yellow cake mix
- 1-1/2 cups water, *divided*
- 1/3 cup vegetable oil
- 3 eggs
- 3/4 cup sugar
- 5 teaspoons cornstarch
- 1/8 teaspoon salt
- 2 tablespoons butter, cubed
- Yellow liquid food coloring

FROSTING:

- 1 cup shortening
- 1-1/2 teaspoons vanilla extract
- 1/2 teaspoon orange extract
- 4-1/2 cups confectioners' sugar
- 1/4 cup milk
- Yellow and red liquid food coloring
- 28 fresh *or* frozen cranberries

For topping, sprinkle gelatin over cold water in a microwave-safe bowl; let stand for 1 minute. Microwave on high for 40 seconds; stir. Let stand for 1 minute or until gelatin is completely dissolved; set aside. In a saucepan over medium-low heat, cook cranberries and sugar, uncovered, for 7 minutes or until slightly thickened, stirring occasionally. Cool slightly. Stir in jelly and gelatin mixture. Cover and chill for 5 hours or overnight.

For cake, process orange in a blender or food processor until finely chopped; set aside. In a mixing bowl, beat cake mix, 1 cup water, oil and eggs on low speed until moistened. Add 1/3 cup chopped orange; beat for 2 minutes on medium. Set remaining orange aside for filling. Pour batter into two greased and floured 9-in. round baking pans. Bake at 350° for 28-31 minutes or until a toothpick comes out clean. Cool for 10 minutes; remove from pans to wire racks.

For filling, combine sugar, cornstarch, salt and remaining water in a saucepan until smooth. Add butter and 1/3 cup chopped orange (discard any remaining orange or save for another use). Bring to a boil; cook and stir for 2 minutes or until thickened. Stir in a few drops yellow food coloring; cool.

Split each cooled cake into two horizontal layers. Place bottom layer on serving plate; spread with a third of the filling. Repeat layers twice. Top with remaining cake layer. Spread the cranberry topping over top to within 1/2 in. of edges.

In a mixing bowl, cream shortening and extracts. Add sugar, 1/2 cup at a time, alternately with milk, beating until frosting is light and fluffy. Using 2/3 cup of frosting, frost cake sides. Tint remaining frosting gold with yellow and red food coloring. Cut a hole in a pastry or plastic bag; insert round tip #8. Fill with gold frosting. Pipe connecting diagonal stripes around side of cake; add cranberries at end points. With star tip #21, pipe a shell border around top and bottom of cake. **Yield:** 12-15 servings.

Editor's Note: This recipe was prepared with Duncan Hines yellow cake mix. Use of a coupler ring will allow you to easily change pastry tips for different designs.

Chocolate Crepes With Cranberry Sauce

With its unique flavor and festive look, this dessert has become a "must" for Christmas at our house. It's an elegant addition to the dinner table. —Lynda Sarkisian Inman, South Carolina

1 package (3.4 ounces) instant vanilla pudding mix
2-1/2 cups milk, *divided*
1 carton (8 ounces) frozen whipped topping, thawed
2 tablespoons vegetable oil
3 eggs
1-1/2 teaspoons vanilla extract
1/4 cup sugar
1-1/2 cups all-purpose flour
2 tablespoons baking cocoa
1/8 teaspoon salt
CRANBERRY SAUCE:
1-1/2 cups fresh *or* frozen cranberries
1 cup cranberry juice
1/2 cup packed brown sugar
1-1/2 teaspoons cornstarch
1/2 teaspoon grated orange peel
1/4 teaspoon ground nutmeg
1/8 teaspoon salt
2 tablespoons butter
1 teaspoon vanilla extract

In a bowl, whisk the pudding mix and 1 cup of milk until smooth. Fold in whipped topping; cover and chill. In a blender container, combine oil, eggs, vanilla, sugar, flour, cocoa, salt and remaining milk; process until smooth. Let stand for 20 minutes.

Meanwhile, combine the first seven sauce ingredients in a small saucepan; bring to a boil. Reduce heat and simmer until smooth and thickened, stirring constantly, about 15 minutes. Remove from the heat; stir in the butter and vanilla. Keep warm.

Heat a lightly greased 6-in. skillet over medium heat until hot. Pour 3 tablespoons crepe batter into skillet and swirl quickly so bottom is evenly covered. Cook until top appears dry and bottom is lightly browned; turn and cook 15-20 seconds longer. Remove and keep warm. Repeat with remaining batter. To serve, fold crepes in quarters; place three on a dessert plate. Top with chilled pudding mixture and warm sauce. **Yield:** 6-8 servings.

Butterscotch Pumpkin Puffs

(Pictured at right)

Yummy things come in these little "packages". The puffs can be made and frozen in advance, then filled before serving. —Michelle Smith, Running Springs, California

2 packages (3.4 ounces *each*) instant butterscotch pudding mix
1 can (12 ounces) evaporated milk
1/2 teaspoon ground cinnamon
1/4 teaspoon ground ginger
1 cup canned pumpkin
1 cup whipped topping, optional
CREAM PUFFS:
1-1/2 cups water
3/4 cup butter
1/2 teaspoon salt
1-1/2 cups all-purpose flour
6 eggs
1/3 cup confectioners' sugar
1/3 cup semisweet chocolate chips, melted

In a mixing bowl, combine pudding mix, milk and spices; beat on medium speed for 30 seconds. Blend in pumpkin and whipped topping if desired. Refrigerate for 1 hour or overnight.

In a medium saucepan, bring water, butter and salt to a boil. Add flour all at once and stir until a smooth ball forms. Remove from the heat; let stand for 5 minutes. Add eggs, one at a time, beating well after each addition. Continue beating until mixture is smooth and shiny. Drop by tablespoonfuls 2 in. apart onto greased baking sheets. Bake at 400° for 30-35 minutes or until golden brown.

Remove to wire racks. Immediately cut a slit in each for steam to escape; cool. Split puffs and remove soft dough. Just before serving, spoon about 1 tablespoon filling into each puff. Dust with confectioners' sugar and drizzle with melted chocolate. **Yield:** 5 dozen.

Black Forest Cheesecakes

As sure as chocolate and cherries go together, so do my family's Yuletides and these no-fuss cheesecakes.
—Jean Olson, Wallingford, Iowa

12 cream-filled chocolate sandwich cookies
2 packages (8 ounces *each*) cream cheese, softened
3/4 cup sugar
1/3 cup baking cocoa
1 teaspoon vanilla extract
2 eggs
1 can (21 ounces) cherry pie filling
1/2 to 1 cup whipped topping

Remove cookie top from each sandwich cookie; crush and set aside. Place cream-topped cookies in foil-lined muffin cups, cream side up. In a mixing bowl, beat cream cheese, sugar, cocoa and vanilla until fluffy. Beat in eggs until blended.

Fill muffin cups three-fourths full. Sprinkle 1/4 cup reserved cookie crumbs over tops (discard remaining crumbs or save for another use). Bake at 325° for 20-25 minutes or until set. Cool completely. Cover and refrigerate for at least 2 hours. Just before serving, top each cheesecake with about 2 tablespoons of pie filling. Top with a dollop of whipped topping. **Yield:** 12 servings.

Cherry Meringue Pie

(Pictured below)

My mother always made cherry pie with a meringue topping, and I think her mother did, too. It's a nice way to finish off a holiday dinner or everyday meal.
—Irene Brill, Manassas, Virginia

1 can (21 ounces) cherry pie filling
3 egg whites
1/4 teaspoon cream of tartar
6 tablespoons confectioners' sugar
1/4 teaspoon almond extract
1 pastry shell (9 inches), baked
1/4 cup chopped walnuts

In a saucepan, heat pie filling on low. Meanwhile, in a mixing bowl, beat egg whites on medium speed until foamy. Add cream of tartar; beat until soft peaks form. Gradually beat in sugar, 1 tablespoon at a time, on high until stiff glossy peaks form.

Remove pie filling from heat; stir in extract. Pour into pastry shell. Spread meringue over hot filling, sealing edges to crust. Sprinkle with walnuts. Bake at 350° for 15 minutes or until meringue is golden. Cool on a wire rack for 1 hour. Chill for at least 3 hours before serving. Refrigerate leftovers. **Yield:** 6-8 servings.

Cranberry-Apple Mincemeat Pies

Traditional mincemeat is too heavy for me, but this fruity version hits the spot. Others agree—few folks who've tried it stop at just one slice!
—Lucinda Burton, Scarborough, Ontario

4 cups fresh *or* frozen cranberries, thawed
4 cups chopped peeled tart apples
1-1/2 cups chopped dried apricots
1-1/2 cups golden raisins
1 medium unpeeled navel orange, finely chopped
1/4 cup *each* red and green candied cherries
2-3/4 cups sugar
1 cup apple juice
1/4 cup butter
1/4 cup orange marmalade
1 teaspoon ground ginger
3/4 teaspoon *each* ground allspice, cinnamon and nutmeg
Pastry for double-crust pie (9 inches)

In a Dutch oven or large kettle, combine the fruit, sugar, apple juice, butter, marmalade and spices. Bring to a boil over medium heat. Reduce heat; simmer, uncovered, for 50-60 minutes, stirring occasionally. Cool completely or refrigerate for up to 1 week.

Line two 9-in. pie plates with pastry; trim and flute edges. Divide filling between crusts. Cover edges loosely with foil. Bake at 400° for 20 minutes. Remove foil. Bake 20-25 minutes longer or until crust is golden brown and filling is bubbly. Cool on wire racks. **Yield:** 2 pies (6-8 servings each).

Editor's Note: Mincemeat mixture may be frozen for up to 3 months. Thaw in the refrigerator.

Glitter Gelatin Torte

This fluffy torte is a nice alternative to heavy holiday desserts. Bright cubes of gelatin shimmer in every slice. —*June Deere, Urbana, Ohio*

1-1/2 cups graham cracker crumbs (about 24 squares)
1/3 cup plus 1/4 cup sugar, *divided*
1/2 cup butter, melted
1 package (3 ounces) strawberry gelatin
3 cups boiling water, *divided*
1-1/4 cups cold water, *divided*
1 package (3 ounces) lime gelatin
1 package (3 ounces) lemon gelatin
1 can (8 ounces) crushed pineapple, drained
3 tablespoons lemon juice
Dash salt
1-1/2 cups heavy whipping cream, whipped
1/4 cup chopped walnuts

In a bowl, combine the cracker crumbs, 1/3 cup sugar and butter; press onto the bottom and 2 in. up the sides of a greased 9-in. springform pan. Refrigerate.

In a small bowl, dissolve strawberry gelatin in 1 cup boiling water; stir in 1/2 cup cold water. Pour into an 8-in. square dish coated with nonstick cooking spray; chill until firm. Repeat with lime gelatin, pouring into another 8-in. square dish.

In a large mixing bowl, dissolve lemon gelatin and remaining sugar in remaining boiling water. Add pineapple, lemon juice, salt and remaining cold water. Refrigerate until partially set, about 1 hour. Beat on medium speed until foamy, about 2 minutes.

Cut strawberry and lime gelatin into 1/2-in. cubes; set aside 1/4 cup of each for garnish. Fold remaining cubes into lemon gelatin. Fold in whipped cream. Spoon into crust. Top with walnuts and reserved gelatin cubes. Cover and refrigerate for at least 6 hours. Remove sides of pan. Cut into wedges. **Yield:** 12-14 servings.

Cherry Pineapple Fruitcake

(Pictured above)

This is the finishing touch to our Christmas dinner. My family always claimed they didn't like fruitcake, but they love this one! For the best flavor, let it sit overnight before slicing. —*SueAnn Bunt, Painted Post, New York*

1 cup chopped candied cherries
1 cup chopped candied pineapple
2 cups chopped pecans
4 cups all-purpose flour, *divided*
2 cups butter, softened
2 cups sugar
6 eggs
2 teaspoons vanilla extract
1 teaspoon baking powder

In a bowl, combine the cherries, pineapple, pecans and 1 cup flour; set aside. In a mixing bowl, cream butter and sugar. Add eggs, one at a time, beating well after each. Beat in vanilla. Combine baking powder and remaining flour; gradually add to creamed mixture. Fold in fruit mixture.

Spoon into a greased and waxed paper-lined 10-in. tube pan. Bake at 300° for 1-3/4 to 2 hours or until a toothpick inserted near the center comes out clean. Cool for 10 minutes before removing from pan to a wire rack. Remove waxed paper while warm; cool completely before cutting into slices. **Yield:** 12-16 servings.

Snowflake Pudding

(Pictured above)

Flakes of coconut give my pudding its snow-like texture and plenty of taste besides! The crimson currant-raspberry sauce is delicious and pretty, too.
—Patricia Stratton, Muskegon, Michigan

1 envelope unflavored gelatin
1-1/4 cups milk, *divided*
1/2 cup sugar
1/2 teaspoon salt
1 teaspoon vanilla extract
1-1/3 cups flaked coconut, toasted
1 cup heavy whipping cream, whipped

SAUCE:

1 package (10 ounces) frozen sweetened raspberries, thawed
1-1/2 teaspoons cornstarch
1/2 cup red currant jelly

In a small bowl, combine gelatin and 1/4 cup milk; let stand for 1 minute. In a saucepan, combine sugar, salt and remaining milk; heat just until sugar is dissolved. Remove from heat; stir in gelatin mixture and vanilla. Refrigerate until partially set. Fold in coconut and whipped cream. Pour into six dessert dishes; refrigerate for at least 2 hours.

Meanwhile, strain raspberries to remove seeds. Combine cornstarch, raspberry juice and jelly in a saucepan; stir until smooth. Bring to a boil; cook and stir for 2 minutes. Chill for at least 1 hour. Pour sauce over pudding just before serving. **Yield:** 6 servings.

Pecan Macadamia Pie

It's bound to be a blue-ribbon Christmas when I serve this rich, nutty pie—it was a prize-winner at our county fair. Even my husband, who can take or leave sweets, can't resist it! *—Anne Simboli, Farmville, Virginia*

1 cup all-purpose flour
2 tablespoons sugar
1/2 teaspoon salt
1/4 cup shortening
3 to 4 tablespoons cold water

FILLING:

3 eggs
1/2 cup sugar
4-1/2 teaspoons all-purpose flour
1/4 teaspoon salt
1 cup light corn syrup
1 tablespoon butter, melted and cooled
1 teaspoon vanilla extract
1 cup coarsely chopped pecans
3/4 cup coarsely chopped macadamia nuts

In a bowl, combine flour, sugar and salt; cut in shortening until crumbly. Gradually add cold water, tossing with a fork until dough begins to cling together. Form into a ball. On a lightly floured surface, roll to a 10-in. circle. Place in a 9-in. pie plate and set aside.

For filling, beat eggs until blended but not frothy. Add sugar, flour, salt and corn syrup; mix well. Add butter and vanilla; mix just until blended. Stir in nuts. Pour into crust. Place in a 350° oven and immediately reduce heat to 325°. Bake for 55-60 minutes or until center is set. Cool on a wire rack. Store in the refrigerator. **Yield:** 8-10 servings.

Candy Cane Cheesecake

This pepperminty cheesecake says "Christmas" at first sight and first bite. The recipe earned me a dairy producer's scholarship. Now, it regularly wins compliments at seasonal parties and teas. *—Gwen Koob-Roach*
Saskatoon, Saskatchewan

1-1/2 cups chocolate wafer crumbs
1/3 cup butter, melted
2 tablespoons sugar

FILLING:

3 packages (8 ounces *each*) cream cheese, softened
3/4 cup sugar
3 tablespoons all-purpose flour

4 eggs
1 cup (8 ounces) sour cream
2 tablespoons vanilla *or* white chips
1/2 to 3/4 teaspoon peppermint extract
Red liquid *or* paste food coloring
Crushed peppermint candy and whipped topping

Combine first three ingredients; press onto bottom of a greased 9-in. springform pan. Chill. In a mixing bowl, beat cream cheese and sugar until smooth. Add flour; mix well. Add eggs, one at a time, beating just until blended. Stir in sour cream. Set aside.

In a small saucepan over low heat, melt vanilla chips. Remove from the heat. Add 1/4 cup cream cheese mixture, extract and a few drops of food coloring; mix well. Pour half of the remaining cream cheese mixture over crust. Top with half of the peppermint mixture; swirl with a knife. Repeat layers.

Bake at 450° for 10 minutes. Reduce heat to 250°; bake 40-50 minutes longer or until the center is almost set. Cool on a wire rack for 1 hour. Chill for at least 3 hours. Just before serving, remove sides of pan. Garnish with crushed candy and whipped topping. **Yield:** 12-16 servings.

Maple Cream Fluff

Maple is the featured flavor in this rich and nutty dessert. It's a nice change-of-pace contribution to a holiday potluck. —Brooke Pike, Pierre, South Dakota

2 envelopes unflavored gelatin
1/2 cup cold water
1 cup maple syrup
2 cups milk
1 cup heavy whipping cream
1 cup chopped pecans, toasted, *divided*
2 cups vanilla wafer crumbs (about 32 wafers), *divided*

In a large saucepan, soften gelatin in cold water; let stand for 1 minute. Cook and stir over low heat (do not boil) until gelatin is dissolved, about 4 minutes. Remove from the heat; slowly stir in syrup. Set pan in ice water; whisk in milk. Continue whisking until mixture has thickened, about 10 minutes; remove pan from ice bath and set aside.

In a mixing bowl, beat cream until stiff peaks form. Fold in 3/4 cup pecans and the maple mixture. Sprinkle 1 cup wafer crumbs into an ungreased 13-in. x 9-in. x 2-in. dish; top with maple mixture. Sprinkle with remaining pecans and wafer crumbs. Cover and chill for at least 6 hours or overnight. Refrigerate any leftovers. **Yield:** 12-15 servings.

Candy Orange Slice Fruitcake

(Pictured below)

My version of Yule fruitcake has a citrusy twist. When you share it, be prepared to pass around the recipe. —Anna Minegar, Zolfo Springs, Florida

1 cup butter, softened
2 cups sugar
2 cups applesauce
4 eggs
1/2 cup buttermilk
1 pound candy orange slices
2 cups chopped pecans
2 cups flaked coconut
1-1/2 cups candied cherries
1 package (8 ounces) chopped dates
3-1/2 cups all-purpose flour, *divided*
1 teaspoon baking soda
1/8 teaspoon salt

In a mixing bowl, cream butter and sugar. Beat in the applesauce, eggs and buttermilk. In a bowl, combine the orange slices, pecans, coconut, cherries, dates and 1 cup of flour; toss to coat. Combine the baking soda, salt and remaining flour; add to the buttermilk mixture. Fold in orange slice mixture.

Pour into a greased and floured 10-in. tube pan. Bake at 300° for 1-3/4 to 2 hours or until a toothpick inserted near center comes out clean. Cool for 10 minutes before removing from pan to a wire rack to cool completely. **Yield:** 10-12 servings.

Chocolate Cherry Cheesecake

(Pictured below)

My love for chocolate-covered cherries inspired this fun and fancy cheesecake that's perfect for Christmas.
—Kathy Speer, La Crosse, Wisconsin

2 cups chocolate wafer crumbs (about 32 wafers)
6 tablespoons butter, melted

CHEESECAKE:
4 packages (8 ounces *each*) cream cheese, *softened*
1 cup sugar
2 teaspoons vanilla extract
4 eggs
4 squares (1 ounce *each*) white baking chocolate, melted and cooled
1 jar (10 ounces) maraschino cherries, drained, rinsed and quartered
1/2 cup chopped pecans

TOPPING:
3 squares (1 ounce *each*) semisweet chocolate
2 tablespoons butter
1-1/2 teaspoons shortening, *divided*
1/2 square (1/2 ounce) white baking chocolate

In a bowl, combine chocolate crumbs and butter. Press onto bottom and 1 in. up sides of a greased 10-in. springform pan. Bake at 350° for 8 minutes. Cool on a wire rack. In a mixing bowl, beat cream cheese until smooth. Add sugar and vanilla; mix well. Add eggs; beat on low speed just until combined. Stir in melted chocolate; mix well. Gently fold in cherries and pecans. Pour into crust. Bake at 350° for 50-55 minutes or until center is almost set. Cool on a wire rack for 10 minutes. Carefully run a knife around edge of pan to loosen; cool 1 hour longer. Refrigerate overnight. Remove side of pan.

In a saucepan, melt semisweet chocolate, butter and 1 teaspoon shortening until smooth. Cool for 2 minutes; pour over cheesecake. Spread over the top and let it run down the sides. Cool. In a small saucepan, melt white chocolate and remaining shortening. Drizzle over the top. Cool. Store in the refrigerator. **Yield:** 12 servings.

Elegant Bread Pudding

At holiday potlucks, our whole family looks forward to my sister-in-law bringing this best-of-the-season dessert.
—Sharon Runyan, Fort Wayne, Indiana

10 cups cubed croissants *or* French bread
1/2 cup raisins
8 eggs
2 cups half-and-half cream
1 cup packed brown sugar
1 teaspoon ground cinnamon
1 teaspoon ground nutmeg
1 teaspoon grated orange peel

CARAMEL SAUCE:
1 cup packed brown sugar
1/2 cup butter
1/2 cup heavy whipping cream
1 teaspoon vanilla extract
Whipped cream, optional

Place bread cubes evenly in a greased 13-in. x 9-in. x 2-in. baking dish; sprinkle with raisins. In a large bowl, beat eggs, cream, sugar, cinnamon, nutmeg and orange peel; pour over bread. Bake, uncovered, at 350° for 30 minutes. Cover with foil and bake 15 minutes longer or until a knife inserted near the center comes out clean.

In a saucepan, combine the first four sauce ingredients; cook and stir over low heat until smooth. Serve bread pudding in bowls with caramel sauce and whipped cream if desired. **Yield:** 12-14 servings.

Swedish Fruit Soup

Our children expect me to make this sweet soup for the holidays. It's a delicious dessert served with pound cake and whipped cream...or offer it as a fruit compote for brunch. —*Dolores Bean Baldwinsville, New York*

4 cups cranberry-apple juice
1/4 cup quick-cooking tapioca
1 medium lemon, thinly sliced
6 whole cloves
1/4 teaspoon ground nutmeg
1 can (20 ounces) pineapple chunks, drained
1 can (11 ounces) mandarin oranges, drained
1 package (10 ounces) frozen sweetened strawberries, thawed, undrained
1/3 cup maraschino cherry juice *or* grenadine syrup, optional
1/8 teaspoon salt

In a 3-qt. saucepan, combine the first five ingredients; let stand for 10 minutes. Bring to a boil over medium heat. Reduce heat; cook and stir for 15 minutes or until thickened and clear. Remove from the heat; discard lemon slices and cloves. Stir in remaining ingredients. Cover and refrigerate for at least 4 hours. **Yield:** 6-8 servings.

French Vanilla Cream Puffs

(Pictured above right)

French vanilla filling dotted with mini chocolate chips is sandwiched in puffy pastry for this elegantly sweet dessert. You could substitute white chocolate or chocolate pudding for the vanilla if you like.
—*Lena Haines, Lawrenceville, Georgia*

1 cup water
1/2 cup butter
1 cup all-purpose flour
1/4 teaspoon salt
4 eggs
FILLING:
1-1/2 cups cold milk
1 package (3.4 ounces) instant French vanilla pudding mix

1 cup whipped topping
1 package (12 ounces) miniature semisweet chocolate chips
Confectioners' sugar

In a saucepan, bring water and butter to a boil. Add flour and salt all at once; stir until a smooth ball forms. Remove from the heat; let stand for 5 minutes. Add eggs, one at a time, beating well after each addition. Beat until mixture is smooth and shiny. Drop by rounded teaspoonfuls 2 in. apart onto greased baking sheets. Bake at 400° for 20-25 minutes or until golden brown. Remove puffs to wire racks. Immediately cut a slit in each for steam to escape. Cool. Split puffs and remove soft dough.

For filling, in a mixing bowl, beat milk and pudding mix on low speed for 2 minutes. Refrigerate for 5 minutes. Fold in whipped topping and chips. Fill cream puffs just before serving; replace tops. Dust with confectioners' sugar. **Yield:** about 2-1/2 dozen.

Buffet Table Tip

Make it easy for guests to identify the food you're serving at a holiday buffet. Write the name of the food or recipe on a small card. Then cut a slit in small pears or apples, lemons or limes, and insert a card in each slit. For a fancier touch, you can spray paint the fruits silver or gold first.

Chocolate Yule Log

(Pictured above)

For many years, this impressive rolled cake has been a favorite Christmas dessert for our family—everyone just loves it! Plus, I'm always asked to bring the rich chocolaty treat to our annual church Christmas function. —*Bernadette Colvin, Houston, Texas*

- 4 eggs, *separated*
- 2/3 cup sugar, *divided*
- 1/2 cup all-purpose flour
- 2 tablespoons baking cocoa
- 1 teaspoon baking powder
- 1/4 teaspoon salt

FILLING:

- 1 cup heavy whipping cream
- 2 tablespoons sugar
- 1/4 teaspoon almond extract

FROSTING:

- 1/2 cup butter, softened
- 2 cups confectioners' sugar
- 2 squares (1 ounce *each*) unsweetened chocolate, melted
- 2 tablespoons milk
- 2 teaspoons vanilla extract

Line a greased 15-in. x 10-in. x 1-in. baking pan with waxed paper; grease the paper and set aside. In a mixing bowl, beat egg yolks until light and fluffy. Gradually add 1/3 cup sugar, beating until light and lemon-colored, about 5 minutes. In another mixing bowl, beat egg whites until foamy. Gradually add remaining sugar, beating until stiff peaks form. Fold into egg yolks, a third at a time. Combine the flour, cocoa, baking powder and salt; fold into egg mixture, a third at a time.

Spread batter into prepared pan. Bake at 375° for 10-12 minutes or until cake springs back when lightly touched. Cool for 5 minutes. Turn cake onto a kitchen towel dusted with confectioners' sugar. Gently peel off waxed paper. Roll up cake in the towel, jelly-roll style, starting with a short side; cool completely on a wire rack.

Meanwhile, for the filling, beat the cream in a mixing bowl until soft peaks form. Gradually add sugar and almond extract, beating until almost stiff. Unroll cake; spread the filling to within 1 in. of edges. Reroll cake. In a mixing bowl, cream butter and confectioners' sugar. Beat in the chocolate, milk and vanilla until smooth. Frost the cake, using a metal spatula to create a bark-like effect. **Yield:** 14-16 servings.

White Chocolate Pudding

I adapted a milk chocolate pudding recipe to suit my preference for white chocolate. Made from scratch, this delicious treat has wonderful homemade goodness. My family requests it often. —*Elizabeth Olds-Barrett East Haven, Connecticut*

- 1/2 cup sugar
- 3 tablespoons cornstarch
- 1/8 teaspoon salt
- 2 cups heavy whipping cream
- 2 cups milk
- 6 egg yolks, lightly beaten
- 3/4 cup vanilla *or* white chips
- 1 teaspoon orange *or* rum extract

In a heavy saucepan, combine sugar, cornstarch and salt. Gradually add cream and milk. Bring to a boil over medium-high heat, stirring constantly.

Reduce heat; cook and stir with a wire whisk 2-3 minutes more or until thickened. Remove from the heat.

Stir 1-1/2 cups hot mixture into egg yolks; return to saucepan. Stirring constantly, bring to a gentle boil; cook and stir 2 minutes more. Remove from the heat; stir in chips until melted. Stir in extract. **Yield:** 8 servings.

Pumpkin Mousse Cheesecake

Fresh from the vine comes my merry after-dinner delight! The scrumptious pumpkin filling makes this cheesecake different from most, and the glaze adds a nice touch. It's a big hit among my family and friends.
—Dawn Oswald, Kailua, Hawaii

1 cup graham cracker crumbs (about 16 squares)
3 tablespoons sugar
1/4 cup butter, melted

FILLING:

3 packages (8 ounces *each*) cream cheese, softened
1 cup sugar
1 cup canned pumpkin
3 tablespoons all-purpose flour
1 teaspoon ground cinnamon
1/4 teaspoon ground nutmeg
4 eggs

GLAZE:

1/2 cup vanilla *or* white chips
1 tablespoon shortening

Combine crumbs, sugar and butter. Press into a greased 9-in. springform pan. Bake at 325° for 8 minutes. Cool on a wire rack.

Meanwhile, in a mixing bowl, beat the cream cheese and sugar until smooth. Add the pumpkin, flour, cinnamon and nutmeg. Add eggs; beat on low speed just until combined. Pour into the crust. Bake for 50 minutes or until center is almost set. Cool on a wire rack for 10 minutes. Carefully run a knife around edge of pan to loosen; cool 1 hour longer. Refrigerate overnight.

In a saucepan over low heat, melt the chips and shortening; stir until smooth. Drizzle over cheesecake. Refrigerate until firm, about 30 minutes. **Yield:** 12-14 servings.

Almond Fruit Squares

(Pictured below)

These sweet squares are easy to fix, thanks to the refrigerated crescent roll dough that serves as the crust!
—Iola Egle, McCook, Nebraska

2 tubes (8 ounces *each*) refrigerated crescent rolls
3 tablespoons sugar, *divided*
1 package (8 ounces) cream cheese, softened
1/3 cup almond paste
1/2 teaspoon almond extract
2 cups halved fresh strawberries
1 can (11 ounces) mandarin oranges, drained
1 cup fresh raspberries
1 cup halved green grapes
2 kiwifruit, peeled, quartered and sliced
1/2 cup apricot preserves, warmed
1/2 cup slivered almonds, toasted

Unroll crescent dough and separate into eight rectangles. Place in an ungreased 15-in. x 10-in. x 1-in. baking pan. Press onto bottom and up sides; seal seams and perforations. Sprinkle with 1 tablespoon sugar. Bake at 375° for 14-16 minutes or until golden brown. Cool.

In a mixing bowl, beat cream cheese, almond paste, extract and remaining sugar until smooth. Spread over crust. Top with fruit. Brush with preserves; sprinkle with almonds. **Yield:** 16 servings.

Lady Lamington Cakes

(Pictured below)

I learned to turn out these dainty no-bake cakes while living in Australia. Named for the wife of a past governor from "down under", they make a lip-smacking snack or dessert. —*Dee Pufpaff*
Raleigh, North Carolina

1 package (10-3/4 ounces) frozen pound cake
1/3 cup water
2 tablespoons butter
1/4 cup baking cocoa
2-1/2 cups confectioners' sugar
4 cups flaked coconut, toasted and chopped

Thaw cake; cut into 3/4-in. slices. Cut each slice into four fingers; set aside. In a microwave-safe bowl or saucepan, heat water and butter until butter is melted. Whisk in cocoa until dissolved. Whisk in sugar to make a thin glaze. Dip cakes into glaze to coat all sides; roll in coconut. Place on waxed paper to dry. Cover and refrigerate. **Yield:** 3 dozen.

White Chocolate Bread Pudding

This delectable dessert features vanilla chips, apples and a sweet caramel sauce. It's a favorite with our boys.
—*Wendy Sleicher, Quakertown, Pennsylvania*

2 cups milk
2 cups heavy whipping cream
1 cup sugar
1 cup vanilla *or* white chips
8 eggs
1 tablespoon vanilla extract
1 loaf (1 pound) egg bread, crust removed, cut into 1-inch cubes
2 medium tart apples, peeled and chopped

CARAMEL SAUCE:
1-1/4 cups sugar
1/2 cup water
1/4 cup light corn syrup
1 tablespoon lemon juice
1-1/4 cups heavy whipping cream
1 cup chopped pecans, toasted
2 teaspoons vanilla extract

In a saucepan, combine the milk, cream and sugar. Cook over medium heat until mixture comes to a boil. Remove from the heat; stir in chips until melted. In a bowl, whisk eggs and vanilla. Gradually whisk in cream mixture. Add bread. Let stand for 15 minutes, stirring occasionally.

Stir in apples. Pour into a greased 13-in. x 9-in. x 2-in. baking dish. Cover and bake at 350° for 45 minutes. Uncover; bake 30 minutes longer or until a knife inserted near the center comes out clean.

Meanwhile, for sauce, combine the sugar, water, corn syrup and lemon juice in a large saucepan. Cook and stir over medium heat until sugar is dissolved. Bring to a boil over medium-high heat; boil, without stirring, until a candy thermometer reads 295° and mixture turns deep amber.

Remove from the heat; stir in cream. Cook and stir over low heat until mixture is smooth. Bring to a boil over medium heat; cook and stir for 4 minutes. Stir in nuts and vanilla. Stir before serving. Serve warm over warm bread pudding. **Yield:** 12-15 servings.

Editor's Note: We recommend that you test your candy thermometer before each use by bringing water to a boil; the thermometer should read 212°. Adjust your recipe temperature up or down based on your test.

Confetti Cream Cake

(Pictured above right)

Luscious layers of cake and creamy filling form this eye-popping dessert. If you're short on time, ready the filling ingredients a day ahead. Then assemble

and frost this wonderful cake right before serving.
—Jennie Moshier, Fresno, California

5 eggs
1 teaspoon vanilla extract
1 cup sugar
1 cup all-purpose flour
1/2 teaspoon baking powder
1/2 teaspoon salt
FILLING:
1 package (8 ounces) cream cheese, softened
1 cup sugar, *divided*
1 teaspoon vanilla extract
1/4 teaspoon ground cinnamon
1 cup (8 ounces) sour cream
1/2 cup finely chopped walnuts
1/2 cup flaked coconut, optional
1/3 cup chopped maraschino cherries
2 milk chocolate candy bars (1.55 ounces *each*), shaved *or* finely chopped
1-1/2 cups heavy whipping cream

In a mixing bowl, beat eggs and vanilla on high until foamy. Add sugar; beat until thick and lemon-colored. Combine flour, baking powder and salt; fold into egg mixture, a third at a time. Pour into two greased and floured 9-in. round baking pans. Bake at 350° for 25-30 minutes or until cake springs back when lightly touched. Cool for 5 minutes; remove from pans to wire racks to cool completely.

In a mixing bowl, beat cream cheese, 2/3 cup sugar, vanilla and cinnamon until smooth. Stir in sour cream, nuts, coconut if desired and cherries. Fold in chocolate. Beat cream and remaining sugar until stiff peaks form; set half aside. Fold remaining whipped cream into the cream cheese mixture. Split each cake into two horizontal layers; spread a fourth of the cream cheese mixture on one layer. Repeat layers. Frost sides with reserved whipped cream. Refrigerate until serving. **Yield:** 10-12 servings.

Keep It Clean

To help keep the serving plate clean when frosting a cake, try this trick. Tuck several 3-inch strips of waxed paper slightly under the cake, covering the plate's edge. Frost as desired, then carefully remove the waxed paper.

Walnut Wedges

(Pictured above)

When you want to serve something light but fancier than cookies, these dainty treats make a beautiful dessert. With a prepared pie crust, they're easy, yet have a special holiday look—the perfect combination for a busy time of year. —*Connie Meinke, Neenah, Wisconsin*

Pastry for double-crust pie
1 cup finely chopped walnuts
1/3 cup sugar
2 tablespoons honey
1 teaspoon ground cinnamon
1 teaspoon lemon juice
1 to 2 tablespoons milk
1/2 cup semisweet chocolate chips
1 teaspoon shortening

Roll out bottom crust to a 10-1/2-in. circle; place on an ungreased baking sheet. Combine nuts, sugar, honey, cinnamon and lemon juice; spread over crust. Roll out remaining pastry and place over nuts. With fork tines, seal edges together and pierce holes in top.

Brush with milk. Bake at 375° for 15-20 minutes or until lightly browned. Cool for 10 minutes. Cut into 16-20 wedges. Cool completely. In a small saucepan, melt chocolate chips and shortening over low heat; drizzle over wedges. **Yield:** 16-20 servings.

Eggnog Trifle

This classic Christmas dessert is too delicious to have just once a year. So our family serves it for birthdays and whatever other occasion we can think of!
—*Cynthia Butt, Winnipeg, Manitoba*

3/4 cup cold milk
1 package (3.4 ounces) instant vanilla pudding mix
2 cups eggnog*
1/2 teaspoon almond extract
1-1/2 cups heavy whipping cream, whipped, ***divided***
1 loaf (10 ounces) angel food ***or*** **sponge cake**
1 cup raspberry jam ***or*** **preserves**
2 tablespoons confectioners' sugar
1/2 teaspoon vanilla extract
Maraschino cherry halves

In a mixing bowl, beat milk and pudding mix until blended. Gradually add eggnog; mix well. Fold in extract and 1 cup of whipped cream; set aside. Slice cake into 1/2-in. pieces; place a fourth in a 2-qt. serving bowl. Top with 1/3 cup jam. Spoon 1 cup of eggnog mixture over all.

Repeat two more layers of cake, jam and eggnog mixture. Top with remaining cake and eggnog mixture. Cover and chill for at least 2 hours. Fold sugar and vanilla into remaining whipped cream; spoon on top of trifle. Garnish with cherries. **Yield:** 8-10 servings.

***Editor's Note:** This recipe was tested with commercially prepared eggnog.

Cranberry Apple-Nut Pie

Wedges of this tangy Christmas-red pie are a feast for the eyes and the taste buds. —*Peggy Burdick Burlington, Michigan*

2 cups fresh ***or*** **frozen cranberries, chopped**
1-3/4 cups sliced peeled tart apple
1/2 cup slivered almonds, toasted
1 tablespoon grated orange peel
1-3/4 cups sugar
1/4 cup all-purpose flour
1/2 teaspoon ground cinnamon
1/2 teaspoon ground nutmeg
1/8 teaspoon salt
Pastry for double-crust pie (9 inches)
2 tablespoons butter, melted

In a large bowl, combine cranberries, apple, almonds and orange peel. In another bowl, combine sugar, flour, cinnamon, nutmeg and salt; add to fruit mixture and toss gently.

Line a 9-in. pie plate with the bottom crust; add

filling. Drizzle with butter. Roll out remaining pastry to fit top of pie. Place over filling; cut slits in top crust. Seal and flute edges. Bake at 400° for 45 minutes or until golden brown. Cool before serving. **Yield:** 6-8 servings.

Ice Cream Tunnel Cake

My son found this yummy recipe a few years ago and now it's a Yuletide tradition. A boxed mix makes preparation easy. For a fun variation, try mint-chocolate chip ice cream. —Holly Jean VeDepo, West Liberty, Iowa

1 package (18-1/4 ounces) chocolate cake mix
1 quart vanilla ice cream, slightly softened
1/2 cup mint chocolate chips*
1/2 cup light corn syrup
1 tablespoon heavy whipping cream
1/2 teaspoon vanilla extract

Prepare cake mix according to package directions. Pour batter into a greased and floured 10-in. fluted tube pan. Bake at 350° for 35-40 minutes or until a toothpick inserted near the center comes out clean. Cool for 10 minutes before removing from pan to a wire rack. Cool completely.

Slice top fourth off cake; set aside. Using a sharp knife, carefully hollow out bottom, leaving a 1-in. shell (save removed cake for another use). Place cake shell in freezer for 1 hour. Fill tunnel with ice cream; replace cake top. Cover and freeze for at least 6 hours.

Just before serving, melt chips and corn syrup in a microwave; stir until smooth. Stir in cream and vanilla. Spoon over cake. **Yield:** 12 servings.

***Editor's Note:** If mint chocolate chips are not available, place 1/2 cup semisweet chocolate chips and a few drops of peppermint extract in a plastic bag; seal and toss to coat. Let stand for 24-48 hours before using.

Paradise Pumpkin Pie

(Pictured at right)

Whenever I take this pie to a holiday party, potluck supper or bake sale, I take along copies of the recipe, too. I'm sure to be asked for it. With the pie's very rich taste, even a sliver is satisfying! —Karen Owen Rising Sun, Indiana

1 package (8 ounces) cream cheese, softened
1/4 cup sugar
1/2 teaspoon vanilla extract
1 egg
1 unbaked pastry shell (9 inches)

FILLING:

1 can (16 ounces) solid-pack pumpkin
1 cup evaporated milk
2 eggs, beaten
1/4 cup sugar
1/4 cup packed brown sugar
1 teaspoon ground cinnamon
1/4 teaspoon salt
1/4 teaspoon ground nutmeg

TOPPING:

2 tablespoons all-purpose flour
2 tablespoons brown sugar
1 tablespoon butter, softened
1/2 cup chopped pecans

In a mixing bowl, beat the cream cheese until smooth. Add the sugar and vanilla; mix well. Add egg; beat until smooth. Spread over bottom of pie shell. Chill 30 minutes. In a mixing bowl, beat filling ingredients until smooth. Carefully pour over the cream cheese layer. Cover the edge of pie with foil. Bake at 350° for 30 minutes. Remove foil; bake 25 minutes longer.

Meanwhile, mix the flour, brown sugar and butter until crumbly; stir in pecans. Sprinkle over pie. Bake 10-15 minutes more or until a knife inserted near the center comes out clean. Cool on a wire rack. Store in the refrigerator. **Yield:** 6-8 servings.

White Chocolate Holiday Cake

(Pictured below right and on back cover)

At our house, we always bake a birthday cake for Baby Jesus on Christmas Eve. The delicious tradition helps remind us all of the true meaning of the season we are celebrating. —Kim Van Rheenen, Mendota, Illinois

1 cup butter, softened
2 cups sugar, *divided*
4 eggs, *separated*
1-1/2 cups buttermilk
6 squares (1 ounces *each*) white baking chocolate, melted and cooled
1 teaspoon vanilla extract
2-1/2 cups cake flour
1-1/2 teaspoons baking powder
1/2 teaspoon salt
1/4 teaspoon baking soda
1 cup chopped pecans
1 cup flaked coconut
FROSTING:
1-1/2 cups butter, softened
6 cups confectioners' sugar
3 to 4 tablespoons milk
3 teaspoons vanilla extract
Poinsettia clay, optional

In a large mixing bowl, cream butter and 1-1/2 cups sugar. Add egg yolks, one at a time, beating well after each addition; set aside. Gradually stir buttermilk into white chocolate; add vanilla.

Combine the flour, baking powder, salt and baking soda. Add to creamed mixture alternately with the buttermilk mixture; mix well. In another mixing bowl, beat egg whites on medium speed until soft peaks form. Gradually beat in remaining sugar on high until stiff glossy peaks form; fold into batter. Fold in pecans and coconut.

Pour into three greased and floured 9-in. round baking pans. Bake at 350° for 30-35 minutes or until a toothpick comes out clean. Cool for 10 minutes before removing from pans to wire racks to cool completely.

For frosting, in a large mixing bowl, beat butter, confectioners' sugar, 3 tablespoons milk and vanilla on low speed until moistened. Increase speed to medium; beat for 1-1/2 minutes, adding additional milk if necessary to achieve spreading consistency. Spread between layers and over top and sides of cake. Decorate with poinsettia clay if desired. **Yield:** 12-16 servings.

EDIBLE POINSETTIA CHRISTMAS CLAY:
Patterns at right
1/3 cup light corn syrup
Red and green gel *or* paste food coloring
10 ounces white candy coating, melted

Divide corn syrup between two bowls. Tint one bowl with red food coloring to a deep shade, and tint the other green. Stir half of the melted candy coating into each bowl just until blended. Spread each color onto waxed paper to 1/2-in. thickness. Let stand, uncovered, at room temperature for 2-3 hours or until dry to the touch.

Remove clay from waxed paper and gather each portion of clay into a ball. Wrap each tightly in plastic wrap; let stand overnight. (Use immediately or store for up to 2 weeks.)

To make cake top poinsettia: Trace the patterns onto waxed paper; cut out. Knead each portion of clay until pliable but not soft. Roll between sheets of waxed paper to 1/8-in. thickness. Remove top sheet of waxed paper. Place patterns over clay.

Using a sharp knife, cut out six large red petals and three large leaves. With point of a knife, score the veins in petals and leaves, but do not cut all the way through. Arrange petals and leaves in the center of cake.

For flower stamens, form three 3/8-in. balls of green clay. Place in center of poinsettia.

To decorate sides of the cake: Cut out small and large petals, small and large leaves and stamens from the remaining clay. Arrange on sides of cake in pattern of your choice.

Cake Clues

Grease and flour baking pans for cakes that will be removed from the pans. Cakes that will be served from the pans should be greased but not floured. Some cake recipes call for the pan to be lined with waxed paper for easier removal of the cake from the pan.

Cool cakes for 10-15 minutes in pan, unless the recipe directs otherwise. Loosen the cake by running a knife around the edge of the pan. Turn out onto a wire rack and cool completely.

If the cake sticks to the pan and will not come out when inverted, return to the oven for 1 minute; turn out again.

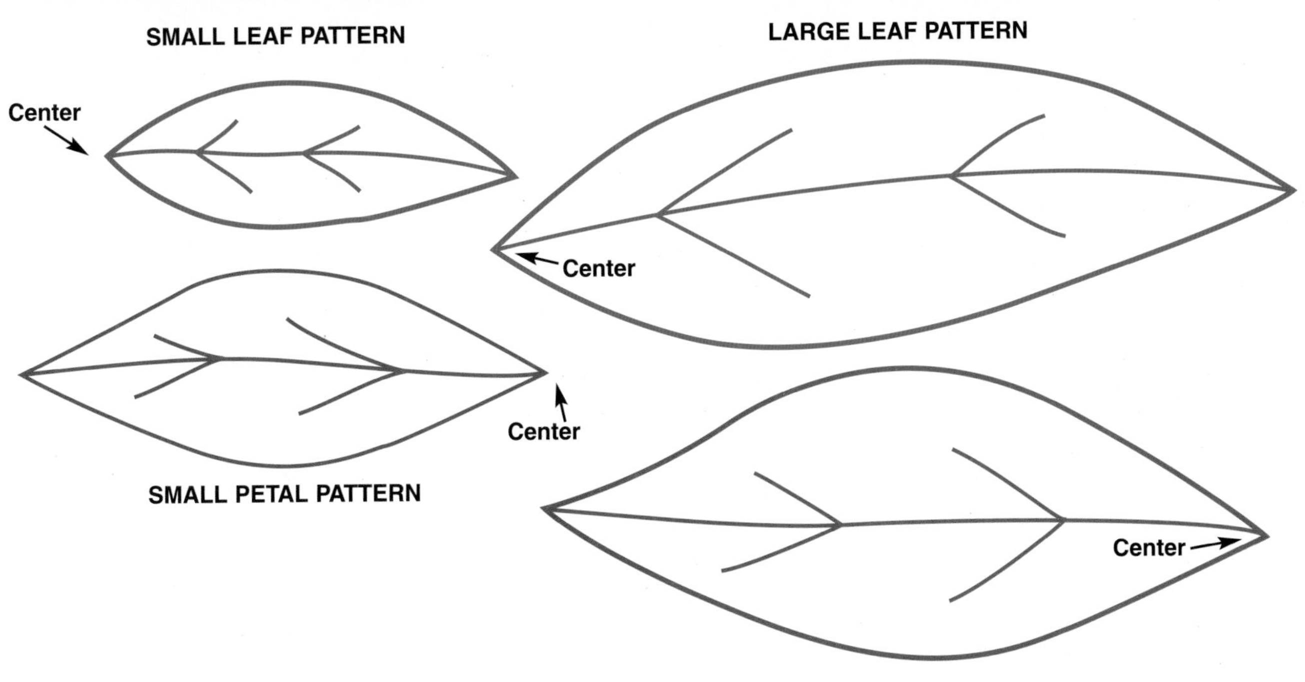
SMALL LEAF PATTERN
Center
LARGE LEAF PATTERN
Center
Center
SMALL PETAL PATTERN
Center
LARGE PETAL PATTERN

Ambrosia Pecan Pie

Orange peel and coconut combine with pecans to make this truly special and rich-tasting dessert. It always wins compliments at Christmas dinner.
—Bernadine Stine, Roanoke, Indiana

3 eggs
3/4 cup light corn syrup
1/2 cup sugar
3 tablespoons brown sugar
3 tablespoons orange juice
2 tablespoons butter, melted
1 teaspoon grated orange peel
1/8 teaspoon salt
1-1/2 cups chopped pecans
2/3 cup flaked coconut
1 unbaked pastry shell (9 inches)

In a large mixing bowl, beat the eggs, corn syrup, sugars, orange juice, butter, orange peel and salt until well blended. Stir in the pecans and coconut. Pour into pastry shell. Bake at 350° for 50-60 minutes or until a knife inserted near the center comes out clean. If edges become too brown, cover with foil. Cool on a wire rack. **Yield:** 8 servings.

Mint Chip Cheese Balls

A friend brought these cheese balls as a hostess gift to our Christmas open house. They instantly caught the fancy of my family. It's like having an appetizer for dessert. *—Robin Dooley, Fort Leavenworth, Kansas*

4 packages (8 ounces *each*) cream cheese, softened
2 cups finely chopped pecans
1 package (11-1/2 ounces) milk chocolate chips, finely chopped
36 starlight mints, crushed
Red and green sprinkles, optional
Chocolate wafers

In a mixing bowl, beat cream cheese until smooth; add pecans, chocolate chips and crushed mints. Divide into four portions. Cover and refrigerate for 1 hour or until firm. Shape each portion into a ball; roll in red and green sprinkles if desired. Serve with chocolate wafers. Store in refrigerator. **Yield:** 4 cheese balls (1-1/4 cups each).

Triple Chocolate Delight

A fitting finale for any special occasion, this fudgy cake has three luscious layers for chocolate lovers to sink their forks into. *—Mrs. Edwin Hill*
Santa Barbara, California

1 cup butter, softened, *divided*
2 cups sugar
4 eggs
5 Milky Way candy bars (2.15 ounces *each*)
1-1/4 cups buttermilk
2-1/2 cups all-purpose flour
1/2 teaspoon baking soda
1/4 teaspoon salt
1 cup chopped walnuts
FROSTING:
1/2 cup butter, *divided*
2-1/2 cups sugar
1 cup evaporated milk
1 jar (7 ounces) marshmallow creme
1 cup (6 ounces) semisweet chocolate chips
Chopped walnuts, optional

In a large mixing bowl, cream 1/2 cup butter and sugar. Add the eggs, one at a time, beating well after each addition. In a heavy saucepan, stir the candy bars and remaining butter over low heat until melted. Remove from heat; stir in the buttermilk. Combine the flour, baking soda and salt; add alternately with the buttermilk mixture to creamed mixture. Fold in the nuts.

Pour into three greased and floured 8-in. round baking pans. Bake at 350° for 30-40 minutes or until a toothpick inserted near the center comes out clean. Cool in pans on a rack for 10 minutes; remove from pans to cool completely.

For frosting, lightly grease sides of a medium saucepan with part of butter. Set remaining butter aside. Combine sugar and milk in the pan; cook over medium heat, stirring occasionally, until mixture comes to a rolling boil. Boil until a candy thermometer reads 234° (soft-ball stage).

Remove from heat; stir in marshmallow creme, chips and remaining butter. Transfer to a mixing bowl and cool to 110°. Beat on medium speed until smooth, about 5-7 minutes. Immediately frost cooled cake. Sprinkle with walnuts if desired. **Yield:** 12 servings.

Editor's Note: We recommend that you test your candy thermometer before each use by bringing water to a boil; the temperature should read 212°. Adjust your recipe temperature up or down based on your test.

Gifts from the Kitchen

Cinnamon Granola

(Pictured above)

Although it's meant for breakfast, my family eats this crunchy cereal by the handful all day long.
—Linda Agresta, Colorado Springs, Colorado

- 2 cups old-fashioned oats
- 3/4 cup whole unsalted nuts
- 2/3 cup flaked coconut
- 1/2 cup sunflower kernels
- 1/3 cup sesame seeds
- 1/3 cup toasted wheat germ
- 1/4 cup oat bran
- 2 tablespoons cornmeal
- 2 tablespoons whole wheat flour
- 1 tablespoon ground cinnamon
- 1/2 cup honey
- 2 tablespoons vegetable oil
- 2 tablespoons vanilla extract
- 1/4 teaspoon salt
- 1 cup golden raisins

In a large bowl, combine the first 10 ingredients; mix well. In a saucepan over medium heat, cook honey and oil for 4-5 minutes. Remove from the heat; stir in vanilla and salt. Pour over oat mixture and toss to coat. Transfer to a greased 15-in. x 10-in. x 1-in. baking pan. Bake at 275° for 45-50 minutes or until golden brown, stirring every 15 minutes. Cool, stirring occasionally. Stir in raisins. Store in an airtight container. **Yield:** 7 cups.

Spiced Cereal Crunch

My mother gave me the recipe for this irresistible party pleaser. I receive compliments every time I serve it.
—Janet Burkholder, Harrisonburg, Virginia

- 3 cups Cheerios
- 2 cups *each* Wheat Chex, Rice Chex and Corn Chex cereal
- 1-1/2 cups pecan halves
- 1-1/3 cups packed brown sugar
- 1/2 cup butter
- 1/4 cup light corn syrup
- 2 teaspoons ground cinnamon
- 1/2 teaspoon salt

Combine the cereals and nuts in a large roasting pan; set aside. In a saucepan, combine the brown sugar, butter, corn syrup, cinnamon and salt; bring to a boil over medium heat, stirring occasionally. Boil and stir for 3 minutes. Pour over cereal mixture and stir to coat.

Bake at 250° for 1 hour, stirring every 15 minutes. Spread onto waxed paper. When cool, break apart. Store in an airtight container. **Yield:** about 3 quarts.

Break-Apart Cookie Bites

These crisp treats lend a different shape to a cookie tray. And they're easy to prepare—just press into a pan, bake and break. My family enjoys them during the holidays and all year long.
—Marcia Wolff
Rolling Prairie, Indiana

- 1/2 cup butter, softened
- 1/2 cup shortening
- 1 cup sugar
- 1 teaspoon vanilla extract
- 2 cups all-purpose flour
- 1 teaspoon salt

1 cup miniature semisweet chocolate chips
1 cup finely chopped walnuts, *divided*

In a mixing bowl, cream butter, shortening and sugar. Beat in vanilla. Combine flour and salt; gradually add to creamed mixture. Stir in chocolate chips and 3/4 cup walnuts. Spread into a greased 15-in. x 10-in. x 1-in. baking pan. Sprinkle with remaining nuts; press down gently. Bake at 375° for 20-25 minutes or until golden brown. Cool completely. Break into pieces. **Yield:** about 8-1/2 dozen.

Bean Soup Mix

An attractive bag of this savory mix makes a tasteful gift for a teacher or co-worker. Remember to attach the soup recipe with a decorative ribbon or cord.
—Elizabeth Clayton Paul, Nepean, Ontario

BEAN MIX:
1 cup *each* dried yellow split peas, green split peas, lentils, pearl barley, black-eyed peas, small lima beans, navy beans, great northern beans and pinto beans

SOUP:
1-1/2 quarts water
1 large onion, chopped
1 large carrot, chopped
2 teaspoons chili powder
1-1/4 teaspoons salt
1/4 teaspoon pepper
1/8 teaspoon ground cloves
1/2 pound fully cooked smoked sausage, sliced
1 can (28 ounces) diced tomatoes, undrained
1 tablespoon lemon juice

Combine bean mix ingredients. Divide into six batches, 1-1/2 cups each. Store in airtight containers.

To make one batch of soup: Place 1-1/2 cups bean mix in a Dutch oven or soup kettle; cover with water by 2 in. Bring to a boil; boil for 2 minutes. Remove from the heat; let stand for 1 hour. Drain, discarding liquid. Return beans to kettle; add 1-1/2 qts. water. Bring to a boil. Reduce heat; cover and simmer for 1-1/2 to 2 hours or until beans are tender.

Add onion, carrot, chili powder, salt, pepper and cloves. Return to a boil. Reduce heat and simmer, uncovered, for 30 minutes. Add sausage, tomatoes and lemon juice; simmer 15-20 minutes longer. **Yield:** 9 cups of mix (six batches of soup—each batch makes 2-1/2 quarts and serves 8-10).

Pretzel Wreaths

(Pictured below)

Youngsters love to lend a hand with this recipe. Our two girls help me measure, pour, stir, shape and, of course, eat the chewy pretzel rounds when they're done!
—Roberta Spieker, Duncan, South Carolina

1 package (1/4 ounce) active dry yeast
1-1/2 cups warm water (110° to 115°)
4 cups all-purpose flour
1 tablespoon sugar
1 teaspoon salt
1 egg white, lightly beaten
Coarse salt *or* colored sugar

In a mixing bowl, dissolve yeast in water; let stand for 5 minutes. Add 2 cups flour, sugar and salt; beat until smooth. Stir in enough remaining flour to form a soft dough. Turn onto a floured surface; knead until smooth and elastic, about 6 minutes. Cover and let rest for 15 minutes.

Divide dough into 16 portions. Roll each portion into a 15-in. rope. Fold each rope in half and twist two or three times; shape into a circle and pinch ends together. Place on greased baking sheets. Brush with egg white; sprinkle with salt or sugar. Bake at 425° for 12-15 minutes. **Yield:** 16 pretzels.

Christmas Spice Mix

Wonderfully versatile, this gift is seasoned for both sipping and sniffing. When mixed with fruit juices, it's a delicious winter warmer-upper. Boiled in water, it makes a "scentsational" potpourri that will add a heavenly fragrance to the whole house! —*Gloria Hoesing O'Neill, Nebraska*

SPICE MIX:

1 cinnamon stick (3 inches)
1 teaspoon ground cinnamon
1 teaspoon whole allspice
1/2 teaspoon whole cloves
1/2 teaspoon ground ginger
1/4 teaspoon ground nutmeg

ADDITIONAL INGREDIENTS FOR CRANBERRY WASSAIL:

1 quart cranberry juice
1 quart pineapple juice
1/2 cup sugar

Combine spice mix ingredients; place in the center of two 6-in. square pieces of cheesecloth. Bring corners together and tie with string or dental floss. **Yield:** 1 spice bag.

To use as a room scent: Place spice bag in a 2-cup microwave-safe measuring cup filled with hot water. Microwave on high for 5-6 minutes or until water boils. Continue to microwave at 30% power to add fragrance to the whole house. (Add more water if microwaved for additional time.)

To prepare cranberry wassail: Combine juices, sugar and spice bag in a 2-qt. microwave-safe bowl. Cover with plastic wrap and cut a vent. Microwave on high for 14 minutes or until mixture boils. Microwave at 50% power 5 minutes longer. **Yield:** 2 quarts.

Editor's Note: This recipe was tested in a 700-watt microwave.

Marvelous Mocha Mix

(Pictured at left)

A tin of this mix with serving instructions makes a ready-to-soothe Christmas gift. My husband and I take it to senior citizens we visit. It perks them right up! —*Shirley Brazel, Rocklin, California*

1 cup instant chocolate drink mix
1 cup powdered nondairy creamer
2/3 cup instant coffee granules
1/2 cup sugar
1/2 teaspoon ground cinnamon
1/4 teaspoon ground nutmeg

Combine all ingredients; mix well. Store in an airtight container. **To make one serving:** Add 4-6 teaspoons mix to 3/4 cup boiling water; stir until dissolved. **Yield:** 3 cups mix (24-36 servings).

Praline Sauce

A can't-miss treat, this topping can be drizzled across pancakes, French toast or waffles or served over ice cream. —*Pat Sturze Campbell River, British Columbia*

1-1/2 cups dark corn syrup
1-1/2 cups light corn syrup

1 teaspoon vanilla extract
1/8 teaspoon ground cinnamon
1/8 teaspoon ground nutmeg
1-1/2 cups coarsely chopped pecans, toasted

In a large bowl, combine corn syrups, vanilla, cinnamon and nutmeg until well blended. Stir in pecans. **Yield**: 4 cups.

Banana Fruit Mini Loaves

(Pictured above)

Plenty of goodies come in these little breads. The recipe is from my aunt, who always used to bake homemade treats for my sister and me when we visited her. Several of her recipes remain favorites of mine today.

—Jean Engle, Pella, Iowa

2 eggs
2/3 cup sugar
1 cup mashed bananas (about 2 medium)
1-3/4 cups all-purpose flour
3 teaspoons baking powder
1/2 teaspoon salt
1 cup chopped mixed candied fruit
1/2 cup raisins
1/2 cup chopped walnuts

In a mixing bowl, beat eggs and sugar. Add bananas; mix well. Combine the flour, baking powder and salt; gradually add to egg mixture. Fold in the fruit, raisins and walnuts.

Transfer to three greased 5-3/4-in. x 3-in. x 2-in. loaf pans. Bake at 350° for 30-35 minutes or until a toothpick comes out clean. Cool for 10 minutes before removing from pans to wire racks to cool completely. **Yield**: 3 mini loaves.

Editor's Note: Bread can be baked in one 9-in. x 5-in. x 3-in. loaf pan for 55-60 minutes.

Creole Seasoning

(Pictured above)

This spicy seasoning adds warmth to the holidays and all year-round. The versatile mix is as good on popcorn as it is on chicken or potato wedges.
—Jan Buchanan, Ventura, Iowa

2/3 cup cayenne pepper
1/2 cup plus 2 teaspoons salt
1/4 cup garlic powder
1/4 cup onion powder
1/4 cup chili powder
2 tablespoons plus 2 teaspoons pepper

In a bowl, combine all ingredients. Store in an airtight container for up to 6 months. **Yield:** about 2 cups.

Fudgy Walnut Sauce

This rich sauce will satisfy any sweet tooth. It tastes great poured over pound cake or drizzled on scoops of ice cream. —Dorothy Bateman, Carver, Massachusetts

1 cup sugar
1/2 cup half-and-half cream
2 squares (1 ounce *each*) unsweetened chocolate
2 squares (1 ounce *each*) semisweet chocolate
1/2 cup butter
2 egg yolks
1 teaspoon vanilla extract
1 cup coarsely chopped walnuts

In a saucepan, combine sugar and cream. Bring to boil over medium heat, stirring occasionally. Add chocolate and butter; stir until melted. Remove from the heat.

In a small bowl, beat egg yolks. Whisk a small amount of the chocolate mixture into yolks. Return all to the pan; whisk until smooth. Bring to a gentle boil; cook and stir for 2 minutes. Remove from the heat; stir in vanilla and walnuts. Pour into jars; cool. Cover and store in the refrigerator. To serve, reheat in a double boiler or microwave. **Yield:** 2 cups.

Nutty Caramel Popcorn

Folks who've tasted my snack are quick to remind me to make it again the following Christmas! The combination of popcorn and crunchy nuts really hits the spot. —Sharon Buchinski, Endeavour, Saskatchewan

4 quarts popped popcorn
1-1/3 cups pecan halves, toasted
2/3 cup whole unblanched almonds, toasted
1-1/3 cups sugar
1 cup butter
1/2 cup light corn syrup
2 teaspoons vanilla extract

Place popcorn in a large greased bowl. Sprinkle the pecans and almonds over top; set aside. In a heavy saucepan, combine the sugar, butter and corn syrup; cook and stir over medium heat until a candy thermometer reads 300°-310° (hard-crack stage).

Remove from heat; stir in vanilla. Immediately pour over popcorn mixture; toss gently. Spread on greased baking sheets. When cool, break into small pieces. Store in airtight containers. **Yield:** about 20 cups.

Editor's Note: We recommend that you test your candy thermometer before each use by bringing water to a boil; the temperature should read 212°. Adjust your recipe temperature up or down based on your test.

Holiday Biscotti

A twice-baked Italian cookie, biscotti makes a wonderful "dunker". A pretty way to present a batch is on a Christmasy plate arranged in wagon-wheel fashion.
—Libia Foglesong, San Bruno, California

1/2 cup butter, softened
1 cup sugar
3 eggs
2 teaspoons vanilla extract
1 teaspoon orange extract
3 cups all-purpose flour
2 teaspoons baking powder
1/2 teaspoon salt
2/3 cup dried cranberries, coarsely chopped
2/3 cup pistachios, coarsely chopped
2 tablespoons grated orange peel

In a mixing bowl, cream butter and sugar. Add eggs, one at a time, beating well after each addition. Stir in extracts. Combine flour, baking powder and salt; gradually add to creamed mixture and mix well (dough will be sticky). Stir in cranberries, pistachios and orange peel. Chill for 30 minutes.

Divide dough in half. On a floured surface, shape each half into a loaf 1-1/2 to 2 in. in diameter. Place on an ungreased baking sheet. Bake at 350° for 30-35 minutes. Cool for 5 minutes. Cut diagonally into 3/4-in.-thick slices. Place slices, cut side down, on an ungreased baking sheet. Bake for 9-10 minutes. Turn slices over. Bake 10 minutes more or until golden brown. Cool on a wire rack. Store in an airtight container. **Yield:** 2 dozen.

Spicy Pecans 'n' Cranberries

(Pictured at right)

Spice up a holiday party with these well-seasoned nuts or keep a batch in the freezer to give as last-minute presents.
—Rene Dalrymple
Hansville, Washington

2 tablespoons butter, melted
2 tablespoons Worcestershire sauce
1/2 teaspoon garlic powder
1/2 teaspoon seasoned salt
1/2 teaspoon ground cumin
1/4 to 1/2 teaspoon cayenne pepper
3 cups pecan halves
1-1/2 cups dried cranberries

Combine the first six ingredients in a large bowl. Add pecans and mix well. Spread in an ungreased 13-in. x 9-in. x 2-in. baking pan. Bake at 350° for 15 minutes, stirring every 5 minutes. Cool completely. Stir in cranberries. Store in an airtight container. **Yield:** about 4 cups.

Wrap It Up

Giving a gift basket of homemade treats this holiday season? Try using nylon netting, fabric or ordinary cellophane for wrapping material. Choose colors and patterns that reflect the season or the contents of the basket.

Instead of struggling to secure the wrapped gift with ribbon, use an inexpensive chenille stem. It's simple to wrap around the gift and give a twist with just one hand.

For the finishing touch, tie on a colorful ribbon, bow or decorative gift tag.

Gift-Wrapped Brownies

(Pictured below)

With a bright green and red frosting "ribbon" piped on top, these chocolaty "packages" are a pretty addition to any holiday gathering. —*Doris Roots*
Big Timber, Montana

1/2 cup shortening
4 squares (1 ounce *each*) semisweet baking chocolate
3 eggs
1 cup sugar
2 teaspoons vanilla extract, *divided*
1/2 cup all-purpose flour
1/2 cup chopped nuts
1/2 teaspoon salt
1/2 teaspoon baking powder
2 cups confectioners' sugar
1/4 cup heavy whipping cream
Red and green food coloring

In a small saucepan over low heat, melt shortening and chocolate; set aside. In a mixing bowl, beat eggs, sugar and 1 teaspoon vanilla. Add the flour, nuts, salt, baking powder and chocolate mixture; mix well. Pour into a greased 8-in. square baking pan. Bake at 350° for 20-25 minutes or until a toothpick inserted near the center comes out clean. Cool on a wire rack. Cut into 2-in. x 1-in. rectangles; remove from pan.

In a bowl, combine confectioners' sugar, cream and remaining vanilla; set half aside. Spread remaining frosting over top of brownies. Tint half of the reserved frosting red and half green. Cut a small hole in the corner of two plastic or pastry bags; fill one bag with red frosting and one with green. Insert pastry tip if desired. To decorate brownies, pipe ribbon and bows as shown in photo or create designs of your choice. **Yield:** 2-1/2 dozen.

Strawberry Orange Spread

(Pictured at right)

I wrap up this refreshing spread with jar toppers made from Christmasy fabric. It looks so festive tucked in a basket alongside homemade bread. —*Rita MacTough*
New London, Connecticut

2 packages (10 ounces *each*) frozen sweetened sliced strawberries, thawed
1/2 cup orange juice
1 tablespoon grated orange peel
1 package (1-3/4 ounces) powdered fruit pectin
3-1/2 cups sugar

In a kettle, combine the strawberries, orange juice and orange peel. Stir in pectin. Bring to a rolling boil over high heat, stirring constantly. Add sugar; return to a rolling boil. Boil and stir for 1 minute. Remove from the heat; skim off foam.

Pour into jars or freezer containers; cool to room temperature, about 1 hour. Cover and let stand overnight or until set, but not longer than 24 hours. Refrigerate or freeze. **Yield:** about 4-1/2 cups.

Apricot Pineapple Braid

(Pictured above right)

Our family can't wait for Christmas morning, knowing this fruit-filled favorite will be on the table. I make several extras for our friends' breakfasts, too.
—*Loranell Nelson, Goodland, Kansas*

4-1/2 to 5 cups all-purpose flour
1/2 cup sugar
2 packages (1/4 ounce *each*) active dry yeast
1-1/2 teaspoons salt
1/2 cup water

1/2 cup milk
1/4 cup butter
2 eggs, beaten

FILLING:
2 cups chopped dried apricots
1 can (8 ounces) crushed pineapple, undrained
1 cup packed brown sugar
3/4 cup water
1/4 cup orange juice

GLAZE:
1 cup confectioners' sugar
1/4 teaspoon vanilla extract
1 to 2 tablespoons milk

Red and green candied cherries, optional

In a mixing bowl, combine 2 cups flour, sugar, yeast and salt. In a saucepan, heat the water, milk and butter to 120°-130°. Add to dry ingredients; beat until moistened. Beat in eggs until smooth. Stir in enough remaining flour to form a stiff dough.

Turn onto a floured surface; knead until smooth and elastic, about 6-8 minutes. Place in a greased bowl, turning once to grease top. Cover and let rise in a warm place until doubled, about 1 hour. Meanwhile, combine filling ingredients in a saucepan. Bring to a boil. Reduce heat; simmer, uncovered, for 10-15 minutes or until thickened. Cool.

Punch dough down. Turn onto a lightly floured surface; divide in half. Roll each into a 16-in. x 8-in. rectangle. Place on greased baking sheets. Spoon filling down center third of each rectangle. On each long side, cut 1-in.-wide strips 2-1/2 in. into center. Starting at one end, fold alternating strips at an angle across filling. Pinch ends to seal and tuck under. Cover and let rise until doubled, about 30 minutes. Bake at 350° for 25-30 minutes or until golden brown. Remove from pans to wire racks to cool.

For glaze, combine confectioners' sugar, vanilla and enough milk to achieve desired consistency. Drizzle over braids. Garnish with cherries if desired. **Yield:** 2 loaves.

Cowboy Cookie Mix

(Pictured above right)

Since half the fun of cookies is baking them, I give this merry-making mix as a gift. The ingredients look so pretty in a jar, and the cookies smell terrific coming out of the oven! —*Rosemary Griffith, Tulsa, Oklahoma*

1-1/3 cups quick-cooking oats
1-1/3 cups all-purpose flour
1 teaspoon baking powder
1 teaspoon baking soda
1/4 teaspoon salt
1/2 cup chopped pecans
1 cup (6 ounces) semisweet chocolate chips
1/2 cup packed brown sugar
1/2 cup sugar

ADDITIONAL INGREDIENTS:
1/2 cup butter, melted
1 egg, lightly beaten
1 teaspoon vanilla extract

Pour oats into a wide-mouth 1-qt. glass container with a tight-fitting lid. Combine the flour, baking powder, baking soda and salt; place on top of oats. Layer with pecans, chocolate chips, brown sugar and sugar, packing each layer tightly (do not mix). Cover and store in a cool dry place for up to 6 months.

To prepare cookies: Pour cookie mix into a large mixing bowl; stir to combine ingredients. Beat in butter, egg and vanilla. Cover and refrigerate for 30 minutes. Roll into 1-in. balls. Place 2 in. apart on greased baking sheets. Bake at 350° for 11-13 minutes or until set. Remove to wire racks to cool. **Yield:** about 3-1/2 dozen.

Pastel Almond Bark

(Pictured above)

Cooks of all ages will find this pretty confection is a snap to prepare. It never fails to take center stage on the goody plates I make for friends. —*Audrey Attoe Lodi, Wisconsin*

1 package (24 ounces) white candy coating, cut into 1/2-inch pieces
2 cups pastel miniature marshmallows
2 cups Froot Loops
1 cup chopped pecans
1 cup flaked coconut

In a microwave or heavy saucepan, melt candy coating; stir until smooth. Stir in marshmallows, cereal, pecans and coconut. Drop by tablespoonfuls onto waxed paper-lined baking sheets. Cool. Store in an airtight container at room temperature. **Yield:** about 5 dozen.

Zesty Snack Mix

Friends and family hint, year after year, that they're looking forward to this well-seasoned snack mix. The sesame snack sticks and shoestring potatoes are fun surprise additions. —*Blanche Swalwell, Thunder Bay, Ontario*

11 cups Cheerios
8 cups Crispix
8 cups Corn Chex
6 cups bite-size Shredded Wheat
1 package (10 ounces) corn chips
1 jar (8 ounces) salted peanuts
1 package (8 ounces) pretzel sticks
1 package (7 ounces) sesame snack sticks
1 package (7 ounces) shoestring potato sticks
1 pound butter
3 tablespoons garlic powder
3 tablespoons onion powder
2 tablespoons hot pepper sauce
2 tablespoons lemon juice
2 tablespoons Worcestershire sauce
2 teaspoons garlic salt

In a large bowl, combine the first nine ingredients. In a saucepan over low heat, melt butter. Add seasonings; stir until dissolved. Pour over cereal mixture; stir to coat. Place in large greased roasting pans. Bake, uncovered, at 250° for 1 hour, stirring every 15 minutes. Store in airtight containers. **Yield:** 12 quarts.

Cinnamon Crunch Triangles

Adding a little sugar and spice to Yuletide is as easy as this recipe. For delivery, wrap the treats in red and green cellophane and stack in a tin or a trimmed-up gift bag. —*Liz Corley, Eufaula, Oklahoma*

12 whole cinnamon graham crackers (5 inches x 2-1/2 inches)
2 cups finely chopped walnuts
1 cup butter
1 cup packed brown sugar
1/2 teaspoon ground cinnamon

Arrange graham crackers in a greased 15-in. x 10-in. x 1-in. baking pan; sprinkle with walnuts. In a saucepan, combine the butter, brown sugar and cinnamon. Cook and stir over medium heat until mixture comes to a boil. Continue cooking, without stirring, for 3 minutes. Slowly pour over crackers.

Bake at 400° for 8-9 minutes or until edges are browned. Cool completely. Cut into 2-in. squares, then cut each square in half to form triangles. Store in an airtight container. **Yield:** about 5 dozen.

Chocolate-Cherry Brownie Cups

It's so tempting to snitch one of these yummy cups, you'll want to double your recipe. That way, you'll have some to munch on right away while you package the others to give as gifts to friends and family. —*Carol Walker Spicer, Minnesota*

1 cup butter
4 squares (1 ounce *each*) semisweet chocolate
4 eggs
1-1/2 cups sugar
1 teaspoon vanilla extract
1 cup all-purpose flour
1-1/2 cups chopped walnuts
3/4 cup chopped maraschino cherries

In a microwave or double boiler, melt butter and chocolate; cool for 10 minutes. In a mixing bowl, beat eggs and sugar. Add vanilla and the chocolate mixture. Stir in flour, walnuts and cherries.

Fill paper-lined muffin cups three-fourths full. Bake at 350° for 20-25 minutes or until a toothpick comes out clean. Cool for 5 minutes before removing from pans to wire racks. **Yield:** 1-1/2 dozen.

Red Beans and Rice Mix

(Pictured at right)

Since there's food galore during the holidays themselves, I like giving this zippy mix as an after-Christmas present instead. I just slip the containers of seasoning, beans and rice into a decorative paper bag. A recipe card completes the package. —*Trudie Hagen, Roggen, Colorado*

1 bay leaf
1 tablespoon dried vegetable flakes
1 tablespoon dried minced onion
2 teaspoons seasoned salt
1 teaspoon ground cumin
1 teaspoon sugar
1/2 teaspoon celery seed
1/2 teaspoon dried minced garlic
1/4 teaspoon cayenne pepper
1/4 teaspoon crushed red pepper flakes
2 cups dry kidney beans
1 cup uncooked long grain rice

ADDITIONAL INGREDIENTS:
4-1/2 cups water, *divided*
1-1/2 to 2 pounds smoked ham hocks
1 pound smoked sausage, sliced
1/2 teaspoon salt
Minced fresh parsley, optional

Combine the first 10 ingredients; place in an airtight container. Place beans and rice in separate containers. **Yield:** 1 batch.

To prepare red beans and rice: Place beans in a Dutch oven or soup kettle; add water to cover by 2 in. Bring to a boil; boil for 2 minutes. Remove from the heat; cover and let stand for 1 hour. Drain. Return beans to pan; add seasoning mix, 2-1/2 cups water and ham hocks. Bring to a boil. Reduce heat; cover and simmer for 1-1/2 hours. Remove ham hocks; cut meat into bite-size pieces and return to pan. Add the sausage. Cover and simmer for 30-40 minutes or until beans are tender and sausage is heated through. Remove bay leaf.

Meanwhile, combine rice, salt and remaining water in a saucepan. Bring to a boil. Reduce heat; cover and simmer for 20 minutes or until liquid is absorbed. Remove from the heat; let stand for 5 minutes. Spoon into bowls; top with bean mixture. Garnish with parsley if desired. **Yield:** 4-6 servings.

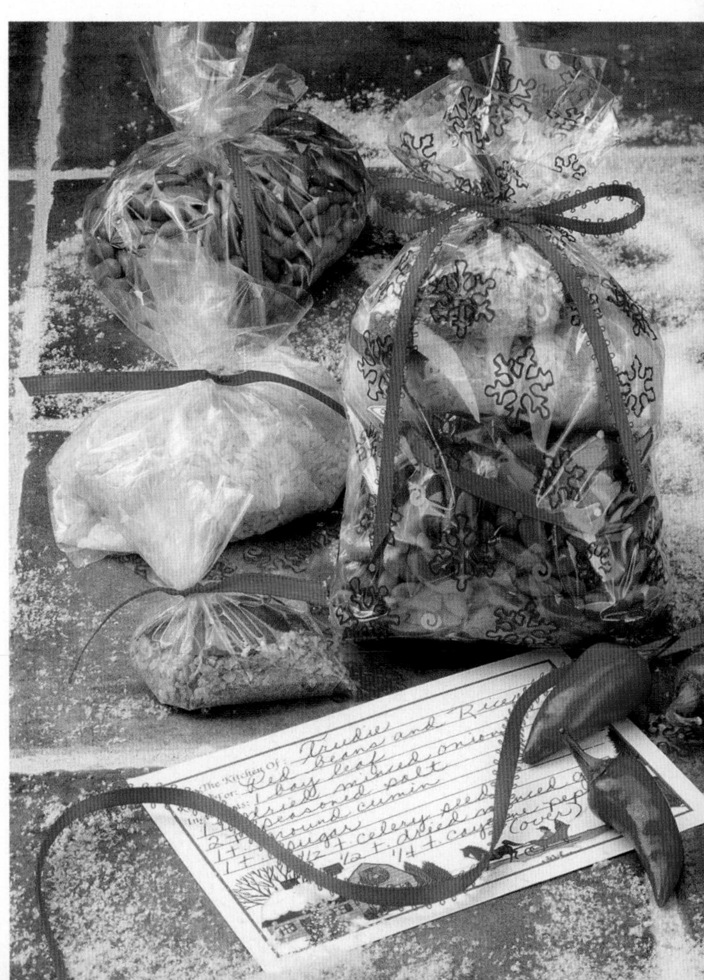

Texas Jalapeno Jelly

(Pictured below)

A jar of this jelly is always warmly appreciated. To add an extra Southwestern accent, I trim the lid with a red bandanna. *—Lori McMullen, Victoria, Texas*

2 jalapeno peppers, seeded and chopped*
3 medium green peppers, cut into 1-inch pieces, *divided*
1-1/2 cups vinegar, *divided*
6-1/2 cups sugar
1/2 to 1 teaspoon cayenne pepper
2 pouches (3 ounces *each*) liquid fruit pectin
About 6 drops green food coloring, optional
Cream cheese and crackers, optional

Puree jalapenos, half of green peppers and 1/2 cup vinegar in a blender or food processor; pour into a large kettle. Repeat with remaining green peppers and another 1/2 cup vinegar. Add sugar, cayenne and remaining vinegar to kettle. Bring to a boil over high heat, stirring constantly.

Quickly stir in pectin and return to a boil. Boil for 1 minute, stirring constantly. Remove from heat; skim off foam. Add food coloring if desired. Ladle hot liquid into hot jars, leaving 1/4-in. headspace. Cover with lids. Process for 10 minutes in a boiling-water bath. Serve over cream cheese with crackers if desired. **Yield:** 7 half-pints.

***Editor's Note:** When cutting or seeding hot peppers, use rubber or plastic gloves to protect your hands. Avoid touching your face.

Thick 'n' Spicy Sauce

With raisins for sweetness and pepper for kick, this spicy sauce is excellent with ham but also lends a nice barbecue flavor to burgers and roast beef.
—Vicki Atkinson, Kamas, Utah

1 small onion, cut into wedges
1 garlic clove
1 cup ketchup
1/3 cup butter, melted
1/2 cup raisins
2 to 4 teaspoons pepper
3 tablespoons brown sugar
2 tablespoons white vinegar
2 tablespoons lemon juice
1 teaspoon salt
1 teaspoon ground mustard

1/2 teaspoon dried basil
1/4 teaspoon *each* dried marjoram, tarragon and thyme
1/4 teaspoon dried rosemary, crushed

In a blender or food processor, combine all ingredients. Cover and process until smooth. Pour into a saucepan. Cook and stir over medium heat for 8-10 minutes or until heated through. Refrigerate leftovers. **Yield:** 2-1/2 cups.

Chocolate Peppermint Pinwheels

My cookie-loving family is never satisfied with just one batch of these minty pinwheels, so I automatically double the recipe each time I bake them.
—Ellen Johnson, Hampton, Virginia

1/2 cup shortening
3/4 cup sugar
1 egg
1 tablespoon milk
1 teaspoon peppermint extract
1-1/4 cups all-purpose flour
1/4 teaspoon salt
1/4 teaspoon baking powder
1 square (1 ounce) unsweetened chocolate, melted

In a mixing bowl, cream shortening and sugar. Add egg, milk and extract; mix well. Combine flour, salt and baking powder; gradually add to creamed mixture. Divide dough in half. Add chocolate to one portion; mix well. Roll each portion between waxed paper into a rectangle about 1/2 in. thick. Remove top sheet of waxed paper; place plain dough over chocolate dough. Roll up jelly-roll style, starting with a long side. Wrap in plastic wrap; refrigerate for 2 hours or until firm.

Unwrap dough and cut into 1/4-in. slices. Place 2 in. apart on greased baking sheets. Bake at 375° for 8-10 minutes or until lightly browned. Remove to wire racks to cool. **Yield:** about 3 dozen.

Eggnog Fruit Bread

(Pictured above right)

Presents from the pantry are a tradition in my family, and this moist, fruity quick bread is a favorite. I wrap loaves in cellophane and garnish with stickers and curly ribbons. *—Margo Stich, Rochester, Minnesota*

3 eggs
1 cup vegetable oil
1-1/2 cups sugar
3/4 teaspoon vanilla extract
3/4 teaspoon rum extract
1-1/2 cups eggnog*
3 cups all-purpose flour, *divided*
2 teaspoons baking powder
1/2 teaspoon salt
1/2 teaspoon ground nutmeg
1 cup candied fruit
1/2 cup chopped walnuts

In a mixing bowl, beat the eggs and oil. Add the sugar, extracts and eggnog; mix well. Combine 2-1/2 cups flour, baking powder, salt and nutmeg; gradually add to egg mixture. Toss the fruit with remaining flour; stir into batter. Fold in walnuts. Pour into two greased 8-in. x 4-in. x 2-in. loaf pans. Bake at 350° for 60-65 minutes or until a toothpick comes out clean. Cool for 10 minutes before removing from pans to wire racks. **Yield:** 2 loaves.

***Editor's Note:** This recipe was tested with commercially prepared eggnog.

Golden Fruitcake

(Pictured above)

Fruitcake has been favored by my family ever since my sister shared this light version. It's filled with goodies.
—Ruth Hempstead, Royal Oak, Michigan

- 2 packages (15 ounces *each*) golden raisins
- 1-1/2 cups shortening
- 2-1/4 cups sugar
- 8 eggs
- 1 teaspoon vanilla extract
- 4 cups all-purpose flour
- 1 teaspoon cream of tartar
- 1 teaspoon salt
- 1/2 teaspoon baking soda
- 1/2 cup milk
- 2-1/2 cups chopped walnuts
- 1-1/3 cups diced candied pineapple (about 8 ounces)
- 1 cup chopped candied cherries (about 8 ounces)
- 1 cup flaked coconut

Place raisins in a bowl; cover with boiling water and let stand for 5 minutes. Drain well and set aside. In a mixing bowl, cream shortening and sugar. Add eggs, one at a time, beating well after each addition. Beat in vanilla. Combine dry ingredients; add to the creamed mixture alternately with milk. Stir in the walnuts, pineapple, cherries, coconut and raisins.

Spoon into nine greased 5-3/4-in. x 3-in. x 2-in. loaf pans. Bake at 300° for 65-75 minutes or until a toothpick inserted near center comes out clean. Cool for 10 minutes before removing from pans to wire racks. **Yield:** 9 loaves.

Editor's Note: Fruitcakes can be baked in two batches. Refrigerate batter until baking.

Mustard Cheese Spread

Wrapped up in a basket with crackers and a decorative spreader, this tangy cheese spread is a distinctive hostess gift. It's also good used as a dip for raw vegetables. —Lilburne Flohr-Svendsen
Barra Bonita, SP, Brazil

- 1 package (8 ounces) cream cheese, softened
- 1/2 cup butter, softened
- 1 medium onion, finely chopped
- 2 garlic cloves, minced
- 2 to 3 tablespoons prepared mustard
- 2 tablespoons paprika
- 1/4 teaspoon salt
- 1/8 teaspoon pepper
- 1 tablespoon caraway seeds

In a mixing bowl, beat cream cheese and butter until smooth. Add the onion, garlic, mustard, paprika, salt and pepper. Spread onto an 8-in. serving platter; sprinkle with caraway seeds. Cover and refrigerate until serving. **Yield:** 2 cups.

Butterscotch Ice Cream Topping

Wonderful homemade goodness and true butterscotch flavor make this sweet rich sauce a well-enjoyed gift. We like it over ice cream or slices of pound cake. It reheats well in the microwave. —*Annie Gingerich Greenwood, Wisconsin*

1 cup packed brown sugar
1/4 cup heavy whipping cream
3 tablespoons butter
2 tablespoons light corn syrup

In a heavy saucepan, combine all ingredients. Bring to a boil over medium heat; cook and stir for 3 minutes. Cool to room temperature. Cover and store in the refrigerator.

To reheat, microwave at 50% power for 1 minute or until heated through. Serve warm over ice cream. **Yield:** 1-1/4 cups.

Chocolate-Dipped Pretzel Rods

Kids of all ages enjoy receiving these fun-to-eat treats for Christmas. Once the pretzels are wrapped with plastic wrap and ribbons, you can tuck them into stockings, tie them onto gifts or slip them inside a glass jar. My whole family looks forward to receiving them each year. —*Kay Waters, Benld, Illinois*

2 packages (14 ounces *each*) caramels*
2 packages (10 ounces *each*) pretzel rods
3 cups chopped toasted almonds
1 pound white candy coating
1 pound dark chocolate candy coating

Melt caramels in the top of a double boiler or microwave-safe bowl. Pour into an ungreased 8-in. square pan or a tall glass. Leaving 1 in. of space on the end you are holding, roll or dip pretzels in caramel. Allow excess to drip off. Roll in almonds. Place on waxed paper-lined baking sheets and allow to harden.

Melt white candy coating in a double boiler or microwave-safe bowl. Repeat dipping procedure with half of the caramel-coated pretzels. Return to baking sheets to harden. Repeat with the dark chocolate coating and remaining pretzels. Store in an airtight container, or wrap in plastic wrap and tie with a colorful ribbon for gift-giving. **Yield:** about 4 dozen.

***Editor's Note:** This recipe was tested with Hershey caramels.

Candy Apple Jelly

(Pictured below)

With a hint of apple and cinnamon, this jelly spreads cheer from breads to bagels to muffins. Its rosy pink color looks lovely blushing through the food jars I save and decorate with fabric-covered lids. —*Betsy Porter Bismarck, North Dakota*

4 cups apple juice
1/2 cup red-hot candies
1 package (1-3/4 ounces) powdered fruit pectin
4-1/2 cups sugar

In a large kettle, combine apple juice, candies and pectin. Bring to a full rolling boil over high heat, stirring constantly. Stir in sugar; return to a full rolling boil. Boil for 2 minutes, stirring constantly.

Remove from heat; skim off foam and undissolved candies. Pour hot liquid into hot jars, leaving 1/4-in. headspace. Adjust caps. Process for 5 minutes in a boiling-water bath. **Yield:** about 6 half-pints.

No-Candied-Fruit Fruitcake

Minus the candied fruit, this traditional cake has a positively natural taste. For those who bake their Christmas giveaways ahead, it freezes beautifully, too.
—Sally Vest, Palatine, Illinois

1-1/2 cups all-purpose flour
1-1/2 cups sugar
1 teaspoon baking powder
1 teaspoon salt
5-1/2 cups pecan halves
2 jars (16 ounces *each*) maraschino cherries, drained
1 can (20 ounces) crushed pineapple, drained
2 packages (8 ounces *each*) pitted dates, halved and quartered
6 eggs
1/2 cup orange juice
1/4 to 1/2 cup corn syrup

In a large bowl, combine the first four ingredients. Add pecans, cherries, pineapple and dates; toss to coat. Beat eggs and orange juice; add to fruit mixture and mix well. Line two 9-in. x 5-in. x 3-in. loaf pans with foil and grease the foil. Pour fruit mixture into pans and press down. Bake at 300° for 1-3/4 to 2 hours or until a toothpick inserted near the center comes out clean. Cool for 10 minutes; remove from pans. Remove foil. Brush with corn syrup; cool completely. **Yield:** 2 fruitcakes.

Apricot-Nut White Fudge

My family looks forward to this luscious apricot-studded fudge every year. It's easy to make and really does melt in your mouth. I like to wrap up small squares of the candy with ribbon and silk holly.
—Betty Claycomb, Alverton, Pennsylvania

1 package (8 ounces) cream cheese, softened
4 cups confectioners' sugar
12 squares (1 ounce *each*) white baking chocolate, melted and cooled
1-1/2 teaspoons vanilla extract
3/4 cup chopped walnuts *or* pecans
3/4 cup chopped dried apricots

Line a 9-in. square pan with aluminum foil. Coat with nonstick cooking spray; set aside. In a large mixing bowl, beat cream cheese until fluffy. Gradually beat in confectioners' sugar. Gradually add the white chocolate. Beat in vanilla. Fold in nuts and apricots. Spread into prepared pan. Cover and refrigerate for 8 hours or overnight. Using foil, lift fudge from pan; cut into squares. **Yield:** about 2-1/2 pounds.

Plum-Apple Butter

(Pictured at left)

I look forward to cooking up this fruity spread each December, using the plums I picked and froze during summer. *—Nancy Michel, Lakeland, Florida*

2 pounds tart apples, peeled and quartered
2 pounds plums, pitted and quartered
1 cup water
3 cups sugar
1-1/2 teaspoons ground cinnamon
1 teaspoon ground nutmeg
1/4 teaspoon ground allspice

Place apples, plums and water in a large kettle; cover and simmer until tender, about 15 minutes. Cool.

Puree in batches in a food processor or blender; return all to the kettle. Add sugar and spices. Simmer, uncovered, for 20-30 minutes or until thickened, stirring frequently. Cool completely. Pour into jars. Cover and store in the refrigerator for up to 3 weeks. **Yield:** 5 cups.

Cherry Almond Mini Loaves

Plenty of good things come in these little loaves featuring golden raisins and cherries. There's a surprise—the creamy almond filling—in every scrumptious bite.
—Connie Simon, Reed City, Missouri

3/4 cup milk
3/4 cup butter, ***divided***
1/2 cup sugar
1 teaspoon salt
2 packages (1/4 ounce ***each*****) active dry yeast**
1/4 cup warm water (110° to 115°)
2 eggs plus 1 egg yolk
5-1/2 to 6 cups all-purpose flour
1-1/2 cups golden raisins
1-1/3 cups candied cherry halves
1 teaspoon grated orange peel
FILLING:
1 can (8 ounces) almond paste
1/2 cup sugar
1 egg white
Confectioners' sugar

In a saucepan, combine milk, 1/2 cup butter, sugar and salt. Cook over low heat until butter is melted. Cool to lukewarm (110°-115°). In a mixing bowl, dissolve yeast in water. Stir in milk mixture, eggs and yolk. Beat in 2 cups flour, raisins, cherries and orange peel. Add enough remaining flour to form a soft dough. Turn onto a floured surface; knead until smooth and elastic, about 6-8 minutes. Place in a greased bowl, turning once to grease top. Cover and let rise in a warm place until doubled, 1-1/2 hours.

For filling, crumble almond paste into a bowl; stir in sugar and egg white until smooth. Punch dough down; divide into 12 portions. Shape each into a 6-in. x 4-in. oval. Place 2 in. apart on greased baking sheets. Melt remaining butter and brush over dough. Divide almond mixture into 12 portions; roll each into a 5-in. log. Flatten slightly and place off-center on ovals. Fold dough over filling; press edges to seal. Cover and let rise until doubled, about 45 minutes. Brush with butter. Bake at 350° for 20 minutes or until golden brown. Dust with confectioners' sugar. **Yield:** 12 mini loaves.

Susie's Hot Mustard

(Pictured above)

My husband enjoys spreading this bold, robust mustard on anything that needs an extra "bite" of flavor.
—Susie Gibson, Alta Loma, California

1 can (4 ounces) ground mustard
1 cup white wine vinegar
3 eggs
3/4 cup sugar
1 tablespoon honey
1 tablespoon molasses
2 cups mayonnaise
1 tablespoon mustard seed, optional

Combine mustard and vinegar in a small bowl. Cover and let stand at room temperature for 8 hours or overnight. In a saucepan, beat eggs. Stir in sugar, honey, molasses and mustard mixture. Cook and stir over low heat until thickened and a thermometer reads 165°, about 20 minutes. Cool. Stir in mayonnaise and mustard seed if desired. Cover and refrigerate for up to 3 weeks. **Yield:** 4 cups.

Christmas Cookies In a Jar

(Pictured above)

With layers of vanilla chips, oats and dried cranberries, this delectable cookie mix looks as good as it tastes! For a special gift, tuck a jar in a pretty basket with a wooden spoon, cookie sheet, kitchen timer and instructions.
—Lori Daniels, Beverly, West Virginia

1/3 cup sugar
1/3 cup packed brown sugar
3/4 cup all-purpose flour
1/2 teaspoon baking powder
1/8 teaspoon baking soda
1/8 teaspoon salt
1 cup quick-cooking oats
1 cup orange-flavored dried cranberries
1/2 cup vanilla *or* white chips
ADDITIONAL INGREDIENTS:
1/2 cup butter, melted
1 egg
1 teaspoon vanilla extract

In a 1-qt. glass jar, layer the sugar and brown sugar, packing well between each layer. Combine the flour, baking powder, baking soda and salt; spoon into jar. Top with oats, cranberries and chips. Cover and store in a cool dry place for up to 6 months.

To prepare cookies: Pour cookie mix into a large mixing bowl; stir to combine. Beat in butter, egg and vanilla. Cover and refrigerate for 30 minutes. Drop by tablespoonfuls 2 in. apart onto ungreased baking sheets. Bake at 375° for 8-10 minutes or until browned. Remove to wire racks to cool. **Yield:** 3 dozen.

Wild Rice Pilaf Mix

We exchange homemade gifts in our family. I give this tasty mix to relatives and friends. It goes well with a variety of entrees, and it's a handy side dish to serve when guests drop in. *—Margaret Snider*
Guernsey, Saskatchewan

3 cups uncooked wild rice
2 cups dried lentils
2 cups raisins
1 cup medium pearl barley
1/2 cup sunflower kernels
1/4 cup beef bouillon granules
3 tablespoons dried parsley flakes
3 tablespoons dried minced onion
2 tablespoons dried minced garlic
1 tablespoon dried basil
1 tablespoon salt
1/2 teaspoon ground cinnamon
1/2 teaspoon pepper

In a large bowl, combine all ingredients; mix well. Store in an airtight container. To make two servings, combine 1/3 cup mix and 1 cup water in a small saucepan; bring to a boil. Reduce heat; cover and simmer for 50 minutes or until rice and barley are tender. **Yield:** 9 cups mix.

Pecan Caramel Bars

These butterscotchy bars bring back fond memories of my grandma who loved to spoil us with good food. Whenever I give these treats away or take them to a buffet, folks request the recipe. *—Trudy Schultz*
Springfield, Missouri

2 cups all-purpose flour
1 cup packed brown sugar
1/2 cup cold butter
1-1/2 cups pecan halves
1 package (14 ounces) caramels*
1/4 cup heavy whipping cream
1 package (11-1/2 ounces) milk chocolate chips
1 cup butterscotch chips

In a bowl, combine flour and brown sugar. Cut in butter until mixture is crumbly. Press into an ungreased 13-in. x 9-in. x 2-in. baking pan. Bake at 350° for 12-14 minutes or until lightly browned. Cool on a wire rack. Sprinkle pecans over top.

In a microwave or heavy saucepan, melt caramels with cream; stir until smooth. Pour over pecans and spread evenly. Combine chocolate and butterscotch chips; spread over caramel layer. Bake 5 minutes longer. Remove to wire rack. Run a knife through melted chips to swirl; cool completely. Cut into bars. **Yield:** 2 dozen.

*__Editor's Note:__ This recipe was tested with Hershey caramels.

Cardamom Tea Bread

A cross between pound cake and fruitcake, this bread is especially nice for folks who dislike the heaviness of regular fruitcake. —Sarah Bedia, Lake Jackson, Texas

1/2 cup chopped mixed candied fruit
2 cups all-purpose flour, *divided*
1/4 cup butter, softened
1/4 cup shortening
1 cup sugar
2 eggs
2/3 cup milk
1/4 cup orange juice
1 tablespoon baking powder
1 teaspoon salt
1/4 teaspoon ground cardamom

Combine candied fruit and 1 tablespoon flour in a small bowl; set aside. In a large mixing bowl, cream the butter, shortening and sugar for 1 minute. Add the eggs, milk, orange juice, baking powder, salt, cardamom and remaining flour. Beat on low speed for 30 seconds; beat on high for 3 minutes. Stir in fruit.

Pour into a greased and floured 9-in. x 5-in. x 3-in. loaf pan. Bake at 350° for 65-70 minutes or until a toothpick inserted near the center comes out clean. Cool for 10 minutes before removing from pan to a wire rack to cool completely. **Yield:** 1 loaf.

Cran-Apple Chutney

(Pictured below)

You can serve this chunky chutney over cream cheese or Brie with crackers, or as a condiment with roast pork or poultry. Either way, its slightly tart flavor and deep red hue lend a festive flair to the table.
—Karyn Gordon, Rockledge, Florida

4 cups (1 pound) fresh *or* frozen cranberries
1 cup sugar
1 cup water
1/2 cup packed brown sugar
2 teaspoons ground cinnamon
1-1/2 teaspoons ground ginger
1/2 teaspoon ground cloves
1/4 teaspoon ground allspice
1 cup chopped tart apple
1/2 cup golden raisins
1/2 cup diced celery

In a large saucepan, combine the first eight ingredients. Bring to a boil. Reduce heat; simmer, uncovered, for 20 minutes, stirring occasionally. Add the apple, raisins and celery. Simmer, uncovered, until thickened, about 15 minutes. Cool. Refrigerate until serving. **Yield:** 3 cups.

Holiday Truffles

(Pictured below)

I like to lavish the chocolate lovers on my list with these sumptuous truffles. They always bring me rave reviews.
—Jennifer Lipp, Bucharest, Romania

- **3 packages (12 ounces *each*) semisweet chocolate chips, *divided***
- **2-1/4 cups sweetened condensed milk, *divided***
- **1/2 teaspoon orange extract**
- **1/2 teaspoon peppermint extract**
- **1/2 teaspoon almond extract**
- **1-1/2 pounds white candy coating, melted**
- **3/4 pound dark chocolate candy coating, melted**
- **1/2 cup ground almonds**

In a microwave-safe bowl, melt one package of chips. Add 3/4 cup milk; mix well. Stir in orange extract. Repeat twice, adding peppermint extract to one portion and almond extract to the other. Cover and chill for 45 minutes or until firm enough to shape into 1-in. balls. Place on three separate waxed paper-lined baking sheets. Chill for 1-2 hours or until firm.

Dip the orange-flavored truffles twice in white candy coating; place on waxed paper to harden. Dip peppermint-flavored truffles in dark chocolate coating. Dip almond-flavored truffles in dark chocolate, then roll in ground almonds. If desired, drizzle white coating over peppermint truffles and dark chocolate coating over orange truffles. **Yield:** about 7 dozen.

Candy Snack Mix

Chock-full of raisins, peanuts and M&M's, this crunchy salty-sweet mix stays fresh for weeks. I keep it on hand to serve to unexpected guests or to fill decorative containers to give as last-minute gifts. *—Mary Newsom*
Grand Ridge, Florida

- **1 package (24 ounces) roasted peanuts**
- **1 package (18 ounces) Golden Grahams cereal**
- **1 package (15 ounces) raisins**
- **1/2 cup butter**
- **12 ounces white candy coating**
- **2 cups creamy peanut butter**
- **1 package (2 pounds) confectioners' sugar**
- **1 package (15 ounces) red and green milk chocolate M&M's**

In a large bowl, combine the peanuts, cereal and raisins. In a heavy saucepan over low heat, melt butter, candy coating and peanut butter; stir until smooth. Pour over cereal mixture and toss to coat.

Place sugar in a large bag; add coated mixture. Close bag and shake to coat. Spread onto baking sheets; sprinkle with M&M's. When cool, store in airtight containers. **Yield:** 25 cups.

Frosted Hazelnuts

Serve these spicy-sweet nuts at your holiday party or buffet. They're a tempting snack for any occasion. *—Kathleen Lutz, Steward, Illinois*

- **2 egg whites**
- **1 cup sugar**
- **2 tablespoons water**
- **1 teaspoon salt**
- **1/2 teaspoon *each* ground cloves, cinnamon and allspice**
- **4 cups hazelnuts *or* filberts**

In a medium bowl, lightly beat egg whites. Add sugar, water, salt and spices; mix well. Let stand 5 minutes or until sugar is dissolved. Add hazelnuts; stir gently to coat.

Spread into two greased 15-in. x 10-in. x 1-in. baking pans. Bake at 275° for 50-60 minutes or until the nuts are crisp. Remove to waxed paper to cool. Store the nuts in airtight containers. **Yield:** 6 cups.

Zippy Dry Rub

Bottles of this spicy blend are fun to share with family and friends. It's a mixture with broad appeal since the rub can be used on all meats or added to rice while it's cooking.
—Gaynelle Fritsch, Welches, Oregon

1 tablespoon salt
1 teaspoon mustard seed
1 teaspoon pepper
1 teaspoon chili powder
1 teaspoon paprika
1/2 teaspoon ground cumin
1/2 teaspoon dried coriander
1/4 teaspoon garlic powder

In a small bowl, combine all ingredients. Store in an airtight container. Rub desired amount onto the surface of uncooked meat. Cover and refrigerate for at least 4 hours before grilling. **Yield:** about 2-1/2 tablespoons.

3 'C' Bread

This sweet bread features carrots, coconut and cherries. That tasty combination ensures each loaf is a welcome gift!
—Edna Robinson Bowland
Lakewood, Colorado

2-1/2 cups all-purpose flour
1 cup sugar
1 teaspoon baking powder
1 teaspoon baking soda
1 teaspoon ground cinnamon
1/2 teaspoon salt
3 eggs
1/2 cup milk
1/2 cup vegetable oil
2 cups shredded carrots
1-1/2 cups flaked coconut
1/2 cup candied cherries, quartered
1/2 cup raisins
1/2 cup chopped pecans

In a large bowl, combine first six ingredients. In a small bowl, combine eggs, milk and oil. Stir into dry ingredients just until moistened. Fold in carrots, coconut, cherries, raisins and pecans. Pour into four greased 5-3/4-in. x 3-in. x 2-in. loaf pans.

Bake at 350° for 40-50 minutes or until a toothpick inserted near the center comes out clean. Cool for 10 minutes before removing from pans to wire racks. Cover and store in the refrigerator. **Yield:** 4 mini loaves.

Peppermint Stick Sauce

(Pictured above)

This pepperminty sauce is one of my favorite Christmas gifts to give. I package it in a decorative jar, then add a container of chopped nuts to sprinkle over the topping.
—Linda Gronewaller, Hutchinson, Kansas

1-1/2 cups finely crushed peppermint candies *or* **candy canes**
3/4 cup heavy whipping cream
1 jar (7 ounces) marshmallow creme

Combine all ingredients in a medium saucepan. Cook over medium-low heat, stirring occasionally, until mixture is smooth and candy is melted. Pour into small airtight containers. Store in the refrigerator. Serve warm over ice cream or cake. **Yield:** 3 cups.

ELEPHANT EARS

(Pictured above)

They'll remember these crispy home-baked pastries long after they've licked the last bit of cinnamon-sugar off their fingers! Great with hot coffee, these make a super gift. —*Susan Taul, Birmingham, Alabama*

1/2 cup warm milk (110° to 115°)
1/4 cup warm water (110° to 115°)
1 package (1/4 ounce) active dry yeast
2 cups all-purpose flour
4-1/2 teaspoons sugar
1/2 teaspoon salt
1/2 cup cold butter
1 egg yolk, beaten
FILLING/TOPPING:
6 tablespoons butter, melted, *divided*
2 cups sugar
3-1/2 teaspoons ground cinnamon
1/2 cup finely chopped pecans

In a bowl, combine the milk, water and yeast; set aside. In a large mixing bowl, combine the flour, sugar and salt. Cut in butter until mixture resembles coarse crumbs. Add egg yolk to yeast mixture; beat into dry ingredients until blended. Cover and refrigerate for at least 2 hours.

Punch dough down; turn onto a lightly floured surface. Knead several times. Cover and let rest for 10 minutes. Roll into an 18-in. x 10-in. rectangle. Brush with 2 tablespoons butter. Combine sugar and cinnamon; sprinkle 1 cup over dough. Beginning with a long side, roll up jelly-roll style; pinch edges to seal. Cut into 1-in. slices.

For each elephant ear, sprinkle a small amount of the remaining cinnamon-sugar on a piece of waxed paper. Place a slice of dough on cinnamon-sugar; roll into a 5-in. circle. Place sugared side down on an ungreased baking sheet. Brush with some of the remaining butter; sprinkle with pecans and cinnamon-sugar. Bake at 375° for 9-11 minutes or until golden brown. **Yield:** 1-1/2 dozen.

Vanilla-Almond Coffee

This recipe is perfect for any coffee lover. Instead of buying flavored coffees, I make my own using flavored extracts for baking. You can prepare this with decaffeinated coffee, too. —*Tina Christensen, Addison, Illinois*

1 pound ground coffee (not instant)
1 ounce vanilla extract
1 ounce almond extract

Place coffee in a large jar with tight-fitting lid. Add extracts. Cover and shake well. Store in the refrigerator. Prepare coffee as usual. **Yield:** 1 pound.

Orange Coconut Creams

Originally a gift from our neighbors, this recipe has become one of our own favorites to make and give at the holidays. —*Julie Fornshell, Bismarck, North Dakota*

1 can (14 ounces) sweetened condensed milk
1/2 cup butter, cubed
1 package (2 pounds) confectioners' sugar
1 cup flaked coconut
1-1/2 teaspoons orange extract
2 cups (12 ounces) semisweet chocolate chips
2 packages (4 ounces *each*) German sweet chocolate
2 tablespoons shortening

In a saucepan, combine the milk and butter. Cook and stir over low heat until the butter is melted. Place the confectioners' sugar in a mixing bowl. Add milk mixture; beat until smooth. Add the coconut and orange extract; mix well. Roll into 1-in. balls; place on waxed paper-lined baking sheets. Refrigerate until firm, about 1 hour.

In a saucepan, combine the chips, chocolate and shortening. Cook and stir over low heat until smooth. Dip balls into chocolate. Place on waxed paper until set. **Yield:** 9 dozen.

Cranberry Butter

(Pictured below)

One of my favorite toppings for toast is this tart spread. It's also great spooned over poultry and ice cream! I've given jars as gifts and have always gotten positive comments. —*Carol Studebaker, Gladstone, Missouri*

10 cups fresh *or* frozen cranberries
2/3 cup apple juice
1/2 to 3/4 cup sugar
1 cup maple syrup
1/2 cup honey
1/2 teaspoon ground cinnamon

In a saucepan over medium heat, bring cranberries, apple juice and sugar to a boil. Cook for 10-15 minutes or until all berries have popped, stirring occasionally. Remove from the heat; cool slightly. Process in batches in a blender or food processor until smooth.

Return cranberry mixture to the saucepan; add remaining ingredients. Bring to a boil over medium heat. Reduce heat; simmer, uncovered, for 10 minutes or until thickened, stirring occasionally. Cover and chill for 8 hours or overnight. Store in the refrigerator. **Yield:** 5 cups.

Cajun Spice Mix

(Pictured below)

You can give fish, beef, pork or poultry a zesty boost with this spicy seasoning. I like to sprinkle the mix on catfish fillets before broiling them. —*Coleen Deon Dover Plains, New York*

2 tablespoons paprika
1 tablespoon chili powder
2 teaspoons onion powder
2 teaspoons garlic powder
1-1/2 teaspoons salt
1-1/2 teaspoons white pepper
1-1/2 teaspoons pepper
1 teaspoon dried oregano
1 teaspoon dried thyme

In a bowl, combine all ingredients. Store in an airtight container in a cool dry place for up to 6 months. **Yield:** about 1/3 cup.

Raspberry Fudge Balls

Here's an idea for a last-minute gift that everyone will think you fussed over. Tasters relish the delectable hint of raspberry and the creamy texture of these fudgy balls. —*Maria Jaloszynski, Appleton, Wisconsin*

1 cup (6 ounces) semisweet chocolate chips
1 package (8 ounces) cream cheese, softened
3/4 cup finely crushed vanilla wafers (about 20 cookies)
1/4 cup seedless raspberry jam
3/4 cup finely chopped almonds

In a microwave or heavy saucepan, melt chocolate chips; stir until smooth. Cool slightly. In a mixing bowl, beat the cream cheese and melted chocolate until smooth. Stir in the wafer crumbs and jam. Refrigerate for 4 hours or until firm. Shape into 1-in. balls; roll in almonds. Store in an airtight container in the refrigerator. **Yield:** about 2-1/2 dozen.

Peanut Brittle Bars

Pairing the old-fashioned flavor of peanut brittle with yummy chocolate chips turns these bars into a satisfying treat and sought-after holiday gift. —*Kristin Gleason, St. John, Kansas*

1-1/2 cups all-purpose flour
1/2 cup whole wheat flour
1 cup packed brown sugar
1 teaspoon baking soda
1/4 teaspoon salt
1 cup cold butter

TOPPING:

2 cups salted peanuts
1 cup milk chocolate chips
1 jar (12-1/4 ounces) caramel ice cream topping
3 tablespoons all-purpose flour

In a large bowl, combine flours, brown sugar, baking soda and salt. Cut in butter until mixture resembles coarse crumbs. Pat into a greased 15-in. x 10-in. x 1-in. baking pan. Bake at 350° for 10-12 minutes or until golden brown.

Sprinkle peanuts and chocolate chips over warm crust. Combine caramel topping and flour; drizzle over top. Bake 12-16 minutes

longer or until golden brown and bubbly. Cool on a wire rack. Cut into squares. **Yield:** about 4 dozen.

Herb Butter

This savory butter makes a thoughtful and versatile gift at holiday time. It's great spread on French bread or chicken before baking, or tossed with hot cooked vegetables or pasta. —Dixie Terry, Marion, Illinois

2 cups butter, softened
1/4 cup minced fresh parsley
2 tablespoons minced garlic cloves
4 teaspoons Italian seasoning
1 teaspoon crushed red pepper flakes

In a mixing bowl, combine all ingredients. Beat until well blended. Cover and store in the refrigerator. **Yield:** 2 cups.

Honey Fudge Sauce

My velvety sauce will sweeten the season for any ice cream lover. The honey and chocolate blend is unbeatable. —Amy Kraemer, Hutchinson, Minnesota

1 cup (6 ounces) semisweet chocolate chips
1/2 cup honey
2 tablespoons butter
1/2 teaspoon salt
3/4 cup evaporated milk
1 tablespoon vanilla extract

In a heavy saucepan, combine the chips, honey, butter and salt. Cook and stir over low heat until chips are melted; stir until smooth. Gradually stir in milk and vanilla; heat through, about 2 minutes (do not boil). **Yield:** 1-2/3 cups.

Almond Coffee Creamer

This tasty creamer has just four simple ingredients, but its spicy almond flavor is so rich and soothing, friends will think you fussed. —Janet Lippincott, Akron, Ohio

3/4 cup confectioners' sugar
3/4 cup powdered nondairy creamer
1 teaspoon ground cinnamon
1 teaspoon almond extract

In a bowl, combine all ingredients; mix well. Store in an airtight container. To use, add to coffee in place of nondairy creamer and sugar. **Yield:** 1-1/4 cups.

Nutmeg Logs

(Pictured above)

The crispy-tender texture and mildly spicy flavor of these cookies will tempt all ages. My whole family enjoys them. —Marjorie Gegelmann, Bismarck, North Dakota

1 cup butter, softened
3/4 cup sugar
1 egg
2 teaspoons vanilla extract
3 cups all-purpose flour
1-1/2 teaspoons ground nutmeg
1/4 teaspoon salt
Additional sugar

In a mixing bowl, cream butter and sugar. Beat in egg and vanilla. Combine flour, nutmeg and salt; gradually add to the creamed mixture. Cover and chill for 1 hour or until firm.

On a sugared surface, shape 1/2 cupfuls of dough into 1/2-in.-thick logs. Cut logs into 2- to 2-1/2-in. pieces. Place 2 in. apart on ungreased baking sheets. Bake at 350° for 12-14 minutes or until lightly browned. Remove to wire racks to cool. **Yield:** about 5 dozen.

in airtight containers. To make one serving, add 1/4 cup mix to 3/4 cup boiling water; stir until dissolved. **Yield:** 6-3/4 cups mix.

Cinnamon Popcorn

Seasoned with cinnamon, this popcorn is the perfect family snack to munch while watching those classic Christmas movies together.
—Katheryne Ann Johnson, Vernon, Texas

4 quarts popped popcorn
1 cup butter
2/3 cup sugar
1 tablespoon cinnamon

Place popcorn in a large bowl. In a microwave-safe bowl, combine the butter, sugar and cinnamon. Microwave on high for 1 minute; stir. Microwave 1 minute longer or until the butter is melted. Pour over popcorn and toss to coat.

Transfer to two greased 15-in. x 10-in. x 1-in. baking pans. Bake, uncovered, at 300° for 10 minutes. Cool. Store in an airtight container. **Yield:** 4 quarts.

Minty Hot Chocolate

(Pictured above)

This hot chocolate mix features a tasty blend of mint and malt. We enjoy some each holiday season, especially after an evening of caroling!
—Esther Lambright Shipshewana, Indiana

2 cups chocolate-flavored malted milk powder, *divided*
1 cup butter mints
3 cups nonfat dry milk powder
1-1/2 cups instant hot cocoa mix

In a blender or food processor, combine 1 cup malted milk powder and mints; process until smooth. Pour into a large bowl. Add dry milk, cocoa mix and remaining malted milk powder; mix well. Store

Spicy Mustard

When I make this mustard, I add fresh horseradish from our garden and vinegar seasoned with homegrown tarragon.
—Joyce Lonsdale, Unionville, Pennsylvania

1/2 cup tarragon *or* cider vinegar
1/2 cup water
1/4 cup olive oil
2 tablespoons prepared horseradish
1/2 teaspoon lemon juice
1 cup ground mustard
1/2 cup sugar
1/2 teaspoon salt

In a blender or food processor, combine all ingredients. Process for 1 minute. Scrape down the sides of the container and process for 30 seconds. Transfer to a small saucepan and let stand 10 minutes. Cook over low heat, stirring constantly, until bubbly. Cool completely. If a thinner mustard is desired, stir in an additional 1-2 tablespoons water. Pour into small con-

tainers with tight-fitting lids. Store in the refrigerator. **Yield**: 1-1/2 cups.

Hidden Mint Morsels

(Pictured below)

Is it a cookie or a candy? No matter which answer folks choose, they find these minty morsels yummy. The recipe makes so much that you can whip up a number of gifts at once. —*Adina Skilbred*
Prairie du Sac, Wisconsin

1/3 cup shortening
1/3 cup butter, softened
3/4 cup sugar
1 egg
1 tablespoon milk
1 teaspoon vanilla extract
1-3/4 cups all-purpose flour
1/3 cup baking cocoa
1-1/2 teaspoons baking powder
1/4 teaspoon salt
1/8 teaspoon ground cinnamon

PEPPERMINT LAYER:
4 cups confectioners' sugar
6 tablespoons light corn syrup
6 tablespoons butter, melted
2 to 3 teaspoons peppermint extract

CHOCOLATE COATING:
2 packages (11-1/2 ounces *each*) milk chocolate chips
1/4 cup shortening

In a mixing bowl, cream shortening, butter and sugar until light and fluffy. Add egg, milk and vanilla; mix well. Combine flour, cocoa, baking powder, salt and cinnamon; add to the creamed mixture and mix well. Cover and refrigerate for 8 hours or overnight.

On a lightly floured surface, roll dough to 1/8-in. thickness. Cut with a 1-1/2-in. round cookie cutter; place on ungreased baking sheets. Bake at 375° for 6-8 minutes or until set. Cool for 2 minutes; remove to wire racks to cool completely. Combine peppermint layer ingredients; mix well. Knead for 1 minute or until smooth. Shape into 120 balls, 1/2 in. each. Place a ball on each cookie and flatten to cover cookie. Place on waxed paper-lined baking sheets; refrigerate for 30 minutes.

In a microwave or double boiler, melt chips and shortening. Spread about 1 teaspoonful over each cookie. Chill until firm. **Yield**: about 10 dozen.

Braided Sesame Wreath

(Pictured below)

"Knead" a gift better than store-bought? This is the all-time favorite bread of everyone I know, and I bake all kinds. I garnish my buttery braided wreaths with festive fabric bows. —Debbie Sadlo, Landover, Maryland

1 package (1/4 ounce) active dry yeast
1 cup plus 2 tablespoons warm milk (110° to 115°)
1/4 cup butter, melted
1/4 cup sugar
1 egg
1 teaspoon salt
4 to 4-1/4 cups all-purpose flour

TOPPING:

1 egg, beaten
1 teaspoon sesame seeds

In a large mixing bowl, dissolve yeast in warm milk. Add the butter, sugar, egg, salt and 2 cups flour; beat until smooth. Stir in enough remaining flour to form a soft dough. Turn onto a floured surface; knead until smooth and elastic, about 6-8 minutes. Place in a greased bowl, turning once to grease top. Cover and let rise in a warm place until doubled, about 1 hour.

Punch dough down. Turn onto a lightly floured surface; divide into thirds. Shape each portion into a 22-in. rope. Place ropes on a greased baking sheet and braid; pinch ends together to form a ring. Cover and let rise until doubled, about 45 minutes. Brush with egg and sprinkle with sesame seeds. Bake at 350° for 20-25 minutes or until golden brown. Remove from pan to a wire rack to cool. **Yield:** 1 loaf.

Butterscotch Dip

This gooey-good dip is an appealing addition to my Yuletide fruit baskets. I just pour some into pint jars trimmed with Christmas ribbons and tuck them in with red and green apples. —Kay Parker Albany, Georgia

2 cans (14 ounces *each*) sweetened condensed milk
2 packages (11 ounces *each*) butterscotch chips
2 tablespoons vinegar
1 tablespoon ground cinnamon
Apple slices

In a heavy saucepan over low heat, combine milk, chips, vinegar and cinnamon. Cook and stir until smooth. Serve warm with apples. Leftover sauce may be reheated in a heavy saucepan over low heat. **Yield:** about 4 cups.

Lime Mint Jelly

You're sure to spread Christmas cheer with gift jars of this holly-green jelly that won me a "Best of Show" at the county fair. Flavored with lime, it's delicious on roasted meats. —Gloria Jarrett Loveland, Ohio

4 cups sugar
1-3/4 cups water
3/4 cup lime juice
7 drops green food coloring, optional
1 pouch (3 ounces) liquid fruit pectin
3 tablespoons finely chopped fresh mint leaves
1/4 cup grated lime peel

In a large saucepan, combine the sugar, water and lime juice; add food coloring if desired. Bring to a boil over high heat, stirring constantly. Add the pectin, mint and lime peel;

bring to a full rolling boil. Boil for 1 minute, stirring constantly.

Remove from heat; skim off foam. Pour hot mixture into hot sterilized jars, leaving 1/4-in. headspace. Adjust caps. Process for 15 minutes in boiling-water bath. **Yield:** 5 half-pints.

Turtle Ice Cream Sauce

Making this rich caramel-fudge sauce is a family affair at our house—the kids love to unwrap the caramels! The sauce can be made ahead and frozen. —Marci Cullen, Milton, Wisconsin

2 cups butter
2 cans (12 ounces *each*) evaporated milk
2 cups sugar
1/3 cup dark corn syrup
1/8 teaspoon salt
2 cups (12 ounces) semisweet chocolate chips
1 package (14 ounces) caramels*
1 teaspoon vanilla extract

In a large saucepan or Dutch oven, combine the first seven ingredients. Cook, stirring constantly, over medium-low heat until the caramels are melted and mixture is smooth (do not boil). Reduce heat to low.

With an electric hand mixer on medium speed, beat in vanilla; continue beating for 5 minutes. Beat on high for 2 minutes. Remove from heat and cool for 30 minutes (sauce will thicken as it cools). Pour into glass or plastic food storage containers. Store in refrigerator. Serve warm or cold. **Yield:** 9 cups.

***Editor's Note:** This recipe was tested with Hershey caramels.

Honey-Mustard Salad Dressing

This zippy recipe is one a friend shared years ago. I like to give the dressing to others in jelly jars trimmed with baling twine. —Jean Keffer, Bend, Oregon

3 cups mayonnaise
1/2 cup sugar
1/2 cup honey
1/4 cup prepared mustard
1/4 cup vinegar
1/4 cup chopped onion
1 cup vegetable oil
1/4 cup minced fresh parsley

In a blender or food processor, combine the first six ingredients. Slowly add oil; process until smooth. Stir in parsley. Cover and chill for at least 1 hour. Can be refrigerated for up to 1 week. **Yield:** about 5 cups.

Pear Raspberry Jam

(Pictured above)

I give this sweet and tangy jam as a Christmas gift. In this part of the country, pears and raspberries are in plentiful supply, but frozen berries work just as well. —Susan Burton, Yakima, Washington

2 cups coarsely chopped peeled ripe pears (about 2 medium)
2 cups fresh *or* frozen unsweetened raspberries
6 cups sugar
2 tablespoons lemon juice
2 teaspoons finely grated orange peel
1 pouch (3 ounces) liquid fruit pectin

In a large kettle, combine the first five ingredients; bring to a full rolling boil, stirring constantly. Quickly stir in pectin; return to a full rolling boil. Boil for 1 minute, stirring constantly. Remove from the heat; skim off foam. Pour hot into hot jars, leaving 1/4-in. headspace. Adjust caps. Process 15 minutes in a boiling-water bath. **Yield:** 6 half-pints.

Pepper Salad Dressing

Friends tell me they can't wait to dip into this zesty dressing. I present it, tied with a plaid ribbon, in recycled glass condiment bottles that I label with my name, the recipe's title and storage instructions. —*Sue Braunschweig*
Delafield, Wisconsin

1 quart mayonnaise
2 cups half-and-half cream
3 tablespoons coarsely ground pepper
2 tablespoons finely chopped green onions
1-1/2 teaspoons salt
3/4 teaspoon white pepper
3/4 teaspoon Worcestershire sauce
1/2 teaspoon hot pepper sauce

In a large mixing bowl, combine mayonnaise and cream; beat until smooth. Stir in remaining ingredients. Pour into salad dressing bottles or pint jars. Cover and store in the refrigerator for up to 1 week. **Yield:** 6 cups.

Fire-and-Ice Pickles

(Pictured above)

These sweet and spicy pickles are great on a sandwich or all by themselves as a snack. The recipe is an easy way to dress up store-bought pickles and make them a special treat! —*Myra Innes, Auburn, Kansas*

2 jars (32 ounces *each*) dill pickle slices *or* spears
4 cups sugar
1 tablespoon hot pepper sauce
1/2 teaspoon crushed red pepper flakes
3 garlic cloves, peeled

Drain and discard juice from pickles. In a large bowl, combine pickles, sugar, pepper sauce and pepper flakes; mix well. Cover and let stand 2 hours, stirring occasionally. Spoon pickles and liquid into 3 pint-size jars; add a garlic clove to each. Cover and refrigerate 1 week before serving. Store in the refrigerator. **Yield:** 3 pints.

Pear Mincemeat

At my house, Christmas just isn't Christmas without mincemeat. This fruit- and spice-filled version is ideal for gift-giving. —*Gay Nell Nicholas*
Henderson, Texas

7 pounds pears, peeled and cored
1 medium tart unpeeled apple, cored
1 lemon, halved and seeded
1 pound raisins
4 cups sugar
1 cup purple grape juice
1 cup vinegar
1 tablespoon *each* ground cinnamon, cloves and allspice
1 teaspoon salt

In a food processor or grinder, chop or grind pears, apple and lemon. Transfer to a large kettle. Add remaining ingredients; simmer for 2 hours, stirring occasionally. Pack hot mixture into hot jars, leaving 1/2-in. headspace. Adjust caps. Process for 25 minutes in a boiling-water bath. **Yield:** about 8 pints.

Ginger Shortbread Wedges

Rich, buttery and lightly spiced with ginger, this shortbread couldn't be tastier. —*Edna Hoffman Hebron, Indiana*

1/2 cup butter, softened
1/3 cup sugar
1 teaspoon ground ginger
1 cup all-purpose flour

In a mixing bowl, cream the butter, sugar and ginger. Add flour; mix well (dough will be crumbly). Press dough into an ungreased 8-in. round baking pan. Using a fork, prick score lines to form eight wedges. Bake at 325° for 32-35 minutes or until edges are golden brown. Immediately cut into wedges along score marks. Cool in pan on a wire rack. **Yield:** 8 wedges.

Coffee Stirrer Sticks

(Pictured at right)

As a holiday novelty, it's hard to lick this lollipop for grown-ups! It doubles as a coffee stirrer, and it makes a special party favor. —*Kelly Pickering, Mesa, Arizona*

1 cup sugar
1/3 cup brewed coffee
1 tablespoon light corn syrup
1/4 teaspoon baking cocoa
1/4 teaspoon ground cinnamon
1/2 teaspoon vanilla extract
12 wooden lollipop *or* craft sticks
Plastic wrap
Red and green narrow ribbon

In a saucepan, combine sugar, coffee, corn syrup, cocoa and cinnamon. Cook over medium heat until the sugar is dissolved, stirring constantly. Cook over medium heat, without stirring, until a candy thermometer reads 290° (soft-crack stage), about 7 minutes. Remove from the heat. Immediately stir in vanilla, then pour into a greased 2-cup heat-proof glass measuring cup.

Working quickly, pour tablespoonfuls into circles on a greased baking sheet. Lay a stick in each circle. Allow to cool until hardened. When cooled, wrap with plastic wrap and tie with ribbon. Store in an airtight container. **Yield:** about 1 dozen.

Editor's Note: We recommend that you test your candy thermometer before each use by bringing water to a boil; the temperature should read 212°. Adjust your recipe temperature up or down based on your test.

Spicy Mixed Nuts

This different nut mix has an appealing kick, thanks to the cumin and chili powder I add. It's perfect for holiday snacking. —*Delores Hill, Helena, Montana*

3 tablespoons butter
1 pound mixed nuts
1/4 teaspoon Worcestershire sauce
1/2 teaspoon salt
1/4 teaspoon paprika
1/4 teaspoon cayenne pepper
1/4 teaspoon chili powder
1/8 teaspoon ground cumin

In a large skillet, melt butter. Add nuts and Worcestershire sauce; cook and stir over low heat for 5-7 minutes. Drain on paper towels. Place nuts in a large bowl. Combine seasonings; sprinkle over nuts and toss to coat. Cool. Store in an airtight container at room temperature. **Yield:** 3 cups.

White Pecan Fudge

(Pictured below)

Each Christmas, I package batches of this rich fudge to send to family and friends. It's just delicious!
—*Marie Draper, Price, Utah*

1 tablespoon plus 1/2 cup butter, ***divided***
2-1/2 cups miniature marshmallows
2-1/4 cups sugar
1 cup heavy whipping cream
16 squares (1 ounce ***each*****) white baking chocolate, cut into small pieces**
2 teaspoons vanilla extract
2 cups chopped pecans

Line a 9-in. square pan with foil. Grease the foil with 1/2 tablespoon butter and set aside. Butter the sides of a large heavy saucepan with 1/2 tablespoon butter. Cut remaining butter into small pieces and place in a large heat-proof bowl; add marshmallows and set aside.

In the buttered saucepan, combine sugar and cream. Cook and stir over medium heat until mixture comes to a boil. Cover and cook for 2 minutes to dissolve any sugar crystals. Uncover; cook over medium heat, without stirring, until a candy thermometer reads 234° (soft-ball stage).

Remove from the heat. Pour over butter and marshmallows; stir until melted. Add the chocolate. Continue stirring until chocolate is melted and mixture is smooth. Stir in vanilla and nuts. Pour into prepared pan. Refrigerate until firm. Lift out of pan; remove foil and cut into 1-in. squares. Store in an airtight container at room temperature. **Yield:** about 3-1/2 pounds (about 6-1/2 dozen).

Editor's Note: We recommend that you test your candy thermometer before each use by bringing water to a boil; the temperature should read 212°. Adjust your recipe temperature up or down based on your test.

Burnt Peanuts

As far as my family's concerned, I can't make this nutty snack too often. In fact, I save pint jars throughout the year as containers for this popular Christmas present.
—*Sue Gronholz, Columbus, Wisconsin*

1 cup sugar
1/2 cup water
1 teaspoon red food coloring, optional
2 cups raw Spanish peanuts with skins

In a heavy saucepan, combine the sugar, water and food coloring if desired. Bring to a boil over medium heat; stir in peanuts. Cook, stirring occasionally, for 12 minutes or until peanuts are coated and no syrup remains. Spread peanuts into an ungreased 15-in. x 10-in. x 1-in. baking pan; separate with a fork.

Bake at 300° for 30 minutes, stirring every 10 minutes. Cool completely. Store peanuts in an airtight container at room temperature. **Yield:** about 4 cups.

Grandma's Peanut Butter

Frequently, I nestle a creamy jarful of this lip-smacking peanut butter beside homemade cookies and candy as a gift "fresh from Grandma's kitchen".
—*Ann Teegardin, Justin, Texas*

1 cup creamy peanut butter
1 cup corn syrup
1/2 cup marshmallow creme
2 tablespoons maple syrup
1 teaspoon hot water

In a mixing bowl, combine all ingredients and beat until smooth. Store in an airtight container. **Yield:** about 2 cups.

Rosy Cider Jelly

For an easy-to-prepare present, try this jelly made with cider and cranberry juice. I got the recipe, now a family favorite, from our local county Extension office. —*Regina Stock, Topeka, Kansas*

3 cups apple cider
1 cup cranberry juice
1 teaspoon lemon juice
1 package (1-3/4 ounces) powdered fruit pectin
5 cups sugar

In a large kettle, combine the first four ingredients. Bring to a rolling boil over high heat, stirring constantly. Stir in sugar. Return to a full rolling boil; boil for 1 minute, stirring constantly.

Remove from the heat; skim off any foam. Pour hot liquid into hot jars, leaving 1/4-in. headspace. Adjust caps. Process for 5 minutes in a boiling-water bath. **Yield:** 6 half-pints.

Cookie Ornaments

(Pictured above right)

What a welcome gift these fun frosted ornaments will make. But beware, the ginger-flavored cookies are so appetizing, they might never make it to the tree!
—*Patricia Slater, Baldwin, Ontario*

1/3 cup butter, softened
1/3 cup shortening
3/4 cup sugar
1 egg
1 teaspoon vanilla extract
2 cups all-purpose flour
1-1/2 teaspoons baking powder
1 teaspoon ground ginger
1/4 teaspoon salt
1/8 teaspoon ground cloves
FROSTING:
1-1/2 cups confectioners' sugar
3 tablespoons butter, softened
1/2 teaspoon vanilla extract
1 to 2 tablespoons milk
Food coloring and colored sprinkles, optional

In a mixing bowl, cream the butter, shortening and sugar. Beat in egg and vanilla. Combine the flour, baking powder, ginger, salt and cloves; gradually add to creamed mixture. Cover and refrigerate for 1 hour or until easy to handle.

Divide dough in half. On a lightly floured surface, roll out each portion to 1/8-in. thickness. Cut with floured 2-1/2-in. cookie cutters. Using a floured spatula, place cookies 1 in. apart on ungreased baking sheets. With a straw, make a hole about 1/2 in. from the top of each cookie. Bake at 375° for 7-9 minutes or until edges are lightly browned. Remove to wire racks to cool.

In a small mixing bowl, combine confectioners' sugar, butter, vanilla and enough milk to achieve frosting consistency. Frost cookies. Decorate with tinted frosting and colored sprinkles if desired. Let dry completely. Thread ribbon or string through holes. **Yield:** about 4 dozen.

Cashew Brittle

(Pictured at left)

I like this easy recipe because it doesn't require a candy thermometer. It also makes a great gift.
—Rhonda Glenn, Prince Frederick, Maryland

1 cup sugar
1/2 cup light corn syrup
1 to 1-1/2 cups salted cashew halves
1 teaspoon butter
1 teaspoon baking soda
1 teaspoon vanilla extract

In a microwave-safe bowl, combine the sugar and corn syrup. Microwave, uncovered, on high for 4 minutes; stir. Heat 3 minutes longer. Stir in cashews and butter. Microwave on high for 30-60 seconds or until mixture turns a light amber (mixture will be very hot). Quickly stir in baking soda and vanilla until light and foamy.

Immediately pour onto a greased baking sheet. Spread with a metal spatula. Chill for 20 minutes or until set; break into small pieces. Store in an airtight container. **Yield:** 3/4 pound.

Editor's Note: This recipe was tested in an 850-watt microwave.

Sweet Pretzel Nuggets

(Pictured above)

This crowd-pleasing snack has been a tremendous hit both at home and at work. The fun crunchy bites have a sweet cinnamon-toast taste and just a hint of saltiness.
—Billie Sue Ebinger, Holton, Indiana

1 package (15 to 18 ounces) sourdough pretzel nuggets
2/3 cup vegetable oil
1/3 cup sugar
1 to 2 teaspoons ground cinnamon

Place pretzels in a microwave-safe bowl. In a small bowl, combine oil, sugar and cinnamon; pour over pretzels; toss to coat. Microwave, uncovered, on high for 2 minutes; stir. Microwave 3-4 minutes longer, stirring after each minute or until oil is absorbed. Cool to room temperature. **Yield:** 12-16 servings.

Editor's Note: This recipe was tested in an 850-watt microwave.

Pistachio Mini Loaves

I bake up this green-hued bread every Christmas. The little loaves have a nice pistachio flavor.
—Joanne Loefgren, Carmel, Indiana

1 package (18-1/4 ounces) yellow cake mix
1 package (3.4 ounces) instant pistachio pudding mix
1 cup (8 ounces) sour cream
4 eggs
1/4 cup vegetable oil
1/4 cup water
3/4 cup finely chopped pecans
3 tablespoons brown sugar
2-1/2 teaspoons ground cinnamon

In a mixing bowl, combine cake and pudding mixes. Add sour cream, eggs, oil and water; beat until blended. Pour into five greased 5-3/4-in. x 3-in. x 2-in. loaf pans. Combine the pecans, brown sugar and

cinnamon; sprinkle over batter.

Bake at 350° for 35-40 minutes or until a toothpick inserted near the center comes out clean. Cool for 10 minutes before removing from pans to wire racks. **Yield:** 5 loaves.

Jambalaya Mix

Keep this mix on hand, and a full-flavored meal is never far away. Add shrimp, smoked sausage and a few other ingredients to the mix to create a speedy skillet sensation. —*Sybil Brown, Highland, California*

3 cups uncooked long grain rice
3 tablespoons dried minced onion
3 tablespoons dried parsley flakes
4 teaspoons beef bouillon granules
1 tablespoon dried minced chives
1 tablespoon dried celery flakes
1-1/2 teaspoons pepper
3/4 teaspoon cayenne pepper
3/4 teaspoon garlic powder
3/4 teaspoon dried thyme
ADDITIONAL INGREDIENTS:
2 cups water
1/2 cup chopped green pepper
1 can (8 ounces) tomato sauce
1 pound fully cooked smoked sausage, cut into 1/4-inch slices
1 pound uncooked medium shrimp, peeled and deveined

In an airtight container, combine the first 10 ingredients. Store in a cool dry place for up to 6 months. **Yield:** about 3 batches (about 3-1/3 cups total).

To prepare jambalaya: In a saucepan, bring water and green pepper to a boil. Stir in 1 cup jambalaya mix; return to a boil. Reduce heat; cover and simmer for 18-20 minutes or until rice is tender. In another saucepan, heat tomato sauce and sausage. Cook shrimp in boiling water until pink; drain. Stir into sausage mixture. Serve over rice mixture. **Yield:** 4-6 servings.

Gingerbread Cake Mix

(Pictured at right)

Put together this mixture to bake moist, nicely spiced gingerbread in no time. —*Ruth Seitz*
Columbus Junction, Iowa

6-2/3 cups all-purpose flour
1-1/2 cups sugar
3/4 cup plus 1 tablespoon nonfat dry milk powder
1/4 cup baking powder
1 tablespoon salt
2-1/2 teaspoons ground cinnamon
2 teaspoons cream of tartar
1-1/4 teaspoons ground cloves
1-1/4 teaspoons ground ginger
1-1/2 cups shortening
ADDITIONAL INGREDIENTS:
1 egg
1/2 cup water
1/2 cup molasses

In a large bowl, combine the first nine ingredients; mix well. Cut in shortening until the mixture resembles coarse crumbs. Store in an airtight container in a cool dry place for up to 6 months. **Yield:** 5 batches (10 cups total).

To prepare cake: In a mixing bowl, lightly beat egg, water and molasses. Add 2 cups cake mix; beat until well blended. Spread into a greased 8-in. square baking pan. Bake at 350° for 35-40 minutes or until a toothpick inserted near the center comes out clean. Cool on a wire rack. **Yield:** 9 servings.

Editor's Note: Contents of cake mix may settle during storage. When preparing recipe, spoon mix into measuring cup.

GENERAL RECIPE INDEX

This handy index lists every recipe by food category, major ingredient and/or cooking method, so you can easily locate recipes to suit your needs.

ALPHABETICAL INDEX

This handy index lists every recipe in alphabetical order so you can easily find your favorite recipes.

A

B

C

D

E

F

G

H

I

J

L

M

N

O

P

Q

R

S

T

V

W

Z